True Grace

Also by Wendy Leigh

The Secret Letters of Marilyn Monroe and Jacqueline Kennedy

Edward Windsor, Royal Enigma

Prince Charming: The John F. Kennedy, Jr., Story

Liza: Born a Star

Arnold: An Unauthorized Biography

True Grace

The Life and Times
of an American Princess

Wendy Leigh

Thomas Dunne Books

St. Martin's Griffin ≈ New York

THOMAS DUNNE BOOKS.
An imprint of St. Martin's Press.

TRUE GRACE. Copyright © 2007 by Wendy Leigh. All rights reserved. Printed in the United States of America. For information, address St. Martin's Press, 175 Fifth Avenue, New York, N.Y. 10010.

www.thomasdunnebooks.com
www.stmartins.com

www.wendyleigh.co.uk

Studio shots courtesy of Photofest

Library of Congress Cataloging-in-Publication Data

Leigh, Wendy.
    True Grace : the life and times of an American princess / Wendy Leigh.
        p. cm.
    ISBN-13: 978-0-312-38194-3
    ISBN-10: 0-312-38194-8
    1. Grace, Princess of Monaco, 1929–1982. 2. Motion picture actors and actresses—United States—Biography. 3. Princesses—Monaco—Biography. I. Title.

DC943.G7 L45 2007
944.9'49—dc22

2006050574

First St. Martin's Griffin Edition: June 2008

10 9 8 7 6 5 4 3 2 1

For Gwen Robyns

—Grace's first biographer—

who blazed the trail for us all, with love and thanks

Contents

Preface

Almost a quarter of a century since her untimely death, Grace Kelly remains a Hollywood icon. Countless stars from Sharon Stone to Gwyneth Paltrow to Madonna have all aped her pristine image, attempting to emulate her, but have failed dismally.

In November 2006, the Internet cited over twenty-five million mentions of her name. Recently, newborn American babies have been christened "Princess Grace," and tourists continue to flock to visit her grave in Monte Carlo. I am only surprised that Monaco—the principality that Grace alone put on the map—doesn't have a Princess Grace Museum.

To many of those who worship her memory, Princess Grace of Monaco is virtually a saint. In fact, even now, decades after her death, a petition to elevate her to sainthood is still lodged at the Vatican.

Yet after spending three years researching her life and talking to more than one hundred people, many of whom knew her well, I encountered a certain number of elements in her history that may well ultimately preclude her elevation to sainthood.

So how should I, as her biographer, have handled this new information, which many of her most fervent fans might consider unflattering?

Given that I'm not in the business of self-censorship, and that (as a biographer) I have a responsibility to report the truth, I had no choice but to do so.

To those fans who prefer to retain their saintly image of Grace, I say, "Read no further. I have no wish to disillusion you or tarnish her memory in your eyes."

But as for the rest of you, read on, for after spending three years researching

Grace's life, I believe that she was a strong, wonderful woman whose story is the quintessential American saga well worth telling. A saga that not only features one of the world's most beautiful Hollywood stars, a style icon, and a twentieth-century legend, but is also a picaresque tale of a child born of immigrants—the daughter of an archetypical self-made American millionaire—whose life encompassed the worlds of postwar Philadelphia, Broadway, 1950s Hollywood, the French Riviera, seventies London, high-society Paris, and, of course, Monte Carlo, yet who—despite all the glamour and the glory—was simultaneously confronted by some of the dilemmas faced by many single girls, mistresses, wives, and mothers today.

Grace Kelly lived four distinct lives: Philadelphia self-made millionaire's daughter, Broadway actress, Hollywood star, and European princess. Along the way—and this has never before been stressed—she crossed paths with the most famous people of her time: Frank Sinatra, Ava Gardner, Rudolf Nureyev, Salvador Dalí, Mikhail Baryshnikov, Marc Chagall, Josephine Baker, Greta Garbo, Gloria Swanson, Joan Collins, Princess Soraya, Sammy Davis Jr., Lauren Bacall, Judy Garland, Edith Piaf, Gregory Peck, King Farouk, Laurence Olivier, Maria Callas, Princess Diana, Prince Philip, Queen Elizabeth, Clark Gable, William Holden, Gary Cooper, Bing Crosby, Richard Burton, Elizabeth Taylor, the Duke and Duchess of Windsor, Aristotle Onassis, Jackie Kennedy, John F. Kennedy, Joe Kennedy, Peter Lawford, David Niven, Charles de Gaulle, Winston Churchill, Gunther Sachs, Andy Warhol, John Wayne, Tony Curtis, the Aga Khan, the Shah of Iran, Ray Milland, Robert Evans, Lee Radziwill, Marlon Brando, Jean-Pierre Aumont, Cary Grant, Alfred Hitchcock, Lord Mountbatten, Rock Hudson, Bob Hope, Zsa Zsa Gabor, Hedy Lamarr, Dwight Eisenhower, Lyndon Johnson, and Prince Charles.

Born beautiful, Grace Kelly had virtually every attractive man of her day at her feet, metaphorically speaking. She had choices, and she made them. The biggest choice of all was that of a husband. She made that choice—and she made the best of it—playing a vital part in the social fabric of her new country, spearheading charities, rendering Monaco a better place for her subjects, and loving and being loved by her children.

At 8 P.M. on Monday, March 6, 1978, in Princeton, New Jersey, she gave a recital, "Birds, Beasts and Flowers, A Programme of Poetry and Prose," and began with the first lines of William Blake's *Auguries of Innocence*: "To see a world in a grain of sand . . ."

In the same vein, I've always believed that there was such a thing as a grain-of-sand moment—a single moment or incident in which the essence—the truth—of a particular human being is revealed. The following story, I believe, is Grace's grain-of-sand moment. . . .

Monte Carlo, August 1975

Princess Grace's friend Baron Enrico di Portanova—Ricky to his friends—was in a fury. Three days before, the baron, who prided himself on his excellent manners, had telephoned one of Monte Carlo's premier florists and ordered a gargantuan bouquet of flowers to be sent to Estée Lauder, in thanks for having hosted him and his wife, Sandra, at a lavish brunch at Bel Abri, her Cap Ferrat villa.

Now, however, after running into Estée, without her acknowledging receipt of the flowers, Ricky reached the inescapable conclusion that the florist hadn't sent the flowers as he'd requested.

Accustomed to having his every whim fulfilled and buttressed by his million-dollar-a-month trust fund, Ricky di Portanova had always lived a gilded existence, jetting between his twenty-eight-room Acapulco villa, a Regency-style Houston mansion, and a luxurious apartment at the Hôtel de Paris in Monte Carlo.

Ricky and Sandra were famous for throwing glittering parties at which they served friends like Frank Sinatra, Rudolf Nureyev, Ava Gardner, and Princess Grace beluga-drenched pasta. The Portanovas cherished the high life and weren't about to offend a luminary like Estée Lauder by failing to thank her properly for her hospitality.

Consequently, when Ricky phoned the florist, he was livid, demanding as to the whereabouts of the "f——flowers." Not mincing words, he carried on, berating the florist, who listened in silence. When he finally finished, she asked him to repeat the message he wanted on the card, then promised personally to ensure that the flowers would be delivered to Estée Lauder.

Ricky, Sandra, and their friends Barry Landau and Princess Soraya, the former Empress of Iran, were at the Red Cross Ball at the Sporting Club the following evening, when Princess Grace approached Ricky, laughing mischievously.

"Did Estée like the flowers?" she said.

Stunned, Ricky asked, "How did you know?"

"You misdialed, Ricky. You called my number by mistake. You thought I was the florist. But I sent the flowers on your behalf anyway."

That, to me—on so many different levels—was Grace Kelly, Princess Grace of Monaco.

Prologue

As Grace Kelly glided down the red-velvet-carpeted aisle of the Romanesque cathedral, her head held high—despite the unfamiliar sensation of six bridesmaids behind her carrying a voluminous train fashioned out of three yards of ivory satin—her step never faltered. She gazed for a second at the huge gold baskets of white snapdragons hanging suspended from the chandeliers between each column all the way to the altar, which was blanketed in lilacs, white lilies, and hydrangeas, and lit by giant white tapers in gold candelabra.

Then her vision was obscured by a barrage of Nikons and Hasselblads, all poised to immortalize her wedding. In the background, the television cameras—which would relay the ceremony to a global audience of thirty million viewers—whirred relentlessly.

This was the third time that Grace Kelly had been a celluloid bride. In her second Hollywood movie, *High Noon*, she married Gary Cooper. In her last, *High Society,* she married Bing Crosby.

Offscreen, in real life, she had once been in love with Gary. Later, she had fallen in love with Bing and wanted so badly to be his wife that—according to his widow, Kathryn—Grace threatened Bing with a breach-of-promise suit when he changed his mind about marrying her.

Her first two cinematic weddings were Hollywood movies with a subtext of reality. This wedding in Monaco was reality fashioned into a Hollywood extravaganza. With Grace and Rainier's agreement—hers given in an attempt to fulfill her MGM contract, his in the belief that the glamour of the event would lend luster to Monaco's fading image—the ceremony was being filmed for an MGM documentary, *The Wedding of the Century*. So the lights blazed white in order to illuminate the proceedings for the benefit of the cameramen, and Grace played her part as the perfect princess bride straight out of everyone's most beloved fairy tale.

Through it all, she was sincere. She wasn't play-acting. She was marrying for life and, despite all the Hollywood hoopla, was entering into this union with Rainier in complete sincerity and honesty. Sincerity and honesty, in fact, were the touchstones of her character. Always were, always would be. For while—in the past—she had been somewhat duplicitous in juggling an assortment of stellar lovers, never allowing one to discover the existence of the other, where it counted she would always be honest, sincere, and ethical.

Inside the cathedral, that far-off day fifty-one years ago, there was a woman who was destined to pay the price for Grace's determination to be honest and ethical. A woman who so loved her that when she witnessed Grace's 1949 Broadway debut in *The Father* she enthused, "When she walked out on the stage, looking so fresh and pretty and breathtaking, I burst into tears. I think it was then that I realized she was going places."

Grace was, indeed. Subsequently, she made eleven movies in six years, won an Oscar, captivated armies of admiring fans who idolized her for her charm, poise, and overwhelming beauty, and she was now marrying into European royalty, becoming a princess.

Little did the woman watching Grace's wedding that day know that less than four and a half years later Grace would send her a letter making a confession so honest, so unvarnished, that the woman's heart would break.

But such was the almost supernatural charisma of Grace Kelly, the depth of the loyalty, and the love that she inspired in her friends and family that—when I interviewed her in April 2005—the woman confirmed Grace's transgression against her, then quickly added, "But it wasn't Grace's fault," and appeared to forgive her.

Part One

Falling in love with love is falling for make-believe . . .

—Lorenz Hart and Richard Rodgers, The Boys from Syracuse

I

The Kellys

Jack Kelly was a macho all-American male in the John Wayne, Gary Cooper, Clark Gable mold. Six foot two, with a muscular body and a wry sense of humor, he rippled with charisma, exuding power and the confidence of a man who has no doubt whatsoever that he is destined to dominate everything and everyone in his exalted universe.

"Jack Kelly was a big man, an extraordinary force. Very good-looking, a terrific personality who always had to be center stage and treated everybody else as a secondary player in his life," remembered Grace's friend and bridesmaid, actress Rita Gam.

Even when Grace became world famous as Princess Grace of Monaco, she was still viewed by her father as being relatively insignificant, her life and desires forever subservient to his own.

Yet Grace's love for her father was so profound that she uncomplainingly accepted her lowly status in his life and after his death insisted, "I only have only the most wonderful memories of him. His motto was: 'Never be the one who takes and gives nothing in return. Everything must be earned, through work, persistence, and sincerity.'"

But while John Brendan Kelly—a Democrat and a politician to his well-manicured fingertips—was brilliant at projecting the illusion that he was a self-made man who had pulled himself up by his own bootstraps, luck and a solid middle-class Irish family background had played a large part in elevating him from failed political candidate to a Philadelphia legend that lives on today in a city where Kelly Drive commemorates the entire Kelly family and not just the late Academy Award–winning actress.

A myth maker, with a talent for self-promotion much like that demonstrated by his fellow Irishman and friend Joe Kennedy, Jack was always eager to relate to the press the story of his family's humble early-nineteenth-century origins, their spectacular rise from Drimurla Farm, County Mayo, on the edge of Leg o' Mutton Lake, in the wilds of Ireland to power and prestige in Philadelphia. In 1956, he recalled to a journalist, "There were five boys in the family and not much money to spare. It was plain to my grandfather that he could not educate them all, so he called them together one day and said: 'Boys, we are going to put the oldest one of you through school, but the rest will have to stay and work the farm and contribute a share to Pat's schooling. At least one Kelly will be educated.' So Pat went to school, and ended up the dean of Dublin University. My own father, John Henry Kelly, never had a day in school himself, but he had a wonderful memory."

Grace, as it turned out, inherited her grandfather's talent, and throughout her career she invariably dazzled her contemporaries in television, the theater, and Hollywood with her virtually photographic memory that enabled her to learn a script by heart after studying it for only an extremely short time. From her grandfather she also inherited a toughness of mind and a determination to follow her own path, whatever obstacles she might encounter, whatever the cost.

By 1868, Grace's grandfather, John Henry Kelly, had survived the harrowing voyage to America in steerage, settling in Rutland, Vermont, where, a year later, he married seventeen-year-old Mary Ann Costello, who had also emigrated from County Mayo in search of a better life in the New World.

By the early 1870s, eager to make a success in his newfound country, John Henry first toiled on the railroads, then moved his family to Philadelphia, where he started work at Dobson's Carpet Mills in the Falls of Schuylkill, just five miles from the center of the city.

His son, John "Jack" Brendan Kelly, was born on October 4, 1890, the youngest son and the last of ten children born to John Henry Kelly and Mary Ann Costello, a woman so healthy that her proudest boast was that she was never sick, except on those days when she gave birth to her children.

She was also a great reader and immensely fond of sitting on the porch holding a book in one hand and rocking her latest newborn's cradle with the other. She could quote whole scenes from Shakespeare verbatim—a fascinating fact, considering that Grace, in the twilight of her life, toured the world giving Shakespeare recitals and once placed a rose on the Bard's grave in Stratford-upon-Avon.

By the time Jack was ten, money was still scarce in the family, so he went to work after school at Dobson's alongside his father and some of his siblings. At thirteen, he left school to join the construction business founded by his brother, Patrick Henry, eighteen years his senior.

He spent three years there as an apprentice bricklayer, devoting his spare time to boxing, and weighed in at 185 pounds. He was well on his way to becoming light heavyweight champion, but—exhibiting a burgeoning vanity that would one day become the talk of Philadelphia—didn't want to risk marring his perfectly chiseled features in a fight. He gave up boxing in favor of sculling, the rowing-related sport in which the sculler drives a fragile wooden shell through a little over a mile of water in less than ten minutes.

Soon, sculling became the passion of his life. As he later recorded, "I was always on the banks, and if I could catch the oar or hold the sweater of one of the great oarsmen of the day, my day was complete."

His sculling career was temporarily derailed by the outbreak of the First World War. Initially, he volunteered for the Air Force but was rejected on account of his bad eyesight, a weakness Grace inherited. And although his peacock vanity was far more overweening than any ever exhibited by Grace, both father and daughter were notorious for failing to wear their glasses and then ignoring someone simply because vanity had prevailed over myopia.

So he ended up in the Ambulance Corps in France, where he spent a relatively undistinguished war plotting his sculling career and dreaming of making his mark on the business world as well. On the way home to America on a troop transport, before his dreams could become reality, he lost his shirt in a craps game and almost jettisoned all his future plans. Fortunately, the family was willing and able to lend a helping hand.

Jack was the little brother of the family, the apple of his mother's eye, and there was no way that his indulgent brothers would sit back and watch him sink into obscurity. His elder brother Walter lent him the substantial sum of $5,000, and his brother George added $2,000, whereupon Jack founded Kelly for Brickworks. He was on the way to making his first million.

Both George and Walter could easily afford to help their little brother Jack rise in the world. As Grace's mother, Margaret, would later put it, "All four Kelly brothers were famous." Patrick Henry, the eldest Kelly brother, graduated from Dobson's via bricklaying to become a big-time contractor who built Philadelphia's Free Library as well as many of the city's most imposing churches and schools. His brother Walter—the first in the family to exhibit the acting talent that Grace ultimately inherited—had earned nationwide recognition by creating the Vaudeville act *The Virginia Judge*, performing monologues in character and winning for himself the accolade of "The Funniest Man in America."

But although audiences laughed themselves silly at the judge's antics, in retrospect, his monologues were racist in the extreme, with one featuring the judge asking a "Negro" if he wanted to make a quarter. "No, suh, I've got a quarter," the judge quoted the hapless stooge as replying. But even though Walter's success was based on racism, offstage neither he nor his brothers ever manifested any.

In fact, the mainstay of the Kelly home for Grace, her siblings, and her parents was Godfrey "Fordie" Ford, their black handyman whom Jack had met as a young bricklayer. "I was trying to make a record with the bricks I carried. Sometimes I didn't have quite enough, so Fordie would have to put some of his in my wheelbarrow," Jack later recalled, going on to hire Fordie to be the Kelly family's general factotum, part butler, chauffeur, handyman and—on Thursday night—babysitter, putting all the children to bed.

Fordie was so at ease with the Kellys that he freely declared to all and sundry, "Mr. Kelly has money to burn, but Mrs. Kelly doesn't like the smell of the smoke. . . ." He was part of the family and a good friend to Grace, who remained loyal to him and stayed in touch with him until the end of his life.

Perhaps because of her early allegiance to Fordie, Grace grew up tolerant and—even in the segregationist fifties and sixties—never displayed an iota of racism. During the sixties, when an American television crew shot a TV program in Monaco, the director objected to filming a scene in the palace grounds where some of the staff's black and white children were playing together. Telling Grace that the program was being shown in the South and there would be an outcry, the director declared that he didn't want the black children in the scene. "We do," retorted Grace. The scene was shot with all the children playing together.

As for Jews . . . when Grace was romantically involved with her Jewish acting teacher, Don Richardson, Jack and Grace's brother, Jack—"Kell"—along with Kell's friends, made Jewish jokes to Richardson's face when he visited Henry Avenue. Yet Grace's younger sister Lizanne went on to marry the Jewish Donald Le Vine, and some of Jack Kelly's closest friends were the Jewish head of Columbia

Records, Emmanuel "Manie" Sacks, the Levy family, which lived next door to the Kellys, and William S. Paley, president of CBS.

But in that far-off era—even among the liberal Kelly family—there was little tolerance for homosexuality. Although Jack Kelly's elder brother George became a Pulitzer Prize–winning playwright for *Craig's Wife*, also winning critical acclaim for *The Torchbearers*, his homosexuality was a closely guarded secret in the family, never to be disclosed to outsiders.

Whenever George, then living in Los Angeles, visited Henry Avenue, bringing with him his lover, William Weagley (whom George had met when Weagley was working as a bellhop in New York) Weagley was passed off as George's valet. Even though George and his lover maintained a fifty-five-year relationship, when George died in 1974, Weagley was not invited to his funeral—but managed to sneak into a back pew at St. Bridget's, where he sat, weeping.

Despite the family assiduously refusing to acknowledge George's homosexuality, his sexual predilections could not have been a secret from Grace. She adored her uncle, characterizing him as a wonderful man, and spent hours listening to him reading poetry and spinning tales of life in the theater. With his courtly European manners and his love for the theater and for poetry, George influenced the young Grace on a number of levels, inspiring her to try for an acting career, teaching her to be wary of the Hollywood studio system, and cautioning her never to be homophobic.

Far from sharing the Kelly family's prejudice against homosexuality, Grace always exhibited a tolerance for the less mainstream aspects of sexuality and gender. In the mid-1970s, her brother Kell embarked on a liaison with blond and beautiful twenty-eight-year-old transsexual nightclub owner Rachel Harlow (born Richard Finnochio). "When Princess Grace came to Philadelphia, she and Princess Caroline had lunch, then dinner with Kell and Harlow," Anthony Cozzi, Harlow's cousin, remembered. "Afterward, Harlow told me that Grace said she was gorgeous and that she loved her. She accepted Harlow completely."

By the time Jack Kelly had become president of his own company, with business booming, he was free to pursue his dreams of athletic stardom. By 1920, already the winner of the sculling national singles, his confidence knew no bounds. He resolved to go to Henley, England, and enter the Diamond Sculls—the world's number one sculling event—and beat the English on their own turf.

He submitted his entry form, bought a new shell, and booked his passage across the Atlantic. Three days before he was due to sail, he received a cable from the Henley stewards informing him that his application had been rejected and that a letter of explanation would follow. Years later, he recalled, "I remember reading that cable over and over, and seeing the tears drop on the paper, and realizing that all my castles were tumbling about my ears . . . the letter never did follow, so I assumed the old rule that a man who worked with his hands could not compete [was responsible]. As I looked through the tears, I felt that my grandfather, who really hated the English, was right and all the disappointment I felt was turned into bitterness towards the English."

Determined not to be cowed or defeated, Jack redressed the balance by entering the Olympics that same year and winning the gold medal in both the singles and the doubles sculling events, the first and only time an oarsman ever accomplished that feat.

When he returned home to Philadelphia, more than one hundred thousand citizens cheered for him in a welcome home parade celebrating his great achievement. He went on to win another gold medal in the doubles sculling event at the 1924 Paris Olympics.

But even that wasn't victory enough for Jack Kelly. He was accustomed to winning every race in the book, and the Henley authorities had prevented him from competing in the world's most important sculling event. He swore to himself that one day his son would be a champion sculler, make it to Henley, and avenge him. His son Kell was now doomed to spend much of his life helping his father live up to that oath—and ultimately suffered the consequences.

By 1924, Kelly for Brickworks had made Jack a millionaire in his own right, and he now directed his iron will toward winning the woman he loved and starting a family with her.

Margaret Majer was nine years Jack's junior, and she could trace her lineage back to the sixteenth century. That Margaret's daughter Grace grew up to play the princess far better than many other blue-blooded princesses to the manner born may well have been partly due to her mother's innate breeding. It is probably not a coincidence that Princess Grace of Monaco became the personification of the ideal fairy tale princess, given that her maternal grandfather, Carl Majer, was born in his father Johann's castle, Schloss Helmsdorf, on the shores of Lake Konstanz, Germany, and had ties to the German nobility.

But after Johann lost his fortune in the late 1800s, he, his wife, and their son, Carl, immigrated to Philadelphia, where in 1896 Carl married another girl of German descent, a saddle maker's daughter, Margaretha Berg. They had three children, Carl, Bruno, and Margaret, Grace's mother. With two German-born parents, Margaret first learned English when she was six years old. Until then, she spoke only German.

"We gave her such grief when she [our mother] tried to teach us German; we'd hide the grammar books. This was round the time of World War II and we'd complain how unpatriotic it was," Lizanne confided to one of Grace's earlier biographers, Steven Englund.

Reviewing the publicity surrounding Grace's career in the early fifties, the press never mentioned her German roots, invariably depicting her as an Irish-American girl from Philadelphia. Nothing could have been farther from reality. Grace Kelly was half German, with a character far more Germanic than Irish, one carefully engendered by her mother. "I had a good stiff German background. My parents believed in discipline and so do I... no tyranny or anything else like that but a certain firmness," Margaret confided to Grace's first biographer, Grace's friend Gwen Robyns, in 1977.

Back in the early fifties, however, just half a decade after the end of World War II, with the majority of Americans still viewing the Germans as the enemy, it was crucial to Grace's success that the studio publicists promote her as an all-American girl of Irish extraction—completely suppressing the fact that her heritage was as German as it was Irish.

Yet as a child, she learned German from her mother and, as her older sister, Peggy, put it, "We were never allowed to sit with our hands empty. We just knew we were expected to knit. We had to knit and to crochet from the time we were three or four years old. We had to because we were German girls... it was expected of us, and we had to do it."

"I met the mother, she was very Germanic and said my hair was too long and that she wanted me to get a haircut," Children of Theatre Street director Robert Dornhelm, Grace's close friend for the last six years of her life, said.

"Oh, that Ma Kelly, she's a tough one, a tough German cookie.... Now, I wouldn't say that Mother's a Nazi... but sometimes I do refer to her as, quote, 'That old Prussian Mother of mine,'" Kell once joked.

If the Irish Kellys—Walter, George, and, to some extent, Jack, who always craved center stage—imbued Grace with a flair for the dramatic, a tendency to dream, a talent to entertain, and a sometimes ribald sense of humor, it was from the German Majers that she derived the bedrock of her character: strong self-discipline, modesty, an ability to mask her emotions, a strong work ethic, the code that her word was her bond, and—above all—frugality.

She was rarely extravagant with herself, adhering to her mother's upbringing regarding thrift and self-indulgence. Years after Ava Gardner made *Mogambo* with Grace, who was then already a rising Hollywood star, Ava told distinguished *Nemesis* author, Peter Evans—during interviews for her autobiography, "We were sitting around the tent and I noticed that there was an enormous hole in the bottom of her shoe. I said, 'Gracie, for God's sake, honey, can't you afford to get yourself another pair of shoes?' She said, 'No. I've had these since high school. And I'll show you something else.' She took it off. The whole sole had come off at one point and she had glued it back herself."

Obeying her mother's teaching, from childhood on, Grace hoarded all her clothes, so that when she moved to Monaco, she brought with her twenty-year-old skirts and ten-year-old shoes. Thanks to Grace, Stephanie wore Caroline's hand-me-downs.

In quest of economizing at the palace, every Christmas, Grace presented each staff member with boxes of soap, albeit expensive ones. The highlight of her trips to London with her childhood friend, former bridesmaid Maree Frisby Rambo, was a visit to the Oxford Street branch of Marks and Spencer, where she purchased bargain-priced scarves and trinkets as gifts.

In her capacity as Princess Grace of Monaco, Grace continually received gifts. She evolved the strategy of rewrapping a gift, setting it aside, and then, a few months later, giving it to someone else. Now and again, one of those recipients received a gift from her that he or she had sent her in the first place. She was so determined not to waste money that, according to her nephew Baron Christian de Massy, "Sometimes people would receive a two-year-old box of chocolates from her that had suffered from deterioration."

Meticulous about finances, she insisted that Gwen Robyns, then coauthoring a book on flowers with her, keep receipts of all related purchases, announcing to her, "You owe me five pounds for stamps."

Although she lived half her life in a principality whose existence was funded mainly by gambling—and her father was cofounder of the Atlantic

City Race Track—Grace herself was a cautious gambler, once admitting that although she liked watching horse racing, she was "far too stingy" to enjoy a bet, however small.

During their childhood, whenever Grace or her siblings failed to finish a plate of calf's liver, Margaret ordered them to remain at the table for hours on end; they were forbidden to get up from the table until they had eaten every mouthful of food. Even as a princess Grace was adamant that food was not to be wasted and, true to her mother's upbringing, insisted that her children clean their plates.

One of her favorite sayings was, "Idle hands are the devil's playmate." She was often seen at the palace embroidering or crocheting or cooking one of her two favorite dishes—a German specialty of pork and cabbage or hamburgers.

She was scrupulous about keeping her word and hard on those who broke it. As a teenager, she and Maree Frisby Rambo signed up for modern dance class, and when Maree failed to attend on some Saturday mornings, she remembered getting calls from Grace sternly chiding her, "Maree, where are you? You promised you'd be here."

"Grace was very honorable. She would not promise something and not do it. She was very precise, very professional, never late, always on time," Robert Dornhelm said.

"Once Grace said she'd do something, she would do it," recalled her former Hollywood agent and friend, Jay Kanter. "She wouldn't get involved in a charity unless she was going to do something about it. She wouldn't get involved in being one of the directors of 20th Century–Fox unless she intended to participate, so she would read all the books and study all the material before each meeting."

Jack Kelly was a Philadelphia legend, a dashing man-about-town, overflowing with charisma and a raw male magnetism, causing Grace to yearn with every fiber of her being to please him. Yet as much as her Irish and German genes dueled within her, it was her German mother, Margaret Majer, who more than anyone else made Grace Kelly what she was and all she would become.

Jack Kelly was twenty-three the first time he saw Margaret, at the Philadelphia Turngemeinde Athletic and Social Club. She was blond, blue-eyed, and healthy, with an athletic body, a strong, Teutonic jaw, and a sultry sex appeal reminiscent of the young Marlene Dietrich.

Then just fourteen years old, Margaret was living with her parents in the Strawberry Mansion section of Philadelphia, a few miles south of the Falls. From the moment that Jack first met her, he intuited the intelligence and strength of will simmering behind the façade of her healthy outdoor-girl good looks. Margaret, however, was too caught up in enjoying her status as one of the most popular girls in the area to be the least bit interested in form-ing a serious relationship with a member of the opposite sex. (In this, Grace was not influenced by Margaret. She began dating in her early teens.)

"When we first met, we did not really take each other very seriously," Margaret later recalled. "But Jack would take me home from the club some nights, and some days he would pick me up after school. Our courtship be-gan in earnest when he came home from World War One."

After graduating from high school, Margaret attended Temple University, where she studied physical education, then became the first woman to instruct University of Pennsylvania co-eds in physical education.

She was a champion swimmer, and she was pretty. Consequently, she was selected to pose for the cover of the *Saturday Evening Post*. It was hardly surpris-ing that Jack was impressed. Soon she was cooking him scrumptious dinners that rivaled those made by his beloved grandmother, whose two-inch-thick steak and salad dinners and cup custard, he always said, fortified him to be-come a sculling champion.

All in all, Margaret Majer was ideal wife material, and whatever else Jack may have been up to during his bachelor years, he was clearheaded enough to recognize that he and Margaret would make a strong team.

For whatever reason—her career ambitions, his womanizing—Jack and Margaret courted for nine long years, until finally, after she converted from the Lutheran religion to Catholicism, on January 30, 1924, she and Jack mar-ried at St. Bridget's in the Falls.

During the early days of their marriage, while they waited for their home at 3901 Henry Avenue to be built, the couple lived in a small apartment at Ridge and Midvale avenues. Their new Colonial-style family home, con-structed with bricks from Kelly for Brickworks—with seventeen rooms, a green slate roof, and a white porticoed entrance—was more suburban house than grand Main Line mansion. As Jack's wealth increased and his power in Philadelphia grew, the family stayed put in the Henry Avenue house, a testament to his success yet not too opulent to disqualify him from his self-appointed role as a man of the people.

Margaret and Jack started their marriage in love, but it was just a matter of time before his unbridled philandering undermined their relationship.

He was handsome, rich, and desirable. An elegant dresser, he was careful never to carry change in his pocket lest it spoil the contours of his hand-made jackets and mar his dashing image. Although his hair thinned early on—he often wore a hat to conceal his hair loss—his lack of hair did nothing to diminish his appeal to legions of women.

Women were his for the asking. One Christmas, he ordered twenty-seven cosmetic-filled handbags from Elizabeth Arden, costing $150 apiece, and sent them to twenty-seven different women, every one of them his girlfriend and proud of it.

The socialite Ellen Frazer captivated him more than most of his other conquests, and for a short time his marriage to Margaret was in jeopardy. As Arthur Lewis, author of *Those Philadelphia Kellys*, revealed, "I've been told that Jack wanted very much to marry Ellen Frazer. She was a marvelous, charming woman, very vivacious, lively and amusing. It is common knowledge that if he'd been able to get a divorce, she and Jack certainly would have gotten married."

Despite the vast array of women eager for Jack Kelly to have his masterly way with them, he still wasn't above making a play for his female employees, as well. "My mother, Marion Holman, worked for Jack. She was very beautiful, a single mother, and I think Jack hired her because of that and then probably hit on her," said Marion's son, the actor Bruce Davison. "She wasn't fond of him as an honorable man. She said that—unlike the majority of other Philadelphia philanthropists she'd worked for—he refused to give anonymous donations to charity. He wanted his name up there. I met him a few times, and he exuded power. I remember him coming by our house and giving me a little leather key chain with clippers and scissors on it. I thought that was really great. He seemed gracious and nice, but he may have just been trying to get in with my mother. She had a lot of va-va-voom, and although she rejected Jack's advances, after which he fired her, she told me that Margaret Kelly was very cold to her."

Margaret was married to a philanderer who was irresistible to other women, and she was powerless. However painful, however humiliating her husband's infidelity, however terrible for her to bear, she would have died before she betrayed any knowledge of it to anyone. Instead, she suffered in dignified silence. It was an example that Grace remembered for the rest of her life.

2

Grace

Grace Patricia Kelly was born on November 12, 1929. Fortunately for the Kelly family, Jack never believed in playing the stock market, so that the crash, which came just weeks before her birth, didn't diminish their financial status.

She was the third child born to Margaret and Jack; Peggy "Baba," the eldest, was born on September 15, 1925, and John Jr. "Kell," on May 24, 1927. Grace spent almost four blissful years as the youngest child of the family, until Lizanne was born on June 25, 1933, usurping her role.

"I was terribly jealous of her," Grace admitted to *McCall's* in 1974. "I loved the idea of a baby but was never allowed to hold it. So I was always on my mother's knee, the clinging type. But I was pushed away, and I resented my sister for years."

Lizanne may well have sensed her sister's jealousy. Years later, when others described Grace as a timid child, Lizanne lashed out, disagreeing with the accepted view of her, telling Grace's biographer James Spada, "Grace was very strong-willed and determined, but very mild about it. She had a way of making people think she needed help. You always thought, 'Oh, I better go over and help her.'"

Margaret Kelly's analysis of Grace was more subtle, less slanted, highlighting the duality in Grace's nature: "She was a shy child but there was a kind of inner tranquility and quiet resourcefulness. She never minded being kept in bed and would sit there with her dolls for hours on end. When you passed near you could hear her talking very quietly to them. She was making up little plays for the dolls. Grace could change her voice for each doll, giving it a different character. Yet, she was a very patient and calm child. She loved attention but did not cry if she did not get it."

Margaret gave Grace a fair amount of attention, teaching her how to cook and sew. Jack, on the other hand, was rarely home, and when he did material-ize tended to devote most of his time to Kell, whom he was forging into an instrument of revenge, willing him to win the Diamond Sculls in his stead, and to Peggy, his first child, the child of his heart.

Unlike Grace, who was shy and understated, Peggy was Miss Personality, bubbly, witty, part commedienne and part beauty queen with big blue eyes, blond hair, and a shining smile that glittered with innate self-confidence.

Peggy's self-confidence was not surprising. She was Daddy's girl, and Jack Kelly adored her, praising her every move and utterance. Arrogant, he never thought to cloak his preference for Peggy from his other children, announc-ing to the adult Kell that he needn't feel demoralized because Kell's first child was a girl, as, "My greatest joy in life has been Peggy."

Given Grace's acutely sensitive nature, she must have felt her father's pref-erence for her elder sister extremely deeply. By turns withdrawn and given to outpourings of emotion, when one of the family's two boxers—who went by the German name of Siegfried—was taken ill and rushed to the vet, she cried her heart out.

While Grace was far from being an abused or neglected child, neither of her parents appeared to consider her brightest star in the Kelly firmament, or the one with the greatest potential to succeed and to thrive. One can hardly blame them. Until around the age of fifteen, she was sickly and frail, with a susceptibility to frequent colds. She wasn't particularly competitive, and—unlike the majority of middle children—had no particular need to entertain the rest of the family or play the clown for their amusement.

However, when she attended her first school, the Convent of the Assump-tion, Ravenhill, because of her youthful beauty and innate serenity she was cast as the Virgin Mary in the school's Nativity play. Shy as she was, timid as she seemed, she happily basked in the applause her burgeoning beauty re-ceived, and loved the limelight.

In summer, the family decamped to Ocean City on the Jersey shore—a seventy-mile drive from Philadelphia—where Jack had built a Spanish-style house right by the ocean on Wesley Avenue. From childhood, Grace always loved the ocean and was unafraid of the waves. After her parents arranged

Saturday morning swimming lessons for her at the Penn Athletic Club in Rittenhouse Square, she became a good, strong swimmer. In fact, one of her earliest innovations as Princess of Monaco was to have a swimming pool built on the palace grounds. Years later, when she was on the board of Twentieth Century–Fox, while visiting Los Angeles she generally stayed at the Bel-Air Hotel, where she swam laps every morning in the hotel's oval pool.

Jack, after bringing a surfboard home from a Hawaiian visit, had the distinction of introducing it to America. He encouraged Grace's love for the ocean, as did her mother. Even when Margaret was in her late seventies, she rose at sunrise every single day, then swam in the ocean before going for a vigorous jog along the beach.

In 1935, Jack ran for mayor of Philadelphia. Like Joe Kennedy, his friend and fellow Irish Democrat—another patriarch with an unquenchable lust for women and power—he didn't hesitate to use his extremely attractive children, glowing with life and vitality, as part of his publicity campaign. When he managed to secure a press call for himself while vacationing in Ocean City, he made sure that his phenomenally photogenic children were on hand as well.

The press photographer focused his camera first on Peggy, then Kell, then Grace. Seeing how especially relaxed Grace was in front of the camera, the publicity savvy Jack seized the moment. He whirled little Grace high in the air, and the cameras flashed, capturing the charm of a loving father playing with his adorable daughter.

For those few seconds, Grace at last experienced the glow of her father's undivided love and attention. The camera had achieved that blissful state for her. The camera was her friend, her ally, and she faced it unafraid, flirting with the lens, her youthful beauty enhanced by its focus. She loved the camera and the camera loved her right back.

It was a match made in heaven between the little girl who longed to be loved by her father and the camera that made him love her, if only for a few seconds. And while her father was to invariably disappoint her, the camera never did, reflecting her own beauty back to her and to the world.

Despite Jack's canny grasp of publicity and his high-level connections, he lost the mayoral election by forty thousand votes. The campaign was fast, furious, and dirty. When Margaret afterward insisted he give up politics, he acquiesced, perhaps reasoning that his life as president of the largest brick masonry firm in the United States, with all the money, power, and prestige that entailed, as well as his almost heroic status as a three-time Olympic gold medal winner, was quite enough.

Instead of sullying himself in the rough-and-tumble of politics, he now channeled all his ambition and will to power into training Kell obsessively, pushing him toward the goal of becoming a sculling champion.

When Jack wasn't forcing Kell to spend grueling hours training on the river, Kell and the other children lived an idyllic life at Henry Avenue, where they had a large back garden, complete with sandbox, cement tennis court, a massive dollhouse big enough to accommodate both Peggy and Grace (but not big enough for Lizanne as well), a skip which—when filled with water—doubled as a swimming pool, and the opportunity of using the larger one owned by their near neighbors, the Levys, as well.

Inside the house, the children ate separately from their parents, generally in the breakfast room next to the kitchen. As soon as Grace learned to read, she spent hours in the third-floor bedroom she shared with Lizanne, reading, spending as little time as possible in the basement, an ersatz Bavarian beer hall, with swinging doors and a vast model train set that her brother loved.

At the age of eleven, Grace appeared with the Philadelphia Old Academy Players in a one-act play, *Don't Feed the Animals*. Despite his self-involvement Jack Kelly loved his children in his own particular fashion and thus was on hand to witness Grace's performance.

"The woman who played Grace's mother forgot her part," he remembered in 1954. "Grace dropped her handbag. As she came up with it, she fed the older actress her lines. Turning to Margaret, I said, 'We've got a trouper on our hands.'"

Given that Jack's recollections were made to the prestigious *Saturday Evening Post* when Grace was already an acclaimed star, he may well have been painting himself as more prescient than he had really been at the time of her first theatrical performance. But he was there, he applauded, and that was good enough for her.

She also adored the ballet. She had lessons from the time she was tiny and longed to become a ballerina when she grew up. By then, however, she was five foot seven, far too tall for the ballet. Nonetheless, she remained body conscious for the rest of her life, never crossing her legs when she sat because, as she explained, "It makes your calves look fat."

As her official photographer, Howell Conant—who began photographing her in 1955—observed, "She had a dancer's awareness of her body; her every gesture, whether she was checking her makeup with the help of her sister, Peggy, or relaxing on the stern of a boat we happened upon on a quiet walk by the water, Grace's arms and legs were as expressive as her face." All in all throughout her life she moved with a fluid elegance, as if she really were the prima ballerina she'd dreamed of becoming.

Her primary interests were artistic, and by the time she was thirteen, her sense of style was well honed. When Gaston Duval, maître d' of Philadelphia's premier hotel, the Bellevue-Stratford, arrived at the Kelly home to cater a big dinner there, Grace insisted on trailing him, rearranging the place settings according to her own blossoming artistic sensibilities.

Gaston had brought a gold service for twenty-four along with him from the hotel and wasn't about to allow the daughter of the house mess with his table settings. Exasperated by Grace's meddling, he complained to Margaret, who—in a telling demonstration of her strict child-rearing methods—gave the maître d' carte blanche to spank Grace if she continued to misbehave. She did, and he retaliated with a Margaret Kelly–endorsed spanking. Grace's reaction is not on record.

Now in her teens, Grace had grown into a great beauty, with luminescent skin, long, elegant limbs, limpid blue eyes, and a full, sensuous mouth. From that time on, her beauty was unrivaled. For a sense of its impact, there is no better witness than Howell Conant who, over twenty-seven years, photographed her thousands of times, spending hours studying her face from all angles. "You trusted Grace's beauty: you knew it wasn't built from clothes and make-up," he explained, adding that she had "a wonderful profile. If Grace's face had one flaw it was her jaw, and she knew it." In later years, when she was a star, he would minimize her jaw by having her "turn her face so it didn't look quite so square. Sometimes a collar would cover it: at other times I would tilt her chin to show more of the cheek."

In September 1943, she entered Stevens School, a small private school in a mansion on Walnut Lane in Germantown. A typical all-American teenager, she had discovered the joys of the movies and, along with Maree, loved outings to the Orpheum, the Colonial, or the Bandbox, where she saw *Casablanca, The Song of Bernadette, The Lost Weekend,* and *Going My Way,* little knowing that one day she would become romantically involved with Ray Milland, the star of *The Lost Weekend,* and Bing Crosby, star of *Going My Way.*

Had the Kellys been Main Line Philadelphia, Grace would automatically have become a debutante and done the "season." "With the deb season coming up upon us, I said to Grace, 'I hear some of your chums are coming out. Do you want to come out too?'" Jack Kelly recalled. "Grace's blue eyes flashed with anger and she flashed, 'I am out. Do you think I have to use those women who sell mailing lists of boys' names to mothers and fathers of girls to get me a date?'"

Grace was already dating and loving it. Both Jack and Margaret Kelly were surprisingly permissive in bringing up their daughters, relishing the attention all three of them got from the opposite sex. On the threshold of Grace's wedding, Margaret proudly boasted, "Men began proposing to my daughter Grace when she was barely fifteen." Grace was encouraged by her parents to date as much as she wanted, and she took full advantage of their laissez-faire attitude.

She was passionate and intense, and her first romance turned out not to be as light-hearted a relationship as her parents might have wished. Harper Davis, one of Kell's classmates at Penn Charter School, was the son of the local Buick dealer. Grace fell for him wholeheartedly. Jack, however, was far from delighted by the prospect of his beautiful middle daughter sailing off into the sunset with a mere car dealer's son, and after a year he insisted that she break off the relationship. Obedient and acquiescent to her father's command, Grace ended the romance. It was a pattern she would often repeat in the future.

Instead of sticking with her first love and consequently displeasing her father, she concentrated on dating the brawny lifeguards in the Ocean City Beach Patrol, an organization that Jack Kelly heavily supported both financially—donating racing boats, surfboards, and trophies—and personally, rowing with the lifeguards and urging the best of them to compete in the Olympics. In 1942, Kell joined the crew, as a result winning his father's approval. All in all, Grace knew that dating a lifeguard was a safe bet and that she'd enjoy it in the bargain.

At first, she and Maree catered to the lifeguards, bringing them lunch.

"Grace was an unbelievably striking girl, but very down-to-earth and friendly, glad to bring us sandwiches," remembered lifeguard Bill Ashmead.

After observing the lifeguards in all their macho glory, Grace accepted a date with another lifeguard, Bill D'Arcy, the son of a wealthy Philadelphia plasterer. She first met the burly seventeen-year-old in the summer of 1944, just months before her fifteenth birthday. Even though more than sixty years have passed, the memory of Grace Kelly hasn't subsided for D'Arcy. "I used to pick her up from her parents' house on Wesley Avenue, and her father would sit and talk to me," he said. "I used to drive there in my father's 1931 convertible Packard, which looked like a German commando car, with a big wheel on the hood. But it didn't have a good battery, so when I drove it, I couldn't turn it off because it couldn't get started again. By September, it was kind of cool, and when I arrived at the Kelly house to pick Grace up for a date, her father cracked, 'Oh, Bill, I see we have the pneumonia car tonight!'

"Grace loved to dance, so we always went to the Convention Hall and danced to the DJ there. She was a great gal, trim, slim and very pretty. She always reminded me of a young gazelle," Bill D'Arcy said. Their romance lasted over two summers.

Back home in Philadelphia, Grace dated other local boys. One, Jack Oeschele, reminisced to Gwen Robyns, "If you wanted to sit, she'd sit; if you wanted to dance, she'd dance. And if you took her to a party she wouldn't float off with another fellow. She was your date and she remained your date."

"Instead of showing off and chattering all about herself like most teenagers, she was attentive to her dates. She made each escort think he was King Bee," Howard Wilkoff recalled.

Grace dated a succession of boys from Penn Charter—all jocks, none alienating her father in any way. She was winning his approval and having a good time in the bargain. Not surprisingly—given her background, her father, and her brother—she had a taste for sportsmen, and one of her more serious teen romances was with Dick Boccelli, starting guard for West Chester State Teacher's College, whom she met on the beach at Ocean City.

Boccelli—who later became the drummer for Bill Haley and the Comets—had a six-month relationship with Grace after one of her ex-boyfriends introduced them with the words, "I just broke up with a great gal, and I'd like you to meet her."

"Grace really was a lovely girl. I used to play basketball with her brother, Kell. I took her out in my father's Lincoln, so her father thought I had money," he said. "Grace knew I didn't, but it didn't matter to her. I took her to shows in Atlantic City, to Vaugham's Comfort Club, where the waiters sang to us and we sang along. She had a great personality, a good sense of humor, was bright, sharp and fun to be with.

"Grace didn't have any pretensions. Although she grew up with a silver spoon, she wasn't in the least bit spoiled. I could have fallen in love with her, but luckily I didn't, because just after my graduation I took her up to West Chester College and introduced her to a football player friend of mine, Joe Mustin. He was the most handsome man ever and could have been a movie star. He took over from me."

Grace's relationship with Joe Mustin also would be short-lived, not because she rejected him but because, as he puts it today, "She was too rich for my blood." Joe took her to a restaurant in Somers Point, Ocean City. "Then she said she had to go home and asked if I would like to go with her, so I did. When we got there, her father put me through the third degree, asking what I did and what my father did. I wasn't welcomed with open arms because I was clearly below Grace's class. She didn't think so, but her family obviously did. We dated a few times, but I was out of her league and, after a few dates, I broke it off."

She was far from heartbroken. She was pretty, popular, sought after, with suitors galore and myriad romantic options. On the surface, she was the quintessential American teen, the perfect date, having a ball with other teenagers. But Grace, the daughter of Jack Kelly, whose love and attention generally eluded her, had deeper, secret hungers that only a father figure could fulfill.

The first time Grace set eyes on an older man who evoked disturbing emotions within her, the submissive teenager who meekly obliged her dates by sitting if they wanted to sit and dancing if they wanted to dance suddenly became predatory, aggressive, clearly grasping for a father substitute. Sadly for her, the first candidate whom she selected for that role in her life was not in the least bit interested in her.

Paul "Skinny" D'Amato was the legendary front for Atlantic City's 500 Club, reportedly fronting for Philadelphia's mob boss, Marco Reginelli, and his successor, Angelo Bruno. From 1942, the 500 Club was the East Coast's epicenter of sin and scandal, and a Mecca for gangsters, former bootleggers, and sundry denizens of the underworld. Urbane, elegant, and charming, Skinny skillfully straddled the worlds of show business and organized crime with effortless cool and was rumored to have been the inspiration for the Rat Pack.

Although—or perhaps because—Skinny had a conviction for running a prostitution racket and was an intimate of mobsters like Sam Giancana, his club attracted performers like Jerry Lewis and Dean Martin, Sammy Davis Jr., Nat King Cole, and his close friend, Frank Sinatra. Not to mention Jack Kelly, who had a permanent table at the 500 Club and could be seen there on many nights, quaffing champagne and holding court with Skinny.

According to 500 Club waitress Rita Marzullo, who told the story to Jonathan Van Meter for his book *The Last Good Time: Skinny D'Amato, the Notorious 500 Club, and the Rise and Fall of Atlantic City*, on one of many occasions, Jack was a guest at a party thrown by Skinny, and with Jack's tacit approval, Grace joined him there.

"She was still young and single and she was chasing Skinny all over the place. And he's hiding in that little alcove, saying, 'Did she leave yet? Did she leave yet?' And now I'm furious because his wife is sitting there with his kids," Rita said.

"Grace Kelly made herself so obvious and I said to Skinny, 'You want me to say anything?' And he said, 'No. Keep your mouth shut. Don't say nothing. She'll leave, she'll leave.' Finally she sees that her father was starting to notice and he reprimanded her. And she finally left and Skinny came out of hiding," she recalled.

Skinny was handsome, married, and unavailable. Despite Grace's attempt to be a regular American girl making out with regular American boys her own age, she threw herself at a man even more piratical and unavailable than Jack Kelly. Skinny D'Amato was the first of a series of unattainable married men she longed to captivate yet failed to snare.

The fact that she made her play for a married man in her father's presence said a great deal about her psyche. Her self-control was such that she clearly could have hidden her incipient passion for Skinny from her father, but instead she flaunted it. Whereupon, in Rita's words, Jack "reprimanded her." Grace had wanted to attract her father's attention and she had succeeded.

Aside from Grace's abortive attempt at seducing Skinny, Jack's continuing

presence at the 500 Club raises other questions. Countless Philadelphia lumi-
naries regularly made the pilgrimage to Skinny's place and Jack Kelly
shouldn't be damned by association. Nevertheless, according to Murray Dubin, a journalist familiar with the Philadelphia Mafia, it is highly likely that
during his rise to power as one of America's leading building contractors, Jack
may well have interacted with organized crime.

Although there is no evidence that during his bid for high political office
Jack was actively involved with organized crime, he was a gambler who loved
power and the powerful. In 1944 he confounded the Atlantic City Race Track,
an enterprise in which he most likely rubbed shoulders with mobsters.

On July 22, 1946, the Atlantic City Race Track—built by Kelly for
Brickworks—opened and became the most popular attraction on the Jersey
Shore. Backed by Frank Sinatra, Bob Hope, and other wealthy stockholders,
the racecourse was Jack Kelly's domain, where he ruled unchallenged.

Grace reveled in her father's powerful status at the track. Kelly family
friend Bill Ashmead remembered, "She'd turn up at the racetrack in a fitted
navy blue suit, wearing a porkpie hat to match, looking very stunning. She'd
present the cup to the jockey and owner who won the main race, then watch
the rest from the box."

Her father was King of the Atlantic City Race Track so that, before she
was even out of her teens, Grace Kelly was already a princess.

In May 1947, she graduated from Stevens. Her graduation yearbook noted
that her favorite actress was Ingrid Bergman; her favorite actor, Joseph Cotten; her favorite summer resort, Ocean City; her favorite drink, a black and
white chocolate milkshake; her favorite piece of classical music, Debussy's
"Clair de Lune" and Grieg's Piano Concerto; her favorite orchestra, Benny
Goodman; and her favorite female singer, Jo Stafford. Even more telling was
the section "Stevens' Prophecy," in which was written, "Miss Grace P. Kelly—
a famous star of stage and screen."

However, although she had acted with the Players right through high
school, and wanted to become an actress, her parents insisted that she attend
college. Bennington College in Vermont offered a four-year dance degree
course, and she planned to apply for it.

But before she did, she took her first trip to Europe, to watch Kell's second try at winning the Diamond Sculls. On the previous trip, in 1946, Jack and Kell traveled to Europe alone. This time, at the end of June 1947, Jack, Kell, Margaret, Grace, and Lizanne all set sail for England together.

In Henley, the family stayed at the Red Lion Hotel. On July 5, they cheered Kell on as he sculled under the colors of the University of Pennsylvania and won the Diamond Sculls. Jack Kelly had his revenge at last.

Twenty years later, Princess Grace of Monaco flew to London to visit her daughter Caroline—then unhappy at St. Mary's School, Ascot—fervently hoping to convince her not to leave the school where she felt she didn't fit in.

Instead of taking Caroline to lunch in Ascot, Grace drove her along the small winding roads to Henley, nineteen and a half miles away, and sat with her by the bank of the Thames.

"Caroline, you must go back to school," she said.

Then, gazing pointedly at the river where Kell had rowed his way to victory, thus fulfilling their father's dream, Grace added, "I hope you understand . . ."

Her meaning was clear. The Kellys were winners. The Kellys never quit.

3

Dynasties

I was talking to JFK about his sisters," Kell recalled to *Philadelphia Magazine*. "Years before, my family had sailed to England with his family, because my dad and his dad were friends. I told him I never forgot that crossing because his sisters were so pretty. Kennedy laughed and told me, 'I was on that ship too.'"

In many ways, the Kellys and the Kennedys were born to meet, mate, and marry. The Kennedy and Kelly children were all blessed with good looks, great vitality, a competitive spirit fostered in them by their fathers, and a sense that they were above the crowd, special, born to make their parents proud. In fact, had you met the Kelly and the Kennedy children at the same time, in the same room, you would have been hard-pressed to know who came from which family.

The similarity between both patresfamilias was striking. Both Joe Kennedy and Jack Kelly were the sons of Irish immigrants, both tall, handsome, dominant, and accustomed to ruling their brood of children, both egoists, brooking no opposition. Charming and powerful, both men were masters of manipulating their public images. Joe Kennedy's motto was, "It doesn't matter what you are. It only matters what people think you are," and Jack Kelly embraced the identical creed.

Both men were adept politicians, both Democrats who ultimately lost their footholds in the party. Joe attained high office and was appointed ambassador to the Court of St. James's, but—after he was exposed as sympathizing with Hitler—lost his post, while Jack failed in his bid for mayor of Philadelphia. Nonetheless, both men remained tacticians, multimillionaires who had settled for channeling their hopes and dreams into their children.

Neither was disappointed. John F. Kennedy fulfilled his father's thwarted political ambitions tenfold, and Kell, of course, reversed his father's failure to
compete at Henley by winning the Diamond Sculls in his stead. Jack Kelly had
made his fortune in the construction business; Joe Kennedy, more illicitly, in
bootlegging. Joe was Mr. Big in Boston, Jack was Mr. Big in Philadelphia. They
were friends and may well have enjoyed raucous evenings together at the 500
Club. Moreover, Joe Kennedy and Jack Kelly were both philanderers married
to long-suffering wives who drowned their disappointment in other pursuits:
Rose made trips to the Paris collections, where she vented her ire at Joe by
spending vast sums of his money on high fashion; Margaret worked with the
Women's Health Center and maintained her physical fitness and her figure.

Whether Grace Kelly met Jack Kennedy before, during, or after the Kelly
family's transatlantic voyage is not on record. However, the fact that they did
meet, is. In the summer of 1953, just weeks before Jack was due to marry
Jacqueline Bouvier, he had a romance with blond Swedish aristocrat Gunilla
Von Post. On their first evening together, at the Hotel du Cap, Antibes, Jack
and Gunilla sat in the twilight, watching the waves of the Mediterranean
crash against the shore. According to Gunilla, "Jack said, 'I fell in love with
you tonight. It's only happened to me once before. Five years ago, I fell in love
with Grace Kelly the moment I saw her.'"

There is no documentary evidence regarding what happened between
Grace and Jack, or why their relationship never evolved into anything long-
lasting. The only clue can be found in historian Priscilla MacMillan's comment, "Joe wanted Jack to marry Grace, but then [Joe] decided that she was
too Hollywood."

In October 1954, Jackie—now married to Jack and unaware of his romantic
past with Grace—met her at a dinner party and enlisted her help in amusing
him, as he was then in the Hospital for Special Surgery in Manhattan, after a
serious back operation.

In an interview with Grace conducted on June 19, 1965, for the Kennedy
Library oral history archive, Grace—as was occasionally her modus operandi
once she became Princess of Monaco—rewrote history somewhat. "The first
time I met President Kennedy was during that year he was in the hospital in
New York with his back. I had been to a dinner party where I had met Mrs.

Kennedy and her sister for the first time," she recalled. "'They asked me to go to the hospital with them to pay a visit and help cheer him up. They wanted me to go into his room and say I was the new night nurse. I was terribly embarrassed. Eventually I was sort of pushed into his room by the two girls. I introduced myself, but he had recognized me at once and couldn't have been sweeter or more quick to put me at ease."

After Grace and Rainier's wedding, Jack and Jackie were looking at the press coverage together. "Jack studied the pictures intently, then frowned and said, 'I could have married her!'" Gore Vidal wrote in his memoirs, adding that he dated Jackie's dislike of Grace from that moment on.

In May 1961, Grace and Rainier were invited to lunch with President and Mrs. Kennedy at the White House. Tish Baldrige, social secretary to Jackie Kennedy, remembered, "Grace had a relationship with the President before his marriage to Jackie, and Jackie knew about it. That, in my opinion, is why Jackie changed the White House meal in their honor from a four-hour black-tie dinner dance to a small eighty-minute-long seated luncheon. A bit of jealousy perhaps.

"Jackie never said anything, but you could tell. She didn't really want to talk about the arrangements and was very offhand about how they were made. Couldn't care less. It was downgraded to an informal visit so there wouldn't be a State dinner. That meant that Princess Grace wouldn't look as gorgeous as she usually did," Tish said.

"I was disappointed in how she looked that day. She wore what I would term a surprisingly dowdy Yves St. Laurent [sic] suit and a white turban with little white flowers that covered all of her hair. The East Wing, acting as fashion observers, concluded that her turban looked exactly like an Esther Williams Aquacade flowered rubber bathing cap, lifted straight from one of the swimming star's movies."

Bill Walton, Franklin D. Roosevelt Jr., Grace, and the President sat at one end of the table and Jackie sat at the other, with Rainier. Jackie was not pleased, whispering to Jack that she wished she were sitting next to him instead. According to Bill Walton, Grace was extremely quiet throughout the lunch. Later, he discovered the reason. "She was so scared of coming to the luncheon that she had two double Bloody Marys and was bombed."

"Grace was like a schoolgirl with Jack," Tish remembered. "She obviously was so thrilled to see him. She batted her eyelashes in admiration of him all the time. It was hero worship. An old boyfriend who was now President of the United States. Why shouldn't she be overwhelmed?"

Nonetheless, Grace looked back on her reunion with Jack with great affection remembering the menu—soft-shelled crabs, spring lamb, and strawberries Romanoff—and kept it because, as she put it, "I'm one of those people who keeps everything."

According to the interview Grace gave to the Kennedy Library, during that same lunch, the President "turned to me suddenly and asked: 'Is that a Givenchy you're wearing?' The astonishing thing was that day that particular dress just happened to be one.

"I said, 'How clever of you, Mr. President. However did you know?'

"'Oh,' he replied, 'I'm getting pretty good at it now that fashion is becoming more important than politics and the press is paying more attention to Jackie's clothes than my speeches.'"

Grace was the Princess of Monaco, the mother of three children, and if she had any regrets that she hadn't seized the moment all those years ago and married Jack, she wasn't revealing her emotions during that interview, except to say of him, "He was almost too good to be true—he was just like the All-American boy, wasn't he, handsome, a fighter, witty, full of charm. . . ."

On the morning of President Kennedy's assassination, not yet aware of the tragedy then unfolding in Dallas, Grace took the children to a carnival in Monte Carlo. There, not knowing that Jack had been shot, when a Monegasque invited her to try her luck at the shooting gallery, she obligingly posed for a photograph, a rifle in her hand poised to shoot. The next morning, the morning after the assassination, that photograph appeared in newspapers around the world.

Mortified, she issued a press statement explaining the circumstances surrounding the photographs but to no avail. She was criticized throughout the world for posing with a rifle the day the President was shot dead, even more so when she and Rainier—perhaps now aware of Jackie's enmity—opted not to attend the State funeral in Washington.

On December 3, 1963, Grace flew to Washington, where she stood by the

President's grave, tears streaming down her face. Then, armed with toys for John Jr. and Caroline, she made her way to the White House to pay a condolence call on Jackie. Jackie flatly refused to see her.

Grace encountered Jackie again, on April 18, 1966, at the feria in Seville. She had been married to Rainier for ten years, Jack was dead, and she had every reason to hope that Jackie no longer harbored any resentment toward her.

Barcelona's mayor, Felix Morena de la Cova, was determined that no tension between the two most famous women in the Western world overshadow the day's festivities. To that end, he traveled to the airport twice to meet each of them in turn, presenting Jackie with a lace mantilla and comb and Grace with a white and rose flamenco dress.

At the opening of the feria, "Grace dressed as a señorita arrived in a carriage, looking incredibly pretty, and Jackie rode in on horseback, looking absolutely stunning in a Matador's outfit. No two women could have looked more different," Gwen Robyns noted.

The last night of the feria was marked by the Red Cross Ball, in which seventy debutantes would be presented to Grace and Rainier. After Grace and Rainier arrived fifty minutes late at the Duchess of Medinacelli's Moorish palace, the atmosphere between Grace and Jackie became frosty in the extreme.

They spent two hours at the table of honor, sitting just a yard apart. The tension between them was so palpable that the next morning, the *New York Herald Tribune* ran a story headed, "Cool Conversation . . . Princess Grace of Monaco and Mrs. John F. Kennedy seem to have little to say to each other at the Red Cross Ball."

An incensed Grace fired off a letter to the paper: "I was delighted to meet Mrs. Kennedy again, for whom I have great admiration and respect. If there was any coolness or fatigue that evening, it was caused only by some of the many dozens of photographers who pushed, shoved and relentlessly pursued us all night."

"That night, at the feria, it was like something out of *Dynasty*. Jackie had it in for Grace, not vice versa," said presidential historian Barry Landau, who was with Jackie at the feria. He added, "Grace couldn't have cared less. But Jackie carried a deep resentment of Grace, knowing that Grace and Jack had dated and that Jack's father wanted him to marry her. Jackie made her feelings about Grace pretty obvious. She wasn't being subtle. Later, at the Marbella Club, in front of a lot of us, Jackie—who was a great mimic—did a flawless impression of Grace in *Rear Window*. Jackie did whole scenes from *Rear Window*, imitating Grace being so obsequious to Jimmy Stewart. It was hysterical."

In July 1947, Grace and the family arrived back in America from England, still intoxicated by Kell's triumph at Henley. However, as the ocean liner docked at New York harbor, she knew it was time to turn her thoughts to her own future, her own ambitions.

However, to Margaret's dismay, they discovered that Grace had been rejected by Bennington, because she hadn't fulfilled their stringent standards with regard to mathematics.

Secretly, Grace wasn't at all upset. It was far too late for her to apply to any of the other East Coast colleges so beloved by her mother. She had always harbored dreams of a career in the theater, but—aware that her parents expected her to go to college—hadn't dared to broach the subject. Now, however, with college no longer an option, she was free to follow her dream.

However, a few obstacles remained. The school of her choice, the American Academy of Dramatic Arts—where Katharine Hepburn, Gene Tierney, Kirk Douglas, and Spencer Tracy had all studied—had already selected its quota of students for the next semester and there were no more available places.

For the first time in her life, Grace knew what she wanted and where she was going, and she resolved to let nothing stand in her way. With the help of an old friend of her mother's, a former actress, she maneuvered her way into an interview with Emile Diestel, the American Academy's admissions officer.

Although she would from then on always work ceaselessly to hone her craft, when it came to getting what she wanted, now she had no compunction about using her Pulitzer Prize–winning playwright uncle's distinguished reputation, artlessly professing on her American Academy application form, "I hope to be so accomplished a dramatic actress that some day my Uncle George will write a play for me and direct it."

She auditioned on August 20, 1947, and although her audition notes of that day contain the criticism that her voice was "improperly placed" and "very nasal," what really mattered was the notation "George Kelly's Niece."

With misgivings, her parents allowed Grace to move to New York and attend the academy, promising that they would fund her studies for a year. She would be living in Manhattan's Barbizon Hotel for Women at Sixty-third Street and Lexington Avenue, an august establishment opened in 1927 for the unmarried daughters of the gentry, which banned men from entering the premises after ten at night. Consequently, Grace's parents felt secure in the knowledge that Grace's virginity wouldn't be stolen by some unworthy man.

Unbeknownst to them, however, it was too late. Just before leaving Philadelphia and launching her new life in Manhattan, Grace lost her virginity.

"It all happened so quickly. I dropped in unexpectedly at a girlfriend's house—I remember it was raining very hard—and her husband told me she would be gone for the rest of the afternoon. I stayed talking to him, and before I knew it we were in bed together," she told one of her next lovers, American Academy teacher Don Richardson, many years later, and he then repeated her comments to James Spada, one of her earlier biographers.

Richardson failed to report Grace's emotions or her conscience in the aftermath of losing her virginity to a friend's husband.

Grace began her first term at the Academy in October 1947, walking from the Barbizon to the school upstairs at Carnegie Hall on Fifty-seventh Street. On her first day there, she met fellow student Herb Miller. They had a brief fling, but she didn't allow it to detract from her dedication to her career. "Grace had somewhat of an open door because of her uncle and her father's friend, Manie Sacks, but she worked hard," said Bettina Thompson, her friend and fellow academy student.

Bettina was her first roommate at the Barbizon, sharing a room so small that, "When one of us dressed, the other had to stand on the bed," Grace later recalled.

"We used to dance along the Barbizon corridors to the tune of Fred Astaire," Bettina remembered. "Grace was famous for doing her 'turtle dance.' She did it at a party at my father-in-law's, and we were all speechless. She got down on the floor, put her head in her hands as if she were in a shell. Then she poked out her head, then her arms, then her tail. That was the turtle dance—and Grace had us all rolling around the floor laughing hysterically."

"I first met Grace when I saw this very pretty girl come out of the revolving door," remembered fellow Barbizon resident Carolyn Scott. "She was wearing a black hat with blue flowers on it, a black coat, and black high-heeled shoes. I thought how pretty she was and how well dressed."

Shy and fragile, with large brown eyes and a tentative manner, Carolyn was a very different kind of girl from Grace's other friends, like the Main Line debutante Maree Frisby Rambo or the Philadelphia-bred actress, Bettina Thompson. Born in Steubenville, Ohio, Carolyn—a former beauty queen—was the daughter of a plant foreman and was in Manhattan to make her fortune as a model, yet despite the differences in their backgrounds, she and Grace became fast friends.

"Grace used to tell me that her father made fun of her when she was in high school. He used to say that she would never get a job. Finally, she got one as a waitress in Ocean City, just to prove him wrong," Carolyn continued. "So even though her father was supporting her at the Barbizon, she always remembered the years in which he kept telling her she would never get a job, so even though he and her mother gave her their blessings, and paid for the apartment, Grace wanted to be independent," Carolyn said.

Soon after Grace moved into the Barbizon, she was invited to a party at Eastfair, the Lloyd Harbor, Long Island, estate of Fairchild Industries tycoon Sherman Fairchild. Sherman had set up a photographic studio at his replica of a Normandy chateau and photographed models and actresses there. The atmosphere at Eastfair—which also boasted a moat, a swimming pool, and an indoor tennis court—was glamorous, elegant, sophisticated.

At Eastfair, Grace met Fairchild's close friend Malcolm Reybold, a divorced advertising executive with an engaging personality and a reputation as a womanizer. Shortly afterwards, Malcolm chanced to meet Carolyn Scott. One date led to another. A few months later, Malcolm, Carolyn, and Grace were invited back to Fairchild's. "Malcolm and I and Grace chatted for most of the weekend," Carolyn recalled. "On Sunday morning, she walked a mile to church. She was very conscious of her religion and believed in it a lot. I am a Methodist Episcopalian and asked Grace about the Catholic religion. I don't think she could think of anything to say right away, so all she said was, 'It's the biggest.'"

Grace's aim was to become self-supporting. She began attending Academy classes in the morning, then working as a model in the afternoon.

Her first modeling job, in 1948, involved the unglamorous task of spraying a room with insecticide for an advertisement for the Bridgeport Brass

Company. "She was obviously well-bred and very much a lady," said the company's advertising manager, William Disea. "From the moment you looked at her and heard her speak, you realized she didn't have to be posing with a spray can for a living." Confiding to Disea that this was her first modeling job, she told him that she thought modeling might prove to be a lucrative alternative to acting—just in case she didn't make it as an actress.

"Grace was lucky when she started modeling, but she took every casting call seriously and believed in it," Carolyn recalled. "I remember going to a cover test for a magazine dressed in a plain jersey skirt and blouse, and there was Grace all dressed up in a Persian lamb coat. I didn't know whether my test was good or not, but the next month, there was Grace on the cover of *Redbook*, looking beautiful. After that, I did a couple of catalogs with her. She was represented by the Walter Thornton Agency and was starting to do very well."

Model supremo Eileen Ford said recently, "Grace was not a big model. She couldn't have cared less about modeling. Her acting took up a lot of her time."

After classes or work, Grace, Carolyn, Bettina, and fellow academy student Sally Richardson often splurged on a visit to the Russian Tea Room. But Barbizon employees recall her spending most evenings in the hotel's dining room, reading a book, studying her lines, or crocheting.

At the end of April 1948, Grace's work ethic paid off. She was selected to attend the academy's senior course, from September 1948 until March 1949, culminating in a series of performances in Carnegie Hall. Her future in acting seemed promising.

4

Actress

Grace did well in her second year at the Academy, but not as well as she would once she had met and been taken under the wing of the Academy's star acting teacher, thirty-year-old Don Richardson, born Melvin Schwarz, a man who had an instinct for finding talent and nurturing it.

"I don't think Grace had formulated anything when she met Don, but he definitely was a stepping-stone for her," said his widow, Laura, to whom Don confided a great deal about his relationship with Grace.

"Don loved playing Pygmalion to Grace," she said. "He felt Grace was vulnerable. He said that she had the ability to make men want to take care of her, and he felt he was doing just that. I don't think it was a manipulative tactic. She was just that kind of a person."

The moment they met, Grace aroused a multitude of emotions in Don. They were in the elevator, and one of the other students was bullying her unmercifully. Don challenged him and made him stop, which he did. But although she was grateful to him, she found it difficult to stop crying. He took her to the Russian Tea Room, but when they got there, he realized that he didn't have any money on him. So he invited her back to his apartment instead.

He left her in the living room while he went to the kitchen to make some coffee. When he came back, she was naked.

She was proud of her body and not the least bit reluctant to show it off to a man she'd just met—an unusual characteristic in a woman in those pre–sexual revolution days.

Don was not the only man to be surprised by Grace's sudden nakedness on their first date. The writer Robert Slatzer remembered his brief relationship with Grace. "The night we first dated in Hollywood, we went back to her apartment. Grace immediately went into the bathroom, then came out stark naked."

"Don told me that he fell in love with Grace sculpturally," Laura said. "He loved her, but I think she used him to get ahead. He was responsible for getting her her first agent."

Don also suggested that she model her accent on that of the British actress Deborah Kerr, star of *The King and I* and *From Here to Eternity*. Determined to rid herself of her nasal Philadelphia accent, Grace spent hours reciting Shakespeare with a clothespin clipped onto the end of her nose.

That accent might have been appropriate when Grace was acting in the theater or in movies, and would hold her in good stead when she played Englishwoman Linda Nordley in *Mogambo*, but she tended to use it offscreen as well, much to the amusement of her family back home in Philadelphia, who ribbed her mercilessly about it until she explained to them that her new accent was crucial to her achieving success in the theater.

"Don never thought Grace was a great actress, but he was convinced that she would make it in the movies," Laura Richardson recalled. "During the relationship, he spent a weekend with Grace at her family's home in Philadelphia and he told them that she was going to be a great movie star, but they all laughed and made fun of him."

In a letter written to her friend, former Barbizon roomate, Prudy Wise on April 13, 1949, Grace expanded on Don's disastrous weekend in Philadelphia, saying of her parents: "They disliked Don immensely and the fact that I could fall in love with a Jew was just beyond them. My mother pops out with the news that he was married and that he was asking his wife for a divorce."

Margaret Kelly had found out that her daughter was dating a married man after jettisoning her ethics and searching through his suitcase, where she found copies of correspondence with his divorce attorney. Appalled, she enlisted Kell's help in ridding the family of Don once and for all. Kell, who as a teenager used to receive compliments regarding his sisters' beauty, to which he invariably replied "three beasts," was protective of Grace and eagerly obliged his mother by bringing three friends home for dinner with Don and the family.

"One was the Olympic Butterfly champion and looked a bit like Kirk Douglas and the other was a big looking guy; a weight-lifting type, who was my partner in rowing races and was also in the life guards at Ocean City," Kell said years later. "There was another chap also a big rowing type. I gave them the word that this fellow was a bit of a creep—which I had deduced from my mother's description. When they came into the room they gave Grace's guy the grip and in a second had him on the floor. My sister was so mad at me for bringing these animals home and embarrassing her that she was quiet for a month."

Grace was furious, but she didn't defend her lover an iota. After the week-end, she still wouldn't brook any criticism of her family, and Don was disgusted by her lack of loyalty to him.

Although he didn't know it at the time, her loyalty also was lacking in other areas—perhaps because she knew that, without her family's approval, she would never marry him. Single and free to play the field, ambitious and determined to make it as an actress, she had other lovers, other mentors.

When the time came for Grace to graduate from the Academy, Don—her teacher, mentor, and lover—took great care in selecting the part she would play in her final performances at Carnegie Hall, that of Tracy Lord in *The Philadelphia Story*, the part created by Katharine Hepburn, first on Broadway, then on screen.

Although she was much younger than Hepburn, and probably not old enough for the part, the role of the petulant Philadelphia Main Line heiress brought to her knees by passion was the perfect one for Grace, and Don, the professional, knew it.

What he may not also have known is that she had already staked her own claim to *The Philadelphia Story*, which would ultimately be adapted into *High Society*, with Grace once more winning the part of Tracy Lord. Whether by accident or design, during her years at the academy Grace dated Philip Barry Jr., whose father was the author of *The Philadelphia Story*.

"Grace met my late husband toward the end of the forties, at a party in Manhattan," recalled Barry's widow, Patricia. "He and Grace started dating, but she had this other man, an older man. It could have been her acting teacher, Don Richardson. Phil told me that Grace was very dear, very sweet. After they stopped seeing each other, and she moved to Monaco, they exchanged notes, and he went there to visit her.

"Did Grace's relationship with Phil have any impact on her being cast as Tracy Lord in *High Society*? Phil was involved in the whole structure of the movie.

I am sure he had an influence on the decision as to who would play Tracy. But it was fait accompli. Grace was perfectly right for the part," she said.

Grace had now moved into apartment 9A at Manhattan House at 200 East Sixty-sixth Street which, like many other East Coast buildings, had been constructed with bricks from Kelly for Brickworks.

Jack and Margaret took great delight in helping her furnish her first apartment. Not realizing that Grace's bathroom was yellow, Jack arrived bearing a gift of white towels monogrammed in pink. But despite the color clash, Grace pronounced her father's gift "cute." Pride of place, however, was an S-shaped couch upholstered in fabric woven with the word "Love."

Among her neighbors at Manhattan House was Carolyn Scott, now married to Malcolm Reybold, the rakish New York ad man twelve years her senior. Sometimes Carolyn and Malcolm played matchmakers, setting Grace up on a date with an eligible man. Malcolm's friend, tennis champion Sidney Wood, was one of those men. "The four of us went to Rothmans in Long Island, where each year they served rhinoceros," ninety-year-old Sidney Wood recalled. "Grace had a bit much to drink, but we started going out and saw each other for two or three months.

"Grace was beautiful, but she was always acting. It is hard to fall in love with someone who is 'on' all the time. She was somewhat artificial, always putting on an act. She would suddenly appear in the apartment and come out with every kind of animal sound—even an elephant's—mimicking them all for her acting. I never felt she was down-to-earth.

"Once, when we were all out together, it was snowing, so I put a snow shovel in Malcolm's car. Afterward, I left it in Grace's apartment. The morning after we broke up, she had the snow shovel delivered back to me. I liked her, but I wasn't in love with her. She wasn't in love with me, either. She was in love with acting."

Carolyn and Malcolm didn't merely play matchmaker to Grace. Carolyn also had an influence on her style. "One afternoon, when Grace was working in television, Malcolm and I were sitting in the living room chatting to Grace, and I gave her a compliment about her hair," Carolyn recalled. "At that time, she was wearing her hair down in a pageboy, parted on the left side, which looked beautiful. But she said she didn't think it was quite right. 'I have such a big jaw—the Kellys all have big jaws—I don't know what to do with my hair,' she said. My mother wore her hair in a French twist, so I said, 'Why don't you accentuate your jaw, rather than try and hide it?' So she tried wearing her hair in a French twist, and she kept it that way."

Ben Dreyfus, who worked in the advertising business, manufacturing point-of-sale displays, met Grace when she was hired as Miss Old Gold, representing the cigarette company. Afterward she cracked, "I was terrible. Honestly, anyone watching me give the pitch for Old Golds would have switched to Camels," but the agency liked her.

After Ben called her to book her for another job, she invited him to accompany her to see José Ferrer perform, then on to the El Morocco nightclub.

"She was absolutely stunning and appeared cool," he remembered. "That night at El Morocco, we were seated at a banquette, when a young man handed me a card identifying him as working for Samuel Goldwyn. He told Grace that he was in town with Mr. Goldwyn and that they were staying at the St. Regis. They were looking for new talent, he said, so could she please make an appointment to see them? Grace didn't hesitate and said, 'I'm sorry, I can't—you'll have to speak to my agent, Manie Sacks.'"

Then head of Columbia Records—part of CBS TV—Manie Sacks had discovered Frank Sinatra and was his best friend, and Jack Kelly's as well. Such was the friendship between Jack and Manie Sacks that the Kelly children called him Uncle Manie. He had been in their lives for as long as they could remember; he was part of their family and a relative of their friends and neighbors, the Levys.

From the time that the Kelly children were small, they considered the Levy house around the corner at 3333 Schoolhouse their second home. When their parents went down to Florida for two weeks every winter, staying at Miami's Golden Inn, while Jack spent most of the time golfing at Indian Creek Country Club, the Kelly children generally stayed with the Levys.

One summer, when Grace was staying with the Levys, according to Ike Levy's nephew Bob, "She had a date whom we didn't like. A friend of mine was over, and he and I waited until Grace and the date came home. She took him into our playroom, where we were hiding behind a sofa. Suddenly we jumped out and sprayed Grace's date with seltzer! She was furious and didn't talk to us for the rest of the summer."

She may have resented Bob Levy interfering with her love life, but she was nonetheless grateful for the range of powerful and successful celebrities whom she met at the Levys'. "You would ring the Levy's doorbell, and Van Johnson or Frank Sinatra would open the door," recalled their friend, Philadelphia businessman Richard Waterman.

Bob Levy confirmed, "Frank was always at our house or our uncle's. He was supposed to marry Ava Gardner there, but then the reporters got wind of the wedding, so he had it at Manie's house instead. Whenever Frank came to Philadelphia, he was always with the Levys or with Manie. Grace was always hanging around and would have met him."

Grace and Anne Levy, who also attended Stevens School, were close friends. On June 29, 1950, when Anne married Herb Siegel at the Levy home, "Frank sang 'Because' that night at the wedding, and Grace was right there, watching him. I am sure they had met before, at the Levys house," Susan Binswanger, one of the bridesmaids, recalled.

Although Frank Sinatra was destined one day to play a major part in Grace's life, that night at Anne Levy's wedding, she had eyes for only one man—Manie Sacks. "Manie was old enough to be Grace's father, didn't look like a movie star at all—was about five foot nine, with curly black hair—but Grace didn't take her eyes off him the entire evening," said Richard Waterman, who sat next to Grace at the wedding. "There were about thirty tables of ten people each. Grace was sitting on my left, and wherever Manie was, she fixed her eyes on him.

"She was not falling over to talk to me. She was skinny, very aloof, elegant, tall—a bit like a glacier—beautiful, but still a glacier. Frank sang, 'Because,' but it was a time in his life when he hardly had any voice, so he only sang that one song. He left at midnight, because he was flying to Spain to join Ava there. Through it all, Grace followed Manie with her eyes. It was as if she was in love with him."

"I know my uncle Manie was very helpful to Princess Grace when she was a model," said his nephew Herman Rush. "He became her surrogate father and gave her advice and introduced her to people. He was a friend of the family and a friend of hers."

Whether or not Grace and Manie Sacks had an affair is not on record. However, he proved to be an extremely useful contact for her, representing her at the start of her career and perhaps—for a time—fulfilling her abiding need for romance with a much older man.

"She had become a career carnivore," Don Richardson observed to Grace's earlier biographer, Robert Lacey. "She was rapacious about getting famous and being important. She'd already talked to me about some of the men she'd been dating, how they helped her to make social contacts, and were teaching her things she needed to know."

But her powerful contacts would have been useless had she not been talented and determined to make it in the theater no matter what the cost. In the spring of 1949, before her graduation from the American Academy, she was chosen from among the other students to take part in the Bucks County Playhouse summer season in New Hope, Pennsylvania. Coincidentally, that July, her first part at New Hope—and her professional stage debut—was that of the ingenue in her uncle's celebrated play *The Torchbearers*. Only four months later, she made her Broadway debut, playing the daughter in Strindberg's *The Father*, which starred Raymond Massey.

At the time, there were whispers that she had won the part merely because her father had pulled strings on her behalf. After the play opened on November 16, 1949, her old Philadelphia boyfriend Dick Boccelli went to see it. "I went backstage after the show, met Raymond Massey and asked him point-blank whether Jack Kelly had persuaded him to give Grace the part. Massey denied it and I believed him," he now attests.

Massey himself made sure to tell the press, "Grace was the third girl I auditioned. I had to see the other twenty-three before I could make my decision. She was just about the most beautiful youngster I ever saw."

Dick Boccelli had suspected Grace had won the part in *The Father* on the basis of nepotism. Chances are she got it fair and square, through her talent. However, there is still another possibility. "Don brought Grace to a party with the producers of a show, the name of which I can't remember," Laura Richardson recalled. "She sat there wearing white gloves, kind of shy and stuffy. Don asked them to hire her and they didn't want to. So he paid her salary, and she never knew it."

No matter why and how Grace got the part, the critics were kind to her, with *New York Times* reviewer Brooks Atkinson writing, "Grace Kelly gives a charming, pliable performance as the bewildered, broken-hearted daughter," and George Jean Nathan dubbing her "charming." Despite that, the show closed after sixty-nine performances, leaving her suffering with the resultant anticlimax. For the next two years, she tried out at more than forty Broadway auditions without winning a single role.

In April 1951, Grace was hired to model at the April in Paris Ball at the Waldorf-Astoria. There she met and was momentarily captivated by the hotel's urbane banqueting manager, Claude Philippe. Philippe had style, sophistication, and a European gloss that Grace found irresistible.

His work at the Waldorf had brought him into contact with the glitterati of the day, and Grace was not averse to mixing with his illustrious friends. In her memoirs, Sheila MacRae, the wife of *Oklahoma!* star Gordon, remembered Edith Piaf driving her and Gordon to Claude Philippe's country house, where Grace was his personal guest. "She had lovely manners," MacRae said.

During this time, Grace also had a brief dalliance with notorious playboy Aly Khan, not yet married to Rita Hayworth. Then one of the world's most glamorous men and reputed to be a great lover, Aly was famous for practicing the erotic technique of *Imsak*, withholding his own sexual pleasure, pleasing his partner for hours, before achieving satisfaction himself.

Few women could resist Aly Khan. Grace was all woman and succumbed to his charms. Yet she felt guilty when he presented her with a series of gifts, including an emerald bracelet which, perhaps hoping for Don's forgiveness, she showed to him. Don was a worldly man, had had other liaisons with beautiful models and actresses whom Aly had also wooed, and had no illusions about the meaning of the bracelet; Aly's modus operandi was to present it to a woman the morning after their first night in bed together. Grace had gone to bed with Aly and Don knew it. "She was like a Patton tank on her way to somewhere. Cold as steel," he said. Their relationship was over, although they would always remain friends.

Consequently, on the evening after Grace won the Academy Award for best actress, she called Don and said, "Thank you, darling."

Through the years, she stayed in touch with him via long, descriptive letters. In the late seventies at a dinner in the Hollywood Hills, Grace—who was in town for a 20th Century–Fox board meeting—called Don, asking to meet his new wife Laura. Consequently, Laura and Don invited Grace to dinner.

"That night, there were about a dozen of us for dinner. Grace requested in advance that we serve fried chicken that night, so we did," Laura recalled.

"She came late, apologized, and had bought a really nice plant so she would look good. She ripped her dress picking it up. I sat at the opposite end of the table from Grace. Don sat next to her and, afterward, he told me that, during dinner, she held his hand the whole time under the table.

"After dinner, she took me aside, and I got the impression that she wanted to make sure I was taking good care of Don. She made it very obvious. It was very sweet, she was being a regular guy, none of that princess nonsense. My husband never called her 'Princess,' sometimes 'Grace,' usually 'Kelly,' like he always had."

After Broadway rejected her in no uncertain terms, Grace—possibly partly drawing on Manie Sacks's pull or that of Ike and Leon Levy at CBS—launched herself on a career in television, then in its infancy and hungry for a beautiful actress capable of learning reams of lines overnight and delivering them on live TV with elegance and ease.

Over a period of three years, she appeared in more than fifty live television shows, including *Studio One, Robert Montgomery Presents, Lights Out, Kraft Playhouse, Lux Video Theater, Playhouse 90, Philco Playhouse, Hallmark Hall of Fame*, and *The Somerset Maugham Theater*.

"It was like working on the edge of a precipice," she later said. "One time I was playing a scene in bed with all my clothes on under the covers so I'd be ready to run into the next scene dressed. But the camera didn't stop in time, and they didn't cut away—so there I was, on screen getting out of bed with all my clothes on!"

Although the work was often arduous, and the waiting between jobs tedious, Grace never regretted her stint as a TV soap opera star, crediting the genre for giving her unrivaled acting experience. When Cary Grant, during the filming of *To Catch a Thief*, asked her how she was so experienced at dialogue, "She told me she had done dozens of soaps. Soaps were live in those days, and you sometimes had to ad-lib. I was awed by her. We all loved her very, very much," Grant said. She would return the compliment, later claiming, "I learned a tremendous amount about motion picture making from Cary. He gave me a great deal of confidence in myself."

"She was fabulous, the only unknown actress I ever knew who wore a mink coat to rehearsal," said Dominick Dunne, who stage-managed some of her television shows. "But if you looked at her closely, you sensed she was on the edge of an act, that she was on the verge of losing it. But she never did."

At the start of her television career, when she was cast as Dulcinea in *Don Quixote*, she made a new friend, actress Rita Gam. "I thought she was very sweet, very nice. She was ambitious, but to be a great actress, not a great star," said Rita.

In the knowledge that the camera made actors look seven pounds heavier than their actual weight, Grace—who generally weighed 126 pounds, the ideal weight for her five-foot-seven frame—tried desperately to lose weight. Consequently, she was often hungry.

"I was the cameraman on *Golden Wings*, an NBC soap," remembered Tony Curcurullo. "Opposite the studio at Rockefeller Plaza there was a drugstore from where I'd buy a strawberry milkshake and a piece of pound cake which I'd take into the studio every morning. I'd put it on the base of my camera and take a bite here, and then a sip.

"One morning, Grace, who was appearing in the soap, came over to me and said, 'That's very cruel of you.' 'I beg your pardon?' I said. And she said, 'I'm so hungry and you are eating that cake right in front of me. And what's that you're drinking?' I told her it was a strawberry milkshake and she said, 'Oh, I love that.' So I told her that I would get a small cup of milkshake and a small piece of cake for her. In the end, I had to force her to eat it. I said, 'You gotta do it my way. Take a small piece of pound cake and a sip of milkshake, then let the cake dissolve in your mouth.' She tried it, and from then on, every day I worked on that show, I bought an extra milkshake for Grace. She didn't want it, she fought me like heck, but she came back looking for it.

"We never became real friends, but I always remember her because she actually came out looking for me and the milkshake and pound cake. There were lots of actresses working on that soap opera, but Grace was very pretty. And so skinny . . ."

Producer George Englund, then an actor, worked with Grace during one of her final TV performances—a pilot for the show *Cads, Scoundrels and Charming Ladies*, in which Grace, in a twist of fate, played the role of a girl who visits Monte Carlo, falls in love there, and ends up getting married. He recalled, "The pilot was written by Michael Arlen and took place in Monte Carlo, which was so prescient. . . . Grace was a big television star, and I had the part of Gerald Moore, who has a romance with Grace's character, very sensual, all misty, and full of mystique.

"I liked Grace, but our love scenes lacked passion. I wasn't rocked by her and thought she was sexless. Once, when we finished rehearsing, I walked her home. It was a long walk and for a while we held hands. But there was no stampede. It wasn't that she was icy, but just that she had a low metabolic rate. But perhaps it was just me. I wasn't animated by her," he said.

Grace probably wasn't animated by Englund, either. Although he went on to marry actress Cloris Leachman and have an extramarital affair with Joan Collins along the way, Englund just wasn't in Grace's league. The Shah of Iran, however, definitely was. They met at the Waldorf toward the end of 1949, when the thirty-year-old Shah arrived in America on an official visit.

Maree Frisby Rambo recalled that the Shah and Grace dated at least six times, with Grace introducing him to the delights of El Morocco and the Stork Club. Although he was a head of state, the ruler of Iran since 1941, the Shah had no intention of hiding his new American paramour away. To the contrary. He invited Grace to accompany him to the opera, amid great pomp and circumstance.

He was besotted by her and demonstrated his feelings in the only way he understood—presenting her with three pieces of Van Cleef & Arpels jewelry: a gold birdcage housing a diamond and sapphire bird, all fashioned into a perfect pin; a gold vanity case with a clasp set with thirty-two diamonds; and a gold bracelet with an intricate pearl and diamond face. Grace's neighbor at the Manhattan House, Valerie Yeomans, recalled, "Grace had a guard outside her front door, and all the Shah's jewels were laid out on her bed. She had called me and Helen Hayes's daughter, Mary MacArthur, over to see them. We couldn't believe it, they were beautiful. But Grace refused the jewelry because she wasn't going to marry the Shah. She sent the jewelry back to him the very next day."

Grace wasn't about to let on to the daughter of one of America's theatrical grandes dames that a serious actress like her could be beguiled—even momentarily—by vulgar jewels, and certainly not that she was tempted to accept them. But accept them, she did.

She may have intended to return the jewels, but in the end, her resolve faltered and she kept them. She stopped short, however, of accepting the Shah's proposal of marriage, which would have made her Empress of Iran.

Her heart and mind were set on an acting career, and she was sensible enough to know that if she accepted the Shah's proposal she would not only be compelled to convert to Islam but would have to retire from acting as well. Knowing that this was unfeasible, she declined his proposal.

Six and a half years after dating the Shah, she finally relinquished his jewels—on the eve of her marriage—by presenting them to her bridesmaids as keepsakes. The subtext was clear: now that she was married to Prince Rainier, all traces of her past loves must be expunged, in particular precious love tokens from another man. Whether or not the prince had decreed that she not keep her souvenirs from the Shah, or whether she jumped to that conclusion of her own volition, is not on record.

Even if Prince Rainier was jealous of his wife's past romance with the Shah of Iran, by 1971 his jealously had subsided sufficiently for him to accept the Shah's invitation for them both to attend the gala celebrations at Persopolis marking the two thousandth anniversary of the Pahlavi dynasty.

Afterward, despite the two decades that had passed since their brief romance and the fact that the brutality of the Shah's regime was common knowledge, Grace fiercely defended the Shah.

In his diary, Richard Burton described traveling in 1971 with Grace, Rainier, and Elizabeth Taylor to the Rothschild Ball at their Ferrières estate, "Grace and E chatted away at the back of the car while I sat in front with the driver. Grace was nice and relaxed and, after the initial awkwardness which I always feel with people like Grace who are in a somewhat false position and know it, everybody talked freely. Grace went into a blow by blow description of the Shah's famous or infamous party.

"Grace defended its extravagance with extraordinary obtuseness though neither of us attacked it. It was meant, she said, as a tribute to the people of Persia and as self-advertisement for the Shah's magnificent governing which was bringing literacy to the illiterate and hygiene to the unwashed and culture to the people. She described the Shah as a marvelous man and once called him a great man which was going a titch too far. She said how monstrous it was of the Western press to be so vulgarly cynical of the whole show, all of them she said she knew for a fact were writing their stuff before the thing had really got going."

In 1950, agent Edie Van Cleve, one of the many agents, including John Foreman, Manie Sacks, and Milton Goldman, who appeared to represent Grace during this period, sent her to audition for *Fourteen Hours*, a movie based on a 1938 incident in which an emotionally disturbed man stood on the ledge of the Gotham Hotel for half a day before jumping to his death.

She auditioned for the small part of Mrs. Fuller, a woman who is in the process of consulting her attorney about a divorce but changes her mind after she sees the man jump. Grace was not immediately cast but instead was asked back for a second audition, this time with a young actor named Robert Evans.

Evans, who ultimately became head of Paramount studios and was the legendary producer of *The Godfather, Chinatown, Rosemary's Baby, The Great Gatsby,* and *Love Story,* working with the most beautiful and gifted actresses of his generation, including Faye Dunaway, Diane Keaton, Sharon Stone, Mia Farrow, and his own wife, Ali MacGraw, briefly dated Grace.

Although he was twenty at the time, one year her junior, and not yet a producer, Evans appraised her with the eyes of a producer, and of a man.

"Grace would know what a guy would say before he would say it. She had instinct. All she needed with a man was half an hour. During that time, she would never take her eyes off him. Then she knew what she wanted from him," he said.

"The only reason she went out with me was because she enjoyed Latin dancing and I was a really good Latin dancer. We'd rendezvous at the Plaza. We also danced the tango together. The guys Grace went out with didn't dance, so we danced all the time.

"She was very sought after. What was the most attractive thing about her? Her profile alone. Her façade didn't have ambition written all over it. She didn't wear ambition on her sleeve. She was very feminine.

"Was she such a good Catholic that she didn't go all the way with men? That isn't true. She wasn't prudish. Quite the contrary. She used Catholicism as a cover. She didn't have the charm of a seductress. She wasn't a femme fatale. She had an aloofness about her. A studious quality that was very captivating. She was rather thin, but had a nice figure, and certainly wasn't a sex object. She knew how to just 'be.' She had good features. She spoke very well and wasn't affected. She had star quality. She was an original," he said.

Grace and Robert Evans didn't pursue their relationship, but throughout her life she remained passionate about dancing. She often danced for Don Richardson, dancing for him naked to Hawaiian or Russian music. And in January 1951, at a party in Albany, marking the last night of *Alexander,* the play in which she had been appearing, when a fellow actor started strumming on a guitar, she threw off her shoes, let her hair down, and broke into a barefoot flamenco. Of all dances, she loved this one best. She danced the barefoot flamenco many times in her life. Once, in the seventies, at a summer party on Roquebrune's Blue Beach in front of sixty friends picnicking under the stars, Princess Grace of Monaco shook off her shoes and danced the barefoot flamenco once more.

Renowned artist Andrew Vicari was there that night. He recalled, "Two Spanish students, dressed in the costumes of sixteenth-century court musicians—looking as if they came straight out of a Velazquez painting—strummed their guitars. We toasted marshmallows, the waves were breaking against the shore, and suddenly, the students began to play the flamenco. Grace, relaxed, happy, in a long summer dress, stood up and began to dance the barefoot flamenco. It was one of the most beautiful things I've ever seen in my life."

5

High Noon

I n early 1950, Grace learned that she had won the role in *Fourteen Hours*. Chaperoned by her sister Lizanne and the Levys, Grace flew out to California, where they all stayed at the venerable Beverly Hills Hotel. After filming began, Henry Hathaway, the director of *Fourteen Hours*, received an on-set visit from Gary Cooper who—like most men—was instantly overwhelmed by Grace's charm and beauty.

"I thought she looked pretty and different, and that maybe she'd be somebody. She looked educated, and as if she came from a nice family. She was certainly a refreshing change from all these sexballs we've been seeing so much of," Cooper enthused afterward.

Gary Cooper, the first major Hollywood star to come into contact with Grace and no mean appraiser of star quality, had, within moments of first meeting her, summed her up extremely accurately and wouldn't forget her.

The movie, starring Paul Douglas, Richard Basehart, and Barbara Bel Geddes, was released in March 1951. Grace failed to excite any comment from the critics, with the *New Yorker* reviewer singling out Basehart for his praise, writing that he "succeeds in conveying the notion that he is indeed sorely beset," and describing Bel Geddes as having given "a nice performance." Grace's Hollywood debut passed without notice, other than making an impact on a high school girl from Oregon who took the visionary step of starting the Grace Kelly Fan Club. At first, she was the club's only member, but Grace took a keen interest in it, tracking any new members, and, on learning that a potential new one had telephoned the club's president from Washington, jubilantly crowed, "I think she's ours. Sewed up."

When Grace returned from Hollywood, she threw herself into her TV and theater acting. For the second year running, she did another season of summer stock at Bucks County and then accepted a ten-week run at Denver's prestigious Elitch Gardens Theater for a weekly salary of $125. During that time, she increased her acting range considerably by appearing in *The Man Who Came to Dinner, Ring Around the Moon*, and *The Cocktail Party*.

Within two weeks of arriving in Denver, Grace had fallen in love with fellow actor Gene Lyons. Rugged, handsome, gentle, and ten years older than Grace, Lyons was not, at first, romantically interested in her. However, when she made her interest in him obvious, he capitulated and soon became obsessed by her. Actress Lee Grant, who had been involved with Gene before he met Grace, revealed to Steven Englund, "Gene told me he was deeply in love with Grace Kelly."

He was sensitive, kind, and by all accounts a talented actor. "You found in Gene a highly sensitive, giving man. In fact he was so sensitive and introverted that I sometimes wondered if he wasn't self-destructive," observed director Ted Post, who worked with him in television. Gene was, indeed, self-destructive: he was an alcoholic. After he proposed to her, Grace played for time.

On August 10, 1952, while Grace was still at Elitch Gardens and grappling with her feelings for Gene Lyons, producer Stanley Kramer—who remembered her from *The Father* and found her refined and pretty—decided she was perfect for the part of the young Quaker bride, Amy, in his next movie, *High Noon*. He sent her a telegram asking her to report to the Hollywood set just eighteen days later.

Kramer, who had just had a cult box office hit *The Men*, starring Marlon Brando, and who ultimately produced *Judgment at Nuremberg* and *Guess Who's Coming to Dinner*, had been encouraged by Hollywood agent Jay Kanter to go out on a limb and hire Grace for *High Noon*, a Western with a strong contemporary subtext, written and coproduced by Carl Foreman, the legendary Hollywood writer once blacklisted as a communist.

However, although Grace was thrilled that Kramer wanted her, she still had to contend with Gene's objections to her giving up the stage and accepting the part. They had often discussed their mutual distaste for Hollywood, a distaste that her uncle George, who loathed the studio system with its autocratic studio heads and sleazy casting couch system, had relentlessly drummed into her. In love with Grace, the ardent stage actress of Elitch Gardens, Gene reminded her that she was contracted to perform in Denver until the end of the season in September and pleaded with her not to abandon the theater, not to abandon him.

Grace listened politely, but only an act of God would have prevented her from flying out to Hollywood and *High Noon*. Although she had always professed that becoming a stage actress was her sole aim in life—being a romantic yet with a pragmatic streak in her nature—it was inconceivable that she walk away from the opportunity to have a second chance at making it in Hollywood. Moreover, Gary Cooper—the quintessential macho all-American movie hero, an Adonis guaranteed to make every girl's heart flutter fast and furiously—was the star. Without any further ado, Grace accepted the part of Amy in *High Noon*.

She flew to Los Angeles from Denver and Lizanne joined her there. Together, they checked into a self-catering apartment in the Chateau Marmont on Sunset Boulevard. A far cry from the more opulent Beverly Hills Hotel, where they had previously stayed, the Marmont—more Hollywood than Beverly Hills—had a distinctive show business insider cachet.

As soon as she arrived, Grace was summoned to an interview with *High Noon*'s director Fred Zinnemann, who had won great acclaim with *The Men*. Zinnemann had not personally selected her to play the part of Amy, so it would have been understandable had he been a trifle peeved that she'd been cast without his approval. However, he was instantly beguiled by Grace's pristine persona, and—in particular—her white gloves, later raving, "She had the personality and manner to go with them. Most actresses are more inhibited." Now not only the producer but also the director of *High Noon* had been captivated by Grace's unique style and substance and were in her thrall.

During Grace and Lizanne's four-week stay at the Marmont, while Grace was filming, Lizanne dashed off a series of letters to her Ocean City boyfriend, Bob Harbaugh, each giving a flavor of the heady excitement whirling around the two Kelly girls at the start of Grace's career.

In the letters, Lizanne described her and Grace's life at the Marmont, where she did the cooking and cleaning while Grace studied her lines. She reported that between the Monday on which they first arrived in Hollywood and Thursday, she and Grace attended three cocktail parties, two lunches, and two dinners. "Not bad for two little girls alone in a great big city, you would say," Lizanne cracked.

In the second letter, Lizanne somewhat caustically wrote, "She had to kiss Gary fifty times today to get the scene right. I bet I'd only have to kiss you once to make it right. Fifty times wouldn't be a bad idea." Then she raved about a restaurant, to which she and Grace were taken by a man whom she airily dismissed as "Mike somebody or other," then—in a contradiction that makes the entire episode slightly suspect—described him as "an old friend of the family."

As the letters continued, she dropped all pretense of transparency or of identifying any of the men with whom she and Grace were socializing, writing that "we went to a friend's house in Bel Air for dinner" and "we went up to Santa Barbara and went on a 104-foot yacht of some friends of ours."

Interspersed with descriptions of how she and Grace were living the high life, she made sure to tell Bob that she and Grace attended Mass on Sunday, and that they went to a private screening at her agent's, who then gave a party for their celebrity clients, including Grace. In a rare moment of honesty, Lizanne told Bob that she and Grace had dinner invitations every single night of the week. Then, on a more down-to-earth note, she described their routine: up at 6 A.M., Lizanne made breakfast, then drove Grace to the studio, Grace arrived home again at 6:30 in the evening, at which point, "She's so tired that we go to bed early."

Lizanne's last letter to Bob ended on a reassuring note: "We've been very good girls this week, going to bed nice and early every night—well, practically every night. . . . Honey, I have to go now. Grace is yelling."

Lizanne's letters ostensibly recorded every detail of the sisters' Hollywood social whirl. But fun as they are, descriptive as they are, she took great care not to name names or give her boyfriend any clues about the men whom she and Grace were seeing.

Had Lizanne revealed the truth about Grace's social life during their brief interlude at the Chateau Marmont, Bob Harbaugh would very likely have been stunned.

Grace's uncle George had warned her about the Hollywood casting couch, and stories of ambitious actresses bartering their sexual favors for a part were legion. Grace, however, didn't need to resort to such tactics. She had already won the part in *High Noon*, primarily because of her talent, partly because of her contacts, and there was no question of her losing it.

Yet Grace Kelly, then a good actress of twenty-two with a solid reputation, a beautiful, photogenic face, and an aristocratic veneer, during the four-week shoot of *High Noon* managed to conduct simultaneous affairs with not only Gary Cooper but also, Fred Zinnemann. He was more than twenty years her senior, married, Austrian, and dripping with European charm. And it didn't hurt Grace that his obsession with her would lead him to include an inordinate number of close-ups in the final cut of *High Noon*, arousing the ire of costar Katy Jurado in the bargain.

But apart from the added career bonus her affair with Zinnemann provided, as well as the kudos of having captivated Gary Cooper, both liaisons would serve to fulfill her ever-present craving for a relationship with a powerful, older man—a father figure.

In the early eighties, Lizanne confirmed to James Spada that Grace "was infatuated with Gary Cooper." Spada also quotes Cooper's friend Robert Slatzer as saying, "Gary told me that he and Grace were having an affair. I was on the set a couple of times, and, when Grace would come up to him, just the way she looked at him you could tell she was melting. She'd embarrass him, sometimes, by coming over and putting her arms around him and being obvious in front of other people."

When I asked Gary Cooper's daughter, Maria—who has published a book commemorating her father and his marriage to her mother, the beautiful actress "Rocky" Cooper—about her father's romantic relationship with Grace, she professed to have no knowledge of it, before adding, somewhat cryptically, "Grace? You should also look at her directors. . . ."

"My father told me that Grace had an affair with Fred Zinnemann," Carl Foreman's son, Jonathan, confirmed, adding that during the making of *High Noon*, his father also had an affair with actress Katy Jurado, Grace's sultry female costar in the movie.

"I loved Gary so much. I will always love him," said actress Patricia Neal in 2005. When *High Noon* was being shot, Patricia was twenty-three years old and in the throes of a five-year relationship with Cooper, who had left his wife for her.

"When Gary was making *High Noon*, I insisted on coming to the set to see him, but he kept trying to put me off. In the end, when they were filming in Sonoma, I went for the weekend and stayed in Gary's room with him," she said.

"On the first evening after I arrived, Gary told me that Grace was having an affair with Fred Zinnemann. I was fascinated, as I had known Zinnemann before. But then we had supper—Gary, Fred, Grace, and I—and Grace sat next to me. She didn't even speak to me. Her fists were clenched and she looked down all the time. It was terrible."

"She and Gary were having an affair, which is why she behaved that way during supper. Gary had told me that Grace was having an affair with Fred Zinnemann, and I believed anything that he said. But of course it was Gary who was having the affair with her."

At the time, Patricia firmly believed that Cooper was using Zinnemann as an alibi to hide his own affair with Grace from her. Cooper may well have been doing just that, unaware that Zinnemann, too, really *was* having an affair with Grace. Or perhaps he knew all about it and, jaded and sophisticated, adhering to the old Hollywood adage "on location, it doesn't count," was sharing Grace with Zinnemann but simply didn't care.

Patricia Neal never confronted either Grace or Gary with her suspicions, but suffered in silence. Today, she describes Grace as "an interesting woman," her throaty voice lingering on the word "interesting," before adding a caveat, "But she did do something great. After I had my stroke, she sent me a religious thing. And she did a jolly good job when she became princess."

Grace didn't succeed in permanently supplanting Patricia in Gary's affections. When they were still on location in Sonoma, perhaps in an attempt to let Grace down lightly from the affair, he introduced her to his friend, Hollywood writer Robert Slatzer, who later claimed that he was briefly married to Marilyn Monroe.

Three years later, when Grace was in Hollywood again and had an apartment of her own, she and Slatzer dated periodically. In 2004, he remembered, "She was easy to get into bed, sexually aggressive. The night we first dated in Hollywood, we went back to her apartment, Grace immediately went into the bathroom, then came out stark naked.

"She liked to cook, and was good at it, but she also loved to eat out. There was a restaurant she liked on La Cienega called The Wild Boar, which served nothing but wild animals like buffalo and game. Grace liked to go there because some celebrities did. So I took her there, and she ordered rabbit. When they brought her order, she said, 'Try this, then some night I'll make it for you at my place. Then you can tell me which was better.'

"Grace had a magnetic quality about her. She was polite, well groomed, and very similar to Marilyn in that she was naïve. She was kind of gullible, easily taken in by men. She seemed very worldly, was well educated, and came from a good background, but she was really very young," he said.

When *High Noon* was released on July 24, 1952, although Gary Cooper went on to win the Academy Award for best actor, and the movie—which cost half a million dollars to make—grossed $18 million, it did not instantly catapult Grace to stardom. *New York Times* reviewer Bosley Crowther showered the movie with praise, describing Cooper as being "at the top of his form," before ending with, "Lloyd Bridges as a vengeful young deputy, Katy Jurado as a Mexican adventuress, Thomas Mitchell as a prudent townsman, Otto Kruger as a craven judge, and Grace Kelly as the new wife of the sheriff are the best of many in key roles."

Yet despite the tepid response to Grace in *High Noon*, her performance has stood the test of time. She is first seen as Quaker Amy Fowler on her wedding day, about to pledge her troth to Marshall Kane, played by Gary Cooper. Wearing a white bonnet and a white wedding dress, Grace is beautiful, and her first words in the movie are, "I do."

Gary Cooper, twenty-eight years her senior, looks much too old for her, and far too tall for her, as well. She smiles up at him submissively, then—when he takes her into another room and they are alone—gazes adoringly at him. Her purity shines through and, from that moment on, she is utterly believable as the high-principled Quaker girl so in love with her new husband that she finally abandons her pacifist principles in order to save him.

When Cooper lifts Grace up in his arms for a public kiss, she giggles fetchingly. However, when he tells her that his nemesis, gunslinger Frank Miller, is bound for the town, planning to kill him, and that—instead of leaving with her on their honeymoon—he intends to stay and fight him, she is devastated.

During her first long speech in the movie, when she pleads, "You don't have to be a hero for me. Will, we were married just a few moments ago. We've got our whole lives ahead of us. Doesn't that mean anything to you?" she uses an English accent as Don Richardson had advised.

When she issues Will with an ultimatum, telling him that if he is determined to stay and fight, she will leave home on the noon train, she is willful, determined, and angry. After Cooper walks out, then returns to the hotel, she is elated, thinking he has decided not to stay and fight. She is simultaneously high-minded, serene, and the epitome of purity. When she finally confronts Mrs. Ramirez, played by Katy Jurado, Grace is strong, courageous, determined, true to her own real-life character.

When she drops her pride, begging Katy to tell her why Will is staying, and Katy spits, "What kind of a woman are you? How can you leave him like this? Does the sound of guns frighten you so much?" Grace erupts, and—in a speech that eclipses her tour de force in *The Country Girl*, the movie for which she would win the Best Actress Academy Award—seeths with righteous anger. Trembling, she says, "No, Mrs. Ramirez, I've heard guns. My father and my brother were killed by guns. They were on the right side, but that didn't help them when the shooting started. My brother was nineteen. I watched him die. That's why I became a Quaker. I don't care who's right and who's wrong; there's gotta be a better way for people to live." As Grace's chin quivers in anger, she bests her rival, the virginal blonde conquering the sultry firecracker brunette.

In the end, Grace proves her love for Will Kane, her pacifist beliefs in shreds, her innocence gone, and her indomitable passion winning her her man. And despite the fact that the critics failed to shower her with praise for her performance, and the Academy ignored it completely, in *High Noon* she proves, without a shadow of a doubt, that she was not only a great beauty but already an accomplished actress.

After the *High Noon* shoot ended, and Grace returned to New York, she stayed in touch with Fred Zinnemann. Toward the end of January 1952, she saw him a couple of times during a week he spent in Manhattan. She was still seeing Gene Lyons as well, and in March attended a screening of *High Noon* with him. At that stage, unsure about the quality of her performance and whether or not she had a future in Hollywood, with Gene's strong encouragement she turned her attention back to the theater.

It appeared that her luck had changed when she was cast in the small part of the daughter in the Broadway-bound William Merchant drawing room comedy *To Be Continued.* Her second try at achieving stardom on the Great White Way did not fare much better than the first. The play opened in Boston on April 8, before transferring to Broadway's Booth Theater on April 23, 1952, but while Grace's performance was described by a critic as having "real style," the play closed within a matter of weeks.

She spent the summer back home in Philadelphia, where she starred in *For Love or For Money* and *Accent on Youth* at the Playhouse in the Park. The theater had been built under Jack Kelly's sponsorship when he was vice president of the Fairmont Park Commission. Grace was on home ground again, the last time in her life she would spend a long stretch in the city of her birth.

6

Mogambo

After *High Noon* was released, and Grace was no longer an unknown actress, *Stagecoach* director John Ford—looking for a British actress to play the second-string female to Ava Gardner in *Mogambo,* a remake of Jean Harlow's steamy *Red Dust*—happened on Grace's black-and-white screen test for the movie *Taxi.* Although she failed to get the part in *Taxi,* John Ford judged it hadn't been right for her in the first place and suggested making another test of her—this time in color.

Grace Kelly, with her translucent skin, blue eyes, and flaxen hair, was born to be shot in color. On September 3, 1952, at MGM's expense, she flew to Los Angeles to test for the part of Linda Nordley in *Mogambo* and was hired at the relatively low salary of $850 a week, along with the proviso that she sign a seven-year contract with MGM.

Grace was now forced to confront her deep-seated misgivings about becoming an indentured slave to the studio system about which her uncle George had issued such grave warnings. Consequently, she drove a hard bargain with MGM by stipulating that before she would sign the contract they agree to two conditions. First, that she be allowed one year out of every two to work in the theater, and second that she be allowed to live in New York. Her conditions were unusual, but she had given a good performance in *High Noon* and Ford badly wanted her for *Mogambo,* so the studio agreed to her demands.

Even then, Grace might still have resisted signing with MGM except, as she put it, "*Mogambo* had three things that interested me. John Ford, Clark Gable and a trip to Africa with expenses paid. If *Mogambo* had been made in Arizona, I wouldn't have done it." Later, she confided to Hollywood colum-

nist Hedda Hopper, "I wanted to go to Africa mainly. I've always been fascinated by it. I had read so many books. I knew everything about it."

Determined to add to her knowledge, before she left for the three-month
location in the wilds of Kenya, Tanganyika, and Uganda, Grace studied
Swahili.

The cast flew to Nairobi, arriving on November 2. They stayed at the New
Stanley Hotel before moving to their main location, seven hundred miles
away in Uganda, in the middle of the African bush, beside the Kagera River,
on the border of Tanganyika and Uganda and 150 miles from Lake Victoria.

Six hundred cast and crew, including pilots, canoe paddlers, guards,
guides, and hunters, and one thousand extras from the Portuguese East
African Makonde tribe and the Congolese Wagenia tribe, set up camp by the
banks of the Kagera River where MGM—prepared to invest their vast re-
sources in what they thought would be a big box office success—had built a
mini city with thirteen dining tents, a movie theater, a games room, a mobile
hospital, and massive kitchens.

Clark Gable was cast as *Mogambo*'s crusty hero, Vic Marswell, the same part
he played in *Red Dust*, while British actor Donald Sinden was playing Dr.
Nordley, Grace's scientist husband. Ava Gardner had the role of the good-
time girl, Honey Bear.

In his memoirs, Donald Sinden recorded his recollections of the first day
of filming on a river steamer, demonstrating John Ford's novel approach to
directing: "Grace—Donald—get below. OK. Donald—come on deck. Look
around at the scenery. Call Grace. Put your arm around her. Point out a gi-
raffe on your right. Get your camera out—quickly. Photograph it—the gi-
raffe. Smile at him, Grace. Grace look at that hippopotamus on your left. Get
Donald to photograph it. A crocodile slides into the water. You're scared. OK.
You're coming into the pier. Look around. What's in store for you?"

While Grace was wrestling with Ford's less than actor-friendly style of
directing, off camera, Ava was coming to grips with the realities surrounding
her year-old marriage to Frank Sinatra, which—amid their mutual insecuri-
ties, jealousies, and the fact that Sinatra's career was in the doldrums—was
rapidly falling apart.

In the hope of salvaging the marriage, even momentarily, Ava had paid
Frank's fare to Africa. But as soon as Frank and Ava arrived there, they bat-
tled ferociously, "cursing and screaming like wild creatures," Donald Sinden

remembered. "There were things being thrown from Ava's tent, pots and things, flying out of the tent, they were throwing things at each other. Then, suddenly, silence. The argument was over and the next thing you heard they were in bed and the bed was creaking. And you've never heard a bed creaking so hard." Grace, too, was acutely aware of the battling Sinatras, and complained in a letter that "Ava is such a mess. . . . Her tent is next to mine, so I can hear all the screaming and yelling."

If the cast and crew were hoping for a catfight to break out in the jungle between the well-bred millionaire's daughter from Philadelphia and the Grabtown, North Carolina, vamp from the wrong side of the tracks, they were doomed to disappointment. Grace had known Frank almost all her life, understood both his attractions and his dark side, and consequently empathized with Ava.

Their friendship was cemented after Ava threw Grace a birthday party at the New Stanley Hotel in Nairobi, at which she and Clark Gable were the only guests. "Gracie never forgot that I gave her a little birthday party when we were in Africa," Ava told Peter Evans. "She never forgot my birthday. No matter where I was she managed to get a present to me till her dying day."

From the first, Ava had been beguiled by Grace. "She was a wonderful girl," she wrote in her autobiography. "If you saw her in a room, she was rather plain. She photographed more beautiful than she actually was. When you talked to her, she became beautiful. Such kindness and warmth. And Donald Sinden, he was so in love with Gracie, oh my God."

Sinden may have fallen for Grace, but she had already set her sights on Clark Gable. Ava, intuiting Grace's emotions, quickly sat her down and gave her the score on him. "Don't be fooled by his looks or interest in you!" she cautioned. "He's been with so many women—you have no idea! I haven't had an affair with him myself, but I know what I'm talking about. Don't fall for it because he'll cast you aside just like he has all the others. You'll be just another girl to him. He likes to conquer, and when he's done, he's through with them and he leaves them."

Ava didn't realize at the time that she couldn't have formulated a better scenario for causing Grace to fall in love with Gable. By casting him as a swashbuckling seducer, a conqueror who reveled in discarding women, Ava had unwittingly thrown down a gauntlet. Suddenly Gable was even more of a challenge to Grace than she had ever imagined. Since Skinny D'Amato, there had never been a man she'd had her heart set on that she'd failed to captivate. Not Gary Cooper, not Fred Zinnemann, not even the Shah of Iran. Clark Gable, she was sure, would be no different.

However, Grace hadn't counted on the fact that Gable wasn't interested in her at all and, instead, was determined to seduce Ava. After Frank received a telegram from Columbia Pictures inviting him to test for the part of Maggio in *From Here to Eternity*—which he was desperate to win—he flew back to America, leaving Ava alone and prey to Gable's advances.

"Gable wanted a night with Ava, but she made it clear that she wasn't interested in him. She slapped him down pretty hard," recalled British show business reporter David Lewin, on location to cover the filming of *Mogambo* for the London *Daily Mail*.

Soon after, Ava discovered she was pregnant with Frank's child, and on November 22 she flew back to London for an abortion. As soon as she returned, Gable resumed his pursuit, still ignoring Grace's rising passion for him.

In moments that would have made Freud cringe, Grace took to calling Gable *Ba*, the Swahili word for "father." He remained impervious, and one day when she was fifteen minutes late for a scene, he berated her and almost made her cry.

Consequently, on December 20, she wrote to her friend Prudy Wise saying, "Aside from a run-in with safari ruts and Clark Gable my weekend has been perfect. The explanation of the latter would take too long. . . . It will have to wait."

Gable aside, in the same letter Grace gave Prudy a flavor of life on location in Africa: "We did a scene where I fall in an animal trap and the second time I did it, I smashed myself all up so they sent me back to camp . . . my native boy—who is about a hundred and three—is busily scraping the mud off my shoes and doing my laundry."

Africa was a revelation for Grace. Afterwards, in an anecdote that spoke of her strength of will, she told Hedda Hopper, "I hate bugs—in a house. The first bug I saw in Africa, I thought: Here is my test. I sort of steeled myself, and after that it didn't bother me. But one day I woke up and saw what I thought was a snake coming in my tent. I watched it closely and discovered it was millions of safari ants—coming on through. Everybody wanted to come to my tent to see them, and some people stepped on the line, scattering ants in all directions. I had them in my tent for a week."

If the *High Noon* set had been a hotbed of sexual intrigue—with Grace in the throes of affairs with both Cooper and Zinnemann, Patricia Neal in love with Cooper, and Carl Foreman having an affair with Katy Jurado—the *Mogambo* set was even hotter. Clark Gable was trying to seduce Ava Gardner, Grace was suffering from unrequited love for Gable, Donald Sinden from unrequited love for Grace, Ava Gardner was having affairs with legendary big game-hunter Bunny Allen—on hand to manage *Mogambo*'s wild animals—and an unnamed prop man, and back in America, Frank Sinatra was expiring of longing for Ava.

Finally, with the prospect of Sinatra returning to Africa for Christmas, putting paid to Gable's chances with Ava once and for all, Gable turned his attention to Grace. "Gable's first choice was Ava, and Grace was only second best," David Lewin remembered. "But Sinatra was about to fly in, so that eliminated Ava for Clark. So Clark decided to use Grace to fill the time.

"As it was nearly Christmas, he wanted to give her presents to ease the way. So he asked her if she would like a crocodile handbag, and she said that would be very nice. Two days later, during filming, on the other side of the river we saw a crocodile sunning himself. So Clark said, 'Get me a gun!' Then he turned round to Grace and said, 'Honey, I'm gonna get you that crocodile bag!' He raised the gun, fired, and hit the crocodile. 'That crocodile is now deader than hell. You'll get your handbag, Gracie,' Gable said. Shortly afterwards, I heard a prop assistant say, 'That's not a croc! that croc's a prop!'" Lewin revealed in amusement.

In quest of winning Gable's respect, not just his lust, Grace graduated from conquering her fear of bugs to conquering her fear of the rugged African terrain. On their nonfilming days, she and Gable got up at four in the morning to beat the sweltering heat, then toured the country in an old jeep, stopping at Lake Victoria to go skinny-dipping. "Being in Africa, with exotic flora and fauna all over the place, and Clark, strong and smiling and completely at home, made her love him more," said Ava.

He taught Grace how to use a rifle; she became a good shot and, in the process, reminded him of his late wife, Carole Lombard, who'd been killed in a plane crash after only three years of marriage.

However, Grace's feelings for Clark were too intense for his liking. "One night she and Clark had a little fight," Ava recalled to Peter Evans. "The tears were pouring down her face and her little nose was red. She ran off into the night. Clark came out of the tent and asked me to look for her. We finally found her behind a little sapling of a tree, not as thick as my wrist. She went back into the tent with Clark. But about half an hour later, he came back to me again, wringing his hands. 'Sugar, can you get up and help me again, she's thrown up all over my tent.' She got drunk and just couldn't hold it. She wasn't a very good drinker."

Frank, still not knowing whether or not he had been cast as Maggio, arrived back in Africa just in time for Christmas. There he resolved to make a last-ditch attempt at winning back Ava. Apart from bringing a mink stole and a diamond ring for her, he decided to give her and the cast of *Mogambo* a Christmas they would never forget.

Almost twenty years later, Grace remembered, "Frank decided to take Christmas in hand. He disappeared for a few days and then returned from Nairobi with I think just about every Christmas ornament the city contained and the one Santa Claus suit. On Christmas Eve, we gathered in a clearing under the starry African sky and there in the center was a huge big mantelpiece. Frank even talked John Ford into reciting *The Night Before Christmas* to us. And this wonderful evening ended with sixty Congolese Africans barefooted, with their blankets around them singing French Christmas carols."

Frank had pulled out all the stops, but by the time he and the cast were back in Nairobi, he had learned of Ava's dalliance with Bunny Allen. At a Sunday night party held at the house of the Randall-Whartons, owners of a U.S. cargo line, Lee Harragin, son of Kenya's Attorney General, witnessed the fallout from Frank's discovery.

He remembered, "Ava and Frank behaved so badly at the party that they had to be put in the study because they were shouting and screaming at each other so loudly, arguing about Ava's affair with Bunny Allen. There was no question that Ava and Bunny were having an affair—and of course Frank had heard about it."

In the midst of all the Sinatra-generated drama, Grace remained calm. "All evening, she sat at Gable's feet, looking at him as if he were a God," said Lee Harragin. "She was incredibly pretty, magical, really, and she only had eyes for Gable. That they were having an affair was common knowledge to the movie people. Watching Grace sitting on the floor at his feet, all of us at the party could draw only one conclusion."

Toward the end of filming, Frank, Gable, Grace, and Ava spent five days in Malindi, on the shores of the Indian Ocean. One afternoon, Gable found

Grace perched on a rock on the beach, reading Hemingway's "Snows of Kili-manjaro," sobbing. "I looked up and saw a lion walking along the beach," she told him through her tears.

As she explained in a letter to Prudy, "It's been a strain on all of us. Ava & I both had dysentery—and three deaths from auto accidents and numer-ous injuries . . . everyone is terribly nervy and on edge."

The stars of *Mogambo* had spent three months together in the wilds of Africa, amid tension, hardship, and high passion, forming lifelong attachments in the process. Grace and Ava remained friends long after filming ended. When Grace invited Ava to her wedding, although other actresses of Ava's stature ad-vised her against attending on the grounds that Grace would inevitably upstage them, Ava refused to listen and went anyway, becoming the only major female Hollywood star who did. Grace never forgot Ava's loyalty. Even as Princess of Monaco, whenever she was in London, Grace always visited Ava in her Hyde Park Gate home.

Despite failing to reciprocate Donald Sinden's romantic feelings for her, years later, during her visits to London, Grace called to suggest they meet for a drink or dinner. "He could never take seriously the way she announced her-self on the telephone as 'Grace de Monaco,'" said Phyllida Hart-Davis, one of her earlier biographers. But he was thrilled to see her, particularly when she surprised him backstage after his performance in *London Assurance* and agreed to present Judi Dench with her birthday present as a surprise.

Long after the debacle of Frank's time in Africa with Ava, Grace would recall with great affection his attempt to brighten up their African Christmas celebrations. In Africa, although Frank still belonged to Ava, their relation-ship deepened.

As for Clark Gable, at the end of January—when Grace flew back to Lon-don with him and the rest of the cast to film the interiors at Elstree Studios—she checked into the Savoy Hotel, anticipating that she and Gable would continue their romance there.

She was in for a shock. "The moment we arrived back in London, Clark was somebody, and I was nobody," she confided to Maree Frisby Rambo in sorrow. "Grace was mad about Gable and crushed when he dropped her," Ma-ree remembered.

Unable to fully grasp that she and Clark had merely had a location romance, and that it had now ended, Grace laid siege to him with such ferocious determination that he fled from the Savoy Hotel to the Connaught to escape her.

Unaccustomed to being rebuffed by men, even a major star like Gable, in a replay of her aggressive pursuit of Skinny, Grace pounded on the door of Gable's suite, desperate to see him once more. Gable, inured to women developing a fatal attraction to him, arranged for a guard to be posted outside the suite to protect him.

Grace then switched tactics. In the hope of winning Gable back by inciting his jealousy, she accepted an invitation from Carl Foreman, then living in London, to join him and Ava at the Café de Paris, where Grace's date would be distinguished *Brief Encounter* producer Sir Anthony Havelock-Allan.

"When my father and Tony walked into the Café de Paris with Grace and Ava, the whole room stopped talking," Foreman's son Jonathan recalled.

Havelock-Allan, a connoisseur of beautiful women who went on to marry the actress Valerie Hobson, and then the glamorous, aristocratic Sara Ruiz de Villafranca, was instantly smitten by Grace and invited her to lunch.

"We had a ten-day romance. She was very beautiful, with wonderful skin, and a wonderful speaking voice. But she was tough, though, no shrinking violet. She was in control of her image," Havelock-Allan confided to me in a 2002 interview.

"Grace used Tony to make Clark Gable jealous," reported Havelock-Allan's widow, Lady Sara, somewhat more bluntly.

Grace's tactics, however, failed to arouse Clark Gable. On February 17, Margaret Kelly arrived in London, partly to chaperone Grace, partly to console her. Although Gable demonstrated a degree of gallantry by inviting Grace and her mother to dinner a couple of times, it was clear that he was romantically involved elsewhere.

By March, Grace had got the message and was devastated by the rejection. She wrote to Prudy that "I have never felt like such a wallflower," then sent her a telex, "feeling very much like someone waiting to be let out of jail," and two weeks later wrote again, "Put two bottles of champagne on ice ... Am not speaking to Clark these days ... Am terribly depressed and anxious to get home."

On April 15, 1953, in a studio-orchestrated photo opportunity, Grace accompanied Gable to Heathrow Airport, from where he was scheduled to fly to America. "When it came to say goodbye to Gable, Ford and the rest of the company, she could not contain herself. She cried," her mother later reported. "As always happens, some people were present. Grace's tears were seen and misinterpreted. As far as the wireless could carry the news, it was reported that she was crying over Gable." Then, in a dizzying volte-face, in the same paragraph she continued, "Why shouldn't she have cried over him? She's an emotional actress, and in spite of her cool, calm exterior, she does have feelings. In many ways, I think she is perhaps more emotional than most people."

Although Gable had treated Grace as if she were a two-bit starlet, a three-month location fling, whom he ruthlessly discarded when filming ended and he was done with her, he was still the King of Hollywood. So almost a year later, when Grace was nominated as Best Supporting Actress for *Mogambo*, she followed the studio's bidding and agreed that Gable accompany her to the Academy Awards. She was a star now, so she and Clark were on more of an even footing. Sensing, perhaps, that her interest in him was now more lighthearted, he invited her to a rendezvous at the Bel-Air Hotel and she accepted, even though by then she had long since replaced Clark Gable in her heart with yet another great love.

Grace may not have believed in sexual fidelity—why should she have when she was forever involved with men who considered monogamy to be an aberration? Yet she did believe in love. She fell in love extremely easily, always had, always would.

In the late seventies, Gwen Robyns gingerly broached the subject to her: "Grace, you seemed to fall in love all the time." Grace, by way of an explanation, retorted, "Well, they were very nice and very charming men."

"Grace was extremely sexual. All she had to do was be touched and she melted. She just couldn't resist all these beautiful men," explained Gwen.

Mogambo opened at the end of the year, with *Time* reporting, "Grace Kelly's blonde beauty remains intact despite the really silly things she is made to say," and *Newsweek* praising her patrician beauty.

Although Grace merely has third billing in *Mogambo* and is first only seen almost twenty-five minutes into the movie, dressed in an unflattering, ill-fitting safari suit, wearing a helmet, and her trademark white gloves, as in *High Noon*, she is believable in the part of Linda Nordley, the prim upper-class English wife who falls hard for Clark Gable's macho white hunter, Victor Marswell.

Like Gary Cooper before him, Gable seems far too old to be Grace's on-screen love interest. Yet the camera captures the chemistry between them. When Grace, her eyes hot with passion, becomes hysterical and slaps Gable's face, she is completely convincing. Her English accent, however, is highly exaggerated, particularly when she meets Honey Bear—Ava's character—and says, "How do you do," in an extremely affected way.

During the jungle scene with Gable, Grace wears an Hermès scarf tied under her chin in the classic style that she and the Queen of England both favored and that would become one of the key components of her ladylike image. Her lust for Gable flames and in one of the movie's most erotic moments, he rips the scarf off her head as thunder crashes in the background. The symbolism is heavy, the meaning clear.

In Grace's next scene—dinner with Ava, Gable, and Sinden—she appears in a waist-cinching purple organza full-skirted dress with a sweetheart bodice, no longer dowdy or dressed in badly fitting clothes, a woman at last and breathtakingly beautiful.

After Grace and Gable have stolen a moment together, Ava senses their growing attraction. During the next scene when the two couples are in the car together, Grace is sly, almost catlike, exchanging furtive glances with Gable. In the confrontation scene with Ava, she is again back in schoolteacher mode, dressed in brown cardigan and monochrome skirt, denying her feelings for Gable yet burning with desire for him.

When she and Gable embrace by the waterfall, Grace—dressed in a shapeless blue skirt and a belted safari jacket—clings to him as if she would die on the spot, were she to let go. Finally, they kiss in the twilight, with Gable kissing Grace in the same masterly manner as he did Scarlett O'Hara after the burning of Atlanta. Grace looks up at him with wide, love-struck eyes.

Clearly, Grace didn't need to stretch her acting ability much during her love scenes with Gable. But given their offscreen affair, and Gable's cynical attitude toward her in real life, there is a terrible irony when, as Victor Marswell, Gable says, "Mrs. Nordling, you are not going to tell me you've been taking all this seriously, are you? It's in all the books. The woman always falls for the white hunter and we guys make the most of it. Can you blame us? When you come along with that look in your eye, there isn't a guy in the world who would . . ." Incensed, Grace shoots him. That scene, as it transpired, was a fitting epitaph to Grace's bittersweet affair with Clark Gable, the King of Hollywood.

7

Scarlet Lady

Grace returned to America emotionally bruised and unhappy. But her spirits quickly revived when, after being cast as Mrs. John Audubon in the TV play *The Way of an Eagle*, her costar, glamorous French heart-throb Jean-Pierre Aumont, a seductive widower twenty years her senior, began to court her ardently. "Jean-Pierre said Grace was so fantastic that it was impossible not to be in love with her," said veteran *Paris Match* journalist Pepita Dupont—the magazine's Monaco correspondent since 1981 who, a few years before his death, interviewed Aumont about his passion for Grace.

Grace and Jean-Pierre had a brief romance, then she left for Philadelphia, where she was appearing in *The Moon Is Blue* at the Playhouse in the Park, spending time with her family as well.

On June 13, she received word that she had been cast as Margot Wendice in the movie adaptation of Frederick Knott's Broadway hit *Dial M for Murder*. She flew out to Los Angeles in July and again stayed at the Chateau Marmont, from where she wrote once more to Prudy, letting slip that she "talked to Fred Zinnemann just before he left for Hawaii on holiday." As always, she had stayed in touch with a former lover, perhaps briefly resuscitating their affair for old times' sake. Zinnemann was one of her earliest mentors, and she wasn't about to forget it.

However, a few months before, she had met Alfred Hitchcock, the ultimate Svengali and the last of her mentors, who would see right into the heart of her, then synthesize every facet of her kaleidoscopic personality and transform her into a Hollywood icon.

Like John Ford before him, Hitchcock viewed Grace's *Taxi* test and was overwhelmed by a sense of discovery. Born in 1899 in East London, England, to a blue-collar family, Alfred Hitchcock had always been ambivalent about the British upper classes, simultaneously admiring and despising them. And although Grace was playing an Irish girl in the *Taxi* test, Hitchcock immediately succumbed to her blond beauty, announcing, "North German or Nordic types, you know they all look like school teachers," he said, adding somewhat feverishly, "but I gather that they are murder in bed. The English woman is the most promiscuous in bed."

Apart from tellingly allying murder to bed, Hitchcock sensed that he could transform Grace into the British upper-class woman of his dreams, then use his camera to defile her, smash through her virginal façade, and unravel her.

Grace, perhaps responding to the slightly sinister subtext cloaked by Hitchcock's courteous manners, recalled her first meeting with him. "I could not think of anything to say to him. In a horrible way it seemed funny to have my brain turned to stone."

"Maybe she has fire and ice and great passion, but she does not flaunt it," Hitchcock later observed somewhat wistfully of her.

Many years later, his voice still pulsating with great glee at the memory of Grace's convoluted love life during the making of *Dial M For Murder*, Hitchcock declared, "That Gryce! She f—— everyone! Why, she even f—— little Freddie, the writer!" Although Grace herself probably viewed her relationships during *Dial M for Murder* in more elegant terms, Hitchcock wasn't wrong about her and Frederick Knott. On August 12, 1953, she said in passing in a letter to Prudy, "Freddie Knott, the author of *Dial M for Murder* is living right here underneath us . . . and has taken a liking to me . . ."

However, Hitchcock hadn't divined the main event in Grace's romantic life, which she intimated in that same letter. "Ray Milland is only sheer heaven," she wrote.

As a teenager, back in Philadelphia, she had swooned over Milland in *The Lost Weekend*. Now she was costarring with him. And what greater triumph for her than to seduce the hero of her teenage years and to make him her own? There was only one problem. Ray Milland had been married for thirty years, and he and his wife, Muriel—known to friends as "Mal"—had a son. Born in Wales, Ray Milland was twenty-four years older than Grace, suave, sophisticated, and an inveterate seducer of young actresses. "You had to run past

'Jack' Milland's dressing room or else," remembered actress Pat Medina, who went on to marry *The Third Man* actor Joseph Cotten.

With Grace, however, Milland was every inch the gentleman, urbane and charming. Grace was in love with him—wife or no wife—within days of first meeting him. Years later, she insisted to Gwen Robyns that at the time of her affair with Milland, she genuinely believed that he was separated from his wife. "He absolutely swore to me that he left his wife. It wasn't till sometime afterwards that I found out that he had fibbed all over the place. I was just one of them. I wasn't THE one," she said.

Soon Ray Milland was squiring Grace all over Hollywood. Ultimately, the salacious gossip magazine *Confidential* exposed Milland's illicit affair with Grace, whereupon he and his wife separated, and Grace was branded a home wrecker. Muriel "Mal" Milland, one of the most popular Hollywood wives, quickly marshaled the support of all her friends, including powerful columnist, Hedda Hopper.

"Mal was in a desperate situation," remembered Doreen Hawkins, the widow of *Bridge on the River Kwai* actor Jack Hawkins. "She and Ray had had a long marriage and they'd been through a lot together. So everyone was on her side and against Grace.

"Grace was through in Hollywood because of her affair with Ray. The word was, 'Out with her. Mal Milland is the most loved woman in town. How can this outsider come in and break up the greatest marriage of all?'"

Grace's reputation was in shreds, her career in jeopardy. Word of her situation filtered back to Philadelphia, but rather than riding to her rescue like the knight in shining armor she'd always longed for him to be, Jack Kelly swiftly dispatched PR man Scoop Conlan to Hollywood to advise her.

Soon after, Grace gave a Hollywood press interview in which she virtually begged the town for forgiveness.

"I think Grace probably wanted to go on with her career and knew she couldn't if she carried on with Ray. She said she was ashamed," recalled Pat Medina Cotten. "She made a public statement, 'I have done the most terrible thing. I have fallen in love with a married man. And I am distraught. I never want to do anything like that again.'

"It was the most marvelous speech. She had admitted what she had done, and after that speech everyone treated her wonderfully. . . . So somebody gave her a party, then somebody else gave her another one."

Very soon after the scandal broke, Ray Milland went back to Mal, who forgave him, while Grace concentrated on her career, and forgave herself.

After the scandal subsided, Grace recast it, putting the blame on Hollywood. "As an unmarried woman I was thought to be a danger," she said later. "Other women looked at me as a rival and it pained me a great deal. Bing Crosby, who starred with me in *High Society*, told me that Hedda Hopper had described me as a nymphomaniac! Thank God everyone soon learned who and what I really was. The persecution didn't last long; I had a circle of good friends. But even so, I hated Hollywood. It's a town without pity."

Her friend, Arlene Dahl, however, has another interpretation of the Milland affair: "The Ray Millands were very good friends of mine. Mal hated Grace like poison. Grace didn't know he was married? Oh, please. Everyone knew he was married. He was one of the most married film stars in Hollywood. Mal was very jealous and they had been married for years and years. I made a film with Ray. Everybody knew he was married."

Jack Hawkins died in 1973, soon after which his widow, Doreen rented their house, Villa Jardin Sur Mer, in St. Jean Cap Ferrat, to Ray and Mal Milland.

"Grace missed people in the business. I suppose she thought, 'I'm Grace of Monaco, now, and the past is the past,' Doreen Hawkins said. "So when Grace found out that Mal and Ray were staying at the villa, she rang Mal to invite them to the palace. But Mal was livid. She hit the roof, then slammed the phone down on Grace."

Through the years, Grace's jealous peers made sure that the stories about her promiscuity were perpetuated. Zsa Zsa Gabor, who was at MGM at the same time as Grace, pronounced in her autobiography, "Even then I was aware that Grace had more boyfriends in one month than I had in a lifetime."

In a dazzling irony, Hollywood siren Hedy Lamarr—notorious for having filmed the world's first cinematic nude scene in *Ecstasy*—also lambasted Grace for her promiscuity. "Hedy told me Grace slept around," her friend Arlene Roxbury said. "Hedy said Grace would sleep with anyone in Hollywood to get ahead. Hedy said that was a known fact, actors, directors, producers, Grace would sleep with them at the drop of a hat."

While there may have been some truth in everything Zsa Zsa Gabor and Hedy Lamarr said about Grace, it is equally true of many of Hollywood's screen sirens past and present. And while the public was utterly unaware at the time of Lana Turner's one-night-stand with a Harlem cabdriver, Ava's propensity for conducting multiple liaisons, and Marlene Dietrich's lesbianism, Grace's tragedy was that, discreet as she was, she trusted two people close to her, each of whom betrayed her.

Grace's affairs with a string of her leading men—Gary Cooper, Clark Gable, Ray Milland, Bing Crosby, and William Holden—would not have been common currency had they not been confirmed by her mother on the eve of her wedding in a ten-part article in which she stripped her daughter of any semblance of privacy. That Grace forgave Margaret is a measure of her feelings for her mother and her good nature.

Moreover, if Don Richardson hadn't kept a journal of all his private conversations with her, then made them public, the details of her promiscuity might never have been disseminated. Consequently, massive damage was done to her reputation. Grace's love life became the stuff of Hollywood legend, a sobriquet forever attached to her name, even when she had become Princess of Monaco and forever after.

Despite the vicious rumors, the truth is that Grace's liaisons were primarily fueled by her passion and her romanticism, not by her ambition. According to actress Betsy Drake, who met Grace during *High Noon* and went on to marry Cary Grant, Grace had no interest in embarking on a sexual relationship with billionaire tycoon Howard Hughes, who made a star of Jane Russell and could have worked his magic for Grace as well.

"When Grace tried to avoid Howard Hughes, she didn't use any makeup and wore glasses. He came to the house specifically to go on the make for Grace, but he didn't recognize her." Betsy said.

Filming the harrowing *Dial M for Murder* fight in which she stabs her would-be killer with a pair of scissors had taken its toll. On September 3, she wrote to Prudy, "Last week we did the murder scene—which went very well and was great fun. I play the whole scene in my nightgown! I am still just covered in bruises."

Her exclamation mark—indicating that she was shocked about playing the scene in her nightgown—was Grace's private joke, which she did not reveal to Prudy. Hitchcock had assumed she would wear a robe in the scene in which she is awakened by a telephone call, then grapples to the death with the killer. But Grace pointed out that wearing a nightgown in the scene was far more realistic than wearing a robe. Acknowledging that she was right, Hitch-cock had her shoot the scene dressed in the flimsiest of nightgowns.

When *Dial M for Murder* was released in May 1954, Hitchcock's influence on Grace's image was dramatically obvious. Her hair is silvery blond, longer and looser than before; she wears a much darker shade of red lipstick than in previous movies, her eyebrows are darker, and—for the very first time on celluloid—she displays her cleavage.

In *Dial M for Murder*, Grace plays the first sophisticated grown-up woman of her career. Under Hitchcock's direction, she is no longer an ardent school-girl. No naïve, unworldly Amy or prim and proper Linda, bursting with un-resolved passion, Grace's Margot Wendice is sleek and poised—the ultimate Hitchcock blonde.

The first time we see Grace, she is at breakfast, reading the *Times*. Dressed in an orange prom dress, with attached lace bolero, she is indescribably beau-tiful and, with her well-modulated, now natural-sounding British accent, ex-tremely regal. For the first time, there are intimations of Princess Grace of Monaco in her performance.

And although the much older Milland radiates a sinister, demon prince aura, when Grace instructs him not to make the martini so watery, we believe that she is strong enough to dominate him, if only for a few minutes.

While the married Linda Nordley, the part she played in *Mogambo*, spent most of the movie fighting to suppress her illicit passion for Clark Gable's character, when *Dial M for Murder* begins, Grace's character Margot Wendice has long since consummated her adulterous passion for Mark, the American writer played by Robert Cummings. Displaying not a shred of guilt, she is so-phisticated, confident, and in control.

In the next scene, she wears a figure-hugging dark brown dress, accentuat-ing her curves. In the scene in which she narrowly escapes being murdered by Captain Legate—played by Tony Dawson, reputedly also one of her off-screen lovers—thanks to Grace's suggestion that she wear a nightgown, she reveals even more of her body. The curve of her bottom and the long line of her legs are shown in sharp relief as Hitchcock's camera caresses her body.

As Grace struggles with her killer, Hitchcock directed his cameraman to linger on every inch of her body—the kicking of her legs, the flailing of her arms—almost as if he were shooting her being raped. Nonetheless, his adora-tion of Grace's beauty, her body—and even her well-muscled back on which the camera dwells for quite a few moments—is evident in every frame of *Dial M for Murder*.

Yet despite the rough treatment Grace receives during the movie, she is projected as regal and composed, even when confessing her adultery.

When Hitchcock photographs her in the last scene, her hair parted, with no makeup, she is suddenly an Ingrid Bergman *doppelgänger*, her resemblance to the star she once named as her favorite utterly unmistakable.

But above all, we are left with an overriding sense of Grace's almost queenly qualities, her glamour and her remoteness.

She loved working with Hitchcock and was eager to repeat the experience; he reciprocated her sentiments. "All through the making of *Dial M for Murder*, he [Hitchcock] sat and talked to me about *Rear Window* all the time, even before we had discussed my being in it," Grace recalled.

Although she had been offered the opportunity to costar alongside Marlon Brando in *On the Waterfront*, Grace—as always—was loyal to those whom she perceived as having enhanced her career or her life. So in October 1953, while she was still considering whether or not to accept the *Waterfront* part, when she received word that Hitchcock had scheduled her for wardrobe fittings for his next movie, Grace unhesitatingly accepted the part of Lisa Fremont in *Rear Window*.

Aware that she would be living in Hollywood for at least another two months and wanting her independence without once again arousing the ire of all the sundry Hollywood wives, Grace rented a two-bedroom apartment in a thirties building on Sweetzer, in West Los Angeles, then cast about for a suitable roommate to chaperone her.

John Foreman, her agent at ICM, came up with the ideal solution. Actress Rita Gam—also under contract to MGM—was staying at the Beverly Hills Hotel while shooting the movie *Attila, the Hun* and was in need of company. Not realizing that Rita and Grace knew each other from their television days in New York, John suggested that Grace call her.

Grace invited Rita for coffee at the apartment, where Rita was struck by her large and heart-warming collection of family photographs, her friendliness, and her good manners. "She wasn't pretentious. She said what she thought and she thought about what she said. She knew what she wanted and she went for it. She also had a great sense of humor. Sort of silly, calling everyone 'bird.' But she also had a kind of stability and a kind of basicness that I didn't have. She wanted to be a mother and she wanted to be married," Rita recalled.

"Once I moved in with her, I discovered that she was never mean or cross but always generous and fun to be with. Because we were so young, life was so free, so full, we were on top of everything. It was like the jazz age in the twenties, a very effervescent time.

"Grace was sloppy, but very clean. She didn't sing in the bath and we never had music on. We didn't have time for those things. The alarm would go off every day at six, then we had orange juice and coffee. Then the studio cars would arrive to take Grace to *Rear Window* and me to my set. When we got home, we were so tired that all we could think about was having a quick and dangerous hamburger—which we'd make for ourselves. Then we'd go to sleep. Grace was a very deep sleeper," Rita revealed.

"Grace loved champagne, so we always kept some on ice. We were invited to a great many parties. Producer Charlie Feldman invited us to one, and when we turned up, only Charlie and the Dominican playboy Rubirosa were there. Just the two of them, nobody else. Luckily, we had brought our own car so we could make a quick escape. Dinner was served, but I was quite ready to leave. When they brought the filet mignon, I turned to Grace and said, 'Let's go.' She said, 'No, let's wait till dessert. It might be good.' So we did, then we left. Grace could deal with everything. In her own way, she was strong. She was sure of herself," Rita said.

"Sammy Cahn invited us to a Christmas party," Rita recounted in her memoirs, "We were dressed to the nines, Grace in a long green satin dress and pearls and, of course, her inevitable white kid gloves. Again, we drove ourselves there in Grace's old Chevy. Everyone murmured admiringly as she drifted up to the buffet table—she looked so fresh, so elegant and ladylike. But when we hit the dessert table, she plunged into the cake like a starving sailor. 'Just one teeny piece for Christmas,' she said as she wolfed it down. She was usually party-shy, but this night she was the hit of the evening, from her astrological predictions to her staged hypnosis of me to stop smoking."

Grace was a Scorpio and attuned to the supernatural, to the paranormal, to tarot cards, and above all to astrology. For more than twenty years, she consulted the astrologer Carroll Righter, whose other stellar clients included Marlene Dietrich. She was proud of being a Scorpio like fellow actress Vivien Leigh and always gravitated toward Leos; Maree Frisby Rambo, John Foreman,

Alfred Hitchcock, Bettina Gray, and Carolyn Reybold were all born under the sign of the lion.

But while Grace adored consulting the stars and enjoyed playing the amateur astrologer at parties, she was also drawn to psychics. "Whenever we had lunch together in Manhattan and passed a sign that said 'psychic,' Grace insisted in going in and consulting her," recalled Maree Frisby Rambo.

"Grace thought she had ESP," said Rita Gam. It is interesting to note that Robert Evans claimed that Grace could read a man's mind and Cary Grant declared, "Grace had the most incredible ESP about her. She could almost read my thoughts." William Holden said, "Every man who comes into contact with her finds she has an uncanny power of understanding men."

In the last year of her life, she would prove, without a shadow of a doubt, that she did, indeed, have psychic abilities.

She was also passionately interested in graphology and, as Princess Grace of Monaco, had her handwriting analyzed by British graphologist Jeanne Heald and wrote the foreword to her book.

Grace spent November and December sharing Rita Gam's Los Angeles apartment while filming *Rear Window*, reveling in the attention and care that Hitchcock devoted to making Lisa Fremont the greatest characterization of her entire career. "Grace adored Hitchcock. They laughed a lot and told jokes— lots of silly ones. Grace had a very good sense of humor," Rita Gam said.

Grace herself recalled to Hitchcock's biographer, Donald Spoto, "One time he turned to me when he had been telling Ray Milland some very raw kinds of things, and he said, 'Are you shocked, Miss Kelly?' I said, 'No, I went to a girl's convent school, Mr. Hitchcock, I heard all those things when I was thirteen.' And of course he loved that sort of answer."

After Grace made the correct judgment call regarding the nightgown in *Dial M for Murder*, Hitchcock learned to trust her wardrobe sense, often consulting her regarding the clothes she would wear in *Rear Window*.

Sometimes, however, their aesthetic sensibilities clashed. "At the rehearsal for the scene in *Rear Window* in which I wore a sheer nightgown, Hitchcock called for Edith Head. He came over here and said, 'Look, the bosom is not right. We're going to have to put something in there.' He was very sweet about it; he didn't want to upset me, so he spoke quietly to Edith. We went into my dressing room and Edith said, 'Mr. Hitchcock is worried because there's a false pleat here. He wants me to put in falsies.'

"'Well,' I said, 'you can't put falsies in this, it's going to show—and I'm not going to wear them.' And she said, 'What are we going to do?' So we quickly took it up here, made some adjustments there, and I just did what I could and stood as straight as possible—without falsies.

"When I walked out onto the set Hitchcock looked at me and at Edith and said, 'See what a difference they make?'"

Despite Grace still being shell-shocked after her abortive affair with the married Ray Milland, she nevertheless developed a massive crush on Jimmy Stewart, who'd been married to wife Gloria for five years and had the reputation of being a steadfastly loyal husband. Inevitably, she flirted with him—if only slightly.

When Stewart's biographer, Lawrence J. Quirk, asked his *Rear Window* costar Thelma Ritter how Stewart had responded to Grace's flirtatious overtures, she said she felt he enjoyed Grace's attraction to him. "I think it took him back to his fancy-free, footloose bachelor days; I don't say he flirted, but he didn't seem to mind it either."

Gloria Stewart was not so sanguine about Grace playing opposite her husband, particularly as Mal Milland was one of her closest friends and godmother of her daughter, Kelly.

Gloria later said, "Jimmy was working with some of the most glamorous women in the world. My constant fear I suppose was that he would find them more attractive than me and have an affair with one of them. A lot of men in Hollywood became involved with their leading ladies. Jimmy was a red-blooded American male so naturally I thought it could happen to him too."

"Gloria was so worried that Grace would make a play for Jimmy that she was on the set every single day," said Van Johnson's daughter, Schuyler, whose mother, leading Hollywood hostess Evie Johnson, was one of Gloria Stewart's close friends.

But although Jimmy Stewart enthused of Grace, "She was anything but cold. Everything about Grace was appealing. I was married, but I wasn't dead. She had those big warm eyes and, well, if you had ever played a love scene with her, you'd know she wasn't cold. She had an inner confidence. People who have that are not cold. Grace had that twinkle and a touch of larceny in her eye," he remained faithful to Gloria.

However, as *Rear Window* assistant director Herbert Coleman put it, "Every man who ever was lucky enough to work with Grace Kelly fell in love with her, me included. Even Hitchcock—although he only was in love with two people, and that was Alma and Pat." "Grace was my father's favorite actress," is all his daughter Pat will say today.

Women, too, always warmed to Grace. *Rear Window* actress Sue Casey, who played a nonspeaking part as a girl in one of the windows, said, "Grace was so well groomed, very gentle and very ladylike."

And when Jimmy Stewart's character in *Rear Window* described Grace's character, Lisa Fremont, as "too talented, too beautiful, too sophisticated, too perfect," he could just as easily have been describing Grace.

When *Rear Window* opened at Manhattan's Rivoli Theater on August 4, 1954, Grace received rave reviews, with *Variety's* critic commenting on the "earthy quality to the relationship between Stewart and Miss Kelly. Both do a fine job of the picture's acting demands."

As Lisa Fremont, wealthy, sophisticated Manhattan fashion model, Grace was playing an independent career woman for the very first time, opposite James Stewart, playing her photographer boyfriend totally incapacitated with a broken leg and reduced to sitting at the window speculating about the goings-ons of his neighbors.

Grace is first seen twenty-two minutes into the movie. In an uncharacteristically slow sequence—perhaps the slowest he ever shot—Hitchcock introduces Grace in silhouette, slowly moving to a close-up of her face, then of her pearls, then more shadow, followed by a close-up of Stewart smiling, then finally focusing on Grace's face, as she leans over to kiss him. The camera lingers on her further as she asks him about his love life, and there is a magical close-up of her perfect profile.

She is in her element, poised, amused, confident, and even more polished and sophisticated than she was as Margot Wendice. For the first time in any of her movies, Grace speaks with an American accent and plays a New Yorker. Both Stewart and the camera gaze longingly at her, every shot perfectly framed, showcasing her charms as never before.

After Lisa gives Stewart a silver cigarette case and orders dinner for him from "21"—one of Grace's own favorite restaurants—she announces, "I am going to make this a week you'll never forget," and brings him his food on a tray. After she unpacks a sheer chiffon peignoir—which Grace later described as making her look like a "peach parfait," although it and the rest of the *Rear Window* wardrobe garnered an Academy Award nomination for Edith Head for best costumes—Grace informs him, "I'm in love with you, I don't care what you do for a living, I just want to be a part of it."

Throughout the movie, her beauty is breathtaking. Audiences throughout the world fell in love with Grace Kelly, for then and always, just as Hitchcock had intended.

8

The Country Girl

At the beginning of January 1954, Grace spent three weeks filming *The Bridges at Toko-Ri* with William Holden, and—given her track record—naturally, fell madly in love with him.

"He was a very handsome man, with a wonderful, engaging smile, a tremendous self-assurance, coupled with a hint of vulnerability. He drank heavily but was very attractive. Grace loved William Holden, and he was very, very fond of her. Their affair was common knowledge in Hollywood," revealed journalist Donald Zec, Holden's friend.

Following in the wake of Audrey Hepburn, who when filming *Sabrina* with Holden the previous year had had a passionate affair with him, Grace had fallen for yet another married costar. At thirty-six, William Holden was the youngest of her married movie star lovers, dazzlingly good-looking, magnetically sexually attractive. "He liked to have affairs, but Grace was really serious, which sort of scared him away in the long run," said Robert Slatzer, to whom Holden confided his feelings.

Although Grace tried to cover up the affair, insisting to a journalist, "As for Bill Holden, he drove up to give me a lift in his white convertible. Everyone reported it. He was taking me to dinner with his wife. That was my romance with Bill," his Cadillac had been spotted on various occasions parked outside her apartment building. Naturally, *Confidential* reported the sighting with great glee.

By then, Holden had jettisoned his fears about Grace. He told his psychiatrist, Michael Jay Klassman, that they had fallen head over heels in love with each other. Together, they braved the Kelly family's disapproval, with Holden paying a visit to Henry Avenue. Given his marital status, it is hardly surprising that the family received him with extreme coldness.

Even though Hitchcock wasn't directing Grace in *Bridges at Toko-Ri,* in each scene she is radiant, each shot of her perfect. Playing Nancy, the wife of a naval officer—William Holden—she is first seen wearing thick stockings, a brown coat, and a white beret.

The offscreen attraction between Grace and Holden is palpable onscreen, and, as they kiss on the quay, his lust for her is unbridled.

The scenes between Grace and Holden in *Toko-Ri* sizzle with chemistry, in particular during the first scene of Grace's career in which she was filmed in bed with a man. Swathed in a white nightgown, the peach duvet setting off her golden complexion, she looks more beautiful than ever. She is also seen in a bathing suit for the very first time onscreen, revealing the perfection of her lissome figure.

When she broaches the subject of Holden's dangerous mission involving the bridges, he changes the subject and talks about the children's piano lessons. She plays along for a bit, placid and pale. Then she explodes and, full of emotion, her voice deepens as she begs, "Harry, you've got to tell me about these bridges."

The movie ends with Grace taking Holden to the boat and kissing him good-bye. He is killed in action, and she isn't seen again in this tragic war movie in which her part is peripheral.

Although Grace's role was minor, when the movie was released on January 28, 1955, *The New Yorker* observed that she played her part "with quiet confidence." With Grace's tacit agreement, there was no glimmer in her performance of the polished Hitchcock blonde of yore.

She was readying herself for her part in *The Country Girl,* in which she would play dramatically against type and win an Academy Award at last.

Jennifer Jones was originally slated to play the part of Bing Crosby's long-suffering wife in *The Country Girl,* but she became pregnant. Grace, who was familiar with the play *The Country Girl,* was desperate for the role. However, MGM balked at releasing her to Paramount.

Finally, Grace threatened MGM that if they didn't give her the release, she would pack her bags and leave for New York for good. "In the end, Grace said to MGM, 'All right, don't release me for *The Country Girl,* then. Fine. You can send my Christmas cards to Philadelphia from now on,'" remembered actress

Kathryn Crosby, who was married to Bing for twenty years from 1957 until his death. In the end, Grace's strong-minded approach vanquished MGM and the part was hers.

Bing Crosby made a great show of not really wanting Grace as a replacement for Jennifer Jones. Yet although, for the benefit of press and public, Bing and Grace enacted the charade of pretending they first met on *Country Girl*, that wasn't the truth. Alan Ladd's wife, Sue, confided to James Spada that during the time Bing's first wife, Dixie, was battling terminal cancer, Bing and Grace had been trysting in the Ladd's home.

While Bing and Grace had a romantic history, and he was set on accelerating their relationship, he was fully aware that costar William Holden—albeit still a married man—was also in the running. "I know Bing talked to Holden and tried to talk him out of seeing Grace. Bing was really crazy about her," remembered Hollywood journalist James Bacon.

Bacon, who first met Grace when Gary Cooper introduced him to her on the set of *High Noon*, had a chilling experience with Grace during the making of *A Country Girl*, which would take on an increasing significance as the years passed. "She once drove Bill Holden and me," he said. "She drove like a stunt driver, swerving around curves at high speed. Holden was a very fast driver himself and he was scared. We were both scared by the way in which Grace drove."

Despite Holden's undeniable appeal, he was married, leaving Bing—now a widower—with a distinct advantage in Grace's eyes. So it was natural that she and Bing embark on a second-time-around romance. Moreover, despite her vast array of past lovers, a deep vein of conventionality ran through her nature. She wanted to get married, and Bing Crosby was the first major star she'd romanced who was free and available.

At least, so she thought. By the time filming commenced on *The Country Girl*, actress Kathryn Grant had been dating Bing for more than a year and was engaged to him. Initially, Kathryn was unaware that Grace was her rival for Bing's affections.

She had first met Grace when she had a small part in *Rear Window* and spent three days filming at Paramount with her. "In the makeup department, Grace ate donuts, tossed jokes about what she'd done before, wasn't stuffy, and was really easy to be with," Kathryn said.

'I was writing a column on Hollywood, so I went on to the *Country Girl* set to interview Bing. Even though Grace was dressed drably, she was gorgeous.

When I interviewed Bing about her, he was very protective about her, about how elegant she was, how sweet and nice. He cared for her. I could tell. In my black little heart, I thought smugly that she was too tall. But I knew that Bing was madly in love with her. So was Holden. Everybody was," Kathryn said.

During filming—irrespective of Kathryn—Bing openly pursued his relationship with Grace. One evening, Rosemary Clooney was invited to his house for dinner. "When I arrived, Grace was already there, sitting in the library, knitting. Knitting! She was wearing low-heeled shoes—Bing wasn't tall—and a skirt and sweater, and she looked amazingly domestic. I thought, 'What the hell is this? Is she auditioning? Is this some kind of test?'" She remembered in her autobiography.

Bing was proud that Grace was twenty-six years his junior. As for Grace, this was the first time that she was able to date one of her famous costars in public without suffering the press's slings and arrows, and she made the most of it. She no longer had to hide and she reveled in the freedom to flaunt her affair with Bing.

During research for her biography of Grace, Gwen Robyns interviewed a source at a Hollywood restaurant where Grace and Bing had dinner together, who recalled them "canoodling" in full view of all the other diners.

Grace was determined to become Bing's wife. But she hadn't reckoned with Kathryn, a tough Texas girl with a hold over Bing that would outlast her own.

Throughout his affair with Grace, although she was unaware of it, Bing continued to swear undying love to Kathryn. Finally, he and Kathryn set a wedding date of September 10, 1954. On September 7, Bing confessed to Kathryn that he'd been having an affair with Grace and didn't want to marry Kathryn after all.

Soon after, he changed his mind once more. Full of remorse, he proposed to Kathryn again, regaling her with every detail of how he broke off with Grace. "I listened to Bing with silent glee while he re-enacted the parting scene: threats of suicide, public exposure, perhaps a suit for breach of promise," she recalled.

Eight years later, the Crosbys, then on vacation in the South of France, were invited by Grace to visit her and the children at Rocagel, their farm outside Monaco. "Grace's secretary advised me to wear a tea gown, so I dressed up to the nines in a chiffon tea gown and a big hat. When we got to Rocagel, Grace was in jeans, making hamburgers on the poolside grill," recalled Kathryn.

When Grace had met her former boyfriend Don Richardson with his new wife, Laura, she covertly held hands with him under the table. In the presence of Bing's wife, she went further. "I sat on the edge of the circle in my tea gown, watching the two of them neglecting to unhand each other. That sort of thing went on for an hour and a half," Kathryn remembered. Then, with relish, she added, "But I got a little of my own back because my daughter, Mary Francis, stole Caroline's shoes, and my son, Harry, kicked Prince Albert in the shins.

"Grace and Bing corresponded for years. I never read the letters, but I know that Grace kept asking Bing to come to the Red Cross Ball. He never did things like that. I know he wrote to her asking about Mary Francis studying ballet in France and she found several ballet schools appropriate for her. He thought Grace was the most beautiful woman, and I hated that."

Despite the fact that Bing's rejection of her during the making of *The Country Girl* reportedly devastated Grace, she quickly consoled herself. "Grace and I had an affair while she was making *The Country Girl*," Tony Curtis—who was married at the time to actress Janet Leigh—revealed. "I first met her at a party given by Charles Lederer at his house behind the Beverly Hills Hotel. Charles was Hungarian, like I am, so he let me use his house whenever I wanted, and I did with Grace.

"I liked her very much. She was articulate, but not as fancy as everyone thought she was. I noticed that when we were together, that Grace Kelly background disappeared. She was very hot. She was a horny Philadelphia girl. But it couldn't go any further with us because she was looking for bigger grapes than me. . . ."

The Country Girl was released on December 16, 1954. Grace was nominated for the Academy Award for best actress.

During her first scenes in the movie, her voice is far deeper than normal, and her flat, expressionless American-accented delivery is redolent of blue-collar factory workers. Her hair is in braids, and she wears glasses, a white shirt, a cardigan, and an ill-fitting skirt. She is stripped of all sex appeal, and when William Holden tells her, "You look like an old lady. You shouldn't wear your hair like that," his words have the ring of truth about them. Free of makeup, her lips pressed tightly together, more than ever she resembles Ingrid Bergman in a dark Swedish art movie, and—with her staccato delivery—even sounds as if she is appearing in one.

As Grace and Holden cross swords, she is grim and stern about her washed-up singer husband, played by Bing. When she stands in the wings, watching Bing on stage, her posture is that of a prizefighter. Her aura is menacing, rather like that of a young version of Judith Anderson in *Rebecca*.

Although Grace's first major movie role in *High Noon* was shot in black and white, after that, audiences became accustomed to seeing her in the glory of Technicolor. The fact that *Country Girl* is shot in black and white serves to diminish her fabled allure somewhat. However, in the next scene at Sardi's, she looks increasingly more glamorous. Her voice begins to lilt slightly upward, although a pugnacious thrust of her chin remains.

In the brief flashback—Bing remembers the day on which he sang "You've Got What It Takes," his little boy conducted the orchestra, and Grace watched, glittering with love and pride—she is herself again. Dressed in monochrome, her face framed by a hat with a veil, she blows Bing a kiss and is as beautiful as ever.

Back in the present again, she interrupts Bing's reverie, all doom and gloom. When she finds his empty liquor bottles hidden under the table, like a jailer she cautions, "No more, Frank."

She is next seen backstage, wearing large horn-rimmed glasses and an unflatteringly large coat. "You smoke too much," she says tonelessly to Holden, in a manner reminiscent of Garbo at her most dour and sits backstage, knitting robotically. After Bing receives dreadful reviews in Boston, and Holden orders Grace to get out of town because she is a bad influence on Bing, he and Grace have a confrontation in which she is strong, contemptuous, and bitter.

She tells Holden the truth, that Bing has demonized her, and she recalls her past feelings for Bing with great tenderness, describing "a pathetic hint of frailty in a wonderful glowing man. That appeals to a lot of us. It did to me. I was so young. His weaknesses seemed touching and sweet, they made me love him more." Here her performance is Oscar-worthy. But when Holden grabs her and she cries out, "You're holding me. Why are you holding me?" her eyes bulge like those of an overwrought silent movie actress.

On Bing's opening night, she is once more beautiful, with upswept hair, horn-rimmed glasses, and a black off-the-shoulder dress with a broach at the waist. As it becomes increasingly clear from the audience's reaction that Bing is a hit, that he's a star again, Holden begs Grace to leave him. She is torn between two lovers, an irony considering the fact that even though Grace was dating Bing in real life, her attraction to the glamorous Holden reportedly had not diminished at all.

In April 1954 Grace flew to Colombia for a ten-day stint to film *Green Fire* with handsome British actor Stewart Granger, in which she was playing the relatively small role of Kathy Noland, the owner of a coffee plantation.

The dashing Granger was then married to British actress Jean Simmons. "My father was used to acting with Ava Gardner and Margaret Lockwood, who were both very much 'one of the boys,'" Granger's daughter, Lindsay, recalled.

"He told me Grace was very different, not down and dirty with the cast and crew, but perfect for the part of princess. He didn't like making *Green Fire*, though. He didn't like the script and he described Grace as being 'cool and aloof.' Jean was then pregnant, so he wasn't in a straying mode," she said.

In his autobiography, Granger cast a slightly different light on his reaction to Grace: "Grace had one phobia, her behind. For me it was the most delicious behind imaginable, but it did stick out a bit and she was very self-conscious. Our last scene was played in a torrential downpour and when the final kiss came we were both soaking wet, which accentuated that fabulous behind. To save her embarrassment I covered it with both hands. She was so delighted at finishing the movie that she didn't even object but if you look closely at that kiss you'll see Grace give a start as those two eager hands take hold."

Grace had a dreadful time making *Green Fire*. As she confided to Hedda Hopper afterward, "It wasn't pleasant. We worked at a pathetic village— miserable huts and dirty. Part of the crew got shipwrecked—it was awful."

Grace has an extremely small part in a film with an extremely thin plot. She looks gorgeous and acquits herself fairly well, but gives nothing extra.

On May 25, 1954, exhausted from the past few months' back-to-back filming of *Rear Window, Toko-Ri, Country Girl*, and *Green Fire*, Grace flew to France to make *To Catch a Thief* for MGM. However, she did not fly there alone.

Department store heir Bernard "Barney" Strauss was initially introduced to Grace by her friend and fellow Academy student Sally Richardson. "Sally brought Grace over to my apartment," Barney Strauss remembered. "I thought she was utterly beautiful, stunning, and I couldn't believe it when she took a shine to me. She was very warm and lovely to me and wanted to know when I would be going to Europe.

"We flew to Paris together. She was going to make *To Catch a Thief* and I was going to play in a tennis tournament there. We went out to dinner together in Paris, then we went down to the South of France, where we both stayed at the Carlton Hotel in Cannes. I was there with her all through the shooting—for six or seven weeks—and then a little bit afterward.

"She was very focused on becoming famous and being a star. She was very self-involved. She could be very loving at times and then very aloof and into her script and studying. She was complicated."

One night, Barney and Grace had dinner with Hitchcock. Often, Cary Grant and his wife, Betsy Drake, joined her and Hitchcock as well. "She wasn't in the least bit intimidated by Hitchcock. He and Grace got along really well, and all of us—me, Cary, and Grace—spent a great deal of time with him and his wife, Alma," remembered Betsy Drake, who was in the South of France during the making of the movie.

"Grace was a very likable woman. She got along well with everyone. She was attractive but not a raving beauty, which is often the case when people photograph beautifully on screen," she said.

From their first scenes, Grace and Grant formed a mutual admiration society. "Grace had a kind of serenity, a calmness that I hadn't arrived at that point in my life—and perhaps never will, for all I know," Cary said years later. "She was so relaxed in front of the camera that she made it look simple. When you played a scene with her, she really listened, she was right there with you. She was Buddha-like in her concentration. She was like Garbo in that respect."

When, in years to come, he was asked to name his all-time favorite leading lady, Cary unhesitatingly replied, "Well, with all due respect to dear Ingrid [Bergman], I much preferred Grace. She had serenity."

"Grace loved and admired Cary and cherished working with him," Prince Rainier attested. "She was also proud and happy about the things Cary had said about her professionalism. But Cary was above all a friend. She valued his friendship."

The Grants, Grace, and her friends, Jay and Judith Kanter (later Balaban Quine) spent Easter weekend 1955, together at the Sahara in Las Vegas. "Mostly we played roulette," recalled Betsy Drake, "because we both believed we had ESP." Once or twice, Grace tried her hand at shooting craps, but when that failed she decided to try and cash in on her photographic memory by playing blackjack. While neither Betsy nor Grace made any big scores, Cary did not gamble at all, instead spending most of the time chatting with fans thrilled to encounter him there.

In 1957, Grace and Rainier visited Betsy and Cary at the Connaught Hotel in London. There, they decided to conduct a séance.

"We decided to try and get in touch with Einstein," Betsy recalled. "So all of us—Grace, Rainier, Cary, and I—all touched fingers and asked, 'Is Einstein there?' The table was still. We asked, 'Is anybody there?' Nothing happened. Cary was making *Indiscreet* with Ingrid Bergman at that time, and she had a kidney problem. It occurred to me to try and reach Freddie Longsdale, a writer I knew who had passed on, and ask him about Ingrid's kidney problem. So I said, 'Freddie, Freddie Longsdale, are you there?' The table started to move. 'Freddie, Freddie, do you know anything about Ingrid's kidney?' The table started jumping around. Of course, it was Rainier and Cary making the table jump."

That experience, however, did not sour Grace on séances. A year later, when Hollywood columnist James Bacon was set to fly to Monte Carlo to cover the gala premiere of *Kings Go Forth*, he received a surprise visit from Cary. "The doorbell rang," Bacon remembered, "and there was Cary standing there. He said, 'Jim, I hear you're going to Monaco. Well, Grace and Rainier are very crazy about playing the Ouija board, so I bought them one. Would you kindly take it over there?' I did and Grace was thrilled when I gave it to her. She thought it was great. They both did."

Their friendship with Grace and Rainier thus cemented, Betsy and Cary flew to Monaco at Easter 1961 to visit them. Delighted, Grace met Betsy and Cary at Nice Airport herself. When she greeted Cary with a kiss, to her horror, a paparazzo captured it.

"When the photograph appeared on the front page of *Nice Matin* the next day, Prince Rainier was furious," reported John Glatt, author of *The Royal House of Monaco*. Although this has never before been disclosed, according to Grace's friend and fellow MGM actress Arlene Dahl, Rainier's jealousy of Cary Grant was justified: "Cary Grant was a very big man in her life. He went both ways. She was able to bewitch him. It was love. A proper romance. Definitely. Cary and Grace bonded on a psychic level. They both thought they knew each other in a past life. He also kept her laughing." Consequently, Rainier was in a bad mood throughout the Grants' stay. Nonetheless, Betsy liked him. "He had a wonderful sense of humor, and he was a sweet, funny man. Grace used to call him, 'My darling little Gemini,'" she revealed.

Grace's performance in *To Catch a Thief* is a soufflé of sex appeal, charm, and elegance. Instead of introducing her with a long, lingering shot as he did in *Rear Window*, the first time we see her—twenty-four minutes into the film—Hitchcock gives us a brief flash of her in the crowd sunbathing on the beach at Cannes, wearing a cream bathing suit, sunglasses, and a turban, and in the process of rubbing suntan lotion into her long, sleek arms.

She is Frances Stevens, an American oil heiress on vacation with her mother. We next meet them in the dining room. Wearing a pale blue chiffon gown, her hair in a Grecian knot, revealing her long, graceful neck, she is even more stunningly beautiful than ever. When she and her mother watch the gambling in the casino, Grace is silent, embarrassed by her mother's vulgarity. Her posture is perfect, her face pale. Utterly still, she projects a tremendous presence.

During the scene outside Grace's bedroom door, when—without any warning—she suddenly kisses Cary, she is the living embodiment of Hitchcock's most cherished fantasy: the well-born debutante who suddenly erupts with passion.

When she arrives at the hotel bearing a picnic for Cary, insisting that she is going to drive him along the Corniche to view a villa, she is dressed in a peach and white dress, sporting her trademark white gloves, and exudes self-confidence, every inch the regal heiress, not too difficult a feat for the former Princess of the Atlantic City Race Track.

She had always prided herself on her psychic abilities, her ESP, but watching *To Catch a Thief* through the prism of the intervening years, Alfred Hitchcock appears to have been equally prescient. Although he was fully aware at the time that Grace hated driving, he insisted that she be filmed driving Cary Grant, and her fear of driving and her inability to properly control a car are captured on film. Moreover, he filmed her driving along the very same road from which she would one day hurtle to her death.

In a second scene in which Grace is seen driving—her feet encased in pale pink sling-back shoes—her car screeches on the pavement and, on a hairpin bend, almost crashes into a coach. Cary clenches his fist in fear as she repeatedly almost drives the two of them over the edge. He looks down at the vast drop, the wheels screech on the road, and Grace brakes sharply to allow a laundry maid to cross. The drive ends. The agony for Cary, and for the audience, is over.

In the celebrated fireworks scene, she is resplendent in a long white chiffon dress. Her breasts are so unnaturally conical that it appears that Hitchcock has finally prevailed upon her to wear a padded bra after all.

After the robbery, when she appears at the door of Cary's bedroom to accuse him of stealing her jewels, just as in her previous collaborations with Hitchcock, she is dressed in a see-through chiffon nightgown that reveals the undulating lines of her body.

As she demands of Cary, "Give them back to me," her diction slips into upper-class British. In haughty tones, she imperiously informs Cary that she has called the police "and told them who you are and what you did tonight." Given that Grace's and Cary's characters clearly had sex that same night, when he cracks, "The boys must have enjoyed that," and Grace flushes with humiliation, it is clear that the role of haughty rich girl being cut down to size suits her extremely well, as evidenced in her final movie, *High Society*.

In filming the masqued ball scene, Hitchcock is once more eerily prophetic regarding Grace's destiny. As costume designer Edith Head explained, "Hitchcock told me he wanted her to look like a princess in that scene." Consequently, the apparition of Grace in a voluminous golden ball gown, wearing long gold gloves, her hair piled high and styled with gold ornaments, prefigures her regal image as Princess Grace of Monaco.

She was not yet a princess, but having jettisoned Barney Strauss for him, she was now romantically involved with aristocratic Russian fashion designer Oleg Cassini, who joined her in Cannes during the early part of June. On June 12, she wrote to Prudy, confiding, "Oleg arrived here last Saturday . . . no violent vibrations . . . but it makes it nice to have company."

Oleg Cassini was the Paris-born son of Countess Marguerite Cassini and the grandson of Czar Nicholas II's ambassador to the United States. Having grown up in Florence, he was courtly and elegant, and while not conventionally attractive, had an abundance of Continental charm, which he managed to parlay into marriage with flame-haired *Laura* actress Gene Tierney, then a major star.

Oleg first saw Grace in *Mogambo* and fell madly in love with her onscreen image. By a strange twist of fate, straight after the movie, he and a friend went to dinner at Le Veau d'Or, where none other than Grace herself was having dinner with Jean-Pierre Aumont.

Mesmerized both by Grace and the magical serendipity of meeting her just hours after being captivated by her onscreen. Oleg resolved to make her his, thus launching into what he later termed "the greatest, most exhilarating campaign of my life, using every bit of fantasy and energy I had. The goal, to get this incredibly beautiful, superficially cool woman interested in me."

After he wooed Grace by sending her vast bouquets of red roses every day—each without a card, thus piquing her curiosity—Oleg's persistence paid off, and she agreed to have lunch with him on the proviso that she bring Peggy as well.

"Grace was reserved and distant," Oleg recalled more than fifty years later. "She used distance to impress America. She frightened them because she gave so little. Once, we were at a black-tie party at my tennis club, with everyone looking at her. One of the male guests was English, and took food from her plate with a spoon. She got up and rushed out. I just managed to catch her in the elevator and she said, 'Who's that disgusting friend of yours?' I told her he was just trying to impress her.

"In public, she was very dignified. In private, she was very warm. She certainly gave the impression that she cared for you. . . . But she was two people. All actresses are two people. She wasn't jealous of my first wife. The fact that I had been married to Gene Tierney made her feel confident that she had made the right choice," he said.

"Grace thought of Oleg as a lapdog. He would do anything she wanted," remembered Rita Gam.

Rita's observations aside, Grace clearly had great affection for Oleg and, according to Betsy Drake, jokingly called him "O Leg O Chicken."

Within a month of first pursuing Grace to the South of France, she and Oleg became engaged.

Back in America to shoot interiors, on July 30, Grace wrote to Prudy, "Oleg drives me to the studio every morning and picks me up at night. We had dinner with Bing one night. . . . My father isn't very happy over the prospect of Oleg as a son in law. . . . But the plan now is to be married the first part of October."

Her haste to marry Oleg, it later transpired, was prompted by the fact that she was pregnant by him. "The couple planned to have a small secret wedding, with Grace taking time off to have the baby," John Glatt wrote. "But at the last minute she changed her mind. Torn between her devout Catholic upbringing, her movie career and her love of Cassini, Grace decided she could not risk a scandal. So instead of going through with the marriage she had an abortion."

When Glatt asked Cassini about Grace's abortion, he remained "defensive and evasive. 'It's too delicate a matter. I don't have to answer this and I will make no comment about that. Absolutely no comment. Let people think what they want to think,' he said."

After making six movies in nine months—and in the aftermath of the abortion—Grace needed a rest. Taking six months off work, she devoted much of the time to moving out of Manhattan House and into a new apartment at 988 Fifth Avenue, which she had decorated by professional decorator George Stacey, who helped her indulge her new passion for French furniture, a taste cultivated in her by Oleg.

The Academy Awards were held on March 30, 1955. Grace, nominated for Best Actress for her performance in *The Country Girl*, was up against Judy Garland for *A Star Is Born*. That morning, she went to Paramount to have her hair done for the ceremony. "Gracie had her heart set on a very special hairdo to go with a very special dress. What she got was less than special. As we walked out, she started to cry," remembered Rosemary Clooney, who was at Paramount that morning having her hair done as well. "I hurried her over to Saks for a salvage operation. And when she stepped up onstage to accept her award for Best Actress, she wore her hair swept back simply, just the way they'd fixed it at the store."

Both Paramount, for whom she had made *The Country Girl*, and MGM, where she was under contract, campaigned heavily for her to win the Oscar. In contrast, Warner Bros., for whom Judy made *A Star Is Born*—perhaps because of her volatile temperament, drug use, and repeated absences from the set—hardly campaigned much for her at all.

Hollywood has always rewarded beautiful female stars brave enough to allow their faces to be stripped of all makeup, their charms shrouded in drab clothes, their hair lackluster—witness Best Actress winners Nicole Kidman for *The Hours* and Charlize Theron for *Monster*— and Grace was no exception.

When William Holden—Best Actor the previous year for *Stalag 17*—tore open the envelope, he was beaming as he announced her name.

Taking the statue from her erstwhile lover, Grace, dazzling in a crystal blue satin evening gown, was close to tears as she said, "I will never forget this moment. All I can say is thank you."

She was sobbing in earnest, when Marlon Brando—Best Actor for *On the Waterfront*, for which Grace turned down the costarring role—was led over for a photo opportunity. A photographer asked Brando to put his arm around Grace and he did. However, when the photographer suggested that Grace kiss Brando, she retorted, "I think he should kiss me." Brando obliged, kissing her a few times.

Afterward, he took Grace aside and told her that, as Edie Van Cleve was also his agent and had lobbied for him to get the part, he almost starred with her in *High Noon*.

According to *Brando Unzipped* author Darwin Porter, Grace responded with a flirtatious, "Too bad you didn't. We would have had fun." Whereupon, according to Porter, who was told the story by Edie Van Cleve, Brando slipped Grace his phone number.

Meanwhile, back in Philadelphia, when a reporter, anticipating a euphoric reaction, called Jack Kelly for a quote in response to the news that Grace had won the Academy Award, Jack replied, "I thought it would be Peggy. Anything Grace could do, Peggy could always do better. I simply can't believe Grace won. Of the four children, she's the last one I'd expect to support me in my old age. How do you figure these things?"

How Grace "figured" her father's insulting response to the most glorious triumph of her life can only be a matter of conjecture.

As Grace later repeatedly recalled, after she slipped away from the post-Oscar party at Romanoff's to her Beverly Hills Hotel bungalow, she placed the statuette above the fireplace and sat there, gazing at it. Years afterward, she declared to director Robert Dornhelm, "That night, I was the loneliest person on the planet."

The image of Grace in her bungalow, with just the gold Oscar statuette and the burning logs in the fireplace for company, alone and lonely, is irresistible. Yet according to Darwin Porter it is not the truth.

Sometime after two in the morning, Porter claims, Brando trysted with Grace at her bungalow. "Apparently, during Marlon's first hour with Grace, he had to listen to her complaints about Bing Crosby," Porter reported after having been told the story by Edie Van Cleve, to whom Brando originally confided it. "Although she'd just won the Oscar for *The Country Girl*, she claimed that Bing had almost denied her the role, since he had approval of his leading lady. 'He thought I was too beautiful,' Grace allegedly told Marlon. 'Not drab enough.'"

At that point, Porter says, Grace told Brando that Bing wanted to pursue a romance with her. She said she was not interested in him, but he refused to accept defeat. She clearly did not tell him that a year before, she, not Bing, had been the pursuer.

Now, though, the tables had turned, and at 3 A.M. Bing suddenly materialized in her bungalow—to find her in bed with Brando.

"That must have been doubly difficult for Bing," Edie observed to Darwin Porter. "Earlier in the evening he'd been denied the Oscar by Marlon, his last chance. Now he finds the same young nude stud in Grace's bed. Reportedly, there were fisticuffs. What chance did an aging, drunken singer have against a well-built young actor who was also a boxer? Marlon was a bit vague, but I gathered that he knocked out the voice behind *White Christmas*."

After Grace called the house doctor and the hotel manager, Bing was marched out of the suite, leaving her alone again with Brando. However, the course of their romantic passion still didn't run smoothly. At around five in the morning, a drunken Judy Garland, who had lost the Oscar to Grace, called her bungalow.

Edie Van Cleve reported to Darwin Porter what happened next. "In a drunken but famous voice, the intruder said, 'This is Judy Garland, Judy Fucking Garland. You Bitch! You took what was rightfully mine. Tonight was my last chance for the Oscar. You'll have many more chances in your future. This was it for me. I'll never forgive you.'" Judy then slammed down the phone on Grace.

A shaken Grace reported Judy's drunken rant to Marlon who, instead of commiserating with her, countered, "She's got a point. You'll probably go on to win seven more Oscars."

Grace was not amused.

Her abortive night with Marlon Brando may have been dramatic in the extreme, but the two of them would remain friends and even have one last foolhardy romantic encounter in the not too distant future, in quite another place.

9

Monaco

Grace had always loved France and everything French, so she was thrilled to be guest of honor at the 1955 Cannes Film Festival, at which *Country Girl* was the American entry.

On May 4, she flew from New York to Paris. Then, rather than change planes and fly directly to Nice, she spent the night in Paris before boarding the Cannes-bound Train Bleu the following morning. Had Grace taken the plane instead, the rest of her life might have unfolded differently.

The next morning, Grace, in a beige cashmere coat, her blond hair piled high, was a vision of loveliness. It was hardly surprising that *Paris Match* editor Pierre Galante instantly recognized her. He was overjoyed at the coincidence, for just days earlier he had been instructed by the magazine's editor-in-chief, Gaston Bonheur, to do all in his power to facilitate a meeting between Prince Rainier of Monaco and the Oscar-winning, Grace Kelly of Hollywood, so that *Paris Match* could run the cover line "Prince Charming Meets Movie Queen."

Pierre Galante was determined to get his boss what he wanted. So he didn't hold back when a mutual friend, Gladys de Segonzac, traveling with Grace, introduced him to her. Apart from his own brand of Gallic charm, Galante had yet another weapon: on the train with him was his wife, Olivia de Havilland, star of *Gone With the Wind*, one of Grace's all-time favorite movies.

Grace was delighted to spend much of the long train journey chatting to the veteran Hollywood star and her handsome husband. When he broached the subject of her spending the afternoon in Monaco and taking part in a brief *Paris Match* photo opportunity there with the principality's ruler, Prince

Rainier, she did not dismiss the possibility out of hand. Nor, however, did she instantly jump at it.

Grace's lack of enthusiasm was understandable. Covering just 370 acres, situated 435 miles southeast of Paris, 10 miles east of Nice, Monaco was in those days considered to be just another tin-pot Riviera resort long past its prime.

Nowadays, of course, thanks to Grace Kelly, Monaco is a glittering fairyland for the rich, an oasis of pleasure, the playground of the gods, famed throughout the world as the epicenter of money, power, opulence, and extravagance, a tax shelter, a gambling Mecca, the residence of multibillionaires, Russian gangsters, Hollywood movie stars, virile athletes, ancient French aristocrats, a fifty-carat jewel of a principality, shimmering with glamour and the fruits of stratospheric success.

Back in 1955, however, when Pierre Galante invited Grace to spend the afternoon in Monaco and meet the Lilliputian principality's ruler, Rainier Louis Henri Maxence Bertrand Grimaldi, the prospect of sacrificing an entire afternoon for a photo call didn't particularly entice her.

But there is every chance that, after agreeing to visit Monaco and meet Prince Rainier, Grace—the girl who studied Swahili before making a movie in Africa—would have read up on the principality and learned all about its darkly romantic past and the Grimaldis, the royal yet sinister family who ruled over it.

If that was the case, an overview of Monaco's star-crossed history will provide a flavor of what she would have gleaned. And it is plain that Grace, an intensely romantic American girl weaned on the relatively recent history of Philadelphia, would have been riveted by the ancient history of Monaco and of its rulers.

Legend has it that Monaco was founded by the Phoenician sun god Melkarth more than sixteen centuries before the birth of Christ. The Phoenicians themselves eventually settled in Monaco, followed by the Romans, with Julius Caesar embarking on his Pompeian campaign from Monaco harbor.

By A.D. 975, the Saracens had settled in Monaco, then were later expelled. Before fleeing, they built a citadel on the rock overlooking the harbor. In 1215, a fortress was built on top of the citadel, which stood on what now is the site of the current palace of Monaco. Until the end of the thirteenth century, Monaco was ruled by an illustrious series of Italian and French princes.

Monaco's story—and that of the Grimaldi dynasty—truly begins on January 8, 1297, when Italian pirate Francesco Grimaldi disguised himself and his men as monks and stormed Monaco's fortress, overwhelming the guards and seizing the palace. Thus was the Grimaldi dynasty born out of bloodshed and deception.

According to Monaco lore, the Grimaldi line was also riddled with adultery, unfaithful wives, cuckolded husbands, and terminally unhappy marriages.

According to legend, Prince Rainer I, a cruel and ruthless man who ruled during the thirteenth century, abducted a fair maiden from Northern Europe, raped, then abandoned her. Instead of expiring from shame, the fair maiden, as the story goes, suddenly morphed into a witch, then issued a dreadful curse on Prince Rainier and all his future descendants: "Never will a Grimaldi find true happiness in marriage."

The witch's curse would reverberate through the years, and only a fortunate few members of the Grimaldi dynasty were ever able to forge a marriage that seemed untouched by the curse. Nor was their destiny untouched by violence and tragedy.

In 1505, the Grimaldi heir Prince Jean II dined with his brother Lucien at the palace. During dinner, Lucien stabbed Jean to death, then seized power, only to be stabbed by another Grimaldi relative shortly afterward.

In 1604, Hercule Grimaldi was stabbed to death and his body thrown into the sea, while his subjects looted the palace.

In 1662, Prince Louis succeeded to the throne of Monaco. Soon after, he married the enchanting Charlotte de Gramont, a siren with an insatiable sexual appetite. Fueled by her voracious passions, Charlotte decamped from Monaco to Versailles, where she caught the eye of Louis XIV.

In 1793, Monaco was annexed to France, but in 1815 when Napoleon was defeated, the principality was returned to the Grimaldis. By then, Louis of Monaco's son, Antoine I, had married the Comte d'Armagnac's daughter, Marie de Lorraine, a beautiful heiress who was blatantly unfaithful to him. Antoine consoled himself by joining the French army. Although he and Marie never divorced, Antoine's marriage was desperately unhappy, yet another example of the curse's untrammeled power.

The curse was finally shattered when Antoine's son, Florestan, married Caroline Gibert, a thin brunette with a talent for finance that dazzled even the most brilliant financial minds of the era, and had a happy marriage with her.

After she gave birth to a son, Charles, she hit on the novel idea of naming the principality's capital Monte Carlo in his honor. But that wasn't all. At that time, gambling was banned in France and Italy. However, after hearing about the vast fortunes pouring into Baden-Baden's casino, Caroline decided that as Monaco was not under French or Italian rule, Monte Carlo should emulate Baden-Baden's example.

In March 1855, she consulted one of her most cherished financial advisers, who agreed with her inspired concept of opening a gambling house in Monte Carlo, but—aware of the power of the church and not wishing to incur its disapproval—advised against labeling it a casino.

In a stroke of brilliance—motivated by a stupendous hypocrisy that endures today—Monte Carlo's newly established gambling den was named Société des Bains de Mer de Monaco, affording Monte Carlo the illusion that it is primarily a spa town, not one dominated by and financed by a casino. Thus respectable Victorian burghers could freely inform their friends that they were visiting Monaco to take the waters, and not to gamble, a far less socially acceptable pursuit.

In April 1856—exactly a century before his descendant, Prince Rainier, married Grace Kelly—Prince Florestan signed an ordinance authorizing a thirty-year gambling concession to two journalists.

A few weeks later, Florestan died, whereupon his son, Prince Charles III, sanctioned the new Société des Bains de Monaco. Monaco was now a casino town, disingenuously marketed as a health resort. And the fact that the Grimaldis would always derive their primary source of income from the gambling losses of Monte Carlo's visitors would forever be obscured behind the marvelously deceptive title of Société des Bains de Mer, known by the abbreviation SBM.

To ensure that the Monegasques did not gamble themselves into ruin, Charles III banned them from gambling at the Monte Carlo casino, at the same time decreeing that they not pay income tax, property tax, or inheritance tax, perhaps some compensation for never being permitted to set foot in the casino.

In 1863, François Blanc, former director of the Bad Homburg casino in Germany, offered his services to Prince Charles, whereupon he was granted a fifteen-year concession to run Monte Carlo's casino,

The Hôtel de Paris, still the heart of Monte Carlo's high life, opened on

New Year's Day 1864, a rococo palace dripping with luxury, with the table silver alone worth almost $200,000 in today's terms.

The SBM grossed two million francs in 1867 and went on to gross two and a half million in 1868. However, the casino didn't always come out on top. Witness the legend of English swindler Charles Deville Wells, who in 1892 played roulette and won so heavily, that he became, in the words of the song Charles Coborn recorded in 1929, "The Man Who Broke the Bank at Monte Carlo."

Then, as now, the casino was a magnet for the rich, the beautiful, the powerful, and the dissolute. The Prince of Wales's mistress, Lillie Langtry, arrived in Monte Carlo with a valet, a secretary, two maids, and two chauffeurs who ferried her around town in a limousine with gold and tortoiseshell fittings, and ended up winning more than $60,000 at the tables in just one evening.

The Romanovs, too, adored Monte Carlo. Dimitri Romanov once threw a dinner at L'Hermitage for six guests, ordering them sixty bottles of champagne and then smashing them against the ornate dining room mirrors.

Then there was Caroline Otero, a Spanish dancer turned courtesan who plied her trade in Monte Carlo and made the memorable comment, "No man with an account at Cartier can be called really ugly."

There was also Diane de Chandel, whose poodle was decked out in a ruby-studded coat and who herself took to strolling through the lobby of the Hôtel de Paris clad in a diamond corset valued at 2,275,000 gold francs.

Given Monte Carlo's burgeoning decadence, it is perhaps hardly surprising that the principality's ruler at the end of the eighteenth century, Prince Albert, turned his mind, instead, to the study of oceanography. Prince Albert I—after whom Grace and Rainier named their only son—was a towering figure in Monaco's history. A scientific genius who in 1911 wrote Monaco's first constitution, Albert was awarded the American Academy of Science's Gold Medal.

Lady Mary Douglas Hamilton, the Duke of Hamilton's daughter, was just eighteen in 1869 when she married Prince Albert and moved to Monaco. According to her great-great-great-nephew, Christian de Massy, just five months after the wedding she and Albert had a raging argument in the middle of the night, immediately after which she fled to Baden-Baden.

De Massy makes the controversial claim that in Baden-Baden, Mary "allegedly became entangled with a Prussian military officer and conceived her son Louis, later Louis of Monaco, Prince Rainier's grandfather." If there is any credence to de Massy's allegations, Prince Rainier's grandfather was the illegitimate son of a Prussian officer and consequently not part of the Grimaldi dynasty at all. However, given that this possibility was never formally broached in Monaco, Rainier's father, and Rainier after him, were permitted to succeed to the throne.

After the birth of Louis, Mary returned to Monaco, but, detesting the climate and the citizens of Monaco who studiously ignored her, she fled the principality. In 1880, the Vatican annulled the marriage between her and Prince Albert.

However, waiting in the wings was New Orleans-born Alice Heine—a blond, blue-eyed enchantress, the great-niece of the celebrated German-Jewish poet Heinrich Heine—the daughter of Michael Heine who co-owned one of the largest banking establishments in France.

When she was seventeen, the Duc de Richelieu fell in love with her. They married and moved to Paris. However, after just four years of marriage, Alice was widowed and left alone in Paris, with her late husband's seventeen-million-franc fortune at her disposal.

She became a brilliant hostess and a patron of the arts, with the greatest geniuses of the day flocking to her Faubourg St. Honoré salon to pay tribute to her. In the words of Marcel Proust, an habitué of Alice's salon, who later used her as a model for Princess de Luxembourg in his masterpiece, *Remembrance of Things Past*, she was "a woman of the soundest judgment, the warmest heart," a description that could just as easily have been applied to Grace.

Alice was beautiful, flamboyant, brazen, witty, and cultured. When Prince Albert I of Monaco first paid a call on her at her salon, he was utterly bewitched. At first, she consented to be his mistress, then, undeterred by his bouts of bad temper—a character flaw inherited by his grandson, Rainier—she set her sights on marrying him.

Willful, determined, and beautiful, with a vast fortune at her disposal—which she made good use of by purchasing a stylish wardrobe, including one thousand two hundred pairs of silk stockings, more than one hundred pairs of handmade shoes, every kind of fur, priceless jewels, and haute couture all showcasing her considerable allure—Alice could be seen daily driving through the Bois de Boulogne in a stately equipage, accompanied by a tiny red satin–clad black page. Moreover, she was also mistress of her own realm, the Château de Haut-Buisson.

In 1885, when Alice was twenty-eight and Albert in his midthirties, he proposed marriage to her, but his father, Charles III, opposed the match because of Alice's Jewish heritage. However, Charles died on September 10, 1889, and Albert ascended to the throne of Monaco on October 31. He and Alice were now free to marry. Alice Heine—the heiress from New Orleans, of German descent, just like Grace Kelly, the heiress from Philadelphia, also of German descent—was now Princess of Monaco.

Thus it was that when Grace married Rainier, and the press and public hailed her as Monaco's first American princess, they were wrong; Grace was Monaco's *second* American princess.

Like Grace, Alice loved the arts and was highly cultured. Repelled by the degenerate gamblers, crooked businessmen, pampered courtesans, and downmarket ladies of ill repute all luxuriating in the carnal delights of Monaco, she vowed to resurrect the principality's reputation by reinventing it as a world-class cultural haven.

With the help of Roumanian impresario Raoul Gounsbourg, who spared no expense in luring world-class artists to Monaco, the Comédie-Française starring Sarah Bernhardt regularly performed there. Alice organized a glittering series of Wagner festivals and elevated the Monte Carlo opera season into one rivaling that of La Scala. Even composer Camille Saint-Saëns made the pilgrimage to Monaco, playing the piano for the enjoyment of the American princess.

The Prince of Wales and his paramour, Lillie Langtry—the glamorous beauty who so loved gambling—were intimates of Alice. Alice and Albert hoped that their friendship with the prince would encourage his mother, Queen Victoria, to honor Monaco with a visit during one of her sojourns in Nice. But the dour Queen Victoria steadfastly refused to set foot in Monaco. After Alice wrote a letter to the Queen venturing that she and Albert might call on her, Queen Victoria responded by inviting the Prince and Princess of Monaco to tea at her Nice hotel instead.

Albert should have been delighted that Alice had transformed Monaco into one of Europe's most cultivated cities. But, indifferent to culture, he was outraged when he discovered she hated sailing and boats—his chief pleasure—and that she flatly refused even to board the two yachts named in her honor, *Alice I* and *Alice II*. But Albert was too besotted by his American princess to consider severing ties with her.

Finally, the willful and reckless Alice took fate into her own hands. Becoming infatuated with Jewish composer Isidor de Lara, a seductively handsome philanderer not even five feet tall, and with a taste for dueling, Alice plunged into a passionate affair with him.

For a while, Albert strove to ignore his wife's infidelity, until one of his courtiers informed on her. Devastated, Albert confronted Alice. Nonetheless mindful of their role as Monaco's rulers, the royal couple struggled to maintain the appearance of a happy marriage, although half of Europe knew the truth about their ill-starred union.

But, in 1901, the illusion of the Prince and Princess of Monaco's conjugal bliss was forever shattered. While attending the first night of the opera, *The Jongleur of Notre-Dame*, Prince Albert accused Princess Alice of being unfaithful to him with his orchestra conductor and, in full view of the audience, slapped her across the face. Alice froze, then stalked out of the building, outraged. She left Monaco the very next morning.

Prince Albert's resolve was now set in stone. Alice Heine, Monaco's first American princess, was banned from ever again setting foot in the principality. Albert decreed that all traces of their twelve-year marriage be expunged from the Royal Archives, her photographs destroyed, and her name excised from every street, ornamental garden, and even the rose that had been named after her.

Alice's existence was eradicated to such an extent that when Grace, fascinated by Alice, attempted to discover more about her, she found very little evidence that she had even existed.

On May 30, 1902, Princess Alice and Prince Albert were granted a legal separation. Alice moved to London, where she spent the rest of her life living in Claridge's hotel, where de Lara also had a permanent suite. There, she recreated her celebrated salon with such success that Rudyard Kipling, Sir Edward Elgar, and Queen Alexandra all came to pay court to her.

After her death in 1925, Alice left de Lara a million francs. He outlived her by ten years and, in his will, left a provision that fresh flowers be placed on her grave every month in perpetuity.

By 1910, the SBM boasted an annual £1 million profit. Thanks to François Blanc and his successor, his son, Camille—who ran the casino with great efficiency

and flair—Monte Carlo was now one of Europe's most fashionable resorts, at-
tracting a motley crowd of rich and disreputable characters from throughout
the world.

Somerset Maugham characterized Monaco as "a sunny place for shady
people," a pronouncement that did not, however, prevent the crusty author
from spending time in Monaco and even from attending Grace's wedding to
Prince Rainier. Nonetheless, his bon mot stuck, simply because it was true.

At the dawn of the twentieth century, Monte Carlo resembled a glittering,
jewel-encrusted carnival. A gypsy fortune-teller became the toast of the town,
earning enough money to retire to her own villa; pawnbrokers made millions,
with Monte Carlo's premier one, Isaac, ending up with a panoply of unre-
deemed items all lodged with him by degenerate gamblers, including a large
boa constrictor deposited by a snake charmer desperate to spend another
night at the tables.

When Camille Blanc's health declined, he sold his vast holdings in SBM
to arms dealer Sir Basil Zaharoff. Prince Louis despised Zaharoff, who remained in control of the SBM until 1923, when his beloved wife died and he
sold his shares to a French banking consortium for more than $8 million.
The wily old arms dealer lived on for another thirteen years, dying of a heart
attack at the Hôtel de Paris.

Meanwhile, the illustrious and the disreputable, the gilded and the greedy
continued to flock to the resort. One celebrated guest, Scott Fitzgerald, who
was banned from entering the casino because he couldn't produce his passport,
retaliated by attempting to hit the doorman, failed, and passed out drunk.

Hungarian-born Ziegfeld showgirl Jenny Dolly stormed Monte Carlo,
where she enthralled her billionaire lovers, bilking them to such an extent that
she was regularly seen in the casino draped in an orchid-garlanded chinchilla
cape over a glittering sequined black gown, diamond bracelets dangling along
the full length of her arm, a seven-string pearl necklace slung around her
neck, and a fifty-carat emerald ring sparkling on her finger. A courtesan with
a proverbial heart of gold, Jenny routinely tipped staff $500, merely for emp-
tying her ashtrays.

Excess was the order of the day in Monte Carlo. When Gloria Vanderbilt's
twin sister Thelma complained that the Hôtel de Paris had run out of
plovers' eggs, her husband had a basket of the missing delicacies flown in
from Paris especially for her. In Monte Carlo, too, the Aga Khan celebrated a

hole in one by tipping his caddie with a sports car. Gertrude Lawrence swanned around the Sporting Club pool in a bathing costume studded with real pearls, and one of the world's richest women, the Maharani of Baroda, whose jewels alone were worth $10 million, kept a permanent suite at the Hô-tel de Paris, where each night she indulged her gambling habits by betting 5,000 francs at a time.

Meanwhile, not wishing to remarry, Louis embarked on a liaison with an Algerian laundress, Juliette Louvette. In 1898, in Constantine, Algeria, Juliette gave birth to Louis's daughter, Charlotte. Louis's father, Prince Albert, refused to recognize Charlotte as Louis's heir, on the grounds that she was illegitimate.

Louis, meanwhile, broke off his relationship with Juliette, joined the For-eign Legion, and later was awarded the Légion d'Honneur for his bravery in World War I.

After Prince Albert died in 1919, Louis finally legitimized his daughter, Charlotte. Charlotte later married Prince Pierre de Polignac and gave birth to Rainier in 1923 and Antoinette in 1921.

In 1929, when Rainier was six and Antoinette eight, Princess Charlotte and Prince Pierre divorced. In an increasingly familiar Grimaldi ploy, which they executed on divorcing their spouses, Prince Pierre, like Princess Alice be-fore him, was banned from the principality.

When World War II broke out, Prince Louis tried to retain Monaco's neutrality, despite heavy pressure from Vichy France and the Italians to do otherwise. In June 1940, Mussolini's troops marched into Menton, just six miles from Monaco, and Prince Louis was threatened with imprisonment. After the Allied landings in North Africa, the entire French Riviera came un-der German occupation.

From that point on, the Gestapo based themselves at the Hôtel de Paris which, like the rest of Monaco, was flooded by black marketeers, gunrunners, and collaborators, wagering their ill-gotten gains at the table. While the SBM didn't have absolute power to ban the Gestapo from entering the casino, they refused admission to anyone wearing a uniform.

Charlotte—*Mamou* to her children—was a passionate admirer of Mus-solini, and, as the Allies stormed toward victory, aware of the consequences of that admiration, went into seclusion in her country house on the outskirts of Paris and, in 1944, renounced her rights to the throne in favor of her son, Rainier.

Afterward, she took a lover, an Italian doctor, Dr. Del Masso, who subsequently tried to leave her for another woman, whereupon she shot him. Fortunately she missed, and he crawled out of the room before she could fire a second shot. In 1947, she married the tennis champion Alec de Noghes.

After the Americans liberated Monaco on September 3, 1944, the Germans fled the principality. When Churchill made his first postwar visit to Monte Carlo, he had dinner at the Hôtel de Paris, where he requested the band play "Lilli Marlene." Life in the pleasure principality returned to normal once more.

Rainier already bore the scars of an unhappy childhood. After the divorce of his parents, he had been dispatched to Summerfield (the equivalent of an American prep school) in St. Leonards on the gloomy windswept South Coast of England, from where he could gaze longingly across the Channel at France. Alone and friendless, he was then thrust into the rough-and tumble of the British public school system. At Rainier's next school, Stowe, he was forced to participate in the archaic custom of making young boys new to the school act as servants to the older boys, who often bullied them unmercifully. Worse, boys who broke the rules were routinely subjected to the humiliating punishment of submitting to six or more strokes inflicted on them with a rattan cane.

Rainier had to endure Stowe only until he was fourteen, at which point his parents whisked him away to the more salubrious surroundings of Le Rosey, in Rolle, near Geneva, where the pampered children of kings and queens, maharajas and billionaires were coached for life at the top. Nonetheless, he was still bruised by his parents' endless battles. He was a loner, with few close friends, introspective, forever an outsider.

Rainier was muscular, with the stocky body of a boxer, was a strong swimmer, and a keen amateur actor. He was also academic and, on his own merits, won a place at L'École Libre des Sciences Politiques in Paris, graduating in 1944. After the fall of France, he joined the Free French, battling the Germans in Alsace. He was brave and fearless, and in recognition of his war service, the French awarded him the Légion d'Honneur and the Croix de Guerre.

In 1948, just a year before he ascended to the throne of Monaco, Rainier attended the play *His Lordship* in Paris and was mesmerized by one of the actresses in it, Gisele Pascale, who played the role of a commoner in love with a young lord. This twenty-three-year-old daughter of a market tradesman was sweet, innocent, and compliant, so that when Rainier invited her on his yacht in Monaco, she had no compunctions about accepting his princely invitation.

When the press besieged her with questions about how she and the prince met, and what happened between them, Gisele smiled shyly and said, "I am living in a dream and nothing can spoil it."

Installing her in his villa, Rainier moved in with her. They were in love and might have become engaged, but due to an ancient Monaquesque law that decreed if the ruler of Monaco didn't produce an heir, Monaco would revert to French rule, Gisele was subjected to a fertility test.

When the Royal Council received the results, they forbade Rainier from marrying her, claiming that she was unable to conceive a child. Strangely enough, after Gisele's relationship with Rainier ended—also partly because, by an incredible coincidence, he had discovered that she was also having a romance with Grace's former flame Gary Cooper—in October 1955 she married actor Raymond Pellegrin and seven years later bore him a daughter.

By the mid-fifties, with the advent of the Cannes Film Festival and the development of other Riviera towns, visitors no longer flocked to Monaco, and the principality went into a sharp decline.

Fortunately for Rainier, there waited in the wings a magician-cum-marauder who was determined to restore Monaco to its former glory. In 1923, a seventeen-year-old boy fled by sea from his native Smyrna, where the Turks had recently defeated Greek forces, and huddled in steerage, alone and friendless.

One starry night, he plucked up his courage and climbed up on deck. As fate would have it, the ship was at that moment sailing toward Monaco. The boy gazed across the bay at the shimmering lights of Monte Carlo. Spellbound, he promised himself that one day he would return.

Half a lifetime later, when he had made his fortune and become one of the world's richest men, wealthy and powerful beyond his wildest dreams, Aristotle Onassis sailed back to Monte Carlo and remembered the first time he saw the pristine beauty of the harbor lights and how their sparkle mesmerized him, obliterating his seasickness and his longing for the land of his birth.

In the early fifties, he made covert inquiries about the financial health of the SBM and then—under the guise of obscure Panamanian companies—

stealthily acquired shares in the paradise of his teenage dreams. After investing less than $800,000, he finally acquired a majority holding of SBM's one million shares.

In September 1953, J. Edgar Hoover characterized Monaco's power structure: "Except for the prince of Monaco, whom the French regard as an inconsequential person whose only real interest is in a reliable source of funds for his pleasures, Onassis may now be regarded as the real leader of Monaco."

In many ways, Hoover was right. When Rainier learned of Onassis's dizzying financial sleight of hand, he was forced to confront the truth that his realm had been hijacked behind his back. Worse still, when just a year later Monte Carlo's biggest bank crashed, threatening the principality's economy, he found himself with greatly depleted coffers.

"With the parliamentary and bank crisis that year...Uncle Rainier needed to bring off a major coup in order to achieve popularity and once and for all prove to the Monegasques that he was a good figure of a man as monarch," his nephew Christian de Massy explained.

Monaco was no longer the most fashionable resort on the Riviera, and the tourists were staying away in droves. A pragmatic man, Rainier swiftly recognized that he needed help from Onassis. Assiduously ignoring the vicious carping that Monte Carlo would soon be named Monte Greco in Onassis's honor, Rainier consulted him on how to resuscitate Monaco's failing economy and burnish its tarnished image.

Fortunately for Rainier, his goals and those of Onassis, who was determined to maximize his investment in Monaco by luring the glitterati back to Monte Carlo, were identical. A showman and a visionary, above all Onassis understood the value of publicity.

With his customary directness, Onassis put forward the suggestion that Rainier marry an American movie star, arguing that if he did, the resultant publicity surrounding the match and the subsequent wedding would focus the eyes of the world on Monaco. Consequently, he argued, Monaco would reclaim its former glamour and the tourists would return. Fourteen years later, Onassis himself would execute a similar publicity-grabbing play by marrying President Kennedy's widow Jacqueline and enhancing his own image and his business empire in the process.

When it became clear that Rainier was receptive to his plan, Onassis compiled a list of suitable candidates for the starring role of Princess of Monaco.

Clearly then favoring blond movie actresses, he listed Eva Marie Saint, Deborah Kerr, and, in a dizzying leap of the imagination, Marilyn Monroe.

According to Gwen Robyns, in whom Onassis's intermediary, Gardner Cowles, confided, Marilyn briefly considered the possibility of becoming Princess of Monaco, but in a show of marked disrespect that may well have disqualified her from marrying him, persisted in referring to Rainier as "Prince Reindeer" clearly rendering a meeting between the prince and the showgirl untenable. Then fate intervened. *Paris Match* editors Pierre Galante boarded the Train Bleu to Cannes and met Grace Kelly.

IO

Prince Charming

On May 6, 1955, Grace, wearing a black silk dress printed with large red and green flowers and sporting her habitual white gloves, settled back in the limousine for the thirty-two-mile drive from Cannes to Monaco. She was accompanied by her friend Gladys de Segonzac and Pierre Galante.

On their arrival at the palace, they received word that Prince Rainier had been delayed. Faced with having to wait for the prince, Grace began to feel nervous. First, she reapplied her powder, then asked Galante how old Rainier was, whether he spoke English, and what she should call him. Then realizing that he was forty-five minutes late, an extremely irritated Grace declared, "Let's get out of here."

At that moment, Rainier made his entrance.

He was thirty-one years old, barrel-chested, with dark eyes, a legacy of his Italian heritage. A chain-smoker, he spoke perfect English, a tribute to his British education. Grace was twenty-five years old, an Oscar-winning actress, in her prime, at her most charming and beautiful.

He escorted her to the palace zoo where, as a demonstration of his courage, he petted a tiger. As he had intended, Grace was impressed. They posed for pictures, then she and her entourage left for Cannes. In the car, she was silent, except to say of Rainier, "He is charming. So very charming."

Of all the adjectives that Grace could have applied to the prince— handsome, brave, courteous, intelligent—it was interesting that she selected the word "charming." As in Prince Charming. And while Grace Kelly was never by any stretch of the imagination anyone's Cinderella, since time immemorial, romantic young women the world over have dreamed of meeting and marrying Prince Charming. Grace, it seemed, was no exception.

When she returned to Cannes's Carlton Hotel, in time for the festival's screening of *The Country Girl*, she was confronted by fifteen thousand people, all eagerly waiting in the receiving line to shake her hand.

She later recalled that momentous day, calling it "pretty wild." "After the reception, I myself gave a dinner party for ten people, after that my movie was screened. To wind things up, Paramount gave a party for me which ended at four o'clock in the morning."

And although she didn't reveal this fact to the press, just before going to bed at dawn, she sat down and in her large, round, Ravenhill handwriting, composed a thank-you letter to the prince.

At the end of the Cannes Film Festival, she reunited with Jean-Pierre Aumont, her lover from her days as an actress in New York, who happened to be on the Riviera. He was eager to see her and primed to propose.

During the stolen few days Grace and Aumont spent together on the Riviera, she attempted to achieve her ambition of meeting Pablo Picasso by making an appointment to see him at his villa in Le Vallauris. "She and Jean-Pierre Aumont waited at the villa for hours, but Picasso never showed up," said Pepita Dupont. "Picasso hated appointments and he didn't care. But when Grace became Princess of Monaco, she met Marc Chagall and they became great friends."

A photographer from *Paris Match* covertly snapped Grace and Aumont basking in the Mediterranean sun, and photographed her kissing his hand. In an attempt to evade the press, they fled to Paris, where they stayed at the Raphael Hotel and went to the theater together. Afterward, they spent a weekend at Jean-Pierre's country house at Malmaison, outside Paris.

However, as romantic as the interlude may have been, Grace ended her relationship with Jean-Pierre before she returned to the States on May 18. "Jean-Pierre was very upset," said Pepita Dupont.

Back in America, Grace began work on a cherished movie project, starring as Princess Alexandra in Ferenc Molnár's *The Swan*. On August 30, 1955, she

wrote to Prudy enthusing about the beautiful clothes Helen Rose had designed for her and that "I am so anxious to start work."

Production on *The Swan*, costarring distinguished British actor Alec Guinness and French heartthrob Louis Jourdan, was slated to begin in Los Angeles in September. Grace rented a small white Regency house in the
Hollywood Hills from Greta Garbo's health guru, Gaylord Hauser.

After two weeks' filming at MGM, the studio rented two DC-7s and flew
the cast and crew to Asheville, North Carolina, where they were due to shoot
at the Biltmore, George Vanderbilt's nineteenth-century chateau and the
largest private home in North America.

According to Grace's friend Gant Gaither, when her agent Jay Kanter visited the set, "Grace was showing him the interior of the castle and the two
were standing on the great stairs in the entrance hall, looking down at the
conservatory and beyond to the library. Grace was a few steps below him
when he remarked facetiously, 'Nice and airy, isn't it?' And, shaking his head,
'A little big for me!'

" 'It's like a palace,' said Grace. 'I love it.' "

The cast and crew spent three weeks in Asheville, during which Grace—
ethereal and beautiful in white lace—played the part of the princess forced to
decide between love and duty.

"Sometimes I saw her just waiting on the set, just looking into space, and
I asked her, 'Grace, are you feeling all right?' Then she came to, but always with
a little start of surprise, as if she'd been far away," Gant Gaither said.

Through it all, she and the prince were in regular correspondence.

Guinness, watching Grace's performance, observed, "This girl is
remarkable—but I wonder what she is doing? What she was doing was first
class, but I suspected that it was accidental.

"After two 'takes,' I realized, with astonishment, that she achieved exactly
the same delicate touches each time we played the scene, that she not only
knew exactly what she was doing, but precisely what she was going to do next.
Then I understood the envy some Hollywood stars have of her—the girl is an
artist, and recognizably one in a city brimful of talent."

Time magazine's critic raved about Grace's charms, noting, "Grace in lace
is every slender, statuesque inch a princess." Then, utterly overcome, he added,
"In the scenes of first love, Kelly is exquisite. She kisses her man as though she
had invented kisses just for him."

Viewing *The Swan* now, it is clear that Grace was rather old for the part of the virginal Princess Alexandra, not that that detracts from her beauty.

In the first scene, she wears a white dress tied with a green sash and a big straw hat, and her hair is arranged in curls on top of her head.

Knowing what lay ahead for Grace, it is difficult not to place extra significance on the lines spoken by her character's mother: "You must prove to Albert on these four days that you have all the qualities he's looking for in a wife. A wife who will share his throne one day. To be gracious, and dignified, warm and charming and amusing. Sweet and unspoiled, that's one of the first duties of a queen, always to put people at their ease"—a description that could have applied in every aspect to Grace's qualifications for becoming Princess of Monaco.

Guinness plays a mustachioed Ruritanian prince, eerily reminiscent of Prince Rainier. However, the scenes with him and Grace are notable only for the lack of chemistry between them.

At the ball, dressed all in white, with white roses in her hair and long white gloves, Grace is a vision of beauty and, as Guinness points out, her character dances "like a queen." She and Jourdan escape in a coach, and driving through the woods, they kiss, and she falls in love with him. Their romance, however, is doomed, and she ends up with Guinness after all.

Throughout the movie, Grace looks innocent, fragile, and is always dressed in white. By dint of the magic of MGM, she is transformed into a virgin once more.

It is interesting to note that the sequence of roles that Grace played during her short career begins with her portraying a wife considering a divorce, a Quaker bride, a scientist's wife, a society wife, a fashion model, a singer's wife, a coffee plantation owner, a naval wife, twice an heiress, and—in her last role but one—a princess, with both *The Swan* and in her final Hollywood movie, *High Society*, starring her in the role of a woman in the process of selecting a husband.

Not long after arriving back in America from Cannes, Grace invited her father's close friends, Texas oilman Russell Austin and his wife, Edie, for drinks in her Fifth Avenue apartment.

As she must surely have known only too well, the Austins were about to leave for Europe. "During cocktails, Grace told Edie and me about meeting the

Prince of Monaco. She didn't seem unduly fascinated, just told me the story as a sort of interesting travelogue because we, too, were going to Monaco," Russell Austin remembered. With the determination of what Don Richardson once termed "a Patton tank on its way to somewhere," Grace had planted the seed.

So when the Austins decided they wanted to attend the Red Cross Ball in Monaco they had no compunction about personally contacting Prince Rainier introducing themselves as friends of Grace and the Kelly family, and asking him for tickets. Naturally, Rainier obliged. Whereupon the Austins issued him an invitation: if he were ever to visit America, they would be delighted if he visited them at their home in Atlantic City, sixty-two miles from Philadelphia.

Sure enough, that November, the Austins received a wire from Rainier's priest, Father Tucker, informing them that the prince would be arriving in America the following month and would very much like to accept their invitation to stay with them.

On December 15, using the name Mr. Grimaldi, Prince Rainier, Father Tucker, and Dr. Maurice Donat, his personal physician, traveled to America.

The official story was that the prince had come to America to have a sinus operation as well as his annual checkup at Johns Hopkins in Baltimore.

The Austins met the prince at the boat, then drove him to their home. Along the way, the prince made a suggestion to the Austins: after Christmas lunch, might they perhaps visit their friends the Kellys so that he could reacquaint himself with their daughter Grace?

Grace's sister Peggy recalled to Gwen Robyns, "When they arrived my father greeted them at the door. The Prince looked very handsome and rather shy. Father Tucker looked like a simply divinely cute parish priest with a twinkle in his eye. My father knew an Irish priest if ever he saw one and said: 'Father Tucker sit down and I'll give you a cigar and let's go on from here.' It was a very lovely dinner and Prince Rainier and my sister sat and talked a lot. I think at first that Grace was a little shy and so was the Prince, but as the dinner progressed everyone seemed to warm up."

Considering the clandestine nature of Grace's past affairs with married men, as well as the tortures to which the Kellys had subjected Don Richardson, Oleg Cassini, and William Holden when she brought them home to Henry Avenue, the prince's extreme eligibility, as well as the warmhearted hospitality that the family afforded him, must have allowed Grace to sit back, relax, and enjoy this novel situation.

After dinner, Jack Kelly drove Father Tucker to the station, from where he was traveling to spend the night at the home of a fellow priest.

When Jack returned home, he took Margaret into another room and broke the news that Prince Rainier was intending to request Grace's hand in marriage, confiding that he had promised the prince to sound Grace out, and if she demurred, he would do his utmost to convince her.

Nonetheless, Jack Kelly later boasted that he wasn't about to be intimidated by a prince, particularly one who was shorter than he was. He was on his own territory, in his own country, in the city where he was a legend, a king. "When I saw the way things were, I laid it down right on the line. I told the Prince that royalty doesn't mean a thing to us," he boasted to a *Daily News* reporter in January 1956.

Then, in an extreme irony given his own marital record, he is purported to have played the heavy father with the prince. "I told him that I certainly hoped he wouldn't run around the way some princes do, and I told him that if he did, he'd lose a mighty fine girl."

Whether or not Jack Kelly actually did lay down the law to Prince Rainier as he said he did, or was just inflating himself and creating an image that would appeal to a reporter, Jack had raised a possibility that the romantic Grace probably hadn't considered. Her future husband-to-be was a prince. And princes have never been renowned for monogamy.

But in those euphoric early days, Prince Rainier's capacity for fidelity was the last thing on Grace's mind. Besides, she'd always been the desirable "other" woman with whom husbands cheated, a Hollywood star whom practically every single man in the universe desired. Why should she even consider the possibility that her Prince Charming might be unfaithful to his Princess Charming?

The following day, Grace and the prince paid a call on her sister Lizanne and her husband, Don LeVine. Lizanne and Don had been in Pittsburgh with Don's family, so she had not yet met the prince. And although she was suitably charmed by Rainier, later in the day, when Grace—without any preamble— informed her that she was getting engaged to him, she was stunned.

"She didn't have time to be really in love. She had been more in love with other people than she was with Rainier when she first met him. I don't know why she decided to marry him so quickly," Lizanne told John Glatt.

Throughout the years that followed, Grace's friends, former lovers, and family would speculate on her motives for marrying a man whom she hardly knew and moving to a country where she'd previously spent only two hours.

The first theory is that, as a great romantic, she simply floated into marriage with Rainier. "She was playing a princess in *The Swan* and she was so naïve and charming, and when the Prince came along, she just drifted into marriage. She was so very romantic," Gwen Robyns concluded.

"Grace could sit in front of the fireplace and stare into the fire and dream about all sorts of things." Robert Dornhelm said. "She told me nothing pleased her more than having dreams while staring in the fire. She was a romantic dreamer and marrying Rainier was romantic, fairy-taleish."

There was also the lure of living in the South of France. "Once I was fortunate enough to have dinner at home with Grace in California before she was married," remembered writer Maurice Zolotow. "Grace served a fine red Bordeaux, a Château Latour 1949 Grand Cru wine. Grace knows and loves French wines and can drink them without any inner torments. In fact, she has always been strongly drawn to French cuisine, French culture, and French literature. French was one of her favorite subjects in school and she has continued to read French poetry and novels. I asked her once to name her favorite writers and she said, 'Balzac and Montaigne.' "

Another—more prevalent—theory is that Grace, ever intuitive, believed that her career in Hollywood had peaked. According to producer David Brown, at the time of her retirement "Grace was a very important actress, but she was not in the league of Garbo or Marilyn. She was on the A-plus list as a star, but she wasn't A-plus at the box office like Marilyn Monroe, Joan Crawford, or Bette Davis. She was extraordinarily beautiful, but she couldn't open a picture by herself. Not without a huge star like Cary Grant, Bing Crosby, Frank Sinatra, Ray Milland, or Gary Cooper. Grace just wasn't huge box office by herself."

"Before Grace left MGM, I was at a lunch party with her," remembered Gore Vidal. "I said, 'Why on earth, now that you've got the Academy Award, you are the number one actress at MGM, are you giving all that up to go off and be somebody's wife at a gambling casino?' She said, 'Well, I think I know what I'm doing. You know about make-up call? Well, I'm still pretty young, so my make-up call is at 7:30. But I get there and there is Merle Oberon who's been in the chair since five, there's Irene Dunne who's been in the chair since

3:30. They're all getting old. Each year my make-up call is a bit earlier. And when I look at the other ladies who've been there since dawn, do I want to live like that? Get me out.' "

"Hollywood is a cruel place, and it's particularly cruel to women," said former Hollywood publicist Dale Olson. "After a time, the allure of a woman wears off. I think Grace knew that the time would come when her physical attractions would diminish. It was time to move on, and this interesting opportunity—of marrying Prince Rainier—arrived and it put her on a different level."

"She felt she was getting older and wanted to get married. She was conflicted about being an actress and wanting to be a normal American woman. She wanted to have children, desperately," Rita Gam said.

"I asked her how much she thought her life would change when she married the prince," said Celeste Holm, her costar in *High Society*, the movie Grace made just before her marriage. "She said she didn't know." According to Grace's friend Arlene Dahl, "The marriage was put together by the priests, by the people who ran Monaco. Grace believed in fairy tales and every young girl wants to grow up to meet Prince Charming. He found her and she couldn't believe her good luck and everybody said, 'Oh go, it's the chance of a lifetime.' I'm sure her mother and everyone was pushing her. But she became trapped."

The last word as to why Grace agreed to marry Rainier must go to Grace herself. She said, "I never wanted just to 'take a husband.' All I ever wanted was to be someone's wife, the wife of a particular man. I needed someone with a strong personality to hold his own against the fame of an actress. I have never wanted to marry a man who would have allowed himself to become Mister Kelly," she said.

In what might have been a more honest moment, she later confessed, "I did not really give much thought to what might lie ahead."

There was still the matter of Oleg Cassini, who believed she might one day marry him. After arranging to meet him on the Staten Island Ferry, she took a deep breath and said, "I know this is going to be a difficult conversation. I want you to know, first of all, that within my capacity for caring, I have cared more for you than anyone I have ever known and will probably continue to do so." Then she gave him the news that she was marrying Prince

Rainier. Stunned, Oleg demanded to know the reason. "I will learn to love him," was all she said.

On December 28, 1955, Jack and Margaret Kelly hosted a lunch for twenty-nine at the Philadelphia Country Club. At 1:40 P.M. precisely, Prince Rainier and Grace—resplendent in a gold brocade dress, a twelve-carat diamond ring on her finger—slipped into the side entrance of the club.

Had anyone asked Jack Kelly what he felt at that exact moment, he probably would have sworn that his feelings did not eclipse the euphoria he experienced when Kell won the Diamond Sculls in his stead.

Nonetheless, it was with pride in his voice that he declared, "We are happy to announce the engagement of our daughter Grace to His Serene Highness Prince Rainier of Monaco."

From the moment Grace's engagement was announced, her marriage was big news throughout the world. The press and public were enthralled by the romance between the Hollywood star and the European Prince, although *Time* magazine's movie critic cattily described their union as that between "a blonde from North Philadelphia and the proprietor of an amusement park."

In Manhattan, her social life became a whirl of glittering activity. On December 30, she organized a dinner party at her Fifth Avenue apartment so that her close friends could meet Prince Rainier. Five days later, she invited Malcolm and Carolyn Reybold to join her and Rainier at the Stork Club.

The next evening, Grace and Rainier attended the Imperial Ball—Night in Monte Carlo, held in the grand ballroom of the Waldorf-Astoria, at which they occupied the royal box, overlooking the dance floor and the one thousand guests who'd each paid $35 to attend. Grace, beautiful in a Dior gown, danced cheek-to-cheek with Rainier, while photographers immortalized the moment, and her engagement ring shone under the lights.

She secretly referred to her ring as "the diamond as big as the Ritz," little knowing that it had not been Rainier's first choice. In anticipation that she would accept his proposal, he had brought a diamond engagement ring to America with him. But an official at the Monacan consulate in New York took one look at it and declared, "You're going to have to do a lot better than that." So Rainier gulped and bought a bigger one.

Rainier's finances were in ruins and, much as he was beguiled by Grace, there is no question that her father's fortune played a large part in his decision to marry her. "It was a business arrangement," said Lizanne. Part of that business arrangement, it transpired, included Rainier's polite insistence that Jack Kelly adhere to the ancient European custom of the bride's father paying the groom a dowry.

And while Rainier's demands for a dowry were couched in the most po-lite terms, it is incontrovertible that no matter how often Jack Kelly might boast of his indifference to royalty, in the face of Rainier's implacable de-mands, he caved in completely and, according to Grimaldi historian, Anne Edwards, paid Rainier a dowry of $2 million dollars. Put bluntly, Jack Kelly bought Grace her royal title. Ultimately, like countless American heiresses before her, including Jenny Jerome who married Lord Randolph Churchill, Grace was bartered by her family in exchange for her getting a title.

In the middle of January, Grace flew to Los Angeles where on January 17 she was to begin filming *High Society* with Bing Crosby and Frank Sinatra. When show business writer Maurice Zolotow asked her if her impending nuptials signaled the end of her Hollywood career, she answered forthrightly, "Of course I'm going to continue with my work. Right now, I'm reading a dozen different scripts, trying to choose among them."

Her *High Society* costar was her former lover Bing Crosby. To the press, he adopted an appropriately paternal attitude toward her, and declared, some-what proprietarily, "I think what happened is her being in love and that this romance with the Prince, old Rainier, helped to bring out this gal's warmness. And isn't it something about Monaco putting her picture on a postage stamp? I also hear they're putting her on a coin. It sure will be the best looking piece of change in the world."

Rainier, then staying at a rented villa in Bel Air, joined Grace and the cast for lunch at MGM. According to costar Celeste Holm, "The lunch went very well, until Dore Schary asked Prince Rainier how big Monaco was. When the Prince told him, Dore burst out, 'But our back lot is as big as that.'" The at-mosphere became decidedly frosty and Celeste remembered thinking that Grace would never work in Hollywood again.

However, Grace had the last laugh in the end. Just before Celeste was due to participate in the 1982 Philadelphia tribute to Grace, she telephoned Grace, asking if it was all right with her if she told the story of Rainier's MGM visit and Dore's withering comment.

"Yes, dear," Grace replied, adding, "but will you also say that today Dore is dead and the Metro back lot sold, but the prince and Monaco are doing just fine?"

She was loyal and true, and countered any attempt to dismiss Monaco as being half the size of Central Park by subtly remonstrating, "As someone once said, you wouldn't want a jewel to be too large...."

Those close to her were acutely aware of her sensitivity to the topic. After director Robert Dornhelm made a crack to me, "Monaco? It was a great movie set," he pulled himself up short and said, "That would have been a joke that Grace wouldn't have appreciated."

During filming of *High Society*, Grace was observed in makeup by contract player Joan Collins, who later wrote, "The biggest star of the Metro lot sat quietly on the side waiting for her turn for the makeup man's magic. Grace Kelly... This fairytale wedding which had captured the imagination of the world, was now imminent. Grace sat quietly in plain gray slacks and non-descript blouse going over lists with her secretary, oblivious to the makeup and hair people who bustled around her. She was truly serene."

High Society, Grace's last Hollywood movie, displays her at her most regal, her most beautiful. In the first scene, she strides into the living room of the Lords' Philadelphia mansion, wearing a beige shirt, beige trousers, and a dark brown belt. Her hair is long. She is willful, disdainful, pugnacious—and a snob.

Sounding like a cross between Deborah Kerr and Audrey Hepburn, in an exquisite irony Grace plays the Philadelphia Main Line socialite the media had always erroneously portrayed her to be.

When she waltzes into the room swathed in a pale blue chiffon dress, toying with a big straw hat garlanded with ribbons, for the first time in her career she shows a marked talent for comedy.

In another career first, she performs a virtual striptease in the pool scene. She starts out wearing a pale yellow Grecian-style gown but is revealed to be wearing a bathing suit underneath that highlights her long, shapely legs to their best advantage.

During the scene in which Grace—as Tracy—chides her father for being unfaithful to her mother who, by some coincidence, has the air of an upmarket German hausfrau and is even called Margaret, it is highly likely that Grace was reminded of Jack Kelly and his infidelities.

Although Grace finally ends up marrying Bing in *High Society*, there is no onscreen chemistry between them. It is only when Frank Sinatra sings "You're Sensational" to her, and—grappling with her rising passion for him—she toys with her champagne glass, that the chemistry truly sizzles.

In 1954, recently separated from Ava, Frank had asked Grace out on a date. "Though involved with Oleg Cassini, she agreed to see him but the date was a disaster because he was already drunk when he picked her up and spent the rest of the evening crying about Ava," James Spada reported.

"Frank, of course, was terribly in love with Grace Kelly," Celeste Holm said, "and there was never a girl he couldn't get if he wanted. At the time he was just fascinated with her."

"Celeste used to tell me that Frank followed Grace around like a lovesick puppy, that he was pining for her all the time," revealed Celeste's husband, Frank Basile.

Grace was engaged to be married to Rainier, so Frank probably didn't make advances to her during *High Society*, but they were friends and always would be. During the filming, his daughter Nancy visited him on set. "Dad took me to lunch. Halfway through, a petite girl wearing blue jeans and a babushka came over to chat. She was in the movie, too. She was pale and pretty with a gentle voice—and Dad called her Gracie. He called her Gracie until the day she died even after Grace Kelly became 'Her Serene Highness, Princess Grace of Monaco,' to almost everyone else," Nancy Sinatra recalled in her memoirs.

In the scene in which Grace gets drunk and sings the lyric "I don't care if you are called the fair Miss Frigidaire," she exhibits her flair for playing light comedy. She would never again have the opportunity to demonstrate it to audiences.

Instead, in the last moments of *High Society*, Grace Kelly plays a bride, getting married in a Philadelphia high-society wedding. Exactly the same type of wedding that had she not met Prince Rainier, she might have had herself.

When *High Society* was released, critics were not particularly enamored of Grace's performance. "Grace Kelly sings a duet with Crosby in a cool, innocuously pleasant little voice, does an alcoholic rumba with Sinatra and looks thoroughly patrician, but she lacks the gawky animal energy that Katharine Hepburn brought to the 1939 play and the 1941 movie," acerbically commented *Time* magazine's critic.

At the 1956 Academy Awards at Hollywood's Pantages Theater, Grace—glorious in a green and white evening gown, her diamond engagement ring and diamond earrings flashing under the spotlight—presented the best actor award to Ernest Borgnine for his bravura performance in *Marty*.

However, it was not the happiest evening for Grace. On stage, Jerry Lewis, whom she hardly knew addressed her as "Gracie" and offended her with his presumptuous familiarity.

After the ceremony, she was escorted to the exit, only to be assailed by the screams of the ten thousand fans crowded in stands on Hollywood Boulevard. Turning to an Academy Awards usher, she whispered, "This is awful. Please get me out."

On the last night before she left for Monaco, she attended a cocktail party thrown in her honor by Monacan Consul General, Marcel Palmero.

Then she and a group of close friends had dinner at "21," the restaurant from where her alter ego in *Rear Window* had ordered food to be delivered to Jimmy Stewart. But this wasn't a movie, this wasn't illusion. This was reality, and in the morning, Grace would be boarding the USS *Constitution*, bound for Monaco, a new husband, and a new life.

II

Swan Song

Grace Kelly was now the most talked about woman in the world, and her wedding was the event of the decade. Eighty-nine years before, her ancestors had made the passage from Europe to America in search of a better life. Now she was reversing the process, leaving America for a new life as a princess in Europe.

Her story was a compelling romantic saga, and it was inevitable that practically everyone was enthralled by it—and by her. The press, naturally, was determined to keep the public informed every single step of the way.

At 9:55 on the morning of April 4, 1956, Grace, dressed in a beige tweed suit and a small white straw hat—accompanied by a party of eighty relatives, friends, and business associates, four trunks and fifty-six other pieces of luggage containing not only her old jeans, sweaters, and old shoes but also her $30,000 trousseau, including a $10,000 full-length sable, a mink, and a leopard-skin coat, as well twenty hatboxes and her black French poodle, Oliver—arrived at Pier 86 in Manhattan to board the USS *Constitution*. There, she was confronted by two hundred reporters, photographers, and newsreel and television cameramen, as well as a large crowd of fans and friends—including Malcolm and Carolyn Reybold, who were flying to Monte Carlo a week later and wanted to see her off.

"There was such confusion, you know. Mounting hysteria everywhere. Leaving New York was frantic," Grace said more than twenty-five years later.

"The scene on the dock was just like a Hollywood version of a boat departing. People on the dock waving. A band playing," remembered reporter

Richard Killian, who traveled on the *Constitution* to cover the four thousand-mile, eight-day trip to Monaco for the London *Daily Express*.

Before the boat sailed, Grace held a press conference—with five press aides by her side—for the benefit of the throngs of reporters and camera crews all clamoring to see her, talk to her, hear her last words before she departed.

Initially, the press conference was scheduled to be held on deck, but due to the rain, it was held in the Pool Café, a tiny room—measuring twenty by fifty feet—in which the two hundred members of the press jostled one another, climbing up on the bar and on tables, just so that they could get a better shot of Grace, screaming her name from all directions as they did.

She handled the mob scene with her customary calm, declaring that she was "very flattered with all this attention," then gently remonstrating, "I wish people would be more considerate of each other. The way you are stamping on each other—it is quite frightening."

In the end, she was virtually pinned in a corner and was almost crushed in the melee. Yet despite the stampede, she said a few polite words, still maintaining her dimpled smile, until to her relief security guards ushered her onto the ship, where the rest of the wedding party eagerly awaited her arrival.

Jack Kelly had paid the first-class fare for seventy-eight of his closest friends and family to travel with him to Monaco on the *Constitution*, a ship so glamorous that it would later be featured extensively in *An Affair to Remember* starring Deborah Kerr and Cary Grant. On board were over seven hundred other passengers, including a large number of disgruntled journalists.

"A whole army of journalists paid first-class fare yet had to share a cabin with two or three other people," remembered British show business writer Donald Zec, who covered the crossing for the London *Daily Mirror*.

Just before the ship set sail, Lizanne, who couldn't travel to Monaco because she was in the last stages of pregnancy, went on board to bid Grace good-bye and present her with her own handkerchief—to represent something borrowed.

Then, as the ship began moving through the heavy fog, Grace climbed up on the bridge. As the Manhattan skyline receded, she stood between her mother and father and slowly waved her last farewell to America.

Then she went downstairs to her stateroom. Filled with flowers sent by well-wishers, the room had been completely redecorated just for her, with the furniture reupholstered in her favorite champagne-colored raw silk, with curtains and bedspread to match.

Inside, she was overwhelmed to find that her black poodle, Oliver—a gift from Betsy Drake, which she so adored that she had even opened a bank account for him—had a new companion, a big Weimaraner puppy sent to her as a farewell present by Philadelphia friends Mr. and Mrs. Alfred Greenfield Jr.

There was another, more practical gift waiting for her. In an inspired move, all Grace's friends sailing to Monaco on the *Constitution* had banded together and brought $14,000 worth of equipment needed to install a private cinema at the palace, so that she could watch movies there and stay in touch with her Hollywood past.

Alfred Hitchcock, however, did not give Grace an extravagant wedding gift, nor was he on the boat. He had declined her wedding invitation because, in the view of his biographer, Donald Spoto, he felt abandoned by her.

However, in her stateroom she discovered a chain leash for Oliver, decorated with white carnations and white bows, and a card: "You'll love Monte Carlo. Happy Barking!" It was signed "Philip." Philip was Hitchcock's dog.

Grace had made three movies for Alfred Hitchcock, each considerably enhancing his reputation. And he now was expressing his contempt for her having jettisoned her movie career in favor of a mere marriage. He had not only declined her invitation to the wedding but hadn't given her a gift, dispatching one from his dog instead. The message was unmistakable.

Later that first afternoon at sea, Grace took part in the ship's mandatory safety drill, during which she was mobbed by other passengers not in the wedding party, all clutching their autograph books and pointing their cameras at her. Good-natured as always, she signed autographs and obligingly posed for pictures.

Early in the evening, she attended the captain's reception with her family, then dined with them in the public dining room. Late at night, while everyone was still carousing in the bar, she put on an old coat and took the dogs for a brisk walk on the top deck. Then she went back to her cabin and, before going to sleep, wrote to Rainier, as she would do every night of the voyage.

During the crossing, she made sure that she posed once for every single press photographer on board, so that they all could claim to their editor that their picture of her was exclusive. She granted each member of the print press a brief interview as well.

Show business journalist Donald Zec recalled, "On the boat she was protected by a whole army of gofers. Every day the journalists received daily bulletins about what she ate, what she drank, and how excited she was.

"She played her cards close to her chest and was never going to be like Marilyn Monroe, capable of a thousand witty comments. So I had to look for clues. I discovered that she loved the idea of celebrity but hated the flipside of it—the intrusion. Grace loved the idea of being a famous actress but hated the idea of being a goddess.

"But she was stunningly beautiful and behaved in an utterly gracious way. Once, we read her horoscope together and it said, 'Don't let money slip through your fingers or be miserly to the point of starvation,' and she laughed," he said.

Grace's friends and family partied the nights away, drinking, dancing, playing charades, and singing show tunes. "On the boat, it was a fairly raucous scene," remembered reporter Richard Killian. "The Kelly family loved to party—and they did. The parties went on day and night, all the way across the Atlantic. Grace didn't seem to participate in them much, though. She tended to stay close to her friends and go to bed early."

Here, on the *Constitution*, in the middle of the Atlantic, she was suspended between her old life in America and her new one in Monaco. As anyone who has ever been on a prolonged voyage will attest, during the journey it is extremely easy to lapse into a dreamlike state, to be lulled into a kind of nirvana by the hypnotic sound of the waves gently lapping against the side of the ship and the ship's regular rocking motion. Time seems to stand still, and even though the ship is inexorably traveling toward its destination, it is easy to forget the outside world. This may well partly explain what Grace did next.

On the penultimate night of the voyage, less than two days before the boat was due to dock in Monte Carlo Harbor, where the Prince would meet her and her new life would begin, Grace reserved the ship's Tattoo Room for thirty-nine of her good friends and proceeded, in the words of Donald Zec, to throw for herself, "the equivalent of a hen party. None of the press were invited."

They certainly were not, with one dramatic exception: Walter Carone, *Paris Match*'s ace photographer, thirty-three-years-old and an extremely handsome daredevil. Grace had met Walter in Paris the previous year, when she attended the fiftieth Bal des Arts with Jean-Pierre Aumont. Walter's strikingly beautiful young new wife Catherine had been with him that night, and, even over fifty years later, still remembers the vision of Grace in an ice blue ball gown.

Although Grace's personal photographer Howell Conant had exclusive access to her during the voyage, Walter was relentless in his pursuit of her. "Howell and Walter were in competition," Catherine Carone, his widow recently recalled. "And Grace laughed and said, 'Walter, you are following me like a dog. I will call my dog 'Walter'!'"

Grace, true to her word, did, indeed, name her Wiemaraner Walter, going so far as to pose with the dog for pictures that later appeared in *Paris Match*.

By the time the voyage was almost over, the trust and friendship that Grace now felt for Carone was such that when she opted to play charades at her hen party, according to Gant Gaither, she was "so desperate to find players for 'The Game' (charades) that she had even cornered Carone, forgetting that he hardly spoke a word of English."

Given that eighty of Grace's close friends and her family were on board the *Constitution*, as well as more than seven hundred other passengers, most of them upright and respectable citizens who would gladly have participated in charades with her, her decision to extend an invitation to a press photographer, a member of the dreaded media, and worse, an employee of *Paris Match*, the publication whose photographers had stalked her during her romance with Jean-Pierre Aumont, was surprising, to say the least.

Naturally, Carone was delighted that Grace had invited him to her "hen party." "He jumped at the opportunity to get close to 'Meez Kelleee.'" Gant Gaither said, "A good sport, Carone had acted out, as best as he could, the phrase he was given. Grace, who loved to practice her French anywhere and at any time, became so engrossed in the conversation with him that momentarily she completely forgot the game. It was then that he charmed her into agreeing to pose for her. Grace agreed to let Walter Carone do an exclusive layout on her while on board ship."

He had been present at what Donald Zec later termed, "a pretty hectic affair. It wasn't until then that it was as if all Grace's strings had been loosened."

And it was also then, either during the party or afterwards, that Grace and

Walter slipped away to her cabin, where she kept her promise to him and granted him his exclusive photo shoot.

The following morning, at breakfast, in the words of Gaither, Walter, "said he had never seen Grace so animated in all the times he'd photographed her. He could hardly believe he had been able to take those wonderfully warm pictures on the voyage. Never once did she object to the clicking of his camera."

On the following night, her last on the boat, Grace didn't have dinner with her friends and family. Instead, she retired to her cabin and—as fellow passengers and friends Judith Kanter and Gant Gaither both chronicled in their books—apart from an hour or so when Peggy manicured her nails, and Judith and Bettina popped in to see her, spent her final evening on board ship alone.

That, at least, is the official version of Grace's last night on the *Constitution*. However, it is not the only one.

"Walter Carone was one of the most beautiful men I have ever met. Everyone at *Paris Match* who knew him has told me that on the last night of the voyage, Grace ended her life as a single woman with Walter," claims *Paris Match*'s Pepita Dupont.

Asked about the possibility that Grace might have had her romantic swan song with Walter Carone, Grace's bridesmaid Maree Frisby Rambo utterly refutes the story. "During the voyage, Grace didn't even dance with another man, never mind have a last fling."

"Grace couldn't have had a final fling on her last night at the party because her hairdresser, Virginia D'Arcy, who always gossiped to me, would have told me," Richard Killian said.

Catherine Carone, now in her sixties, is beautiful, charming, and still passionately in love with her husband, Walter, who died in 1982. "Did Grace flirt with Walter? He said she didn't but that she was a coquette," she said in 2005, adding, "Walter told me that Grace was charming but not very exciting. Most of all, he said that she wasn't full of the joy of getting married. He said she didn't seem to be happy. She didn't seem to be in love with Rainier, he said."

The following morning, according to Howell Conant, as the *Constitution* was not scheduled to dock at Monte Carlo, "Most of the press had to disembark early, in Cannes. *Paris Match*'s Walter Carone stayed aboard."

Judith Kanter, Grace's bridesmaid, who detailed the voyage in her book *Bridesmaids: Grace Kelly and Six Intimate Friends*, written under her married name of Judith Balaban Quine, is one of Grace's most fiercely loyal supporters, and described what happened when the *Constitution* entered Monte Carlo Harbor. "Without warning, Walter Carone, the *Paris Match* photographer who had been on shipboard with us crossing the Atlantic, wedged his muscular, athletic frame through a porthole and flung himself dramatically into the sea. Carone only had a short way to swim until his magazine's launch circled him in the water and hoisted him aboard. We laughed and cheered at a job well done. Walter had his scoop and was simply delivering it in the most expedient way possible.

"Grace came out on deck and was told of Walter's leap. Hooting with laughter, she finally calmed herself enough to add, 'Ah, those Latin men.' Walter had given new meaning to the words 'Special Delivery'! Then she turned her eyes toward her new homeland."

At 10:30 on the morning of April 12, 1956, Prince Rainier's white yacht, the 1,340-ton *Deo Juvante II*, sailed into the Bay of Hercules toward the USS *Constitution*. Suddenly, a yellow seaplane shot through the azure sky, dropping thousands of carnations, all in the Monaco flag colors of red and white, right onto the deck of the ship, Aristotle Onassiss's welcome to Grace. Moreover, he donated one million francs to the Monaco Red Cross and, to top it all, later presented Grace with a ruby-and-diamond tiara as a wedding gift.

As showers of carnations drifted on the deck around her, Grace, dressed in a navy blue sheath dress, a blue faille coat lined in white, and a white organdy and Swiss lace hat with a brim so wide—the equivalent of a veil, thus preventing photographers from capturing close-ups of her face—clutched Oliver in her arms as if he were a lifeline.

A myriad fireworks exploded from the deck of Onassis's pleasure palace, the *Christina*, the world's most luxurious yacht. Aristotle Onassis's welcome to Grace was spectacular. Rainier could not hope to match it. The Greek tycoon had made his point.

The *Deo Juvante* pulled alongside of the *Constitution*, and as the ship's band played Monaco's national anthem, and yet more carnations, mingled with confetti, rained down on Grace, hundreds of flashbulbs flashed, freezing the moment forever. She was now wearing a large pair of horn-rimmed sunglasses to shield her eyes from the sun as well as her emotions from the press and—perhaps—from the prince awaiting her.

Taking careful, measured steps, her parents following behind her, Grace was escorted across the gangplank from the *Constitution* to the *Deo Juvante*, where Prince Rainier waited to greet her. She turned and smiled back at her friends and the rest of her family, still on the ship behind her.

At that moment, it is highly likely that she gazed at the narrow mouth of the harbor that appeared to have virtually closed behind her, like pincers. Then back at Monte Carlo and the palace on the rock above it. And although she may not have known it at the time, for Grace, from now on the world had become smaller.

After the *Deo Juvante* docked, to the sound of the cheering crowds all along the streets, standing on the roofs of buildings, hanging over balconies, Grace and Rainier disembarked.

A green Chrysler Imperial flying Prince Rainier's standard whisked them through Monaco's small and winding streets to the pink palace where, in the Court of Honor, Rainier's family was waiting to meet the Hollywood star whom he had selected to be Monaco's princess.

Prince Rainier's nephew Christian de Massy was present at Grace's arrival at the palace and at the reception that followed. Noting the frostiness flickering in the eyes of his grandmother, Princess Charlotte—Christian concluded that her hostility was partly caused by the presence of her former husband, Rainier's father, Prince de Polignac, and partly by the fact that "she was compelled to receive an American movie star as her son's future bride. . . . She used to talk about *Les Américaines* with great disdain."

Princess Charlotte, the illegitimate daughter of an Algerian washerwoman, was a snob who thought that Academy Award–winning actress Grace Kelly wasn't fit to be her daughter-in-law.

Even without having met Grace, Princess Charlotte had found her wanting and would quickly make her disdain for Grace extremely clear to her. Laura Richardson remembered, "In one of her letters to Don, Grace talked about meeting her mother-in-law and said that 'the palace is cold, but not as cold as my mother-in-law.'"

From the first, the brassy self-made American Kellys alienated the blue-blooded royal European Grimaldis. When Margaret Kelly shook Princess Charlotte's hand, announcing, "Hi, I'm Ma Kelly," Charlotte practically turned to stone. From that moment, according to Christian, her distaste for the Kelly family equalled that which she already felt for Grace.

"Mamou was critical of Jack Kelly about what she called 'turning the palace into a post office,'" Christian revealed in his book *Palace*. "She found it inappropriate that he went down to the main Monaco post office, bought a huge quantity of special commemorative wedding stamps, and proceeded to distribute them to his own guests for the wedding, who numbered nearly one hundred. . . . She also commented negatively on the gesture used by some of the members of the Kelly entourage of turning wine glasses upside down to indicate that they didn't want wine, and on Peggy's drinking a glass of milk while eating a dozen escargots."

Grace also managed unwittingly to offend her future sister-in-law, Princess Antoinette. After breaching European etiquette by inviting her to be one of her bridesmaids, Grace compounded her error by presenting Antoinette with the identical yellow organdy outfit made for her bridesmaids. Whereupon Princess Antoinette, who had long ago had her haute couture gown made for her by a Paris fashion house, had an underling convey to Grace in no uncertain terms that it was utterly against protocol for a member of the royal family to act as a bridesmaid. "Grace broke into tears, crying, 'I was only trying to be nice. And I brought her dress all the way from America,'" Christian recalled.

Grace spent her first two days at Monaco in the palace. On April 14, she went out to have lunch for the first time with Rainier and her parents at Princess Antoinette's villa in Èze.

On the following morning, she attended Mass in the palace chapel. In the evening, she and Rainier went to a white-tie gala held in their honor at the Sporting Club, where they were entertained by Russian ballerina Tamara Toumanova, singer Eddie Constantine, and magician Channing Pollock, who made Grace laugh by pulling a dozen white doves out of his fingertips and his buttonhole. The evening ended on an intensely romantic note as fireworks formed into the intertwined initials R and G exploded into the balmy Riviera night.

The days before the wedding were a constant whirl of celebration and ceremony. On April 17, Grace helped the prince host a noon champagne buffet for the palace staff held in the palace courtyard. In the afternoon, Grace was present at a palace ceremony at which she received a Rolls-Royce sedan, a gift from the people of Monaco.

Later that day, she was delighted when Kell and his wife Mary, who had flown from New York to Nice, arrived at the palace for dinner. Kell had never been a fan of any of Grace's boyfriends but after meeting Rainier reported that he liked him very much.

Grace's sisters, however, were not impressed and didn't feel that the impending nuptials were a fairy tale come true. According to Christian de Massy, Peggy said, "It was never a fairy tale romance," and Lizanne said, "It was just a very nice agreement." "They thought it was a farce, that it was such an arranged marriage," said Gwen Robyns.

And if the Grimaldis viewed Grace as a latter-day Cinderella whom Rainier was elevating through marriage and assumed that her family would be awed in his presence and dazzled by the magnificence of his realm, they were sadly mistaken.

"Peggy thought Monaco was populated with stupid fools trying to make her feel bad for wearing shorts in the lobby," Gwen Robyns remembered. "But she wouldn't let them make her feel bad. She—and the whole family—just didn't go along with the whole Monaco thing. They thought Grace was very silly going into this kind of marriage. They thought she was worth more than just Monaco. They weren't thrilled at all. They weren't dazzled at all. They felt Rainier had to prove himself."

And if, as many of her earlier biographers have attested, Grace's major motivation for marrying Rainier was to impress her father and win his love and admiration at last, it was dismally clear that she had failed. Despite having paid Grace's dowry, and experiencing the euphoria accompanying the celebrations, Jack Kelly was not impressed. "He hated Monaco, where you have servants all over you. He'd say to them, 'Go away! I'll call you,'" Arthur H. Lewis later reported in his book *Those Philadelphia Kellys*.

In later years, on Jack's rare visits to Monaco, it was patently obvious that he also felt upstaged by Grace. As Rita Gam had remarked Jack had always considered everyone else—including Grace—to be a second-string player in his life.

Moreover, he had always been the alphamale but now his son-in-law, Prince Rainier, was more famous than he was, his daughter, Princess Grace of Monaco, had eclipsed him utterly and completely—and Jack Kelly didn't like it one bit.

At 11 A.M. on April 18, eighty guests gathered in the sixteenth-century lily-and-lilac-garlanded crimson and gold palace throne room, to witness the civil ceremony conducted according to Monegasque law.

Grace wore a rose silk dress, a chiffon turban decorated with matching silk roses, and pink gloves instead of her ubiquitous white ones. The girl from Philadelphia who dreamed of becoming a great actress—and had become one—was now about to become Princess Grace of Monaco as well.

The minister of state of Monaco, Marcel Portanier, cited Articles 181, 182, and 183 of the Napoleonic Code, which prevailed in Monaco, and read, "The husband owes protection to his wife, the wife obedience to her husband. The wife is obliged to live with the husband, and to follow him everywhere he judges it suitable to reside." There was worse to come, even in those pre-feminist days.

In going through the civil ceremony, Grace had taken a fateful step that she could never retract. As Judith Balaban Quine pointed out, "Monaco's civil matrimonial law, together with European custom, made it clear what would happen if Grace's union with Rainier failed. It was all spelled out for her. She could leave. She just couldn't take her children with her. They belonged to their father and to Monaco.

"What Grace had to promise to do, there before the eyes and ears of the entire world on April 18, was unthinkable. She had to agree that if push came to shove she would give up her children. Marriage to Rainier meant not only abdicating her career, it also meant abdicating her possible future rights to her offspring."

That evening, Grace and Rainier attended a gala at Monaco's opera house. Grace, who so revered French culture, was thrilled to discover in the program *Compliments,* a short love story that the august, multi-talented Jean Cocteau had composed specially. She and Rainier opened the ball, dancing to "A

Woman in Love," the song that Sinatra sang in *Guys and Dolls* and that Grace had designated as "their song." In later years, her favorite song would become the equally romantic "All the Things You Are."

That night at the opera house, she was an apparition in a Lanvin gold embroidered white organdy ball gown studded with mother-of-pearl and gold sequins, a diamond tiara resting on her golden hair, and a white mink stole around the perfect shoulders over which Alfred Hitchcock's camera had once so adoringly lingered. On this night of all nights, Grace was the fairy princess incarnate, and she and Prince Rainier were now husband and wife.

Part Two

Having once embarked on your marital voyage, it is impossible not to be aware that you make no way and that the sea is not within sight—that, in fact, you are exploring an enclosed basin.

—*George Eliot*, Middlemarch

12

The Wedding of the Century

April 19, 1956, was Grace's wedding day. However, her marriage vows would be drowned out by the whirr of the movie cameras, and the blinding flashbulbs would obliterate any solemnity pervading Monaco Cathedral.

"When Grace arrived at the Cathedral, this lovely church looked like a movie set," said Lizanne's friend, Philadelphia television personality Gene London.

"It was a media circus, with the quality of an insane happening. The wedding was an MGM production, but the Palace agreed to it. And as much as Grace and Rainier complained about it afterwards, I'm sorry, it was their call," pointed out Rita Gam.

It certainly was. For unpalatable though the truth may be, it is incontrovertible that, in April 1956, Prince Rainier and Grace Kelly had made a business arrangement with MGM, virtually identical to the one that countless celebrity couples today, like Michael Douglas and Catherine Zeta Jones, make with *OK* Magazine or *Hello*, bartering the rights to make a visual record of weddings in exchange for publicity, money, and services.

In payment for the rights to film the wedding for a documentary, *The Wedding of the Century*, the studio provided Grace with the following: a $7,226 wedding gown, designed by *The Swan* costume designer, Helen Rose; MGM hairdresser Virginia D'Arcy to style her hair for the wedding; and MGM publicity executive Morgan Hudgins to handle the media. Moreover, Grace and Rainier would also receive 50 percent of the profits left after deduction of the 30 percent distribution cut.

Grace and Rainier's wedding thus became an MGM production, bought, paid for, and orchestrated by the studio.

While there was very little Grace could have done to prevent the 1,600 journalists from throughout the world from flooding into Monaco to report on the ceremony, it seems utterly alien to her character that she, who so valued her privacy and always fought for her independence from the studio system, relinquished the rights to her wedding to MGM and allowed them complete control over it.

Part of the reason was that she was still under contract to MGM, who played tough with her, driving a hard bargain and insisting that they would only release her from her contract if she agreed to allow them to film her wedding. Moreover, they also agreed to pay her a $65,000 bonus for 1956, which would have greatly gratified the money-conscious Grace.

But even if Grace had kicked against accepting MGM's terms, Prince Rainier had every reason to convince her to accept them, and given that the Palace, not Grace, brokered the final MGM deal, he was bound to have done all in his power to persuade her to do so.

Apart from the fact that he was desperate to publicize Monaco to the world, he didn't intend to squander Grace's dowry on a lavish state wedding befitting the union between the Prince of Monaco and the Queen of Hollywood. And while Jack Kelly clearly did pay for part of his daughter's wedding, Rainier did not intend to contribute, so he was happy for MGM to pay in his stead. Moreover, *The Wedding of the Century* would serve his dual need to promote Monaco to the world and further replenish the principality's coffers—and his own, as well.

Thanks to the deal with MGM, Grace would now share her wedding day with thirty million television viewers around the world. For those viewers, it would be as if they were seeing a fairy tale come to life. For Grace, however, her wedding day was more of a nightmare.

"Not only was there pressure before the wedding, but the tension during the ceremonies was quite unbelievable," she said, looking back in 1960. "The atmosphere reached such a pitch of frenzy that people were dropping like flies under the emotional strain. It was just too much."

"I was told how magnificent the flowers were at my wedding, but all I remember is that the flower arrangements in the cathedral were filled with Rolliflexes, Hasselblads, and Nikons with telephoto lenses and flashbulbs," she told Gwen Robyns.

"After the wedding was over, I just didn't think about it. I never even read a press clipping for over a year, because it was a nightmare, really, the whole thing. There were one or two moments that were marvelous—the actual marriage and then a few private moments. But it was a difficult time to go through, for the Prince and myself," she confided to *Ladies Home Journal* shortly before her death.

"Sometime after, when I was older, Aunt Grace told me that the royal wedding day and the whole period that preceded it were among the worst ordeals she had known," reported Christian de Massy.

Years later, Prince Rainier recalled, "Grace kept saying: maybe we should run off to a small chapel somewhere in the mountains and finish getting married there. I wish we had, because there was no way either she or I could really enjoy what happened."

"My parents hated their wedding. They didn't even look at pictures of it for a year," Princess Caroline told the *Today* show in 1985.

At 8 A.M. on the morning of the wedding, limousines picked up the six bridesmaids—Sally Parrish Richardson, Bettina Gray, Maree Frisby Rambo, Rita Gam, Carolyn Reybold, and Judith (later Balaban Quine), as well as Grace's sister Peggy, the matron of honor—outside the Hôtel de Paris, where they were staying.

At the palace, the bridesmaids took part in a photo opportunity, to the background of roaring cannons fired in celebration of the wedding by all the battleships in the harbor. The sky was blue, the sun was shining, and a slight breeze was in the air.

Crowds of people from all over Europe had flooded into Monte Carlo to witness the wedding.

"I was stationed in Germany in April 1956. On a lark, I drove to Monaco in my Opel, so I would be there when Grace Kelly was married," remembered American serviceman Mac Macintosh. "The entire town was open twenty-four hours a day. Drinking parties and many people, like me, sleeping in their cars just so they could catch a glimpse of Grace."

A long red velvet carpet led up the stone staircase of Monaco's Romanesque cathedral, while on either side a row of firemen and policemen in
full dress uniform formed a cordon of honor. Across the street, sailors from
three battleships, currently berthed in Monaco's harbor, stood at attention.

Inside the cathedral, large gold baskets of white snapdragons hung from
chandeliers between the columns supporting the vaulted ceiling. At the end
of the nave, the altar was covered in hydrangeas, lilacs, and white lilies.

Inside, the six hundred guests awaited the arrival of the bride. Yet although
Grace was a Hollywood star, the only other Hollywood stars who bothered to
attend her wedding were David Niven, his wife, Hjordis, Gloria Swanson, and
Ava Gardner, who sat in the congregation, an empty seat next to her. She and
Frank Sinatra had recently filed for divorce. So although Frank had accepted
Grace's invitation and had gone so far as to have white tie and tails made for
him in London, at the last minute—afraid of upstaging the bride if the press
spied him and Ava at the wedding together—he canceled.

Erroneously declaring, "Too many movie stars," the Queen of England
had flatly refused to attend the wedding, in private making it eminently clear
that she considered Grace to be a Hollywood starlet marrying a small-time
prince. The only crowned head who accepted the wedding invitation was the
Aga Khan. However, there was also a sprinkling of aristocratic guests, including the Duchess of Westminster and Grace's former boyfriend Sir Anthony
Havelock-Allan.

"European high society thought the wedding was a joke," said *Tatler*
columnist Taki. "They all thought, 'What kind of marriage is this?' You don't
marry a Hollywood actress and have newsreels and a thousand photographers
at the wedding. It was a joke."

It said a great deal about how the great and the good viewed the nuptials
of Grace and Rainier—as well as Monaco's place in the world—that President Eisenhower didn't attend the wedding of America's most famous
princess-to-be but instead sent as his representative not a congressman, not a
senator, not a governor, but the hotelier Conrad Hilton.

At exactly 10:30 A.M., when Grace—ethereal in an ivory *peau de soie* gown
with a lace-and-seed-pearl-embroidered bodice constructed from century-
old Brussels lace, a three-yard-long train, on her head a skullcap of lace and
pearls, a white tulle veil bordered in lace partly covering her face, a bouquet

of lilies of the valley and a Bible clasped in her hand—entered the cathedral on Jack Kelly's arm the congregation gasped in admiration.

Protocol now decreed that Jack Kelly return to his pew, leaving his daughter standing alone at the altar, but he remained firmly rooted to the spot, standing tall next to Grace while she waited for Rainier's arrival.

Rainier entered the cathedral dressed in a Napoleonic marshal–style military uniform that he'd designed himself, with all his medals on show, which later gave rise to a great deal of mockery from observers unaware that he had been awarded many of those medals in recognition of his war service. Nonetheless, glittering with gold leaf and gold epaulettes, wearing ostrich feathers and a red and white sash, Rainier resembled a Ruritanian prince straight out of a Strauss operetta.

At 10:41 precisely, Monsignor Giles Barthe, Bishop of Monaco, began the ceremony, culminating in the question, "Rainier Louis Henri Maxence Bertrand, will you take Grace Patricia here present for your lawful wife, according to the rite of our Holy Mother the Church?"

His voice hardly audible over the whirr of the cameras, Prince Rainier answered, "Yes, Monsignor."

"Grace Patricia, will you take Rainier Louis Henri Maxence Bertrand here present for your lawful husband, according to the rite of our Holy Mother the Church?"

Grace replied in the affirmative.

Her words too were drowned out by the clicking of cameras, her eyes almost blinded by the flashbulbs.

Emerging into the brilliant sunlight to the cheers of the crowd Grace and Rainier made their way down the cathedral steps and into the waiting black and cream convertible Rolls.

As they were driven through the streets of Monaco, their subjects lined the pavements, blowing kisses, even crying as the bridal procession passed, while the bridesmaids followed in another car. "It was the nicest experience of the whole day, and very moving," Carolyn Reybold said later.

The guests gathered at the Court of Honor at the palace. However, protocol forbade them from taking their seats until the prince and princess made their entrance. Meanwhile, inside the palace, Grace, Rainier, and the immediate family posed for photographs.

After what, to the guests, seemed an interminable time, Grace and Rainier descended the grand stairway into the court, where they joined their guests at the champagne buffet.

Afterward, they both clasped a ceremonial sword and, with it, cut their magnificent six-tier wedding cake, each tier decorated in icing piped into the shape of scenes from Monaco's history, and topped by two sugar cherubs, each one wearing a replica of Monaco's gold crown.

Afterward, Grace retired to her bedroom to get ready for the honeymoon, aided by her bridesmaids. They were aware they were witnessing the start of her new life, the end of her old, that she was now Princess of Monaco and no longer Grace Kelly.

Overwhelmed by the finality of it all, vivacious, light-hearted Peggy, always a barrel of laughs, was close to tears. Then her pride came to the fore. Forcing a megawatt smile in Grace's direction, and reverting to one of their childhood rituals, she cracked, "See you later, Alligator."

Before Grace could answer, Rainier materialized in the doorway. "In a while, Crocodile," he replied on her behalf.

At 4:30, cheered by a crowd of five thousand adoring Monegasques, Grace and Rainier once more boarded the *Deo Juvante II*, this time as husband and wife. The sun shone down on Monaco harbor, where dozens of boats—all flying the red and white flag of Monaco—sounded their sirens in farewell to the royal couple. At 5:20, as the yacht set sail on the month-long honeymoon cruise, bound first for Majorca, then Corsica, the sun began to set behind the Corniche and two rockets unfurled the American and the Monegasque flags into the amber sky.

It was crystal clear that Onassis's publicity ploy to restore Monaco's fading glory had worked miracles. The civil ceremony had been broadcast all over the world. The cathedral wedding had been watched by a global audience of thirty million. Stamp collectors clamored to buy Monaco's newly issued commemorative stamps featuring Grace and Rainier. And while much of the world had formerly confused Monaco with Morocco, now tourists flocked to the tiny principality in droves.

Meanwhile, on the honeymoon, Grace immediately caught a cold. In Corsica, she and Rainier explored coves and deserted beaches, but once back on board, and for much of the rest of the voyage, she was violently nauseous.

Worse, she was also starting to confront the stark realities of her marriage lurking underneath the façade of all the publicity and all the euphoria.

By the time the yacht docked in Monte Carlo, in the first week of June, Grace and Rainier had been alone together for more than six weeks, affording her ample time to divine the character and emotions of her new husband, to learn what drove him, what pleased him, and what did not. It proved to be a sobering discovery.

At the time of the marriage, Rainier was thirty-two, and the head of Europe's longest-reigning royal family, a bachelor prince accustomed to having the world at his feet and everyone he dealt with doing his bidding without hesitation or quibble. Nonetheless, at the time of the wedding, he felt sure that he was ready for marriage and that he was utterly equipped for the role of husband.

"Rainier undoubtedly saw himself with the easygoing, tolerant self-regard of a Professor Higgins who had 'let a woman in his life,'" said Grace's previous biographer Steven Englund. "The truth was that he (like Higgins) had very strong ideas [about a whale of a lot more subjects] than he realized. It was his world Grace entered."

Even before Grace returned to Rainier's world—Monaco—the bridal couple's differences were already apparent. Whereas Grace was seasick throughout much of her honeymoon, and never really managed to find her sea legs, Rainier adored the ocean, loved skin diving, racing sailboats and, as president of the International Commission for Scientific Exploration of the Mediterranean, was fascinated by marine science, in particular Monaco's Oceanographic Museum, the world's largest. "He liked cowboy movies, football, and business talk with his friends. They had nothing in common," said Gwen Robyns.

In contrast, Grace adored the ballet and opera. Eventually she came to realize that Rainier did not. On the rare occasions when she managed to convince him to accompany her to the opera or ballet, he embarrassed her by not only falling fast asleep as soon as the curtain went up but also snoring his way through the entire performance. Whereupon Grace, Christian de Massy reported, "would look alarmed and prod him with her elbow. He would wake up with a start and sometimes immediately begin applauding loudly, not aware that the performance was still going on."

Yet he was far from a stupid man. "Rainier was one of the most brilliant men I've ever met in my life," said Bernard Combemal, president of the SBM from 1977 to 1981. "I have extraordinary letters from him about politics, education, and art. He was a Renaissance man."

"Rainier was very close with a lot of writers like Colette," said Pepita Dupont. "They used to correspond. Rainier loved to write, and wrote a lot of letters. Some people say that he kept a diary and that he wrote his autobiography."

Rainier's favorite authors were Graham Greene, Paul Gallico, Gerald Durrell, John Steinbeck, and Marcel Pagnol, while Grace adored poetry, which didn't interest Rainier whatsoever. When, in her late forties, she forged a career in giving poetry readings throughout the world, he refused to attend all but one of them. Even then, soon after Grace began to read, he fell fast asleep.

As for temperament, he and Grace were poles apart. For although she had grown up at the heart of the competitive Kelly family, Grace understood how to be a good loser. Rainier did not. After asserting to a *Collier's* magazine reporter that he felt that there was "nothing more disagreeable to a man than to have a wife who knows more than he does on every subject," he added, "even worse than being beaten at tennis."

His horror of losing at tennis became apparent to Grace's friends David and Micheline Swift when they joined him and Grace in a doubles game at the palace. Rainier and Micheline were paired off against Grace and David, who was an extremely strong player.

"Rainier hit every ball, as hard as he could, straight at Grace," the Swifts revealed to Robert Lacey, Grace's earlier biographer.

"Oh, it hurts!" Grace cried as one ball hit her in the face.

"Keep your eye on the ball," growled Rainier and kept on hitting hard at her.

"He was just desperate to win," Swift said.

"Rainier's Golden Labrador was equally agile when his master missed a golf stroke and went to hit the dog with his club in his frustration," Lacey wrote.

While Grace was placid, hated confrontation, and rarely lost her temper, Rainier was childish, moody and—as Grace may well have discovered during her honeymoon—possessed of a fiery Latin temper.

During their marriage, he frequently exploded, berating her in front of the servants for making innocent mistakes, like filling a vase with chrysanthemums which, as he reprimanded her, in Europe are considered to be flowers fit only for a funeral.

"My uncle was very fast-tempered," his nephew Christian de Massy confirmed, "He was totally autocratic. You couldn't contradict him. He was well-intentioned, with a great sense of humor, but you would never take him head-on. You always had the impression that he was permanently on an election campaign."

Witnessing Rainier's temper tantrums and his lack of self-control, many of Grace's friend, like Judith Balaban Quine, felt embarrassed for her. In the early years of her marriage, Grace tended to defend Rainier, apologizing for his fireworks, excusing him with, "He's just frustrated, so many things pressing on him."

There was also the matter of his moodiness. Even at the wedding, and during the celebrations that followed, Rainier's face was often clouded and his manner taciturn. Afterward, columnist Dorothy Kilgallen noted, "The thing that flabbergasted everybody was his glumness. It had to be seen to be believed. Day after day, night after night, Rainier became gloomier and more fidgety as he attended the festivities designed to do him honor. . . . He is singularly lacking in *joie de vivre*."

Once Grace and Rainier returned to Monaco from their honeymoon, she was confronted with the realities of creating a life for herself inside a dirty sixteenth-century palace. "When Grace arrived back in Monaco, the palace was supposed to have been cleaned for her, but it was done in a rush," said Pepita Dupont. "So everything was dusty and not fantastic at all. Monaco wasn't at all fascinating, either."

Grace was moving into a palace that contained over two hundred rooms, many of them too cold in winter and too hot in summer and all in need of modernization. The brocade covering the walls was fading, the lighting was insufficient, and the entire interior of the palace was dank and dark. It was hardly surprising, as it had been two hundred years since any member of the Grimaldi family had taken up permanent residence there.

Worse still, Rainier turned out to have retained the autocratic attitudes of many of his ancestors and did not always handle Grace with the love and respect to which she had always been accustomed. "It was not easy at the start living in a new country with new people, a different language and far away from home and friends. But then everything new is hard," she later acknowledged.

Grace "was in a trap," Gwen Robyns revealed. "From being a movie star with absolutely the whole world at her feet, she dropped to second place. Rainier was the Serene Highness and very much a macho man. Grace had always been able to twist men around her little finger. But not Rainier. He was his Serene Highness, and she was just a girl from Philadelphia. She was miserable from day one."

"They started out having problems; she cried a lot and called her friends cross-Atlantic and said Rainier was terrible; difficult to get along with. She was homesick and he's a strong-willed person," Jack Kelly's friend Bill Hegner told Arthur Lewis.

"The problem for Rainier was that when Grace arrived she didn't speak much French, and in the beginning, the people of Monaco didn't like her. She was very refined, and that's not the Monegasque people," said Pepita Dupont.

"She certainly had difficulty adjusting to life in Europe because at the beginning she didn't speak French," said Bernard Combemal. "She could never get rid of her American accent, which was all right. I found that very charming.

"And, you know, Monaco is not very fun to live in. In summer, it's all glamorous, but you have the fall and the winter and the spring and there aren't many people. It's not like living in a big city. I'm sure that that was difficult for her at the beginning," he said.

Three months before her marriage, in the days when she was Grace Kelly, not Princess Grace of Monaco, she had been asked by the journalist Maurice Zolotow if she would retire from Hollywood now that she was moving to Monaco. Her answer, spontaneous and not spun in any way by a palace publicist, was, " 'Why,' she said, laughing, 'there isn't anything to do in Monaco, you know. It's such a little country.' "

It certainly was. She was born in Philadelphia, had lived in New York and Los Angeles, and Monaco was, indeed, far too small for her. Even had she been living in London, Paris, or Berlin, it was inevitable that she would miss America and all things American.

After issuing an SOS to her family, she regularly received care packages from Philadelphia, filled with soft American toilet paper—so different from the rough paper in use all over Europe, even at the palace—packages of Betty Crocker mixes so that she could bake angel food cakes, ham, capons, nylon stockings, a complete set of American cooking utensils to replace the palace's tarnished antique ones, dog biscuits for Oliver, and Rainier's favorite drink, Kentucky bourbon.

To the disdain of the stuff, along with American merchandise, Grace imposed a certain amount of American style on the palace—filling vases with a

A winning family: Jack, Margaret, Peggy, Jack,
five-year-old Grace, and Lizanne, two.
(Courtesy of Photofest)

The Princess of Fairmount Park
and her father, the King, 1954.
(Courtesy of Photofest)

Do not forsake me, oh my darling. Grace and Gary Cooper in High Noon. *(Courtesy of Photofest)*

Grace and Clark Gable—the man that got away—in Mogambo. *(Courtesy of Photofest)*

Producer Sir Anthony Havelock-Allan, Grace's ten-day London romance, many years later. (Courtesy of Lady Sara Havelock-Allan)

Grace and Ray Milland in Dial M for Murder. *Their off-screen affair nearly killed her career. (Courtesy of Photofest)*

The Rivals: Grace, with William Holden and Bing Crosby, in a shot from The Country Girl, *which mirrored real life.* (Courtesy of Photofest)

Carolyn Reybold, in her modeling prime. (Courtesy of Nyna Reybold)

Grace and Marlon Brando, triumphant as Best Actor and Best Actress Academy Award winners. (Courtesy of Photofest)

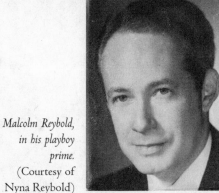

Malcolm Reybold, in his playboy prime. (Courtesy of Nyna Reybold)

Grace and James Stewart in Rear Window.
(Courtesy of Photofest)

*Grace and Cary Grant in a
passionate moment from*
To Catch a Thief.
(Courtesy of Photofest)

*Grace with then-fiancé,
fashion designer
Oleg Cassini.*
(Courtesy of
Photofest)

Frank Sinatra romancing Grace in High Society. (Courtesy of Photofest)

Monaco, the enclosed basin. (Courtesy of the author)

The bride and groom at the Civil Ceremony. (Courtesy of Photofest)

Jack, Margaret, Rainier, Grace, and Carolyn Reybold, her bridesmaid. (Courtesy of Photofest)

Frank Sinatra and Peter Lawford visiting Grace at the palace. (Courtesy of Mirrorpix)

The Princess and Rainier with the President and the First Lady at the White House. (Courtesy of Photofest)

True Love: Grace and David Niven at the Red Cross Ball. (Courtesy of Photofest)

Graham Binns, Elizabeth Taylor, and Grace at Elizabeth's fortieth birthday party in Budapest. (Courtesy of Rex Features)

Robert Dornhelm in 2004. (Courtesy of the author)

mixture of real and plastic flowers and importing from Manhattan House her trusty sofa embroidered with the word "Love" all over it.

Two years into her marriage, Grace continued to miss America and all things American to such a degree that she even wrote to Hollywood columnist James Bacon asking him to bring her some traditional Pennsylvania Dutch Ponhaus, a kind of scrapple, on his upcoming visit to Monte Carlo. "I got the feeling she was homesick for America," he said.

"I don't think people understood how hard it was for her to be cut off from her family and friends in America," Rainier once conceded to Gwen Robyns.

As far as her new subjects were concerned, first and foremost Grace was an American, which was not necessarily an asset. To the Monegasques, with their memories of GIs liberating Europe, but then—in the words of a World War II saying—becoming "overpaid, oversexed, and over here"—Americans were undesirable. Years later, Grace confirmed to Barbara Walters that at the start she faced a "definite anti-American feeling. Naturally, I was a stranger coming into their midst, and to many people I am considered a foreigner and will always be," she said.

When she presided over staff meetings, she got down to business as quickly as possible. Her subjects resented the fact that she ignored some of the niceties to which the Monegasque people were accustomed, like asking after everyone's health and that of their family, or commenting on the weather. They considered her abrupt, cool, unfriendly. Moreover, perhaps confused by all the Cinderella-laced publicity dubbing her a bricklayer's daughter made good, many of the Monegasque persisted in believing that she came from an impoverished family and had no education or breeding.

Yet she felt no need to defend or explain herself, even when she met with a similar brand of snobbery from her own countrymen. When she encountered a visiting American who snidely informed her, "Your father used to work for me," she simply retorted, "How lucky you were."

During Grace's first few months in Monaco, she developed conjunctivitis, then was racked by hay fever, a condition that would continue to plague her for the rest of her life. Taki, who sat next to her at 1966 palace dinner, remembered, "We spoke nonstop about hay fever. In those days, there were no pills except the kind that would put you to sleep, which Grace couldn't take. So I recommended her to a doctor in Paris. After that, every year she would send me a Christmas card, thanking me for introducing her to him."

Never comfortable in hot weather, she suffered in the claustrophobic atmosphere pervading Monaco and even went so far as to tell reporter Pete Martin of the *Saturday Evening Post*, "I am subject to attacks of claustrophobia and at times I get a little panicky in crowds."

Although she never admitted it then or later—except in her letters to Don Richardson—her new in-laws did not welcome her with open arms, and Rainier did not spend a great deal of time with her, either. But although she felt alone, she was rarely left alone. From being free to fly from coast to coast in a private jet, to window-shop at Bergdorf's, to act on a whim and have her hair styled at Saks, to sip cocktails at the Beverly Hills Hotel Polo Lounge, or to make hamburgers at the Chateau Marmont, she was now virtually a prisoner, her freedom of choice and movement forever curtailed.

There was also the matter of the servants, who dogged her every move, obsequious yet ever present. When former bridesmaid Bettina Thompson came to visit her, she noted, "There was too much bowing and scraping. It was pervasive, especially later. Grace had trouble adapting to a protocol-ridden life at the palace."

Never permitted to leave the palace unless in the company of a lady-in-waiting and a security guard, Grace was continually under surveillance, always under the watchful eye of palace retainers, she was no longer allowed to be spontaneous, and was forever deprived of her liberty.

"Loss of liberty is something you come to terms with," she said years afterward. "It is odd now to think of the days when I knew what it was to walk down a street and not have anybody know who I was."

Yet however difficult it may have been for her to come to terms with all the dramatic changes in her life, she never betrayed any discomfort at her new circumstances. "I wouldn't have been able to do my job as well as I do it now had I not been an actress," she admitted to her friend Bill Allyn.

When she made a stab at altering the palace status quo, she quickly fell afoul of the staff. For more than thirty years, the staff had been overseen by the same major domo, who wasn't the least bit amenable to altering his ways for the new American princess. When Grace asked him to dim the bright lights in the dining room by putting lower wattage bulbs in the chandeliers, he did so—for one day—then replaced them with the old ones.

"There was an elderly gentleman there who had been responsible for arranging the flowers for decades and . . . Grace had a point of view about arranging them. I mean, this guy was p——off. He was Mr. Flowers at the Palace and who was this American movie star coming in and telling him how to do the flowers," remembered Judith Balaban Quine in the documentary *Life After Grace*.

In 1979, Grace looked back at her first year at the palace and acknowledged all the difficulties she had faced. "After my days as an actress I had to become a normal person again, and at the beginning I suffered a personality crisis. My husband was determined to turn me into a real princess and it was with so much patience and understanding that he showed me the way."

Rainier had every reason to be patient and understanding with her, for on her wedding night she became pregnant by him.

"I did exactly what they wanted me to. Nine months and three days after the wedding, the baby came. That's what they wanted," Grace later told Gwen Robyns.

13

An Enclosed Basin

Grace was thousands of miles away from home, and during the first months of her pregnancy she not only suffered from morning sickness, but also remained bitterly homesick.

True to form, however, she didn't betray her emotions. "Can you believe I'm pregnant? . . . everything has happened so quickly that I can hardly believe it," she wrote to Prudy on August 30.

At the end of August 1956, she and Rainier got ready to leave for Paris, where she was due to see a doctor and buy her maternity wardrobe. There, she and Rainier visited her favorite store, Hermès, where he bought her a crocodile handbag, which—unlike the one Clark Gable gave her—was fashioned from real crocodile skin.

She wrote to Prudy, "Am so fat it's hysterical—but it is all so wonderful. I feel very well now except for getting tired. . . ." Whenever she spied a photographer about to snatch a picture of her, she covered her bulge with her new Hermès handbag. After she was repeatedly photographed with it, Hermès dubbed that particular model of handbag the "Kelly bag." High society scrambled to buy it, and it became a status symbol.

Perhaps because Grace's homesickness for America had become unbearable, in September 1956, she and Rainier sailed there, ostensibly so that she could close up her Fifth Avenue apartment, buy baby clothes, and spend a few days in Philadelphia with the family.

The pandemonium she had experienced at the dock as she set sail for Monaco on the *Constitution* was nothing in comparison with the hysteria that erupted wherever she went in America. When she stepped out on the Ocean

City boardwalk, she caused a riot. During a shopping spree at Saks in Manhattan, she was mobbed and had to be hustled out of the store by worried security guards. For a moment, she was afraid. She was pregnant, determined to protect her unborn child, and had hoped no one would bother her in her native America.

But it seemed that everyone wanted a piece of Princess Grace of Monaco. She was so world famous that an average of two hundred letters a week flooded in to Henry Avenue, begging for funds or for permission to use her face or her name in advertising campaigns. Fashion designers wanted her to wear their clothes, manufacturers wanted her to endorse their products, and painters clamored to be commissioned to paint her portrait—and went to any lengths to gain her agreement to pose for them.

A few weeks before Grace and Rainier arrived in America, society painter Ralph Wolfe Cowan, who was living in a four-story walkup on Manhattan's Seventy-second Street, read in the paper of their impending visit to New York.

He immediately made a $50 bet with a friend that he would become the world's first artist to paint a formal portrait of Princess Grace. He hired a model bearing a slight resemblance to her and then photographed her. Next on the pretext that Rainier's sister had commissioned him to paint a portrait of Grace, he contacted MGM, which hadn't yet released any stills from *The Swan*, and convinced the studio publicist to send him a few. From those photographs, and the ones he took of the Grace look-alike, he painted the portrait, completing it just before Grace and Rainier arrived in America.

He arranged for an eight-by-ten transparency to be hand-delivered to Grace's press agent, Rupert Allan, who had accompanied the royal couple to the States. Clearly impressed, Allan called Cowan and made an appointment to see the original.

Ralph Wolfe Cowan recalled, "At four in the afternoon, the buzzer rang, and a voice said that it was Rupert Allan and friend. I saw them coming up the stairs and I recognized Rainier. He looked right past me, said, 'Hello,' and then went to look at the painting. Then he came back to me and said, 'Mr. Cowan, I'm very jealous of you!' 'Oh, my God,' I thought to myself. 'My first Prince and I've messed it up.' Then he said, 'It's the most beautiful painting I've ever seen. There's a look of love in her eyes that I thought was only for me, and you've seen that look.' Later, we became good friends, and I discovered that Rainier has a great sense of humor, so he was just teasing.

"Then he told me that he wanted me to paint a tiara into the picture and showed me exactly where on the picture he wanted me to paint it. I did that, then we had one formal sitting over breakfast a couple of days later. Rainier gave Grace my portrait as her Christmas gift."

In a difficult rite of passage, Grace emptied her apartment at 988 Fifth Avenue, supervising the crating of her eighteenth- and nineteenth-century antiques that she was shipping to Monaco along with what she termed her "good paintings." In relinquishing her apartment, she was losing her final foothold in America.

At the same time, she made it abundantly clear that she would always maintain ties with her old friends. She and Rainier and Rita Gam and Judith, accompanied by their spouses, went to see *St. Joan* on Broadway and, on another occasion, attending the *Ice Follies* and then *High Society* at Radio City Music Hall, slipping in by a side door to avoid the fans. "Rainier was enchanted with the whole thing. Especially with the Rockettes. He'd never seen anything like them in his life. They put on an underwater show and I thought for a moment he was going to get up on the stage and swim with them," Grace recalled to Hedda Hopper. In another first, they also visited Chinatown with Malcolm and Carolyn Reybold, where Rainier ate melon soup for the very first time.

They spent two weekends in Ocean City, where Grace showed him her old haunts and introduced him to her friends. But while she braved the elements and took a dip in the ocean, he demurred. "He prefers the warmer waters of the Mediterranean," she laughingly explained.

In Philadelphia, they attended a luncheon in her honor hosted by the mayor, and another at the National Stamp Museum, which Rainier, an avid stamp collector, thoroughly enjoyed.

They also made a side trip to Washington, where they paid a courtesy call on President Eisenhower. Grace was disappointed that Mamie was sick and unable to see her, but was mollified by the president chatting with her and Rainier for an hour, rather than for just five minutes, which she had expected after his failure to attend their wedding.

Then it was back to Manhattan, more shopping, more evenings with friends, on one of which she confided to Judith how much she loved Manhattan and missed it when she was in Monaco. One of the highlights was a visit to Malcolm and Carolyn Reybold at their Long Island home, to which Rainier drove Grace, Judith, and Jay in a rented green Chevy.

During that same trip, she confided to Hedda Hopper that she was showing her pregnancy so early on because "all the Kelly girls do," adding, "My father is hoping for a grandson. His five grandchildren are all girls and he's looking to me to break the spell."

They returned to Monaco laden with purchases, particularly baby clothes. "The Prince laughs at me and tells me I have enough clothes for six babies," she said to Hedda, "but I haven't finished yet. I've brought over trunks of clothes and the palace dressmakers are just starting on more. They've waited till now so they won't duplicate my American shopping."

She was in the last months of her pregnancy, still suffering from daily bouts of nausea, as well as a number of food cravings. "At first, it was Chinese food. Normally I don't like it, but one day when we were in Paris, we had to search for a Chinese restaurant because I simply longed for this type of food. Then I craved for spaghetti and starchy food. But all that starch made me put on twenty-eight pounds. So when we got onto the boat, the Prince, who had also put on weight, and I went on a high protein diet. No salt, and no shell fish," she told Hedda.

Her first Christmas in Monaco was a happy one. "We had a lovely Christmas," she wrote to Prudy on January 10, 1957. The whole week between Christmas and New Years was devoted to parties for the children of different groups. . . . Because I am the size of a house and not feeling up to par we spent a very quiet New Years. . . . We are now getting anxious about the arrival of the baby. . . . I still can't get used to being a wife let alone a mother."

At 9:27 A.M. January 23, in the library of the palace and without any anesthetic, Grace gave birth to her first child, Caroline Louise Marguerite. While she had not fulfilled her father's request for a grandson, or her husband's for a male heir, Monaco and the Grimaldi dynasty were secure at last.

The names Caroline and Louise were, of course, chosen to honor the memory of Rainier's illustrious ancestors Queen Caroline, who introduced gambling to Monte Carlo, and Prince Louis, Rainier's grandfather.

In the spirit of their MGM-orchestrated wedding, immediately after Caroline's birth, publicity-hungry Rainier filmed her and Grace, then rushed the film to the local television station. Within a few hours, it was broadcast.

The nursery that Grace set up for Caroline—and later, Albert and Stephanie—was furnished in white wicker furniture, the floor covered in white marbled linoleum and a yellow rug. A Cocteau poster designed to promote the Oceanographic Museum of Monaco hung on the walls, as well as Picasso's portrait of a happy king. The pièce de résistance was a toy castle that doubled as a toy cupboard. After Albert was born, pride of place in the nursery was also given to a color photograph of Princess Grace cradling the newborn Caroline in her arms.

Like her mother, Caroline would grow up to be intelligent and strikingly beautiful, but with a far more stubborn and willful nature than Grace's. After all, Caroline was born and raised in the palace of Monaco, not on Henry Avenue, Philadelphia.

Grace did her utmost to prevent Caroline from becoming spoiled. "Remember that your grandfather was a bricklayer, and your great-grandmother was a laundress," she regularly reminded her children, evoking the memory of Jack Kelly and of Rainier's grandmother, Juliette. However, despite her attempts to keep Caroline's feet on the ground, Caroline was every inch a princess and proud of it. She was arrogant and, when she was a teenager, far more vain than Grace had ever been. Although Grace dressed Caroline and her siblings in casual clothes, Caroline was forever gazing at her own image in the mirror, fiddling with her hair.

From the first moment he saw Caroline, Rainier was besotted by her. "Princess Caroline is adorable and already has a special smile for her daddy," Grace wrote at the time to *Celebrity Bulletin* publisher Maggi Nolan.

She was to write Maggi an equally warm letter during the seventies, when Maggi's feckless ex-husband Jim was bound for Monte Carlo. Maggi wrote to her asking her not to fall for his Irish charm.

Grace replied to Maggi's letter, reassuring her that she had not encountered her errant ex-husband, telling her that she empathized with her plight as a single mother. "For a woman alone raising children under the best conditions is never easy," she wrote.

Despite the opulent circumstances of Princess Caroline's birth and a succession of nannies who helped look after her, it would never be simple for Grace to raise her either. The press clamored daily for news and pictures of Caroline. Grace and Rainier were fiercely protective of her and, later, Albert and Stephanie. Todd Allan, nephew of Rainier and Grace's personal press agent Rupert Allan, recalled, "Rainier was very specific about some of the things he wanted done or not done in the press about his family. He just didn't want to splatter them all over the tabloids and for people to have access to them all the time."

However, despite professing to Rupert Allan, and later to the press itself, how much he despised the media, Rainier always remained mindful of the importance of publicity in maintaining Monaco's high profile—the same high profile he had created by marrying Grace in the first place.

In an illustration of the palace's extraordinarily press-friendly policy, London *Daily Express* photographer Bill Lovelace recalled what happened when, in the autumn of 1956, he snatched a picture of a very pregnant Grace.

Sydney Smith, the *Express*'s foreign correspondent and a tough man who didn't take kindly to working with photographers, had convinced the palace to allow him and Lovelace to tour the palace on behalf of their paper, on the condition that they not bring any cameras in.

"Needless to say, I took a Leica in my pocket just in case. We were in the courtyard when along one side walks Princess Grace, looking very pregnant. Behind her, carrying some dresses, were three maids," Lovelace recalled before his death.

"Sydney Smith gave me a look, as if to say, 'Quick! Take a picture.' And I thought, 'My God. I can't take any pictures having been told not to and with the captain of the guard standing there too.'"

At that moment, Bill Lovelace found himself between the devil and the deep blue sea, aware that Sydney Smith would report him to his editor if he didn't take the photograph, and that the captain of the guard might arrest him if he did. "I pulled out the camera and took the shots. The captain of the guard was dumbfounded," he recalled.

Within moments, Lovelace was seized and marched into the Guard Room, where the chief of staff read him the riot act. Meanwhile, terrified as he was, Lovelace still had the presence of mind to reach into his pocket, open the Leica, remove the film he had taken of Grace, and slip it into another pocket.

When the furious chief of staff demanded the film, Lovelace produced a second camera, pulled out the film, opened it to the light, and handed it over. To Lovelace's relief, the chief of staff accepted it, believing it to be the pictures he had snatched of Grace.

What happened next demonstrates the palace's ambivalent attitude toward the press. "I thought it would make things bad for me at the palace, but it didn't at all," Bill remembered, reporting that when Caroline was due to be christened, his editor demanded that he attend the photo call at the palace.

Convinced that he would be banned from doing so, Lovelace contacted the palace press officer and was told by him, " 'The prince was most upset. He nearly sacked me, in fact.' I said, 'I was terribly sorry, but I had my reasons. If there's anything I could do to put it straight.' He replied, 'No. It's straight now.'

"And from then on they knew me. They thought, 'We've got to watch him. He means business.' In a strange sort of way, it helped. In the christening, for instance, I had a bad position in the church and I complained about it and they immediately changed me to the best position." No matter how much Grace and Rainier would in the future complain about press intrusion, Bill Lovelace's story tells quite another tale.

After the christening, Grace wrote to Prudy, "I was very tired and nervous after the baby was born. . . . But old Caroline is just divine . . . and gets cuter every day . . . I really can't quite believe that she is mine. . . . She smiles and giggles and gurgles."

On August 12, 1957, she wrote to Prudy that they now had "an adorable chalet in the Swiss Mountains," in Schonreid, which they had rented on a long-term basis.

There, she sometimes took to the slopes. "I used to go skiing with Grace," remembered David Niven Jr. "She looked better than she skied . . . the great thing about Grace when she was skiing was that you would have had no idea it was her. She wasn't surrounded by any kind of security."

That first season in Schonreid, she enthused to Prudy in a letter, "The air is delicious & has been a wonderful change for the baby—she is so sweet that I can hardly believe it. Oliver is a father!" Then, in a rare display of irritation at Monaco's thriving tourist trade, which given the vast amount of money tourists invariably blew at SBM's hotels and the casino, is surprising, she wrote, "Monaco is lovely in autumn because all of the white shoes & straw hats are gone."

In another letter, she wrote to Prudy on the subject of Oliver's puppies, "There are six puppies and all adorable. . . . We have promised some of them but now Rainier loves them so much he wants to keep them all."

In the fall she wrote Prudy, "Many thanks for your very sweet thought on my birthday. Rainier organized himself a little party for me and planned the menu of everything I love—it was a wonderful evening. I now have to be on a strict diet."

That year Grace's life took a turn for the better when Rainier purchased a small Provence-style farm in Rocagel, France, high in the mountains above Monaco. Set on sixty acres of land, the farm was an escape from Monaco, a place where Grace and Rainier could enjoy family life away from the prying eyes of the servants and the constant stream of tourists desperate for a glimpse of Monaco's adored princess. "Rocagel is where we close the door to the world," Grace explained to *People*'s Fred Hauptfuhrer.

At Rocagel, Rainier could play the gentleman farmer, supervising the planting of four hundred fruit trees, working in the vegetable garden, and taking pride in the fact that the palace kitchen would now cook with produce grown there.

Down the line, he would install a small dairy, with cows whose milk would be churned into butter for the family, while Grace grew roses in the garden. Gradually, through the years, they expanded Rocagel, so that it came to resemble an American ranch to such an extent that the locals took to dubbing it "The Ranch."

The American ambience was enhanced after Grace decorated the ranch with imported American wallpapers and carpets, and even installed an American-style kitchen, shocking her more conservative Monegasque visitors who considered its aquamarine hues garish. Finally, Grace put her own particular stamp on her Rocagel bathroom, covering the walls with stills from her movies. "Rainier banned Grace's films from being shown in Monaco for quite a few years after he married her," said Christian de Massy. Whether or not this irreverent placement of memorabilia from her days as a Hollywood star was an attempt to placate Rainier's hatred of Hollywood is an interesting question.

"Grace told me many times that Rainier was jealous of all her Hollywood friends," remembered Gwen Robyns. "He hated them coming to see her and made a scene every time they did. She said, 'Those friends are a part of my life and I miss them so much. When they come to see us, I long just to sit and talk Hollywood.' But Rainier used to say to her, 'We're not having any of that Hollywood talk tonight.'"

Doreen Hawkins remembered Rainier's behavior at a dinner she and Jack had with him and Grace, and David Niven and Peter Ustinov and their wives. "All these actors—David, Peter, and Jack—were sitting around the table, rivaling each other to see who could tell the best story. There was Ustinov, who was very funny, Jack, who was very entertaining, and David, who was past master of telling great anecdotes.

"The lunch was a riot, but Rainier sat at the head of the table looking totally bemused. I felt sorry for him because there was all this quick-fire banter going on and although he was laughing, too, it was impossible for him to really understand it. But Grace was loving it—it was her world, her old environment."

On another occasion, David and Hjordis Niven hosted a dinner attended by Sir Laurence Olivier and his wife, actress Joan Plowright, who recalled in her memoirs, "After the niceties of who wanted black or white and who did or did not take sugar, and some comments on how pretty the garden looked through the French windows, there was a lull. And Rainier fell fast asleep on the sofa and began to snore.

"The rest of us sipped our coffee without speaking and avoided each other's eyes, trying to control a mounting hysteria and wondered who, apart from his Serene Highness, would dare to break the silence. Princess Grace, who could have done it, seemed paralyzed.

"Then Larry, who was seated next to her, decided to come to the rescue and asked loudly, 'Have you ever played Detroit, Ma'am?' Niven bolted from the room on the pretext of fetching more coffee. Grace looked surprised at the idea that she might have played Detroit, but was grateful for any distraction from the shattering noise still coming from the sofa. When Niven returned, Larry was telling Grace about the movie he had made with Marilyn Monroe." Rainier, presumably, was still asleep on the sofa.

He had married a Hollywood star, yet he appeared to despise Hollywood and all who worked there. But perhaps there were other, more complex emotions governing his disdain for Grace's former Hollywood compatriots. "He was especially awkward in the presence of Grace's Hollywood set, uncomfortable with them perhaps because they were associated with a time when he wasn't with Grace," Christian de Massy explained.

In short, Rainier was jealous. Grace was now his possession. In his view, she belonged to him, and nothing, not even her past, was permitted to undermine that reality for him. "She was frightened of Rainier. She would never

say it in those words, but she would say, 'I have to be careful of Rainier,' "
Gwen Robyns recalled.

Her unhappiness was later apparent to her friend and former 988 Fifth
Avenue neighbor Emi Sawada-Kamiya, who stayed with her in 1958 for three
months at the palace. "She said that the Princess was so sad and lonely and
that Princess Grace told her that she could feel the people of Monaco didn't
like her, an American," her friend, Jean-Claude Baker, reported in his biography of his adopted mother, Josephine Baker. "She told me that one day,
Princess Grace left the Palace to do some shopping. When she came back, she
stood in front of the palace guards for twenty minutes, not able to bring herself to go back inside. Finally she did. She went back inside the Palace, then
cried in Emi Sawada's arms."

14

Broken Vows

On March 14, 1958, Grace delighted Rainier, her father, and the citizens of Monaco by giving birth to an eight-pound-eleven-ounce heir to the Grimaldi dynasty. They named him Albert Alexander Louis Pierre. "Our little boy is really too sweet for words," Grace raved in an April 2 letter to Prudy Wise. "He is gaining weight rapidly and will soon be a big fatty. Caroline loves him but gets very upset when he cries."

Yet despite her joy at Albert's birth, Grace was left feeling debilitated; her resistance was low, and she constantly suffered a sore throat. Despite Grace's assertion that Caroline loved Albert, in fact Caroline had quickly developed a deep jealousy of him, once even ripping up her own favorite coloring book merely because he had touched it.

"Caroline and Albert were very close together in age and, therefore, always quarreling—Caroline had a nasty habit of biting," Grace told British broadcaster Terry Wogan. "One day, we were on Onassis's yacht and they were playing. She wanted something. Albert wouldn't give in, so she bit him! He let out a howl, so I grabbed Caroline and bit her! Now I had two screaming children and a shocked Onassis crying, 'What kind of mother are you?' But Caroline never bit Albert again."

Stephanie, too, was a victim of Caroline's jealousy. According to her cousin Christian de Massy, "Grace once caught Caroline putting Stephanie's head in the toilet. She told her to stop that at once."

By the time Caroline and Stephanie were in their teens, according to *The Wilder Shores of Love* author, Lesley Blanch, Grace confided in her that, "I have no power over my daughters. They give me endless trouble." And then she added, "But I've never had a moment of difficulty with my son."

Her husband, however, was quite a different story. The previous year, Grace unwittingly betrayed to a journalist the tensions simmering under the surface of her marriage. "The biggest change in my life wasn't the Palace," she said, "it was the adjustment to marriage itself. I lived alone in New York and in California, and the entire schedule of my life centered around my work. I had to get to the studio on time; I had to arrange my meals to fit my schedule. My career was the central focus of everything I did. Now, my life centers around my husband."

Grace's life may have centered round Rainier, but sadly for her despite the fact that she had presented him with a son and heir, his life did not center around her.

As early as three months after the marriage, she heard rumors that her new husband was keeping a mistress. Then another one. Then another. Princess Grace of Monaco, the world's adored fairy tale princess, a Hollywood screen goddess, a great beauty, desired by millions, had been loved by some of the most handsome, sexually attractive men of her time. Yet for her husband, she wasn't enough. "He never stopped having mistresses," said Gwen Robyns.

"Most Sundays, Rainier would leave the Palace, telling Grace he was off to watch a local soccer game. Instead he would go straight to the bed of his long-time French actress mistress for an afternoon of passion," author John Glatt revealed. "The Prince had a close friend monitor the soccer games and brief him later to provide him with an alibi. Then he would return to the Palace and discuss the finer points of the game with Grace."

When Grace married Rainier, her father—the consummate philanderer—boasted to a newspaper reporter that he had laid down the law to Rainier, telling him "that I certainly hoped he wouldn't run around the way some princes do, and I told him that if he did, he'd lose a mighty fine girl." Sophisticated and worldly—perhaps more so than Grace—Jack Kelly also knew his history. He knew that since time immemorial, kings and princes have considered infidelity their divine right. Even after they married queens, princesses, or even Hollywood movie stars, it was a forgone conclusion that they also would take a mistress or two. And who could blame Rainier for following suit or be surprised when he did? After all, he was Prince Rainier II, the absolute ruler of

the Principality of Monaco, scion of the Grimaldi royal family, which had been
in power for more than seven centuries. He was entitled to follow the siren call
of his own sexual appetites wherever—and to whomsoever—they might lead.

There was, however, something else at play. Rainier, a keen student of his
family's history, knew that his ancestors—Prince Antoine I, Prince Louis I,
and Prince Albert I—were cuckolds every one of them, and he clearly had no
intention of following in their footsteps.

There was also the matter of Grace's past. Before making his final decision to marry her, Rainier had initiated a thorough investigation into her
background and no doubt received a voluminous dossier on those past lovers:
the Shah of Iran, Gary Cooper, Clark Gable, Ray Milland, William Holden,
Jean-Pierre Aumont, and Oleg Cassini, whose names had been whispered in
the press. To top that, on the eve of the wedding, in a long series of articles
published throughout America, Margaret Kelly had reiterated the names of
many of Grace's lovers with evident relish.

And, as Rainier's jealousy of Grace's Hollywood friends demonstrates, he
was insecure, possessive, and acutely aware of her allure for other men, her
warm and passionate nature.

As a result, he was the one who fired the first shot, as it were. Two years after Grace married Rainier amid pomp and circumstance, and with the blessings of the Catholic church, she knew without a shadow of a doubt that he
had been unfaithful to her.

"I know he has affairs with other women. That's very frustrating to me,
and it makes me very, very unhappy," she confided in one of her many long
telephone conversations with Hollywood hairdresser Sydney Guilaroff.
Arlene Dahl, Grace's close friend said, "I really felt so sorry for her at the end.
What she had to put up with, what she had to go through with both Rainier
and the children. Of course she knew Rainier was so unfaithful. Of course.
Of course. She knew, but she didn't want anybody else to know. But we would
have tea alone together in the Palace and she complained to me. I knew how
unhappy she was. She was in a trap."

She was devastated by Rainier's infidelities. She had spent her entire childhood observing the searing pain and humiliation her mother suffered in
the face of her father's infidelity. Now she was suffering in exactly the same
way.

For Grace, proud, beautiful, and once courted by some of the most glamorous men in Hollywood, the agony was almost too much to bear. Consequently, I believe that what transpired next was entirely justifiable.

On June 14, 1958, in Monte Carlo, Frank Sinatra gave a concert before the premiere of his movie *Kings Go Forth*, which was held under the auspices of Grace and Rainier, in aid of the UN Refugee Fund. Among the guests that night was former MGM star and Frank's fellow Rat Packer, debonair British actor Peter Lawford.

But this was indisputably Frank Sinatra's movie, his night. Grace was delighted that the gala was taking place in Monaco and that she was seeing him once more. He was powerful, charming, attractive, and masculine, with a combination of macho swagger and romantic tenderness that women found irresistible. Ever since she had first met him, in her early teens, there had always been a frisson between them, a spark of attraction that the camera captured when it flared in *High Society*.

During their time together in Africa, she had seen the best of Frank and the worst. The Frank who erupted in fury at the slightest provocation. The down-and-out singer utterly unraveled by the faithless Ava, whom he loved to distraction. The romantic, creative spirit who made Christmas far from home tolerable through his kindness and generosity. The great lover of whom Ava once—after flipping up the tunic of a passing African to reveal his vast endowment—declared, "Frank is bigger than that." The sensitive, considerate soul who didn't attend Grace's wedding because he didn't want to upstage her. Above all, he was an American, a fellow Hollywood star, a loyal friend who remembered her from the days when she was starting out and the world was new. It was only natural that when Frank came to Monaco with Peter, Grace invited them both to the palace for cocktails.

"I have a gorgeous picture of Grace, Frank, and Peter when they were up at the Palace for cocktails," his widow, Patricia Seaton Lawford, said. "Peter told me that Grace was rather unsettled in her life at that time. She didn't know if she was Grace Kelly of Hollywood, or Grace de Monaco. Peter and Grace were extremely close friends but not lovers. He liked her, but he said she was cold, frosty."

Frank, however, felt differently about her and always had. "Peter told me that when Grace and Frank met at the palace, they started having an affair.

Frank was smitten with her. Frank was just crazy for Grace and she for him," Patricia Seaton Lawford volunteered.

At the time of the *Kings Go Forth* premiere, Frank and his entourage—including his fifty-eight-piece orchestra—were all staying at the SBM-owned-and-run Hôtel de Paris. Reporters swarmed through the town, covering the star-studded gala. Moreover, Prince Rainier had eyes all over Monaco; security cameras were on every street corner, phones were constantly tapped, and a police force of three hundred dogged the steps of every citizen or tourist under suspicion of even the slightest infraction. So the possibility of Princess Grace of Monaco managing to indulge in an illicit tryst with Frank Sinatra seems remote.

Then again, Grace was clever, brave, and fearless, and given Rainier's own extramarital affairs, she may well have felt vindicated in seeking consolation with an old and trusted friend.

And as Frank Sinatra's valet, George Jacobs—who charted Frank and Grace's love affair when he was in Monaco with Frank after the 1964 filming of *Von Ryan's Express*—attests, there was always a way. "When they were alone on the balcony of the palace after a reception there, I had overheard Mr. S. and Gracie make elaborate plans to meet at some villa near the David Nivenses in Cap Ferrat," George reported. "When I went to the palace and was served a fabulous lunch in the state dining room, the prince said that the princess was at the flower market. I was told by Mr. S. to say he was rehearsing. I knew he wasn't.

"He called her 'Gracie' and she called him 'Francis.' Whenever we were shooting in Europe, Mr. S. would go down to Monaco. Sometimes he would arrive in his yacht, other times we would stay in a hotel in Nice. Then he would see Gracie," George recalled to this author in 2004.

"He would send me up to the Palace to bring Prince Rainier cases of special Jack Daniel's. The Prince was very nice to me. He took me down to the garage and showed me his collection of vintage cars, and took me for a spin one of them. Sometimes Grace would show Mr. S. the French Riviera. She would take him out to lunch or a drink or two. Sometimes the Prince would join them. Sometimes he wouldn't.

"Later on, I took part in a dating game and won the first prize of an all-expenses trip to Monaco. The show ferried me and my date around Monaco in a Rolls. Just as we stopped outside the Palace, Grace happened to come out. She saw us and said, 'My God! How are you doing? How's Francis?' Then she asked us to have coffee with her and her secretary in a little coffee shop outside the Palace gates. She wanted to know if Mr. S. was doing well, if he was in good shape. She was always very nice to me, and when I used to come to Monaco with Mr. S., she would ask me about different jazz musicians because she knew I grew up in New Orleans. She was a great lady. Mr. S. used to call her his 'dream girl.' "

Sinatra's relationship with Grace would endure through the years, and her attraction to him would never diminish, nor his for her. At her request, he traveled to Monaco again to perform at the Sporting Club on June 9, 1962. When on June 13, 1971, he gave the first of many farewell performances at the Los Angeles Music Center, Grace was on hand to applaud. And when in 1976 he married his fourth wife, Barbara Marx, there were those who remarked on her striking physical resemblance to Grace.

Even the press were aware of the cracks in Grace and Rainier's marriage with *The New York Times*'s Judy Klemesrud noting their contrasting temperaments and tastes. "Once, as they approached a long line of diplomatic guests, Rainier's face was like a thunderstorm. Grace took one look at her husband and sailed blithely into animated conversation. 'What a wonderful morning we had today,' and then she said, 'I hear all the hotels are full.' "

"After a few minutes of this, Rainier took his cue from his wife; he agreed that Monaco was booming and permitted himself a smile.

"Sometimes, however, it is he who has to curb his wife's enthusiasm. Not long ago, diners at Le Pirate, one of the Riviera's most famous restaurants, were highly amused at the sight of the Princess of Monaco, half out of her seat with excitement, clapping to the beat of a gypsy orchestra and the Prince pulling her back in her seat.

" 'Eventually,' said one of the witnesses, 'I saw him kiss her hand lightly and quickly. She immediately calmed down. This is obviously a fellow who knows how to handle his wife.' "

The subtext was clear. He was bad-tempered, she wasn't. She was spontaneous, he reined her in. It was hardly the recipe for lifelong marital bliss.

On April 2, 1960, seventy-year-old Jack Kelly, who had been feeling gravely ill for over a year, was rushed to the hospital, suffering from stomach pains. He was diagnosed with stomach cancer and had two operations, but to no avail. During the first week of June, a distraught Grace flew to America to visit him in a hospital in Philadelphia, so grief-stricken that the nurse taking care of him at first did not recognize her.

Sad and dispirited, she also spent time in Manhattan. There, she made the worst mistake of her life, one that she would forever bitterly regret.

Grace Kelly was a woman of principle, a woman of integrity, who had never knowingly hurt another human being, a kindhearted woman who will always be remembered for her charity and the goodness of her soul.

She had been brought up a Catholic, although, as Lizanne told Steven Englund, "having a Catholic education was never terribly important to our parents."

However, Grace believed in the precepts of the church. "I know for certain she went to confession regularly—I sometimes accompanied her to the church—and I believe she was often troubled in her conscience," Oleg Cassini remembered.

She was true to all the commandments except one: Bing Crosby, Ray Milland, Tony Curtis, and William Holden were all married when she had affairs with them. And even before her days as a Hollywood star, she had demonstrated her willingness to have affairs with married men. According to James Spada, Don Richardson told him that Grace had confessed that before leaving Philadelphia to begin her acting studies in New York, she lost her virginity to the husband of a friend.

In Grace's words, as reported by Don Richardson to Spada, "It all happened so quickly. I dropped in unexpectedly at a girlfriend's house—I remember it was raining very hard—and her husband told me she would be gone for the rest of the afternoon. I stayed, talking to him, and before I knew it we were in bed together."

The identity of that man has never been revealed. But whoever he was, there is no doubt whatsoever that he was married to one of Grace's friends and was the first of her friends' husbands with whom she went to bed. The second was Malcolm Reybold—the husband of her friend and bridesmaid Carolyn Reybold—with whom she had an affair, most likely when her father was on his deathbed.

During those dreadful days where Grace was compelled to grapple with both the impending loss of her father and the death of any hopes she retained that she might finally win his love and approval, Malcolm Reybold provided a solid shoulder for her to cry on.

"Women adored my father," Malcolm Reybold's daughter Patricia recalled. "He was a dashing man-about-town. He was very creative, played the piano beautifully and was extremely charming and very proud of his Southern heritage."

He was a multifaceted man, an advertising executive at J. Walter Thompson, then McCann Erickson. He had a quick and inquisitive mind, and in the seventies he wrote a novel, *The Inspector's Opinion: The Chappaquiddick Incident*. He was courteous, well read, erudite, sophisticated, good-looking, dapper, a polished dancer and an ace tennis player. Gregarious and convivial, he had friends in high places like *Time* magazine publisher Henry Luce and billionaire Sherman Fairchild, at whose Long Island estate Grace had first met him.

"Malcolm was a wonderful guy, very interesting, sweet, and lovely. He and Carolyn would talk about Grace Kelly constantly," remembered Edward Ory, his friend and neighbor at Manhattan House.

"Malcolm was a genuine, honest man. He was a character and a half," recalled his friend Susan Andraesen. "His whole philosophy was that a woman was a very special creature and should be treated specially. He really knew the workings of a woman and I think every woman realized that when she was around him. He told me that he and Grace were close friends, that he had given her career advice, told her how to handle herself and how to succeed in her career when she was a model. He said that she had drive and a special sparkle. That when she put her mind to something, she would do it."

During Grace's Manhattan House days, Malcolm often entertained her, Carolyn, and all their friends by reading from *The Pursuit of Destiny*, a book of astrological interpretation. And it was at Malcolm and Carolyn's apartment that Grace first initiated Rainier into her cherished game of charades.

When Grace made her Broadway debut in *The Father*, Malcolm and Carolyn were in the audience, cheering her on. "When she walked out on the stage, looking so fresh and pretty and breathtaking, I burst into tears. I think it was then that I realized she was going places," Carolyn said.

As far as Grace was concerned, the Reybolds were family, and when their first child, Jyl, was born in 1951, followed by her sister, Robyn, in 1953, she adored their children as well. Grace was Jyl's godmother, showering the little girl with characteristic kindness, marking her birthdays with thoughtful gifts and notes.

Grace and Carolyn had always remained close, although at the time of the wedding there were tensions in their relationship.

When Carolyn couldn't afford the trip to Monaco, NBC's *Home Show*, in exchange for her granting them a postwedding interview, offered to fly her and Malcolm there, free of charge. When she asked Grace's permission to accept, Grace agreed somewhat reluctantly. At the wedding, Carolyn and Malcolm committed a major *faux pas*: having failed to respond formally to invitations, they nevertheless turned up at the celebratory events.

Yet Grace cared about Carolyn, saw her whenever she came to America, and empathized with her when Malcolm initiated a family move to Long Island. After the Reybolds set up home there, Malcolm started to spend many nights alone in Manhattan, and Carolyn began to feel isolated and afraid.

Without Malcolm's knowledge, she began to take secret trips to Manhattan, where she underwent psychoanalysis, then afterward hid the bills from Malcolm. By the late fifties, although they were still husband and wife, Malcolm and Carolyn were leading very different lives. Thus it is highly likely that when her father was dying, and Grace was in Manhattan, Grace and Malcolm met there alone, without Carolyn.

In April 2005—at Nyna Reybold's invitation—I accompanied her to visit Carolyn in her Long Island nursing home and, in Nyna's presence, interviewed her there on tape.

During the interview, I showed Carolyn the following passage from *Bridesmaids*, Judith Balaban Quine's book for which Carolyn's eldest daughter, Jyl, granted an extensive interview: "Grace was not fond of Malcolm Reybold and never had been. In the early sixties, she'd learned he and Carolyn had separated when Cholly Knickerbocker's column reported, 'Malcolm Reybold, who at one time was a big name in Grace Kelly's life (in fact Princess Grace "confessed" to his wife that there had been a romance), has now moved quarters to the elegant Colony Hotel in Palm Beach . . . to establish residence for a divorce from his pretty brunette wife, Carolyn, who was one of Grace's closest friends.' Grace had met Malcolm before he and Carolyn knew each other, but she had never gone out with him. She couldn't imagine why he would prolong this fiction of a romance between them, especially at a time when it might so wound Carolyn."

Carolyn's response was to recall visiting Grace in a Manhattan hotel: "She told me it was over and said, 'We are no longer an item.' I cried all the way to the therapist, but afterwards, he made me feel better." Then, turning to Nyna, she said, "Daddy was very tricky. He must have persuaded her. It wasn't Grace's fault."

Perhaps it wasn't. As far as Grace was concerned, Malcolm was a long-standing friend, a relic of the good old days at Manhattan House when she was savoring success for the very first time. His very presence would have evoked bittersweet memories of her past.

Her father had never given her the degree of love that she craved from him. Now he was in the twilight of his life and there was little hope that he ever would. So if Malcolm, twenty years her senior, was there to comfort her and temporarily provide her with love and consolation, how could Grace— then at her most vulnerable—reject his advances? As Carolyn put it, Malcolm was very tricky. He must have persuaded her. It was not her fault. The letter, however, was quite another story.

In August 1960, Aileen Mehle—the respected columnist *Suzy*—was in Hyannis Port staying with Morton Downey and Peggy Hohenloe. "We went over to dinner at the Kennedys, and everyone was agog over a letter Princess Grace had just written to Carolyn Reybold," Aileen recalled. "Everyone was talking about the fact that Princess Grace had written a letter—a full confession—to Carolyn Reybold, her friend and bridesmaid, telling her that she loved her but that she would never be happy, could never live with herself if she did not confess to Carolyn that she had had an affair with Malcolm. She said that she was sorry. She was seeking expiation.

"I don't know how everyone knew about the letter that weekend, but they did. Someone had a copy. We all said, 'How stupid, how stupid, how stupid of Grace, to get things off her chest and hurt somebody in the bargain. Why did she have to? She wasn't talking to a priest.'"

Father Peter Jacobs, a Catholic priest who became Grace's friend a few years before her death, is adamant that she would never have written a letter of confession to a friend telling her that she had had an affair with her husband. "Grace would never have done that. That was committing murder. I don't believe she did that," he insisted.

In 2005, Nyna Reybold confirmed that her mother had repeatedly told her about Grace's confession, but added, "I've always questioned it because my mother wasn't so stable and I thought she imagined it."

When asked about the existence of the letter of confession Grace wrote to her mother, Nyna's elder sister, Jyl—who is writing her own book about her mother and her relationship with Grace, which she described as being "very shocking"—revealed in a telephone conversation with me that she did not have the letter in her possession, "but I have that on taped interviews from a number of her close friends." Her cousin Jack also confirmed to me that he had also heard that Malcolm had had an affair with Grace.

Not long after her split from Malcolm, Carolyn took Robyn and Nyna on a pilgrimage to Lourdes, but in the middle of the trip she ran out of funds. Although Carolyn had received the proceeds of the sale of the Long Island house, she had squandered it on a combination of bad investments and donations to Christian evangelists. Finding herself penniless in Lourdes, she telephoned Grace, desperate for funds to pay for tickets back home for her and her daughters. Grace instantly obliged.

Then, in January 1979, the final blow fell: twenty-six-year-old Robyn was killed in a car crash. When Grace heard the news, she immediately called Jyl and sent Carolyn a condolence letter.

By 1981, Carolyn Reybold—former Ford model and Princess Grace's bridesmaid—was homeless and living in a Manhattan women's shelter.

Grace and her other bridesmaids learned of Carolyn's fate at that time. Grace's reaction to the news, as quoted by Judith Balaban Quine in her book *Bridesmaids*, was, " 'Isn't it odd that there's something about Carolyn's life I actually think of enviously? Please don't take that wrong,' Grace cautioned, 'I know it might sound awful and insensitive, but the thought of just getting up all day and doing what that day brings you sounds wonderful to me in certain ways. I've also watched street people in New York and Paris and envied them, so I must be going gaga with the change.' "

In an interview for this book, her friend, director Robert Dornhelm, confirmed that she had expressed similar sentiments to him.

In 1988, Malcolm Reybold died. The following year, Carolyn's tragedy was made public after her daughter, Jyl, revealed the entire story of her homelessness in an interview with Judith Balaban Quine, who published the details in her book.

Jyl went on to give an interview on the subject to *Hard Copy*, asserting, "My mother doesn't have an alcohol problem. She's not incoherent." Then, without elaborating, she added, "Something happened to her several years ago that made her the way she is, but it's not for me to say just what it was."

After the *Hard Copy* interview was aired, Carolyn's story became worldwide news. Then living at the hostel for homeless women at New York's former National Guard Armory on Park Avenue, she slept in a large dorm, patrolled day and night by armed guards. During the day, she tramped the city, lingering in parks where she painted pictures of flowers and animals. "Carolyn rarely speaks to any of the other homeless women. Occasionally she shows staff her drawings. They really look professional, even though she only took up drawing several months ago. Sometimes she seems aware of what you're talking about and sometimes she doesn't," one of the shelter's staff explained to *Hard Copy*.

When Carolyn's story was made public, it seemed logical to those in the know to assume that her tragedy was precipitated by the trauma of Grace's shocking confession.

"Receiving that letter was the beginning of the downfall of Carolyn Reybold," Aileen Mehle said. "I met her and I knew her—a little, not a lot. Sometimes you look at certain women and there is a look about them, a fragility, a victimhood, something that is almost part of their persona, as if they are asking to be kicked, and there was something of that about Carolyn."

However, at the time Grace made her confession to Carolyn, Carolyn was already in psychoanalysis, a cry for help in the days when consulting a psychoanalyst or psychiatrist was considered by many to be beyond the pale and done only in extreme desperation. This suggests that Carolyn was already deeply disturbed before receiving Grace's letter. So when the letter came, it might have been the last straw for her. She was already fragile and unstable, and it had always been just a matter of time before she cracked up completely.

Although Grace visited America after she learned of Carolyn's fate, she did not see her again. According to Eileen Ford, to whom Jyl Reybold revealed the information, Grace left Carolyn money in her will. Since the publication of Judith Balaban Quine's book, none of the bridesmaids has ever spoken publicly about Carolyn again.

However, Balaban Quine ended her book with a posthumously written open letter to Grace in which, addressing her directly, she makes the curiously cryptic comment about Carolyn that, "There is no way that she will fault anyone for anything, at least not anyone she or I ever really knew," almost as if she were reassuring Grace, beyond the grave, that Carolyn has indeed forgiven her.

Speaking to Carolyn Reybold today—now no longer homeless, but in a nursing home—there isn't a glimmer of bitterness in her voice when she talks about Grace, something she does freely and with warmth. Carolyn is still beautiful in her late seventies, her eyes as big and haunting as in the days when she and Grace were the toast of Manhattan. She is a voracious reader, any mental problems she might once have had, are now, by dint of modern medicine, under control.

Her mind is sharp and her voice rarely trembles, except when talking about Grace's affair with her husband. Then her body stiffens. "Daddy was very tricky. He must have persuaded Grace. It wasn't her fault," she said.

15

Grace of Monaco

On June 20, 1960, Jack Kelly breathed his last. Margaret Kelly lived on for another thirty years without him. Desolate at her father's death, Grace flew back to America for the funeral. Then she returned to Monaco. She was inconsolable, yet protocol dictated that she immediately resume her duties as Princess Grace. Soon after her return, she and Rainier attended a Chopin concert at the palace, during which she was overcome by emotion and left the concert, her face streaming with tears as she cried for the memory of the father whom she'd loved so much but who had never really loved her back.

Along with Jackie Kennedy, the Queen of England, Marilyn Monroe, and Elizabeth Taylor, Grace was now one of the most famous women in the world, and her image burnished Monaco's reputation to such a degree that the pocket-handkerchief-sized principality thrived beyond the wildest dreams of Aristotle Onassis and Prince Rainier.

"Grace made a sinking boat beautiful again," Oleg Cassini said. "She attracted people. The cult of Grace Kelly. They were coming to Monaco like the Arabs came to Mecca. It was a pilgrimage of the affluent to Monaco. Grace grabbed all the successful people to come and everybody wanted to be there. That was *the* spot. She did it."

Yet Grace was far from being just a magnet for tourists or a mere figurehead of the principality. During the sixties, she employed both her creativity and her humanity in the service of Monaco, introducing to the principality a variety of innovations that enhanced the lives of the Monegasques.

Thanks to Grace, every Monegasque mother giving birth in the principality is sent a medal commemorating the birth, and at Christmas all Monegasque children receive one toy and one item of clothing as a gift from the Grimaldis.

Due to Grace, Monaco now has an International Television Festival, and, after she became honorary president of the World Association of Friends of Children, she founded Notre Dame de Fatima, a day nursery for the children of working Monegasque mothers.

In 1964, she created the Foundation of Princess Grace, which supported young dancers, and in order to encourage local artists and craftsmen, she acquired two shops in the principality in which local crafts and works of art are sold.

She created Monaco's International Bouquet Show, became president of the Association of the Welfare of Children, founded the Garden Club of Monte Carlo and the International Arts Festival of Monte Carlo, played an active part in the La Leche League—encouraging mothers to breast-feed— and founded the Académie de Danse Princesse Grace.

With the arrival of Grace—and her Hollywood star power—the International Red Cross Ball became a world-class high-society extravaganza, a draw for the rich and famous flooding into Monte Carlo in their Rollses and Ferraris, with their valets and maids, their glittering jewels, couture gowns, furs, and ever-expanding bank accounts.

Grace didn't merely initiate events. With a military efficiency and an attention to detail, perhaps stemming from her German background, "She organized all the big SBM events, like the Red Cross Ball, all the other big parties—and never missed anything," Bernard Combemal reported in admiration. "She had the most amazing sense, we redid all the SBM china for L'Hermitage. The serving plates featured a woman in a crinoline, carrying a parasol. Grace immediately saw that the padding was too big in the back. She had us reduce it and had the parasol tilted at a different angle because she thought it would look better. She had an eye. This didn't take hours, she just looked. She never said, 'I want.' She always said, 'Don't you think?' She was never confrontational.

"For example, the Monte Carlo Opera cannot make money because there are only five hundred seats and the price of those doesn't cover the cost of a production," he continued. "So you have a loss. Once in a while, though, you put on something less expensive. Consequently, I put on a program based on an opera by a Danish composer but done on tape instead of by live orchestra.

The music was taped, but it was not disturbing, and I thought the performance was entertaining.

"When Princess Grace came downstairs from her box after the performance, I was waiting at the foot of the stairs and said, 'Well, ma'am, what did you think?' And she said, 'Mmmm . . . but it's time to say good night.' I gathered she hadn't liked it, but she didn't make long speeches.

"She was charming. And she was so beautiful. Sometimes she would ask me to come to the palace at eight o'clock in the morning to discuss something that needed to be dealt with urgently. She would receive me in a marvelous housecoat. Very proper and very elegant, but without any makeup and she was ravishing. Her skin! I thought she looked more beautiful without any makeup than when she was dressed up at night."

She also worked hard at imposing her personal touch on the palace and its staff. She redesigned the maids uniforms in white poplin and also supervised the redecoration of the prince's ground-floor rooms, replacing the dingy furniture with elegant antiques and the faded drapes with more stylish ones. But despite whatever changes she was able to make in terms of the palace furniture and decorations, she was unable to banish archaic customs like the one preventing her from taking her seat at the dinner table until the prince had taken his.

However, thanks to her charm, dedication, and plain hard work, half a decade after her marriage, all the Monegasques' bitter criticisms of her American taste and style had completely subsided, and they—and the rest of the world—fully accepted her as their princess.

"She showed from the first a natural aptitude for being a princess, a quality of belonging that I've found to be rare in people suddenly risen to such a position," famed society hostess Elsa Maxwell noted.

"She was such a great actress that when she married Prince Rainier, she carried on acting the part she had played in *The Swan* just a few years before. She became quite regal," said Reinaldo Herrera, who attended many events in Monaco. "She played the royal very well. She was always sparkly, neat and clean. But she was fun. She could be very raunchy. It wasn't as if she were being vulgar, because it didn't come out vulgar."

Although Rainier may not have been tremendously attached to Grace personally, he acknowledged her taste and intelligence, sometimes even turning to her for advice. It was Grace who prevailed upon Rainier not to permit shady international financier Adnan Khashoggi to base his European head-quarters in Monaco by arguing that the specter of his arms-dealing past would reverberate onto the principality's reputation. When it came to dealing with Aristotle Onassis, the SBM's other big shareholder, Grace was by Rainier's side, socializing with the Greek tycoon.

On August 28, 1960, Tina and Ari Onassis hosted a dinner party on board the *Christina*, then berthed in the harbor and festooned with sparkling lights. That night, Rainier and Grace were guests of honor. The other guests included Greta Garbo, in a print afternoon dress, her eyes shielded by dark glasses; the Maharani of Baroda, as always glittering with priceless jewels; Prince Aldobrandini; Count and Countess Bernadotte; Reinaldo Herrera, and a female British aristocrat.

Grace arrived at the party with her arm in a sling—not an ordinary one, however, but a silk scarf emblazoned with Monaco's coat of arms. Earlier that day, she had been stung by a bee and had suffered an allergic reaction. And while she had forced herself to attend the party, she was pale and clearly in pain, and consequently was far from amused when the British aristocrat—displaying startling enmity toward her—greeted her by sarcastically inquiring, "Did you forget to feed your dog?"

Tension between Grace and the British aristocrat, who was patently envious of Grace, escalated after the aristocrat's dinner partner, Reinaldo Herrera, seeing that Grace was unable to cut her meat because her arm was so swollen, cut it for her.

Overcome by jealousy that Reinaldo was paying so much attention to Grace, the aristocrat muttered that Reinaldo was cutting it "for your bitch." Grace and Rainier left the party early, disembarking at midnight.

At the time of the abortive party, Onassis was having an extramarital relationship with renowned opera star Maria Callas. And while contemporaneous newspaper reports claimed that Grace was scandalized by Onassis's affair with Maria and intended to banish her from Monaco, nothing could have been farther from the truth. From the start, Grace liked and admired the legendary diva, a New Yorker of Greek origin and as much a star in her arena as Grace once was in Hollywood.

"I think Maria Callas is a very great artist, and as a person I find her to be a nice, warm and very honest, forthright person. She says what she thinks and what she feels, which is a quality I admire very much," Grace confided to *Playboy*. Then, when asked if she did the same, in a revealing comment, she replied, "Not quite as openly, perhaps."

She had great admiration and respect for Maria's talent, and on December 7, 1960, she and Rainier attended the glittering opening of La Scala, witnessing Callas's bravura performance in Donizetti's *Poliuto*.

From that time on, she made sure to attend as many of Maria's opening nights as possible, including her *Norma*, which she viewed from the royal box, along with the Onassises and the Aga Khan.

Grace's relationship with Onassis, however, had not always been so cordial. She had first met the Greek tycoon when she was on the Riviera making *To Catch a Thief* and he invited Cary Grant and Betsy Drake for dinner on the *Christina*, and she came too. According to Hollywood mythology, Onassis hadn't recognized Grace, instead assuming that she was Cary's secretary, and later complimented him on how good-looking she was.

Whatever the truth of that story, in the wake of Onassis's ostentatious welcome to Grace—showering the *Constitution* with red and white carnations as the ship sailed into Monaco harbor—Grace and Onassis were finally formally introduced.

After she returned from her honeymoon—slightly appalled that the palace did not yet have a swimming pool—she reluctantly took to accepting Onassis's invitations onto the *Christina* where she could swim to her heart's content in the massive pool which, in the evening, was transformed into a discotheque, then electronically raised to deck level.

The *Christina*, then the world's most luxurious yacht, also boasted two gourmet chefs, a fireplace fashioned from lapis lazuli, a formal dining room furnished with priceless French antiques, not to mention what for Onassis was the pièce de résistance, bar stools upholstered in the skin of a whale's penis, affording him the opportunity of informing unsuspecting guests that "you are sitting on the world's biggest penis."

While Grace had always adored swashbuckling self-made men, she required that they possess some varnish and consequently wasn't attracted to Onassis. He, on the other hand, definitely was attracted to her. "Onassis unquestionably made a pass at Grace," said *Nemesis* author Peter Evans, who collaborated with him on his autobiography. "He made a pass at all women, looked on all of them as potential mistresses. It would be inconceivable if he had not made a pass at Grace. But she rejected him."

By 1961, now that Onassis's relationship with Maria was out in the open, Grace was finally able to relax in his presence and he was now invited to lunch or dinner at the palace twice a month.

Although Grace still had a tendency to suffer from seasickness, mollified by the *Christina*'s stabilizers, she agreed to go on a four-day cruise with Rainier, Maria, and Onassis to Palma, Majorca, to attend the opening of the Hotel Son Vida, in which Rainier had invested.

At a party at the hotel that night, thrown in the ornate ballroom, Onassis sang love songs, Elsa Maxwell accompanied him on the piano, Callas played the maracas, Rainier banged the drums, and Grace conducted the motley little orchestra.

The following morning, they all attended a bullfight in the Plaza de Toros, during which, to Grace's horror, Rainier suddenly jumped over the railing and made a mock charge at the bull.

Whether she was so disturbed by his combination of recklessness and macho exhibitionism or the plans had already been made, during the voyage back to Monte Carlo, she requested that the boat stop so that she could go ashore in France and, from there, join a two-day pilgrimage to Lourdes.

Later that same year, she boarded the *Christina* again for a cruise around the Greek islands with Maria and Onassis. "The men visited some of the monestaries [*sic*] at Mt. Athos. Callas and I went as far as the shore and tried to see as much as possible without getting out of the boat . . ." she wrote to Prudy on October 30.

After Maria's relationship with Onassis ended, Maria moved to Paris. Whenever Grace was there, she had dinner at Maria's home every week. "Maria used to be in a depression, and Grace called her a lot. She helped her. She was very loyal to her friends," said Pepita Dupont.

By 1963, the friendship between Onassis, and the Grimaldis had begun to cool considerably. "Onassis wanted to use the SBM for his own business purposes, which were totally legitimate, but his point of view was totally different from the prince's," Bernard Combemal explained. "Prince Rainier wanted to strengthen the principality, strengthen the government and the country's financial structure, but Onassis didn't agree with that."

Worse, after Onassis arrogantly proclaimed that he "only had two toys:

Christina and the SBM," Rainier became increasingly aware that Onassis now considered Monaco to be as much his private fiefdom as was his luxurious yacht, a jet-set playground over which he reigned.

By the midsixties, Rainier was under no illusion about the fact that Onassis's viewpoint on Monaco was diametrically opposed to his own. Unlike Rainier—a forward-thinking Americophile who intended that Monaco become a tourist destination complete with Holiday Inns for middle-class Americans—Onassis firmly believed that Monaco should cater to the three thousand wealthiest individuals on the planet and that the principality's aura of exclusive opulence should be preserved at all costs.

"Onassis was more interested in maintaining a kind of nineteenth-century Monaco. He wanted to be the prince of Monaco himself," Bernard Combemal said.

Paradoxically, it was Onassis, the nouveau riche pirate—not the head of its ruling family, whose reign went back seven centuries—who was far more attached to Monaco's glittering past than to modernizing the principality and dragging it into the twentieth century.

"Onassis didn't want to expand the casino and fill it with one-armed bandits," observed Taki. "But Rainier wanted to change things and make Monte Carlo extremely profitable for his subjects. I sided with Onassis because I wanted to keep the place exclusive. But I think in the long run, Rainier was right."

Rainier launched his fight against Onassis during his New Year's address, in which he made a veiled attack on the SBM's shortcomings, attributing them in part to Onassis. Onassis failed to rise to the bait. Refusing to be ignored by someone whom he considered to be an upstart, Rainier executed a cunning piece of strategy: exercising his divine right as Monaco's ruler, he created six hundred thousand new shares in SBM, all of which fell under his control, now making him the SBM's chief shareholder.

The piratical self-made entrepreneur had been outwitted by the scion of an effete dynasty. Incandescent with fury, declaring that he had been robbed, Onassis petitioned the Supreme Court, asking it to rule the legislation unconstitutional.

The instant Onassis learned that his petition had failed, he boarded the *Christina* and commanded the captain to set sail. The gilded principality that had shimmered through his teenage dreams, and over which he had once ruled, was now lost to him forever. He returned to Monte Carlo only in the twilight of his years, when he was a broken man, contemplating divorce from Jackie, and gravely sick.

Whenever Grace and Rainier needed a respite from Monaco, they invariably escaped to Rocagel, their haven where Grace delighted in making spaghetti with her own special sauce which, Rita Gam said, "wasn't a particularly unique spaghetti sauce, but she was very proud of it."

In Rocagel, Grace rode horses, had barbecues, and went swimming in the pool that she and Rainier had specially installed.

They also had a spell at the glamorous Splendido, one of Europe's most beautiful hotels, high above Portofino, and a photograph shows them in an informal setting, reveling in the beauty of the place, just like any other vacationers.

On an average day at the palace, Grace's routine began with her getting up by eight, splashing rosewater on her face—a secret she learned from Lady Bateman, who always wintered in Monte Carlo and was eighty years old with beautiful skin—then breakfasting on grilled grapefruit, a boiled egg, and tea without sugar (she never used it, or ate white bread, either).

After making breakfast for Rainier and the children, she answered correspondence in her office, which was furnished in pale green Louis XV furniture, with pale green walls decorated with banners imprinted with comic slogans, including, "In God We Trust. All Others Pay Cash" and "We'd Love to Help You Out. Which Way Did You Come In?" as well as the gold record she and Bing won for their recording of "True Love" from *High Society*.

In her office, every morning she met with her chef, housekeeper, major domo, and gardeners. Her diary was filled six months ahead, so that she constantly had people to receive, meetings to chair, engagements to attend. Occasionally she was able to steal a few moments to relax by doing needlepoint, particularly when she was on planes and at the hairdresser. She also enjoyed solving jigsaw puzzles.

As often as possible, she had lunch with the children or took them to swim in the sea at the Monte Carlo Beach Club—which could be a hazard, as it was open to the public, who practically went into shock if they happened to recognize her underneath her disguise of sunglasses and large scarf.

In the evenings, she read the children the stories of Hans Christian Andersen and Lewis Carroll.

She kept in touch with America by subscribing to *The New York Herald Tribune*, *The New Yorker*, *Architectural Digest*, and *Celebrity Bulletin*, a newsletter that listed the names of visiting celebrities visiting Paris.

Now that Monaco was international society's most beloved destination, there were parties galore. Despite Grace's incipient shyness, she loved them and generally threw herself into the spirit of the evening.

In August 1961, she and Rainier attended Elsa Maxwell's costume ball held to celebrate the opening of the Hôtel de Paris's swimming pool. Both good sports, Rainier wore a bald wig and a Victorian villain's mustache, while Grace wore false braids and flippers. The guests wined, dined, and watched fireworks, and at 4 A.M. went swimming in the newly opened pool.

Yet—her willingness to make an appearance at Monaco's most illustrious social events aside—she was nervous about forming friendships with her Monegasque subjects. As she explained in an interview with Barbara Walters exactly ten years after her wedding, "We are not doing them [her Monegasque subjects] a favor to be friendly with them. Monaco is such a small town that there are inevitable jealousies."

She felt safer making friends among the American ex-pat community living in the region. One of them, her pretty lady-in-waiting Harriet Groote, lived with her husband in a villa in Roquebrune, high above Monaco. "When I used to see Grace up at the Grootes' house, it was like being with any other nice, attractive actress, the sort of person who you were very happy to know," remembered former Saint Paul de Vence resident Ken Annakin, director of *Monte Carlo or Bust*.

She also was friendly with Texas socialite Lynn Wyatt, who kept a house in Cap Ferrat and threw a Texan barbecue in her honor, at which Grace—in a cowboy outfit like the other guests—did the square dance with gusto, though Rainier refused to join her on the dance floor.

Then there was Jeanne Kelly Van Remoortel, a vivacious Southern belle whom Grace first met during her New York days, and whose maid of honor she was in 1962, when Jeanne married Edward Van Remoortel, conductor of the Monte Carlo Symphony.

Jeanne, owner of The Texan, Monaco's Tex-Mex restaurant, remembered, "Grace owned a London taxi, and she and I used to put our bicycles in the back, then Grace's driver, Paul Raimondi, would drive us into the countryside where we'd get out and bicycle.

"Once, though, we gave Raimondi the slip. He took us to Nice and thought we'd gone into a little shop. But we sneaked out and into Galeries Lafayette. But everyone recognized Grace, and started to gather round in a mob, so we hid under a counter until the security guards rescued us. Grace was scared to death," she noted.

"Rudolf Nureyev was also a great friend and had a farm close to Rocagel. He would often come to dinners there with Grace and Rainier. Grace and I used to bicycle up to his place, as she liked him very much and loved to dance with him."

Jeanne was sometimes the target of Rainier's somewhat crude sense of humor. She remembered one night when she and Grace and Rainier "went out to dinner with an Arab friend called Khalil something or other. He was in Monaco a lot, and every time he'd see Grace, he'd give her a piece of jewelery. She usually didn't wear much jewelery at all. She'd wear a strand of pearls, only. Or a pair of earrings only.

"That night, though, as a joke, she came to dinner wearing beads, diamonds, broaches, rings, bracelets—every single piece of jewelry that Khalil had ever given her. Rainier turned to me and said, 'Darling, give me your hand. I don't want you to feel left out.' He put on my finger a gold band that said on it 'F——" Jeanne laughingly recalled, adding, "The prince wasn't an easy person, but he was lovable. And he was crazy about her."

Greta Garbo was also one of Grace's great friends, and she and Grace would lunch alone together by the palace pool. "Princess Grace would listen as Miss Garbo began to talk, at first haltingly as if she were not used to expressing herself, and then more animatedly," remembered Serge Fliegers. The conversation between the former Grace Kelly, the Hollywood star who retired in her prime, and Greta Garbo, the Hollywood star who retired in hers, must have been fascinating.

Some of the British residents of Monaco and the surrounding region were also among her closest friends. "Grace was never royal when she came to the house," asserts Doreen Hawkins. "She always invited me when she was opening art galleries and would always kiss me and be very sweet and casual."

British author Anthony Burgess, who with his Italian wife lived near L'Hermitage, was a friend and, before his death, remembered Grace with fondness: "My last memory is of her composing Irish songs to play and sing at the James Joyce Centennial banquet. I was at the piano and she was leaning over it. Her beauty and vivacity were never meant to be awesome, but, despite her friendliness, they always were." Before her death, however, his praise of her was mixed with a degree of cynicism. "Princess Grace was more gracious and royal than any of the British royal family, except for Princess Di. But then she was a trained actress," he said.

In the years that lay ahead of her, Grace would need every iota of acting ability at her disposal.

16

True Love

In January 1962, debonair English actor David Niven, Academy Award winner for *Separate Tables*, bought Lo Scoglietto, a two-story seven-bedroom villa on its own peninsula in Cap Ferrat, directly across the bay from Monte Carlo. From the time that he moved there, his relationship with Grace, which dated back to Hollywood in the late forties, flourished and endured until her death.

Niven has always been identified as having been an extremely minor element in Grace's romantic past, with James Spada claiming in his biography of her that she and Niven had "a brief and very discreet affair" in the spring of 1955. None of her subsequent biographers mentioned her relationship with Niven at all.

Broaching the subject of Grace's affair with Niven during their time in Hollywood, after citing Spada, Niven's authorized biographer, Graham Lord, wrote, "Several of Niv's friends—Leslie Bricusse, Bryan Forbes, John Mortimer—told me they thought so too, and Tom Hutchinson told me that Niv had once said to him that Grace was, 'a very ardent lover.'"

Niven, a brilliant raconteur, gloried in telling Sir John Mortimer and other friends the story of attending a palace dinner during which Rainier demanded to know which woman out of all his Hollywood romances was most accomplished at sex. "Gracie," David blurted, then immediately realizing what he said, amended his comment to "Gracie Fields."

Like all Grace's previous biographers, apart from Spada, I concluded that it wasn't worth devoting space to Grace's brief relationship with Niven. Reasoning that everything there was to say about Niven's insubstantial affair with her had been said, I categorized him as a bit player in her life and did not intend ever raising Niven's name with sources who knew Grace well. There were far too many other fascinating topics to explore.

Then, over lunch with an old show business friend in London, I mentioned that I was about to begin researching Grace Kelly's biography. Her immediate reaction was to blurt out, "David Niven! Are you going to write about David Niven? He and Grace were in love right through her marriage to Rainier and until the end of her life. I have letters from David talking about how much he loved Grace and how much she loved him," she said.

At the time, still working as a journalist, I was assigned by the *Mail on Sunday* to interview Schuyler Johnson, the daughter of Van and Evie Johnson, for a feature about her Hollywood childhood. During that interview, I mentioned to Schuyler that I was researching a biography of Grace Kelly. This was her immediate reaction: "My mother knew David Niven very well, and she knew Grace as well. She told me that they really were in love. It was a last hurrah for both of them. It wasn't just a fling. It went on for many years, until her death."

"I believe David Niven was Grace's lover right through her marriage to Rainier. I believe they remained lovers, I really do," said Peter Evans, one of Niven's friends.

"David Niven was a light in Grace's life," Rita Gam said.

"I would say that David must have been a very, very lucky guy. I would say that it was a love affair till the end. They loved each other," said director Ken Annakin, who was close to Niven, before adding a proviso, "but I think both of them were sensible enough that they wouldn't have done anything at that time in their lives in Cannes and Monte Carlo where they could be caught."

"David Niven spent quite a few evenings with Grace in Paris and was charming and wonderful just like in the movies. Grace loved him," said Robert Dornhelm. "They were very close, very good friends."

"David was one of Grace's closest friends. He was very fond of her," said Phil Kellogg, his friend and sometime agent.

David's younger son, Jamie, who was fifteen years old when David moved to Cap Ferrat, confirmed that his father and Grace were extremely close, but added, "My father was very protective of both Grace and Rainier. He was extremely loyal. I don't think my father and Grace had a love affair while she was married to Prince Rainier, I really don't believe that. I just don't think it is true. I would know.

"My father had a lot of lady friends. He would go out and shoot a movie and be gone for long periods of time. He pretty much told me everything in his life. I was, without a doubt, very close to my father. There wasn't a thing we didn't discuss. I mean, everything. I knew about all the finances, all the deals, and all the relationships. It's not possible. It just wasn't the case. I think it would have been lovely if it had been true. I really, really loved Grace," he said.

Jamie's brother, David Jr., said that he believes that his father and Grace had a platonic relationship. "They definitely loved each other and were very, very close to each other."

With sources divided as to whether, during her marriage to Rainier, Grace and David Niven were friends or lovers, it is still worth charting the course of their relationship, as well as the importance of Niven—who was nineteen years her senior—in her life.

Their relationship began when Grace was launching her Hollywood career. "I always used to see Grace in the MGM canteen all the time. She was always with that British actor, David Niven," recalled George Jacobs, who worked as an extra at the studio during the early fifties.

"I first met Grace in the early fifties when she used to visit my father at his house on Amalfi Drive in Pacific Palisades," remembered David Niven Jr.

"David told me he had an affair with Grace in Hollywood," reported distinguished *Rumpole of the Bailey* author Sir John Mortimer. "He loved her," Lady Mortimer added.

At the time of moving to Cap Ferrat in 1962, Niven had been married to Swedish actress Hjordis Niven for fourteen years. A strikingly attractive woman, Hjordis had a strong personality but was a borderline alcoholic and led the even-natured Niven a merry dance and in the process alienated many of his closest friends. All except Grace, whom Hjordis considered to be her best friend.

According to David Niven Jr., "At first, Hjordis and Grace were friends and they used to play canasta together, but then Hjordis got tricky. During the difficult years, you didn't know whether she was going to turn up for lunch or not, and she was so tricky that people would say, 'Let her stay in her room and not come down.' My father's marriage to Hjordis was a nightmare."

"Grace was very friendly with Hjordis Niven. No one could understand why Grace would bother with her. She was an alcoholic," said Bernard Combemal.

"Grace wasn't nice about Hjordis, she wasn't nice about her at all," said

Gwen Robyns. "She said, 'She is terrible. She drinks too much.' I said, 'look at that wonderful hair.' Grace said, 'That's not her hair. That's a series of wigs.' Hjordis wasn't her best friend at all."

Talking to Graham Lord about Grace's friendship with Hjordis, Lauren Bacall, who knew Hjordis well, said that she thought it was "all to do with men because Grace Kelly was very active with men and I think that's what Hjordis wanted."

According to credible sources, Hjordis was wildly unfaithful to David. In a dazzling irony, one of her lovers in the early sixties was Grace's old flame, President John F. Kennedy.

"Hjordis told Grace about her infatuation with Kennedy. She told her, me, and no one else," Hjordis's friend Pat Medina Cotten said. "She was giving Grace the guts to go away and have a go on her own. I'm not sure that Grace didn't catch a little of Hjordis's infidelity," she added, insinuating that Grace followed Hjordis's example, but not necessarily with David.

David was kind, witty, charming, intelligent, and wildly attractive to women. He had a colorful romantic past that included sharing a house, dubbed "Cirrhosis by the Sea," with swashbuckling actor Errol Flynn. Together the two men cut a swathe through countless winning Hollywood women. Through the years David was linked with a series of beautiful women, but Grace was always close to his heart.

From the moment that he moved to Cap Ferrat, he spent a great deal of his life interacting with her on a variety of levels.

According to his friend Peter Evans, "We were having lunch at David's beautiful house across the bay from Monte Carlo one day, and he told me that he had brought the house for £10,000 but couldn't understand why the bargain was so good. Then he discovered the reason why he got it so cheaply was because developers were going to build up the bay across from the house and destroy the view. He was horrified. He told me he didn't know what to do about it, so he called Grace. And Grace said, 'Leave it with me.' And she had the whole development plans scrapped."

Jamie Niven, however, said that Grace did no such thing, and that David—along with his neighbors—had fought the development through conventional channels, petitioning local authorities to have it scotched.

David may not have disclosed to Jamie the whole story of Grace's intervention; he was famous for sacrificing the truth in quest of embellishing his stories. So while Grace may not have intervened with the developers on his behalf, it is interesting that he wanted Peter Evans, then an important show business editor, to believe that she had.

On one occasion, in an amusing incident recounted to Graham Lord by journalist Roddy Mann, "David said, 'We are going out to dinner in Monte Carlo but I want to pick a chum up.' A chum! It was Grace, and I fell instantly in love with her. She was adorable, a knockout, and they were huge friends. So we were charging around Monte Carlo in the dark and he gets lost and goes up a one-way street and Grace said, 'David, you'll get into trouble, it's a one way street.' And he said, 'How can we get into trouble? You own this place.' "

On a more serious note, Roddy Mann confided to Graham Lord, "I think Grace was lonely for friendship in Monaco, and Rainier was a dull man."

"We called Hjoridis 'Jaundice,' " remembered David's friend Sir John Mortimer who, with his wife, Penny, went to a dinner with David at Rocagel. "David used to take us out of the house to avoid being with her. We were all invited to Rocagel but Jaundice didn't go," Sir John said.

"Before we went to Rocagel, David seemed slightly worried about how I would behave because I was unconventional," remembered Lady Mortimer. "He said to me, 'Grace would love it if you could bring yourself to drop a little curtsey.' When we got there, she was sort of serene, correct, slightly grand, with her hair in a bun and the whole dinner was quite formal. Grace had a grandness about her."

"Grace and Rainier didn't seem to be talking to each other much," said Sir John, adding, "Rainier seemed to me to be a totally artificial person, talking in an old public school English. When he offered me a drink, he said, 'Would you have a jar, old bean?' He talked like Niven talked."

Even when Grace was away from Monaco traveling, she and David still met. "When we were in Lausanne in 1977, Grace said, 'Let's go to see David Niven in Gstaad,' " *Children of Theatre Street* choreographer Oleg Briansky remembered.

Rainier liked David so much that he was prepared to endure him and Grace trading Hollywood reminiscences. "David and Grace both shared a nostalgia for the old Hollywood studios and a certain regret for the glamor of the days that had totally gone from California in the 1960s," Rainier said. "She and Hjordis always got on very well together, but David was one of the few men I could simply ring up and say, 'come over for dinner tonight.' "

While David relished the pomp and circumstance of Monaco, most of the time Grace—either with or without Rainier—visited him in Cap Ferrat. As his official biographer Graham Lord put it, "His social life was full and he spent a great deal of time with the Rainiers and often with Grace alone."

"I think what gave Grace an enormous sense of comfort was the ability to leave the palace and her house at Rocagel and come down to our house," Jamie Niven said. "The house was always full of people who were in the movie business, therefore the talk around the table was always about Hollywood or *Variety*. There was no one there from the outside. There she was again amongst people who were Hollywood.

"I think of her as being someone who was really close to our family because she was there a lot with my father and stepmother," Jamie recalled. "She and my stepmother were very close. My father was also very close to Rainier and very close to Grace. I remember that all of the couples, they were around the most.

"Rainier was a really funny man. I saw him less than I saw her. He loved my shenanigans. I was a wild boy and he loved the idea that I was this wild kid letting it rip in the South of France. He would always say, 'How's it going? Who are you doing these days?'

"I used to love seeing Grace. I just couldn't wait for her to come over," Jamie went on. "She genuinely made you feel she cared about you. She was a wonderful person. I adored her. I thought she was just great. She was kind, thoughtful, and was wonderful to me. I saw her a lot because she used to come to my father's house a great deal.

"As I got older, if she needed an extra man for one of her nieces from Philadelphia, she would ask me to sit at their table at the Red Cross Ball. When the American Olympic swimming team came to Monaco, she invited me to lunch with them, and also when the Yale chorus came over and sang in the palace garden. I am a Scorpio so Grace would always invite me to her Scorpio party every year.

"I always looked forward to her coming to the house and sitting up by the pool with her. I could sit and talk with her about anything. I married someone from Philadelphia, and we talked about that a lot. My wife was Main Line Philadelphia, and Grace said, 'I didn't grow up the way your wife grew up.'

"Before Grace died, my father got really ill and was too sick to go to her funeral. When she died, he was devastated. He called me and was very, very upset. They were really, really close."

"When Grace used to come to our house in the South of France it was a sort of summer camp for her, in a way. It was totally relaxed there," David Jr. remembered. "If they were having a romance, I don't know where the hell they would have gone. They couldn't do it in Daddy's house and they couldn't do it in the palace and the two of them couldn't check into a hotel. But it is always possible that they met in the house of a third party. They loved each other. But you can love someone without physically doing the deed.

"I don't think their relationship was sexual. They had a number of things in common. They had both won their Academy Awards, were both living in the South of France, were part of the old Hollywood thing, and had both moved out of Hollywood. And were both very glamorous. And they lived ten minutes apart." As Arlene Dahl recalls, "David Niven kept her laughing. God knows she loved to laugh. David was one of the cornerstones of her loves over the years."

17

Hollywood Comeback

On January 23, 1961, Caroline celebrated her fourth birthday with a party at the palace for eleven children. Already aware of her royal prerogatives, and showing early talent at ballet, she had taken to telephoning her father in his office each night, chidingly reminding him that it was late and she was waiting for him to say good night to her before she went to bed.

On February 26, Grace was distraught when Oliver, whom she had taken on vacation with her to their chalet in Schonreid, was involved in a fight with a rabid dog and mauled to death. "As you can imagine I am a wreck as it has been such a dreadful shock. . . . I am grateful at least that he [the dog] didn't go after one of the children but we will miss Oliver so terribly," she wrote to Prudy the very next day.

By June, she had recovered from her sad loss and, full of joy, prepared for her first state visit abroad—a trip to Ireland, her ancestral home, an experience that she would later term one of the most profound of her life.

Arriving at Shannon airport, Grace—fittingly dressed in a shamrock green Dior suit—was mobbed by a crowd of twenty thousand, all desperate for a glimpse of the woman they considered to be the most beautiful and famous Irish colleen of them all.

During all the official and unofficial celebrations that followed, and in the press coverage thereof, no mention was made that Princess Grace was only half Irish. As always, there was not even a whisper of her German heritage.

At Dublin's Gresham Hotel, where Grace and Rainier began their stay in Ireland, attending a banquet and ball, the tumultuous crowds went so wild and, intent on seeing Grace for even a second, jostled so violently that some of them were injured and ended up being rushed to hospital.

In County Cork, Grace and Rainier were mobbed again, and in County Kerry, then in County Mayo, where Grace visited the thatched cottage from where her grandfather John Henry Kelly had embarked on his pilgrimage to America. There, at Drimurla, Grace was served Irish tea and scones by the cottage's new owner, Ellen Mulchrone, met her cousin Paddy Quine, a boat builder, and must have marveled at how far the Kelly family had come. Inexpressibly moved, Grace demonstrated her attachment to her Irish roots fifteen years later when, after Mrs. Mulchrone died, she bought the cottage for £8,000.

In Ireland, too, she purchased from a retired Irish diplomat five hundred books—all written by Irishmen—which would become the basis of Monaco's Princess Grace Irish Library, opened in 1984 and now housing more than eight thousand books, part of her enduring legacy.

In a startling December 1961 *Cosmopolitan* feature, Maurice Zolotow ripped away what he called "a silken curtain of myth" that he claimed had begun "to descend around Grace Kelly."

Zolotow, who had known her well during her Hollywood years, reported, "She was now only to be seen filtered through the distorting screens of high-powered public relations. There would always be publicity men at her side, guiding the questions, dictating the answers, slowly creating an image of a woman that is partly true and partly fictional, and suppressing so much of the untold truth."

Citing friends "in and out of the palace," Zolotow went on to write that she was suffering from "an almost neurotic fear of crowds and hates to meet strangers..."

He described her as "a sleepless woman who wanders often during the long nights through the silent corridors of the palace, a prey to insomnia and ennui.... She hates the climate of Monaco.... When the hot winds blow across the Mediterranean, she becomes depressed and gloomy and does not talk much."

In another passage, equally evocative of her unhappiness, Zolotow described her as "a shy, self-conscious, introverted, oversensitive human being. A friend told me that Grace suffers for days before any large public banquet or great social event in or away from Monaco. She can't eat. She can't sleep. She is tormented by it all.

"Grace has been so utterly wretched that she's prayed to get very sick so she could get out of the responsibility. She hates all the rigmarole she has to put up with. Besides being very nervous—and it always goes to her stomach when she gets emotional and can't eat—she is also horribly bored by it all." Zolotow's article also contained the revelation that she "so often finds her existence so aimless and empty and longs to be acting again in motion pictures."

The following month, she confided to Prudy, "I was completely worn out and literally falling apart. Eye troubles, tummy troubles, etc."

Although she recovered somewhat after she and the children had a brief vacation in Switzerland, Rainier—who had not traveled with them—was so concerned about her deteriorating physical and mental state that he made the revolutionary decision to permit her to make a Hollywood comeback.

Thus it was that on March 18—with no prior warning—his spokesman made the sudden shock announcement that "Princess Grace has accepted to appear during her summer vacation in a motion picture for Mister Alfred Hitchcock to be made in the United States. The Princess has previously starred in three movies for Mr. Hitchcock (*Dial M for Murder, Rear Window* and *To Catch a Thief*). The movie to start in late summer is based on a suspense novel by the English writer Winston Graham. It is understood that Prince Rainier will most likely be present during part of the film making depending on his schedule and that Princess Grace will return to Monaco by the beginning of November."

The night before the announcement was made, wildly happy and excited, Grace rushed into her office and presented her personal assistant with a large box of chocolates, warning her to be prepared for an onslaught of press enquiries the following morning. She was thrilled. Not since her wedding day had she looked so radiant.

However, while Rainier may have approved Grace's return to movies, in interviews given at the time, his ambivalence was obvious. "She is merely spending part of her time in America making a film for an old friend," he told Donald Zec. "She is not making a comeback. There will be no Hollywood ballyhoo for her. And she will not undertake the role if it is cheap or superficial—any more than I would approve it."

On a patronizing note, in another interview he went so far as to describe

Grace's participation in Hitchcock's upcoming movie, *Marnie*, as "my little holiday treat" and, in the same patriarchal tones, went on, "I love lots of golf on holiday and that does not interest her very much. I know she would like to see whether she can still act as well in the way that took her to the top. She spent a great deal of time and effort in establishing her career and winning an Oscar—then she gave it all up to marry me. Mind you, she has been sweet enough not to bother me about it, knowing I have had plenty of worry and troubles of my own."

More troubles and worries were ahead, both for Rainier and Grace, once the Monegasques digested the news that she was about to make a Hollywood comeback.

"In a flood of letters and petitions, the citizens of Monaco protested at the prospect of seeing their princess in love scenes," said Patrick McGilligan, author of *Alfred Hitchcock: A Life in Darkness and Light.*

"At first, Rainier thought Grace making *Marnie* was a great idea. Then the reaction came in from three thousand five hundred Monegasques who refused to see her being kissed onscreen. So Rainier changed his mind and said she couldn't do it after all," said Rita Gam.

"She never thought for one moment that she wasn't going to go back to acting. And when she found out she couldn't do *Marnie*, she was undone and we talked about it. I told her there wasn't much she could do about it. This was a bargain she had made. And she didn't believe it at first. She was really unhappy about that. She missed acting very much. I think that was a black hole in her life," Rita said.

Laura Richardson adds, "Don showed me Grace's letters so I got the impression that when she married Rainier she thought she could go back and forth between two worlds—Monaco and Hollywood. I knew she wasn't happy in Monaco or in the marriage."

Had Grace been permitted to accept Hitchcock's offer of Marnie—the role ultimately played by Tippi Hedren—she would have portrayed a kleptomaniac struggling to overcome her frigidity.

In the movie's most explicit scene, Sean Connery, playing Marnie's husband, bangs on the door of her bedroom. After reluctantly opening the door clad only in a small bath towel, Marnie declares, "I want to go to bed."

"So do I, so do I very much," Sean Connery says, before ripping the towel from her body and forcing himself on her.

Watching that scene in *Marnie*, enacted by the darkly handsome Sean Connery, then in his macho prime and exuding raw, animalistic sexuality, one can only conclude that in offering Grace the part of Marnie, Hitchcock was being supremely sadistic. Princess Grace—the world's foremost Catholic princess, married to the ruler of Monaco—could never, by any stretch of the imagination have played Marnie. That Hitchcock offered her the part can be explained only as a cruel and heartless practical joke, not too far removed from the one he once played on an impoverished cameraman—paying him to spend the night chained to a camera and, after chaining him up, feeding him a drink laced with laxative.

The fact that Grace agreed to star in *Marnie* says everything about her burning desire to return to Hollywood. That Rainier endorsed her decision speaks only of his lack of attention to her life in general.

After she was compelled to reject Hitchcock's offer, those around her were intensely aware of her sadness. "She was shocked beyond all measure . . . and in grave danger of breaking down," revealed Rainier's close aide Georges Lumkowski.

"Caroline told me that when her mother learned that she couldn't be in the movie, she locked herself in her room, cried for a week, and wouldn't come out," said Pepita Dupont. "She was very artistic and needed an expression for this, but Rainier took away everything she wanted to express herself. He caged her. She was a bird in a gilded cage."

"Just knowing Grace and Rainier, I thought from the beginning that theirs was a fraught relationship," Donald Zec said. "My feeling is that she delivered up to a point the thing that Rainier wanted, which was great for him but not for her. She had a longing for the roar of the crowd. I think the dream faded more rapidly than she would have wanted."

"She lived in a terribly small world. I really felt that. It was like suffocation, in a way," said Doreen Hawkins, "but she knew what she was doing. She wasn't a quitter."

"I sometimes used to have dinner with Grace at the palace," recalled Lesley Blanch. "I think Grace tried to be idealistic, but I understood from a great friend of mine, her press attaché Rupert Allan, that she became very unhappy—although she never made her sadness public."

On February 21, 1963, Grace wrote to Prudy Wise complaining, "I have not been feeling too well . . . was very tired when we arrived and then have had a streppe [*sic*] throat for two weeks." In fact, she was pregnant with her third child, but after four months she miscarried, on July 9, 1963, writing to Prudy Wise in sorrow, "It was a terrible experience and has left me shaken both mentally and physically."

One of her few consolations, it seemed, was seeing visiting Hollywood stars. In 1963, John Wayne moored his yacht in Monaco for the night. It was after midnight when Wayne, his wife, and their daughter, Aissa, were woken by a crew member: " 'It's Princess Grace!' he announced. 'It's Princess Grace! She's coming on board.'

"Running to the mirror, my father said, 'Jesus.' He was positively rattled. Rushing to peel off his pajamas, his thick fingers fumbling at the little buttons, he finally cursed and quit in exasperation. While my mother lagged behind a little longer, John Wayne marched out to greet the Princess of Monaco, wearing his silk pajamas hidden under his clothes," his daughter remembered.

Making a surprise visit to John Wayne's yacht was not Grace's only attempt to recapture the glory of her Hollywood past. In 1963, Marlon Brando spent a few weeks on the Riviera filming *Bedtime Story*. *Brando Unzipped* author Darwin Porter reported Edie Van Cleve as telling him, "I know for a fact that Marlon and Grace slipped off together to spend at least two secret weekends together on the French Riviera when she was reigning over Monaco." "Two secret weekends" may have been an exaggeration—and was clearly an impossibility on the Riviera, given Grace's status and high visibility—but as Brando consistently confided in Van Cleve, it is highly likely that he and Grace had some sort of a romantic reunion, however brief.

Another former flame, Tony Curtis, also visited Grace in Monte Carlo, and although their encounter was not romantic, he was aware of her longing for her old life. "She asked me if Dominic's was still the restaurant of choice in Hollywood," he remembered in his autobiography. "I said yes. Dominic's was a little chop house on Beverly Boulevard. Another time, she said, 'Do you still go dancing?' I said, yes, and she asked me what places were still around from the old days, and I said, 'Well, Mocambo for one.' She looked up and away and just said, 'I remember Mocambo,' with a wistful tone in her voice."

While Grace loved and missed Hollywood desperately, she was clearly beguiled by certain elements of European society, in particular the British royal family, and, one of its senior members, Lord Louis Mountbatten, First Sea Lord of the Admiralty, former Viceroy of India, a great-grandson of Queen Victoria. She claimed to have kept a photograph of him in his white naval uniform right next to her bed before her marriage to Rainier.

When she finally met Mountbatten, she told him about the photograph. Mountbatten was utterly disarmed, and from that moment on was besotted by her.

"As we'd heard from others who knew them, Prince Philip and, particularly, Lord Mountbatten were a little gaga over Gracie," Judith Balaban Quine said. "Mountbatten was always making passes at Grace," Jeanne Kelly Van Remoortel told me.

Grace did not succumb, but that didn't deter Mountbatten or dampen his ardor for her. Perhaps aware that he was too old for her, he was thrilled when his own nephew, Charles, fell for her charms.

On September 15, 1964, he recorded in his diary, "Dinner at the Royal Yacht Club. Prince Charles came to ask me whether I knew Grace, and, on hearing I did, said he particularly wanted to meet her and I promised to fix it. When Grace eventually did arrive, she sat between King Gustav of Sweden and me and I never had a look in for the first twenty minutes, for they never drew breath talking to each other. Then I had a dance with Grace and finally brought Charles over to sit next to her. They got on like a house on fire, but every time I suggested, in a whisper, that he should ask her to dance, he was too shy to do so, and he wouldn't let me help him either. So he finally went away without having asked her."

Had Grace known of sixteen-year-old Prince Charles's interest in her, she would have done everything in her power to redirect it toward her daughter Caroline. "In her wildest of dreams, Grace wanted Caroline to marry Charles," Christian de Massy confided. "She liked the British royal family."

"Grace was quite keen that Caroline marry Charles. But when they met, nothing developed between them," Pepita Dupont said.

Grace remained undeterred by her failure to make a match between Caroline and Prince Charles, but still had a yen to make a match between the Grimaldis and the Windsors. According to Christian de Massy, she arranged a blind date between him and Charles's sister, Princess Anne.

Without revealing her intentions, one August day, Grace telephoned de Massy, inviting him to dinner at the Hacienda Restaurant in Roquebrune, cautioning him to be on time. "Grace was very mysterious about the guest of honor," he remembered, noting that she was "an exceptionally good mood."

When Princess Anne finally arrived, Christian discovered that he was to be seated next to her. "I could see Grace checking on me with a twinkle in her eye . . . it was obviously important to her that I represent the family correctly," he said. However, while he and Princess Anne had a pleasant evening, their relationship did not progress.

Not only did Grace's matchmaking efforts fail, but her hopes of making a Hollywood comeback never came to fruition either. Out of the blue, producer Spyros Skouras offered her the role of the Virgin Mary in the epic *The Greatest Story Ever Told*. After being informed that Maria Callas was slated to play Mary Magdalene, Grace reportedly laughed and said, "The Virgin Mary? No way! Mary Magdalene, yes!" knowing full well that her possessive subjects would never countenance her playing either.

That same year, she was pregnant again and almost miscarried, writing to Prudy, "I ate something that gave me terrible intestinal cramps and I was so sick it brought on contractions and I . . . have been practically immobile for a month."

Fortunately, she was able to survive her bout of sickness, carrying her baby to term, and on February 1, 1965, she gave birth to her third child, Stephanie Marie Elisabeth.

"Our Stephanie is a dream—after a difficult pregnancy I was rewarded by a quick and fairly easy birth." Grace wrote to Prudy on March 10.

Stephanie's birth may have been easy, but from the first she was even more willful than Caroline and ran rings around the placid, good-natured Albert. As the Grimaldis' youngest child, she was spoiled, petted, and indulged to a horrifying extent. Grace was so lenient with Stephanie that the child was allowed to scream her head off and even spit at visitors without being reprimanded or punished.

Rainier, too, was impossibly soft with Stephanie, adoring her fiery temperament and making no attempt to curb it. "Stephanie was her daddy's baby. She could get around her mother and father like you couldn't believe," Lizanne told Gwen Robyns.

As Stephanie grew older, Grace began to see her more clearly. "Stephanie is an interesting child, a very interesting child. Quick to learn, gifted, but I'm afraid strong-willed and not easy to handle. In other words, quite a handful!" she said.

Yet, "Grace was insane about her two daughters and called them her 'jewels,'" Laura Richardson remembered.

In September, Grace and Rainier went sailing on Rainier's 133-foot twin-screw diesel cruiser, the *Albecaro*—so named before Stephanie's birth—stopping at the Aga Khan's holiday paradise Porto Cervo in Sardinia, where they picnicked on the beach with the Aga Khan and Princess Margaret and Lord Snowdon, who were vacationing there.

Despite living the high life as Princess of Monaco and queen of the jet set, Grace's social conscience hadn't gone into abeyance and was in evidence during the Vietnam War. Two of her cousins were stationed in Vietnam, and in order to enhance her children's awareness of the suffering there, Grace, Rainier, and all the children each wore a bangle engraved with the name of an American POW. One Christmas during the war she went even farther and invited ten Vietnam veterans to Monaco, where they were guests at the palace.

The following year, she managed to coax Rainier into allowing her to come out of retirement at last. He agreed, simply because *The Poppy Is Also a Flower*, the movie about the evils of drug addiction in which she'd been asked to make a brief appearance, was commissioned by the United Nations Children's Fund.

She took part in the movie for a token fee of $1, insisted on doing her own makeup and said, "It's good to be back."

"She just lit up before the camera," said director Terence Young. "You could tell it was a wonderful and moving moment for her. The extraordinary thing is she looks better today than she ever did. There is an excitement in her face now, a marvelous maturity."

Sadly for Grace, once shooting had ended, the excitement also subsided, leaving her bereft and lonely. At the end of the year, she granted an interview to the ever-perceptive Barbara Walters, who observed, "'Happy' is not the word I would use to describe Princess Grace at all. Nor does she use the word herself. I asked her point-blank before I left, whether she is happy.

"She replied, 'I've had happy moments in my life, but I don't think happiness—being happy—is a perpetual state that anyone can be in. Life isn't that way. But I have a certain peace of mind, yes. My children give me a great deal of happiness. And my life here has given me many satisfactions in the last ten years.'"

Then, on a lighter note, Barbara Walters added, "The happiest I saw Princess Grace during my stay in Monaco was at the much publicized baseball game during American Week. There she was, the usually sedate Regent, in a T-shirt, bobby socks, sneakers and baseball cap, having the time of her life running the bases. She said it was the first time she'd played baseball in twenty years."

On March 31, 1967, Elizabeth Taylor and Richard Burton, who had just completed filming *The Comedians* in Nice, came to the palace for drinks with Grace and Rainier, then to a banquet at the Hôtel de Paris, held in aid of the British American Hospital.

Afterward, Burton recorded in his diary, "He was tubby and smiled kindly and seemed nice. She was pretty and young-looking. Her eyes indeed are terribly weak and at the end of the evening were shot bright with blood."

That same June, Grace was pregnant again, but a month later, while attending Expo 67 in Montreal, she lost the baby. Fortunately, by the end of August she was sufficiently recovered to be photographed at the Red Cross Ball dancing with Bobby Darin and looking radiant once more.

In September, Grace and Rainier attended a masqued charity ball in Venice's Rezzonico Palazzo, mingling with Cornelius Vanderbilt, Elizabeth Taylor, Richard Burton, Rose Kennedy, billionaire J. Paul Getty, and an enfeebled Aristotle Onassis.

"The night before the ball, there was a dinner for twenty. Grace attended, wearing a bejeweled veil and looking beautiful in a gold lamé dress, while Rainier came as a gondolier," remembered society jeweler Kenneth Jay Lane. "I wore a black velvet suit with a lace jabot, with a diamond-encircled ruby pin stuck in the jabot. After dinner, Grace said, 'Oh, my God, Kenny, that's some ruby!' And I said, 'Well, it's a famous ruby. It even has a curse!' 'That's probably why it's raining so hard,' Grace said. So I said, 'Oh, my God, you're right!' We were standing on a balcony overlooking the Grand Canal and I tore the ruby pin out of my shirt and threw it into the canal. Grace was horrified and went, "Oh, oh, oh!' She thought it was real. I told her not to worry, it was only worth fifty cents!"

In the late sixties, too, Grace managed to escape from Monaco and spend a few days in Hollywood, staying at the home of director Mervyn LeRoy and his wife, Kitty. There, she attended a party thrown in her honor by Rupert Allan, at which Rock Hudson was one of the star guests. As Rock recalled to cowriter, Sara Davidson, who went on to publish his autobiography posthumously, "The LeRoys had left the party early and Grace and Rock had stayed on, drinking, until Rock said, 'We were ripped to the tits.' Grace said, 'I can't go back to the LeRoys like this,' and Rock said, 'Let's go to Ollie Hammond's they're open late.' So Grace, in her long gown and Rock in his tuxedo, were shown to a booth at Ollie Hammond's. When the check came, Rock turned to Grace. 'I'm sorry, I don't carry money.'

" 'Princesses don't carry money. I guess we'll have to do the dishes,' Grace said.

"Rock called the manager. 'Neither of us has any money. Could I leave my wallet?'

" 'No, no,' the manager said. 'We're honored to have you as our guests.' "

"Grace told me how shocked she was by the changes in Hollywood," remembered Dominick Dunne, who met her again at Rupert Allan's party. "She missed the old days. I always felt she missed being a movie star. I always felt she was sad. I think she felt underused. She was a star and she needed to shine. After a while it wasn't enough for her to wave at people. That's a six months' kick, but that can't be what life's about once you've achieved what she achieved."

In 1968, when director Ken Annakin requested an audience with Grace to discuss his upcoming movie *Monte Carlo or Bust*, which he was intending to film in Monte Carlo, she jumped at the opportunity to participate, if only behind the scenes.

"She received me in the Throne Room and was as beautiful as one would have expected. She listened to my ideas as a princess rather than an actress," remembered Ken Annakin. "She said, 'I think the film will be very good for the principality. I will explain to Rainier what you need and what you are going to need, and maybe, on your next visit, he will show you his collection of cars.' I said I knew he was a car buff and wondered if he would lend us some of his vintage cars. Smiling, she said she would ask him nearer the day. I left feeling we would be given all the facilities we needed in Monte Carlo. Indeed, for the shooting, Grace was a patron to us.

"We used some of Rainier's cars and he watched some of the shooting. Grace knew very well the pictures I had made. We got on very, very well, not just because I was the director, but for two or three years after—while I was living in Saint Paul de Vence, only a few miles from Monaco—my wife, Pauline, and I, Grace, the children, and her lady-in-waiting Harriet Groote would spend every New Year's Day together. We would have a few drinks, then go for a two- or three-hour walk in the hills, chatting as we walked.

"Grace loved fun, and one year—before we left for the walk—we had a New Year's cake, stuffed with coins and trinkets. In my slice, I found something that said, 'You are King for the Day.' I remember looking across the table and saying to Grace, 'You have to bow to me today because I am king for the day.' She did. She joined in any fun. She was very happy in her situation. I think she felt that she had a fine career in movies and that she was very lucky to finish up with her kids in the palace in Monaco.

"She and Rainier held a wonderful premiere for *Monte Carlo or Bust*. She behaved so nicely and warmly to me. She was a very close friend and I couldn't have asked for anyone to be more helpful to me. She had lovely blue eyes and a nice smile.

"I was closer with Grace, apparently, than my wife was. Grace was a very feminine woman. She responded very well if you attracted her at all. I felt that I attracted her. I am quite sure she always kissed me on both cheeks, which may have spread closer to the mouth...," said Annakin, even almost forty years later sounding slightly love struck.

On March 11, 1968, in a dramatic act of rebellion, Kell abandoned his wife, Mary, and six children and moved into a luxury twenty-seventh-floor Philadelphia penthouse. Like his father before him, Kell had not been a monogamous husband and had finally decided to leave his wife and live a playboy lifestyle. However, despite his having quit the family home, he and Mary stayed married—yet separate—for the next eleven years.

In November, Grace accompanied Rainier to England, where he drove his 1903 De Dion Bouton vintage convertible in the famous London-to-Brighton vintage car rally. Before Rainier set off, ten-year-old Prince Albert, aware that drivers drive on the left in England, took care to stick a note on his father's windshield on which he had drawn a picture of a clown, along with the words, "Don't drive on the right or you will be a clown."

However, although Grace started out riding with Rainier, by the time they had reached the little village of Coulsdon, Surrey, just fourteen miles outside London, she was shivering with cold and got into the bodyguards' car following them, driving to Brighton, where she waited at the finish line for Rainier.

On November 12, 1969, at the end of the decade during which she had suffered so much unhappiness, Grace marked her fortieth birthday by inviting sixty of her closest friends to a lavish Scorpio Ball at the L'Hermitage. The invitations were issued only to fellow Scorpios, or those who were married to or partnered by Scorpios. All the guests were requested to wear the traditional Scorpio color, red.

Grace and the guests celebrated under the watchful eyes of the late, lamented Scorpios Edgar Allan Poe, Auguste Rodin, and Queen Marie Antoinette, whose portraits Grace had specially selected to adorn the ballroom walls in keeping with the theme of the party.

Amid all the glittering festivities, Grace was grappling with an overwhelming sensation of doom and depression. She was about to begin her fifth decade and, partly because whenever she felt unhappy she would drive across the border and gorge herself on Italian pasta, was gaining weight. "She had a thing about her shape. She was always worrying about that. She asked me how I kept so thin," remembered Doreen Hawkins.

Grace was petrified of her once willowy figure turning to fat and began a lifelong battle with her weight, dieting as rigorously as she could and spending fifteen minutes each morning on her exercise bike. Two years later, with her friend Fleur Cowles, she spent a week at Dallas's Greenhouse, where she lost weight but failed to keep it off.

Above all, she knew that her youth was over. "Forty is a marvelous age for a man, but for a woman it's torture, the end. I think turning 40 is miserable. I'm an absolute basket case. I can't stand it. It comes as a great jolt. It really does. It hits one right between the eyes," she admitted to William B. Arthur of the *Daily Sketch*.

She had never been one to wallow in self-pity and she had never been self-centered, so that same year, when she read that black American entertainer Josephine Baker had gone bankrupt and had lost Les Milandes, the home of her Rainbow Tribe of underprivileged children from all over the world, she contacted her, and—with the help of the Red Cross—purchased a villa at Roquebrune, just outside Monaco, for Josephine and the children.

Jean-Claude Baker, Josephine Baker's unofficial adopted son, said, "Princess Grace, a white American, the president of the Red Cross in Monte Carlo, feeling guilty for the way white Americans treated black Americans, reached out her white hand to help a black woman. Princess Grace was a great actress and recognized in Josephine a great professional."

Six years later, in August 1974, Josephine repaid Grace for her kindness and generosity by stepping in when, at the eleventh hour, on the night of the Red Cross Ball, headliner Sammy Davis Jr. suddenly pulled out because he felt snubbed after Grace and Rainier failed to include him in that afternoon's palace tea party thrown for a group of champion tennis players. Josephine replaced him and gave the performance of a lifetime.

The following year, on April 8, 1975, Grace attended her show at the Bobino in Paris. Days after, Josephine collapsed and was rushed to the hospital. "Princess Grace knelt beside the bed, praying, as a priest gave Josephine the last rites," Jean-Claude remembered.

"During Josephine's funeral at the Madeleine, Grace was there, but because of all the press commotion, thought the events of the day were unseemly. From the beginning, Grace had thought the funeral should be held in Monaco, so a compromise had been reached: there would be one funeral in Paris, another—more dignified one—in Monaco. So Josephine's body was flown to Monaco. It always seemed to me that Grace kidnapped it," he said.

"At the funeral in Monaco, Grace handled all the arrangements for the ceremony. No press were allowed in the church. Princess Grace wore black with dark glasses and a single strand of pearls. In the Catholic church, only the coffin of a blue-blooded person can be put to the left of the nave. Grace did something that moved me very much. She put Josephine's coffin there. She gave her a beautiful funeral, with a chorus of young boys singing in her honor."

Josephine's funeral was followed by an unusual train of events. "The funeral in Monaco was in April. By September, Josephine's body was still in the gardener's shack at the cemetery of Monte Carlo. There was a great scandal in the French newspapers because it was one hundred degrees and Josephine's body had been there for five months, unburied. The princess gave an official answer that she was looking for the right black marble for the tomb. Josephine was finally buried on October 2," Jean-Claude said.

18

The Englishman

The seventies marked a new and fraught phase in Grace's marriage. During the first few years of Rainier's reign, the principality had come close to sinking into bankruptcy and obscurity, which could have meant the end of the Grimaldi dynasty. Acting on Aristotle Onassis's advice, Rainier had married Grace partly in order to publicize and glamorize Monaco. That plan had worked its magic.

Thanks to Grace and only Grace—now Monaco's crowning glory—the principality had become wildly fashionable, internationally renowned, and a magnet for tourists flocking there in the hope of catching a glimpse of her from afar, or even of meeting her in person. Because of Grace, tourism was booming in Monaco, and the Grimaldi dynasty had a male heir, alive, well, and flourishing. Consequently, Rainier no longer felt the need to be so vigilant or to concentrate all his energies on the principality.

He was now freer, more relaxed, with time to fully indulge his desires in every aspect. In a great irony, the miracle that Grace had wrought—the wedding that lent Monaco its luster and the prosperity that ensued—was indirectly responsible for undermining and almost destroying the union between her and Rainier.

"In the seventies, so many yachts came to Monte Carlo—Khashoggi's, Sam Spiegel's—all those people invited Rainier onto their yachts," said Dewi Sukarno, the widow of the President of Indonesia, who spent a great deal of time in Monaco during the seventies. "Rainier sailed to St. Tropez on Sam Spiegel's yacht, and there were girls on board that yacht and all the others. I think Rainier was really having fun. He would spend the whole day on a yacht and then would come home and Princess Grace wouldn't have done anything all day. I think she was very, very, very unhappy."

Grace had once told Sydney Guilaroff that she "resolved to build her life around her children and her subjects, and Rainier could do whatever he chose, but discreetly," but now he no longer bothered to hide his infidelities. "In Monte Carlo restaurants, people would point out Rainier's girls," Dewi Sukarno said. "Everybody knew. Everybody talked about it. Everybody. People told Grace about it. Rainier was killing her pride."

Source after source confirmed that starting in the early seventies, Rainier's infidelity was common currency in Monaco.

"Obviously, Rainier had mistresses or the odd girl," said Taki, who spent a great deal of time in Monaco, where he socialized with Grace and Rainier.

"It was common knowledge around the 'in' group in Monte Carlo that her relationship with Prince Rainier was troubled," Yolande Turner, widow of *Network* Oscar-winning actor Peter Finch, wrote in her memoirs. "We knew that her husband had returned to the companions of his bachelor years and excluded the princess from his personal life. Except for their appearances at Royal weddings and charity functions when they presented a united front, their lives were increasingly separate."

"We all knew Rainier was a huge playboy. He always was. He lived a perfectly free life in a perfectly privileged way," Lesley Blanch said.

"Monaco is a very small place, and everybody knows everything. Everybody has said that Rainier was quite a seducer. But at the beginning, the couple was very in love, and then things changed," Pepita Dupont said.

"In the early 1970s, Grace's relationship with Prince Rainier had lost some of its magic. Her marriage had its infidelities," said playboy and television personality Massimo Gargia.

And in a tragicomic irony, as David Niven's friend Sir John Mortimer recalled, "David said that Rainier had asked him to get a flat in Monte Carlo so Rainier could use it for his mistresses." Whether or not David Niven obliged is not on record.

Later in the decade, while strolling through the rose garden with Gwen Robyns, Grace confided, "You know, I have come to feel very sad in this marriage. He's not really interested in me. He doesn't care about me."

Even Grace's loyalest supporters, who always endeavored to mask any unpleasant aspects of her life in Monaco, like Steven Englund, let slip, "Rainier spent much of his spare time on the yacht, while Grace was never happier than walking in the mountains and along the coast, sometimes alone, sometimes with Monsieur Kronlein or a member of the Garden Club, collecting flower cuttings for her collages and enjoying nature."

Moreover, as the loyal and highly protective Judith Balaban Quine admitted, Rainier still erupted in bouts of temper. "Grace had suffered silently over the years on the occasions when he barked at her without reason. She had counted on Rainier's anger subsiding as he aged. But that had not been the case. Instead he grew moodier than ever."

Whenever possible, Grace escaped from the oppressive, hothouse atmosphere of Monaco. In November 1970, she flew to London where, at the Royal Festival Hall, she made her first stage appearance in fourteen years, introducing none other than Frank Sinatra at *The Night of Nights,* a concert in aid of Lord Mountbatten's most cherished charity, United World Colleges.

It all began after Sir Noël Coward, slated to introduce the show, was suddenly taken ill just days before the concert, and Mountbatten's assistant, Jeffrey Archer—later the best-selling author and British politician who fell from office—suggested that Princess Grace would make an ideal replacement. "She had long retired from Hollywood, but that didn't stop Mountbatten," Archer recalled. "So he just called and asked her. No one ever said no to Mountbatten. She immediately said yes, with the proviso that she was informed of all the details. So I flew over the next day to see her at the palace. It was clear that she was nervous. She said to me, 'I'm an actress, I'm no good at ad-libbing,' and she asked me to write a speech for her, which I did. After that, Frank Sinatra sent his private jet to pick her up and fly her to London.

"When she arrived at Heathrow airport, two hundred fans were there to greet her. 'Funny,' she said, 'I was here last week shopping and no one even noticed.'"

Grace turned up at the first rehearsal wearing a green sweater dress, pearl earrings, heavy dark glasses, and an Hermès scarf. She slipped into the side door of the Festival Hall. Wringing her hands and brushing a nonexistent wisp of hair from her eyes, she was clearly nervous. Then she walked on stage where thirty-nine musicians waited for Sinatra. "Is Frank here?" she asked, only to be told that he would be arriving any second. She took a second-row seat in the auditorium and waited.

Fifteen minutes later, Sinatra materialized on stage, all alone. Looking out into the dark auditorium, at first he didn't see her. But when he did, he said, "Gracie," and came down to hug her. For a few moments, they chatted. He went back up on stage and sang a few numbers, then motioned her up on stage. "She was nervous about where she would stand, and what she would do. She walked on stage and felt it. Where the box where she'd be sitting during most of the performance was, where the orchestra would be, and how she would stand and where she would walk," Jeffrey Archer remembered.

At first, she seemed lost on stage, didn't seem to know what she was supposed to do, then Frank said, "We'll have Her Highness come on from the left over there." He glanced at her for approval, "That okay, Gracie?" She nodded but didn't look particularly confident. Then she checked her speech, which she'd scribbled on a sheet of paper, and tried out one or two lines. Frank seemed pleased and said, "Right, we're okay, then." She smiled and started to walk out of the auditorium. As she did, Frank called after her, "See ya later on, Gracie."

On November 16, in front of a high-octane audience including Prince Charles, Princess Anne, Princess Alexandra, and Tony Bennett, Grace—in a white marabou-trimmed gown—glided on stage looking every inch a princess. It was fourteen years since she'd last trod the boards. As the audience greeted her with tumultuous applause, she smiled a glittering, happy smile, "blushed, then relaxed," said Jeffrey Archer.

Then, in dulcet tones, she recited the speech that Archer had written for her, a retelling of the Christmas Frank had created for her, the cast, and the crew of *Mogambo* in Africa, describing Frank as "generous and warm-hearted."

She went on: "It was a wonderful Christmas thanks to Frank. Frank and I made one film together, *High Society.*" At the mention of the movie, the audience applauded wildly. And once more, Grace smiled contentedly, fulfilled and happy, the way she'd always been whenever she was on stage, in the days when Monaco was merely a tiny speck on the map and meant nothing to her.

"I even had the nerve to sing a song. Of course, I was slightly supported by Bing Crosby, and that reminds me of a story. . . . One time Frank was in Monaco for a benefit for children and he came to visit us and there proudly displayed was a golden disc. . . . When Frank saw that, he said, 'Who's is that?' And I said, 'Mine.' And he said, 'How did you get that?' And I said, '*High Society.*' And he said, 'Well, I was in that picture and I didn't get one.' Then he turned to my husband and said, 'How do you like that? She opens her mouth once and gets a gold record and I've been knocking myself out for twenty years and don't have one.' Of course, that was long before 'Strangers in the Night' and the many others that followed. Ladies and Gentlemen...Mr. Frank Sinatra."

"During Princess Grace's speech, Frank was in the wings and Kenny Clare was beside him," remembered musician Don Lusher. "Frank didn't know what she was going to say. Kenny said that he got all choked up at the nice things she said about him."

Without any further fanfare, Frank was up on stage, striding by her, then he turned and stopped short and said, "Princess..." By the time she had left the stage, the applause had finally subsided and the orchestra was playing the first bars of "You Make Me Feel So Young," her favorite Sinatra song. Looking toward the Royal Box where she had now taken her seat, Frank sang to her.

"Before the show, I watched him walk the paces. It took him fifteen paces to get up to the box and hit the word 'You'," Archer said. "Frank sung it directly to Grace, looking at her all the while he sang it. It was clear they were very close."

She was forty-one now, and her thoughts often strayed to the past. "She told me she wanted to write a truthful autobiography," said Peter Evans, then show business editor of the London *Daily Express*, whom Grace contacted in November 1970, requesting that he meet her to discuss the possibility of him ghostwriting her autobiography.

"We met for tea at Claridge's, where she was staying. She was still attractive then, because she hadn't started to put on weight. There was still a sexual edge to her, almost a flirtatiousness. I say 'almost,' because when you were sitting there you felt you were in with a chance. It didn't manifest itself, alas! A few months later, I got a communication from her saying she wanted to go ahead with the book, but she wanted it to be about flowers. I was the last person to do a book about bloody flowers, so it didn't come to anything," he remembered.

The following year, in December 1971 she was back among her show business peers when, along with Elizabeth Taylor and Richard Burton, she attended the Proust Ball, thrown by Guy and Marie-Hélène de Rothschild at their Ferrières estate outside Paris. In the early hours of the morning, Grace asked Burton to escort her upstairs and help her remove an antique choker.

Afterward, he recorded in his diary, "This I did, nearly strangling Grace to death while trying to get the necklace off."

"So down the stairs we went. At the bottom, alone, was Sam Spiegel. 'Where are you going, you two?' 'For God's sake,' said G, 'Don't Sam, say a word to Elizabeth. She's at the ball, she's dancing, she's happy, let us go. Richard will let Elizabeth know. It's going to be a shock, but . . . these things happen.' For a full half minute, Sam, because of Grace's normal seriousness and because of her very good piece of acting and my deliberately stricken with guilt face, was taken in. We made off. Found Grace's car not before a lot of waiting in the piercing cold and she was going. She was quite the nicest she's ever been and David Rothschild expressed astonishment that she should be so gay. She had always, he said, been a bit of a dead weight. On the contrary, we said, but she does need a little drawing out. Actually it is the nicest she's been in all the years since we've known her as a Princess."

Grace had been alone that night at the ball. Rainier did not escort her, preferring to stay in Monaco. Two months later, it was the same story again. On February 25, 1972, Richard Burton threw a gigantic party in Budapest to mark Elizabeth's fortieth birthday. In a typically generous gesture, he had chartered a 150-seat Trident to fly his and Elizabeth's relatives to Budapest where he was filming *Bluebeard*. Ringo Starr, Michael Caine, Victor Spinnetti, Susannah York, Guy de Rothschild, Princess Elizabeth of Yugoslavia, and Grace were among the guests invited to the three-day, $60,000 festivities at the Hotel Duna.

"Elizabeth instructed the designer to redecorate some of the hotel suites for the more important guests, such as Princess Grace," Kitty Kelley recorded in *Elizabeth Taylor, the Last Star*. "She even arranged for him to visit various homes throughout Budapest to borrow antiques and paintings he would need. 'We can't move out of our suite because it would take weeks to get my things out of there, so make a royal one for Grace,' said Elizabeth. 'Make it pretty enough for a Princess . . . but remember she is just like us.'"

Richard installed all the guests at the Duna Hotel, booking the entire first floor. "In each room we found a huge bouquet of out of season blooms, champagne on ice and a bar stocked with the best wine and spirits," his brother Graham recalled in *Richard Burton, My Brother*. "Cards identifying us as belonging to the Burton party entitled holders to free access to all the hotel services. Elizabeth even arranged for the hairdresser to stay open on Sunday so that the ladies could look their best for the big night."

On Saturday evening, at a small informal family dinner, to the background of a band playing Hungarian pop music, the guests supped on Chicken Kiev, followed by fruit salad and chocolate. Richard's brother, Verdun Jenkins, a fifty-four-year-old steelworks fitter, sat next to Grace. When he complained to her that the collar of his new shirt was too tight for his neck, she advised, "You must change. You can't sit there all evening looking as if you are about to have a seizure." Verdun left the table for a few moments, but came back wearing the same shirt, telling Grace that he had forgotten to take out the cardboard stiffeners.

Matching Richard Burton's family beer for beer, Grace quickly won the admiration of all of them—Tom Jenkins, a retired miner; Will Jenkins, a gas fitter; David Jenkins, a former police inspector; Graham Jenkins, who ran a sports shop; and Burton's sisters Cissie and Cassie and their spouses—and promptly invited them all to come and stay at the palace.

After dinner, Elizabeth received her birthday gifts: intricate gold jewelery, precious ornaments, priceless antiques, valuable paintings, all eclipsed by Richard's gift, a Cartier diamond-and-ruby pendant engraved with the words, "eternal love till death." However, one gift above all excited and amused her: a small flat white pebble, hand-painted with abstract blue squiggles, a birthday gift presented to her with great flourish by Graham Binns, Richard's friend from Oxford, who had painted it.

The painted pebble was simple and pretty, with a purity about it that instantly appealed to Grace, who would go on to make art out of wildflowers, pressing them, then forming them into a collage. As photographers snapped Grace and Elizabeth laughingly examining the painted pebble, Grace was torn, not knowing what to admire more—the pebble or the disarming man who had created it.

Graham Binns was the prototypical Englishman, tall, handsome, charming, courtly, polite, yet with a flamboyant streak that manifested itself in the brightly colored shirts and matching ties and handkerchiefs he always wore, as well as his habit of kissing a woman's hand when first he met her, and the seductiveness of his shy smile. Extremely erudite, he had cut a striking figure at Oxford, where he directed plays and was theater critic for *Isis*, the university newspaper. "He was a deeply creative man. He drew all the time and he wrote poetry. And he was so heartfelt in everything he did. Very passionate, very emotional and very warm," his friend for thirty years, Karen Amiel, remembered.

He was also an accomplished womanizer, a serial seducer who had a wife, two sons, an open marriage, and a string of lovers in his thrall. At the time of his first meeting with Grace, Graham was in his prime, urbane, winning, desirable. After her birthday party, Elizabeth Taylor wrote of him to Professor Nevill Coghill: "Graham was such great fun—all the ladies had a pash on him. He was a whirling Dervish."

She was alluding to Graham's wild dancing at the Sunday night ball held in the Duna's rooftop nightclub, decorated with masses of white lilacs and red tulips, as well as thirty-five hundred gold helium-filled balloons flown in especially from Paris.

However, Graham did not dance alone. In his diaries, Burton recalled, "Nobody had ever seen Grace let her hair down—literally and figuratively— as much as she did. Grace confesses that she never knew she had it in her. She danced wild Hungarian dances."

Richard Burton was too discreet to record in his diaries that Grace danced those wild Hungarian dances with 'whirling Dervish' Graham Binns, intoxicated by him. She would have quickly learned of his reputation, that he was married, that however courtly and academic he seemed, he was also a playboy. But that didn't prevent her from becoming romantically involved with him.

Graham's wife of twenty years, Jillian, was not with him in Budapest that weekend. He was alone, seemingly eligible, with carte blanche from his wife to live out his wildness. "We always had the feeling that both Graham and Jillian had their close 'friends.' And as we grew older, we saw that there was a little more to it," Graham and Jillian's son Matthew explained.

In Budapest during Elizabeth Taylor's birthday party celebrations, Graham clearly made another "close friend," one who meant so much to him that when he died twenty-five years later, his sons found a souvenir of that long-ago weekend, which he had carefully preserved ever since. "It was a little note on a pinkish-orange faded Duna Hotel card, and said, 'See you at 11 by the pool.' The writing was flowing, and the card obviously meant a lot to my father. He had kept it for all those years. He wasn't usually sentimental, but he kept that card for over a quarter of a century," Matthew Binns said.

Grace's romance with Graham Binns began in Budapest, in February 1972. In May 1973, Antonia Williams, former daughter-in-law of eminent playwright Emlyn Williams, one of Richard Burton's closest friends, rented a room in her terraced Victorian house at 73 Stephandale Road, Fulham, in

London, to Graham Binns. She remembered, "At that time, Graham was just starting up Capital Radio, in London. During the week, he stayed with me in London, and at weekends went home to his wife and sons who lived in Brighton on the South Coast of England.

"Graham had an open marriage, and—during the year in which he was my lodger—he always confided in me. One evening, he told me he was going out. 'I'm going to see Grace,' he said. 'Grace who?' I asked. And he whispered, 'Princess Grace.' He told me that he was meeting her at the Sheraton Park Towers Hotel.

"I got the impression that he was going straight to her suite. Then he left. He didn't come back that night," said Antonia, who claims that on three occasions in the space of a year Graham told her that he was going to the hotel to see Princess Grace. "He saw her whenever she was in London. He wasn't boasting, though, but he always told me everything, and it was quite possible he didn't tell anybody else."

"My parents had an open marriage, although they always had a dynamic passion," the Binns' son Jonathan recalled. "My father went to Elizabeth's birthday party alone. Afterwards, when I saw the pictures of him dancing with Princess Grace, I could see the attachment they had and that they were having such fun together. But he never told me that they had an affair. He and my mother were really good at underplaying and protecting us children from what was going on outside their marriage. My father had his own social life and didn't flaunt it."

19

Paris

Grace's own social life was beginning to shift to Paris, where she appeared to feel happy and free. In 1973, she made her first public appearance there without Rainier. As she took her seat in the royal box at the Theatre des Champs-Elysées, "All of Paris was waiting to see Grace. They all looked at her with critical eyes," remembered Dewi Sukarno, who was there that night. "*Le Tout* Paris inspected her and afterwards, everybody raved about her."

In May 1973, back in Monaco, Grace was guest of honor at the world premiere of Franco Rossellini's *The Driver's Seat*, held there after Rossellini— whose movie had been rejected by the Cannes Film Festival in favor of one directed by his archrival Franco Zeffirelli—"called my old friend, Princess Grace, and arranged to have the premiere of my movie on the same night they showed the Zeffirelli movie in Cannes," Rossellini explained to Bob Colacello. "And, as you know, darling, when Grace and Rainier invite, the entire Cote D'Azur comes. There's not going to be a star left in Cannes that night!" he added gleefully.

On November 14, Grace flew to London to attend Princess Anne's marriage to Captain Mark Phillips. Horrified by what they considered Grace's flouting of convention by wearing white, British commentators like columnist Marjorie Proops sniffed, "Guests shouldn't wear white at a wedding. It simply isn't done." Grace was reportedly so hurt by the criticisms that she never wore that outfit again.

By 1974, she was spending more and more time in Paris, staying in Rainier's former bachelor apartment on the Avenue Foch. There, one of her neighbors was glamorous German playboy Gunther Sachs, one of the wealthiest men in Europe, whose first wife was Brigitte Bardot.

On one occasion, for some inexplicable reason, Salvador Dalí convinced Sachs to play a cruel practical joke on Grace. As Daniel Peres reported in *W*, "The plan was to put a live pig in the bathtub of Sachs' Avenue Foch apartment and trap it there. When Grace, who like Bardot was an animal rights activist, came to the house, she would hear it squealing and run into the bathroom, where a powerful light would be rigged to flash in her eyes and give her the scare of a lifetime." And although Dalí ultimately scrapped the plan, on learning of it, Grace didn't talk to Sachs again for half a decade.

Back in New York in April, she made a brief speech at a gala tribute to Hitchcock held at Lincoln Center in front of an audience of two thousand eight hundred. She and Hitchcock remained close always. "When I had dinner with Grace and Hitchcock, he was in his eighties and was very sweet," director Robert Dornhelm recalled. "He was very fond of her, ever holding her hand. He treated her very well and was extremely sweet to her and happy for her to be there."

On April 20, in the first television performance to which she had agreed since participating in the Sinatra concert (which was televised), the British ITV network aired an episode of *Stars on Sunday*, in which she read a few verses from the Bible. She had decided to participate after the show's producer Jess Yates flew to Monaco. Given the religious nature of the program—and the fact that Yates was introduced to Grace by a cardinal who described the Grimaldis as "the ideal Catholic family"—Rainier had no objections to her participation.

The following month, Rainier celebrated the silver jubilee of his reign. During the two-week festivities, Grace hosted a Texas barbecue at Prince Louis II Stadium's soccer field, to which every single citizen of the principality received an invitation.

Two months later, the new $2 million Sporting Club, complete with roof that slid back to reveal the stars, opened. That August, the Red Cross Ball was held at the new club, and illustrious guests, including Henry Ford, Gregory Peck, and David Niven, supped on caviar, consommé, beef, and peach surprise, washed down with 1969 Brut champagne.

Grace was always on hand for Monaco's most high-profile events, but otherwise her virtual separation from Rainier was the talk of Europe, and by June 7, 1975, after an article titled "Princess Grace's Marriage on the Rocks" was published in the *National Star* (now *Star Magazine*), the story had reached America as well.

Quoting Kell as saying, " 'My sister has definitely moved out of her husband's apartment on the Avenue Foch and into an apartment she owns,' " the story went on, "Rainier has been seen living it up at jet-set nightclubs in the plush Spanish resort of Marbella, on the Costa del Sol . . . Grace no longer appears at affairs of state in Monaco and Rainier makes only infrequent trips to see his wife, who has been staying most of the year in Paris, supposedly to keep an eye on her frisky older daughter, Caroline." It ended with a final epitaph for Grace and Rainier's marriage; "They don't see each other for weeks, sometimes months at a time."

The article would never have seen the light of day in Monaco, where Rainier's censors checked every single imported publication and would have immediately pulped it. It is unlikely that it would have been published in France, where even today privacy laws protect public figures to such an extent that, before publishing a photograph of a celebrity, other than one taken in a public place, that publication must receive written permission from the celebrity in question, and, after that celebrity has died, from his or her heirs.

Now, however, the story that Grace and Rainier's marriage was on the rocks was spreading through Europe like wildfire. An outraged Grace took matters in her own hands. James Brady, then editing the *National Star*, remembered, "I got a handwritten note from Grace from Monaco, written in a wonderful American private school handwriting. The handwriting was impeccable and it was obviously on very good stationery, with the exposed seal of the palace.

"Somebody had told her about it and she was absolutely furious; she said that I was a disgrace and asked why would I deal with such things . . . that there was no truth to them . . . that she had always heard that I was a fairly responsible journalist and certainly I had broken all the rules, and so forth.

"As a journalist, I'm accustomed to getting those letters. But the extraordinary thing was that her spelling was terrible! I mean, she misspelled not complicated words, you know, but words in everyday use. I thought to myself, 'My God, she's got this fine school handwriting, but she can't spell.' In any event, I knew her brother Jack, so, just to be sure, I sent him a facsimile of the letter with the envelope and a note, 'Is this really your sister who's pissed off at me, because if it's someone else pretending to be Grace I won't do anything about it. But I would like to respond if this is legitimate.' And he called and said that that was her handwriting and that's her stationery and that he was sure she wrote me the letter. So I wrote back to her rather apologetic, the typical journalist response to an angry celebrity in the news. But the only thing that really makes it different from the usual screed was that it was so nicely written and yet so poorly spelled."

That fall, back in America again, there was yet more trouble brewing for Grace's family. Just when forty-eight-year-old Kell was deciding whether or not to run as the Democrats' mayoral candidate against Frank Rizzo, Margaret scuppered his chances by announcing that she would not only support Rizzo against her son, but back Rizzo financially as well. Kell withdrew from the race.

Her motivations for destroying his political career before it was in full flight were crystal clear: she was determined to avoid public exposure of his liaison with a transsexual. And not just any transsexual, but one who was the spitting image of his sister Grace.

The transsexual in question was born Richard Finnochio, who renamed himself Rachel Harlow and finally had a sex change operation on June 8, 1972. "She was operated on by the best doctors in New York. She was very gorgeous and you would never have thought she'd ever been a boy," her cousin Anthony Cozzi said.

Rachel Harlow was twenty-eight, blond, blue-eyed, and beautiful, and owned a glamorous Philadelphia nightclub on Second and Bank. In fact, she was so famous and popular that she was known simply as Harlow, which became the name of her club.

Such was Harlow's beauty that it even caught the eye of Truman Capote, who in *Answered Prayers* dubbed her "a swan," citing "Garbo, Barbara Cushing Paley, the three Wyndham sisters, Diana Duff Cooper, Lena Horne, Richard Finnochio (the transvestite who calls himself Harlow), Gloria Guinness, Maya Pliesetskaya, Marilyn Monroe" as sublime examples of the species.

Anthony Cozzi remembered how Kell and Harlow met. "The first night after the operation, Rachel was back at Harlow's, and came down the steps in a slinky silk red dress, exactly like Jean Harlow used to wear, clinging to her body. Everybody in the room stood still, the whole bar stopped serving, and everyone applauded. It was a magnificent time. And that's when Jack Kelly Jr., "Kell," met her and started going out with her.

"Harlow was very classy. She and Grace were the same type: pure blondes, fair skin, blue eyes. She was very, very fair, she had pure white porcelain skin. She was absolutely gorgeous. Just like Grace Kelly. In fact, the night that Kell met Harlow, he said, 'You look just like my sister, Grace.'

"Kell loved his sister. She was his life. They were very very close. So when Princess Grace came to Philadelphia, she and Princess Caroline had lunch and dinner with Kell and Harlow. Afterward, Harlow told me that Grace said she was gorgeous and that she loved her. She accepted Harlow completely.

"If you had seen Harlow, you would never have believed that she was a boy at one time. Never in your life. Kell was crazy about her. He and Harlow were together for over a year at least. He said he didn't care about what she was or what she did or anything. Was their relationship physical? I think so, yeah. She had everything a woman had. The only thing she couldn't do was have a baby. Kell wanted to marry Harlow, but his mother said that she would disinherit him if he did."

After Kell's relationship with Harlow ended, he never again considered running for political office. Instead, after remarrying in 1981, in 1985 he was elected to a four-year term as president of the U.S. Olympic Committee. Three weeks later, he died of a heart attack while jogging in Philadelphia.

In 1976, citing as a reason the necessity for Stephanie to be educated in Paris rather than Monaco, Grace and the children moved into 26 Square de l'Avenue Foch, with author Marcel Pagnol her neighbor on one side and Mrs. Arthur Rubinstein on the other.

Previously, Grace had always stayed at Rainier's former Paris apartment. Now she put down roots at this new address, making it her own and personally selecting the eighteenth-century furniture, the delicate china, and the variety of flowers grown in the apartment's minuscule garden.

"She loved Paris. She used to go to bookstores a lot," Pepita Dupont remembered. "In London, she would go to Habitat. She said that one time there were a lot of paparazzi in front of the store. She asked them to carry her packages and said, 'For once they can be useful.' So all the photographers carried her packages."

In Paris, she and the children tried living as normal a life as possible. She often left the house with her hair hidden by a turban and dark glasses covering her eyes, hoping not to be recognized. Once she was so successful that the manager of La Samaritaine department store wouldn't accept her personal check because she didn't have any ID on her.

And when she and Caroline went to see a Monte Python movie at a local cinema, Grace laughed so loudly that the manager, who didn't recognize her, asked them to leave.

Although Grace loved eating at home, she also enjoyed lunching at the Plaza Athénée's Relais Plaza, where she generally sat at table 10 in the corner and ordered *Escalope de Veau Genoese*, and the Brasserie Lipp on the Left Bank. In Paris she also was able to indulge her love for haute couture and attend all the collections, sometimes with Caroline.

However, despite Caroline's forays into high fashion, "She never looked well dressed," Pepita Dupont recalled. "Her mother was so beautiful, so perfect. She could wear something white from morning to evening. She was immaculate, and Caroline said, 'Next to my mother, I look like a tramp.'"

However, despite sometimes feeling overshadowed by her mother, Caroline was now more beautiful then ever and was beginning to understand that she had power. As Caroline reveled in the impact she was having with both Parisians and the media, Grace continually worried about her and Stephanie. "Grace knew that life wasn't a fairy tale, but she wanted a fairy tale for her children," said Pepita Dupont. "She was like a mother hen. She looked after them, even when they went out. She'd call at one in the morning to find out what was going on. She didn't like them smoking, though, and fought with them over that."

By now, she was increasingly aware that she needed an outlet for her creativity. So when Gwen Robyns suggested that she give a poetry reading at the Edinburgh Festival, she eagerly agreed.

That September, at St. Cecilia's Hall in Edinburgh, Grace, in a crimson chiffon gown, with British actor Richard Pasco and American actor Richard Kiley by her side, gave four readings titled "American Heritage," celebrating the bicentennial. After one of the readings, journalist Michael Thornton was introduced to her. "She was utterly charming but very tense. I said to her, 'What a fairy story it's been!' She looked at me with an old-fashioned look, then did a double take like, 'Can you be for real?' and said, 'You have no idea what hard work fairy stories can be.'" Arlene's husband, Marc Rosen, commented that: "I noticed when you went to Monaco, in those days, other than a plate with Grace and Rainier, there was hardly a souvenir. I mentioned it to Grace and she said, 'Oh, you are absolutely right. I'd love to work with you on something like that. We have a porcelain works in Monaco that could make it.'

We decided we were going to make a collection of porcelain that I would ghost design and she would work with me on it and she would promote it. I met with her several times in New York at Vera Maxwell's apartment – she was staying with her. Finally it got to the point that we were going to make this a business arrangement. I got a call from an executive of the SBM, very good-looking (probably Bernard Combemal). He made an arrangement to meet with me at Grace's house in Paris. We spent the day together. Finally when the chips were down, he said to me that he and Rainier had no intention of letting Grace dabble in this foolish enterprise. He was basically saying that this was some foolish fancy of hers and that Rainier didn't want her to work and he didn't want to spend the money on something that was just one of her flights of fancy. I thought it was shocking that he would say this to me. He knew that Arlene was a personal friend. He said this to me, boy to boy. It was such a put-down."

She had always loved flowers, and after Mrs. Henry King, a friend from Philadelphia, introduced her to the art of pressing flowers, began to create collages out of them. She pressed fresh flower petals between the pages of phone directories, forming designs out of maple leaves, roses, and wildflowers into collages and signing them G.P.K.—not G.P.G.—almost as if her collages had been created by the person she was before she married Rainier. Eventually, she gave a show of all her collages in Paris, and although all her designs sold, Judith Balaban Quine reported Rainier made fun of them.

However, neither she nor Rainier found anything to laugh about when that summer Caroline met playboy Philippe Junot at Régine's exclusive club on Rue de Ponthieu in Paris and fell in love with him at first sight.

He was thirty-seven, a businessman working in finance and a tennis player, who thought nothing of clubbing till four or five in the morning, then getting up at eight-thirty the next morning and starting all over again. "Caroline loved my energy, my zest for life," he once said.

Seventeen years her senior, Junot was old enough to be her father. Caroline had fallen in love with a father figure, just as Grace often had. Dominant and determined, he was a ladies' man, wore tight trousers, and—when he wasn't addressing Caroline as "Fatty"—had a well-honed line in flattery that she, and almost every other woman, found irresistible. "He was a very charming man. I think he was very much in love with Caroline," Bernard Combemal said.

At the same time that Grace was underwhelmed by the prospect of one day having Junot as a son-in-law, she was also yet again forced to struggle with the temptation to make a Hollywood comeback. Her former Hollywood agent Jay Kanter was aware of her great love for the ballet, and he suggested that she consider playing a part in the upcoming movie *The Turning Point*. The part of dancer Deedee Rodgers—a former ballerina who gave up her career to have a family—was perhaps slightly close to the bone. "Grace read it and thought the script was absolutely wonderful but said, 'I just can't do it,'" Jay Kanter explained.

"But when the picture was finished, I asked her if she would consider having a gala premier for it in Monaco, and she was very gracious about it and said, 'Absolutely.'"

One can only imagine Grace's bitter regrets as she watched Shirley MacLaine on screen playing the part that she could have played as well, if not better. "It was a wonderful movie, and it's an interesting movie, beautifully done," she somewhat wistfully said to Judy Klemesrud of *The New York Times*, before adding, "but I made a decision long ago, a decision I had to take."

In November 1976, Grace became the first woman ever appointed to the board of 20th Century–Fox for an annual salary of $10,000 plus $300 and expenses every time she attended a board meeting in Hollywood. That same year, she flew there for two days, during which she attended eleven screenings. The board meetings took place four times a year, providing the perfect excuse for her to leave Monaco. She stayed on the board until 1981, when Fox was sold to oilman Marvin Davis.

Former chairman and CEO of Fox, Dennis Stanifill, remembered, "She was committed, thoughtful, and she did her homework. She had the very perceptive judgments of a clear-thinking businesswoman. I admired her and sought her counsel. We all did. She went out of her way to attend board meetings, and that was hard coming all the way from Monaco. The jet lag alone must have been killing. She had such a sound business sense. I really admired it. Did that woman know Hollywood! It was very seldom that she would suggest an idea that she wished to be personally involved in. I just don't think she had time. But when other ideas were brought to her for consideration, she could make these fine, balanced judgments between the creative process and the bottom line. A very competent woman."

20

Children of Theatre Street

She was back in Hollywood again, if only in an administrative capacity. Then, in 1976, she finally made something of a comeback at last. Russian choreographer Oleg Briansky was working on *Children of Theatre Street* about the children of Leningrad's famed Vaganova Institute, formerly the Russian Imperial Ballet School.

"When the movie was in the can, Earl Mack, the American producer, said we needed a narration," Briansky remembered, "We thought of Betty Ford, Joanne Woodward, but I had an intuition—Grace Kelly. I didn't know her, but we sent her a telegram and within three days she replied that she would like to do the narration.

"Monaco is very provincial. She was bored. That's why she accepted so quickly when I asked her to be in my movie. She was so excited that she accepted at once. She wasn't happy at all. She found herself in an environment which she didn't like at all. She wanted to be surrounded by people of her own profession," he said.

However, before she would finally commit to doing the narration, she asked to view the film. Best-selling novelist Beth Gutcheon had been hired to write the narration of *Children of Theatre Street* and was at the screening Grace attended in Paris.

"Grace arrived with her lady-in-waiting and my first impression was that she looked dowdy," Beth remembered. "She was wearing a tweed skirt, a sweater, a scarf, and very little makeup. Her accent wasn't pure American—she was aiming at something like Deborah Kerr.

"It was eleven in the morning and we began showing Grace the first of five reels. After we had shown her two, she gathered her purse and said, 'It's lovely. Is it over?' We didn't understand that she had been ready to do the film in the first place as she wanted to use the fee for a ballet school in Monaco."

That day Grace also met the documentary's director, the twenty-seven-year-old Romanian Robert Dornhelm, who remembered, "I barely spoke English. I had seen *High Noon* and *Dial M for Murder,* but offscreen, in reality, Grace was very different, like most actresses are. She was less glamorous, more plain, very plain. She was very easygoing and joyful and giggled and laughed while she saw the documentary. So we had some vodka and I knew we had a deal."

After the screening, Grace invited him to fly to Monte Carlo to talk about the movie. Although he didn't like Monte Carlo, he accepted.

"Robert was very left wing, but while I thought of Grace as an American movie star, he had such reverence for her as a royal," Beth remembered. "He was half in love with her before he met her. But although she was adorable, to me she was a Hollywood movie star. But Robert, the revolutionary, saw her as a royal."

"On the night that I arrived in Monte Carlo, Grace had left a ticket for me to the ballet that night and told me she would see me at intermission," Robert said. "When I got there, everyone was dressed to kill, while I was wearing a faded blue blazer and gray trousers. So there I was, sitting in the second row, dying, not even thinking of getting out of my chair because I was feeling so shy and insecure. Then someone tapped me on the shoulder and asked me to join the princess in the Royal Box. So I go there, shy, barely speaking English, lost and out of place. I was so embarrassed, but I know Grace loved it. She loved every moment of me feeling totally lost, because deep down she was a simple person. She was very lively and the opposite of the white-glove image."

Grace's narration was filmed in Paris over two days. "We filmed her French narration at the Paris Opera. She was very stiff," Oleg Briansky said. "She had a few words to say in French, and she made one mistake, two mistakes. The secretary didn't say a word, the cameraman didn't say a word. I said, 'Grace, I hope you don't mind . . .' She said, 'Of course not,' so we started again. She made two mistakes at another place. I couldn't let it go. So I told her. She did it a second time. After that, she realized I was a professional and we became very, very good friends. Everybody else was in awe of her, bowing down in front of her."

Everybody except Robert Dornhelm, that is. "I was always honest with Grace and she appreciated me for being honest. I used to tease her that in her wildflower collages she was pressing the life out of flowers. I said it was a way of celebrating death. I got away with certain things somebody else would have been slapped for saying," he said.

During Robert's visit to Monaco, a policeman spotted the belt buckle he was wearing, with the Communist Party emblem—a hammer and sickle—engraved on it. The policeman demanded to see his papers, but he refused to show them. Whereupon he was taken to police headquarters. From there, he telephoned Grace, who arranged for him to be released. However, when he demanded that the arresting policeman be disciplined, she erupted in peals of laughter and said, "Certainly not. We're going to give him a medal."

At a formal event during his stay in Monaco, he was introduced to someone with the words, " 'This is your king.' I said, 'My king? I have no king.' They said, 'Well, this is King Michael of Romania.' And I said I didn't recognize him and tried to get out of the unpleasant situation by saying, 'Well, Your Highness, I wasn't born when they chased you out of the country,' meaning 'I'm sorry, otherwise I would have recognized you.' And he took it as the worst insult ever and turned around and left. Grace was laughing forever. She said. 'You know, I can't take you into society if you make such a....' "

"The premiere of *Children of Theatre Street* was held at the Paris Opera. It was a black-tie event," Robert said. "Grace and a group of ministers were in the royal box, and I was in the audience. At intermission, Grace said, 'I'll see you at dinner afterward,' and I told her I hadn't been invited. She said, 'Well, that's not possible. It's bad enough you are not sitting where you should be sitting—in the box—but this is your evening. What's going on?'

"So she went to ask the director of the opera about dinner, and he told her that it was a dinner for twenty-four, just her and the ministers. She said, 'Wait a minute, the director and the choreographer are not going to the dinner?' The director apologized and Grace said, 'Well, I'm sorry,' and did not attend the dinner. Instead of getting into the car that was sent to pick her up at midnight and take her there, Junot, Caroline, Rainier, my mother, Grace and myself got into the taxi and we all went out to dinner at a restaurant together."

In her onscreen narration in *Children of Theatre Street*, Grace looks decidedly middle-aged, nervous, her face is slightly bloated, her hair is short, her voice is deeper than in previous films, yet she still enunciates like a well brought up schoolgirl.

Nonetheless, after the documentary was released, it was nominated by the Academy as Best Documentary. Grace did publicity for the film, and with Dornhelm traveled to Lausanne and then to Manhattan, where it was screened at the Beacon Theater.

In Manhattan, they had dinner with Oleg Briansky and his wife at their apartment. "I asked Grace if she wasn't tired of shaking hands and didn't she sometimes wish she didn't have to?" Oleg recalled. " 'It is part of discipline and of being who I am and what I represent,' she said."

Oleg makes no bones about that fact that he was extremely beguiled by her. "She was very sexy. She had tremendous charisma. I liked her, of course, I liked her very much," he said.

While they were in Manhattan, Grace, Robert, and the crew attended a private party for the film's ballet dancers. Beth Gutcheon remembered, "Baryshnikov was there that night, and Grace danced with him." Yet although Grace—once a little girl who longed to become a prima ballerina but grew too tall—must have been thrilled to dance with Baryshnikov, she reserved her emotions and her passion for Robert. "They danced as if they were lovers," Beth observed.

From that time on, as Dornhelm put it, "Grace and I traveled together in Europe, America and, when she came to Los Angeles for 20th Century–Fox board meetings, I would see her then, and in Paris."

Robert Dornhelm—now married and the successful director of *RFK, The Sins of the Father,* and *Rudolph*—categorically denies that he and Grace were lovers. When asked if she was in love with him, he insists that she was not.

However, when Grace's old friend and confidante Maree Frisby Rambo, who spent a great deal of time with Robert and Grace in America, was asked if Grace was in love with him, she put finger in front of her mouth and answered with a nod.

Gwen Robyns remembered that when Grace was staying with her and her husband in Oxford, "Robert rang during lunch and Grace talked to him for an hour."

Once, when Grace's chauffeur, Paul Choisit, drove her and Gwen and Robert up in the mountains overlooking Monaco, Grace suggested they all take a walk together. Then—as if it were an afterthought—she solicitously said that she thought the walk might be too long for Gwen. Gwen, sensing that Grace wanted to be alone with Robert, obligingly stayed in the car with Paul, while Grace and Robert went off on their expedition.

When they finally returned more than an hour later, Grace's face was flushed, and her hair was in disarray. "Oh, darling," Grace said later, when she and Gwen were alone again, "it was so lovely, just being with him."

"She started telling me about the taste she was starting to have for young men while she was married to Rainier," said Rita Gam, "and I told her not to tell me. But she was happy having those flirtations."

In 1977, Grace wrote to Don Richardson, describing Robert as "a dear boy who reminds me a bit of you. He could almost be our son."

In whatever light Robert Dornhelm's six-year relationship with Grace is cast, it is undeniable that during that time he came to know and understand her extremely well. "There was something about her that was slightly larger than life, but not in a negative way. She was serene and her title fitted her like clockwork. She could be very quiet or she could be quite chatty," he said. "She could be depressed, but she wasn't a moody person. She was genuinely elevated in trying to be kind and understanding, by not judging.

"I met stars in her house like Lauren Bacall and Bette Davis, and Grace was less real. They were more real people. She was shy, hated being the center of attention. Unlike other strong women, she wasn't threatened by other women. She was a strong personality and most of her friends were women. She was superstitious, and astrology was a big issue. We were once in China-town and she went to a gypsy palm reader there. It was amusing.

"I didn't find her vain at all. She was proud of every wrinkle she had. But her hair was an issue, a problem. She had thin hair in areas and had to wear extensions.

"She was as American as they come. She remained totally American. She loved hamburgers and Bloody Marys. She was a total Democrat, even though she was a Republican by her associations. She loved to joke, to tease me about my lefty politics. I would tell her to get rid of her right-wing friends, Henry Kissinger and Alexander Haig. But she was a Democrat in a sense that when she was on set she wanted absolute equal treatment of everybody from the last extra to everyone else and she checked that everyone was looked after.

"She definitely missed Hollywood. She cast a movie for me about Raoul Wallenberg, the script of which Richard Chamberlain later inherited. She taught me about movies and to have patience and respect, by never getting impatient herself, and not making it a problem if she had to wait. She taught me not to take yourself too seriously, to have the ability to laugh at yourself. If she made a mistake while we were recording, she would say, 'You can fire me now.'

"I saw her in Paris and her life there was avoiding public life as much as possible, taking many walks every day, and having a lot of visiting friends. The ones I met in her house were Lauren Bacall, Hjordis Niven, Madame Rubinstein, and David Niven, who spent quite a few evenings with her. I took her to a cheap Romanian restaurant in Paris. We took the metro to get there. She wore a scarf and no one recognized her till we got to the restaurant, then they couldn't believe it. In New York, we went to fashionable restaurants together. We went shopping in Bloomingdale's for little knickknacks and Christmas presents. She always went to New York before Christmas."

About Grace's marriage to Rainier, all Robert Dornhelm will say is, "The marriage was like any marriage after many years and three children. She referred to him as her 'Old Bear.' She had a very sympathetic, sweet way of calling him. He is a stiff Mediterranean macho man.

"What did Grace teach me about life? To be forgiving. I would have liked her to teach me about generosity, which wasn't her forte. It's that kind of old-fashioned German frugality.

"My happiest moments with Grace were dancing with her. I'm not a dancer, but I had the courage to dance. I danced with her in all sorts of places, from balls in Monte Carlo to New York. She was wonderful, a very good dancer."

In July 1977, Grace—who had always adored Shakespeare—was thrilled when producer John Carroll asked her to give a poetry ready as part of a program, "A Remembrance of Shakespeare," in Stratford-on-Avon. While she was there, Grace placed a rose on the Bard's grave.

The following month, on August 25, Grace and Rainier announced Caroline and Junot's engagement. On the evening prior to the announcement, Grace called Gwen Robyns, now a trusted friend, imploring her to come up to Rocagel to be with her and Rainier. "We need you here. We need friends with whom to commiserate," she said.

Grace had dreamed of Caroline marrying into royalty, as she had, marrying a prince of the blood, like Prince Charles, like her own husband. She felt that Caroline was far too young to marry. She wanted her to have a career, explore her potential and not tie herself to someone whom she considered to be a high-society wastrel.

Rainier took the marriage as badly as, if not worse than, Grace did. She wrote to Don Richardson, confiding that Rainier didn't like "his baby marrying anybody" and that, as a result, had gone into decline. Rainier wrote to Rupert Allan, "I'm not very happy with the choice that Caroline's made for many reasons, but what can one do? It is so delicate and difficult to be responsible for the deep and lasting unhappiness of one's child."

He could have banned Caroline from marrying Junot, but he may well have been afraid that if he did she would simply walk away from Monaco and the family and marry him anyway.

On the night of the engagement, Christian de Massy was at Régine when, just after midnight, Junot turned up alone. Rubbing his hands in triumph, he turned to his Parisian high-society friends and declared, "It's in the bag, my friends! We've taken the town."

"It was a joke," Christian de Massy says today, "but Junot paid for it all his life. Everyone was on an anti-Junot trip. Grace said to everybody, 'Now at least Caroline will be ready for her second marriage. . . .' And when someone asked Rainier what his future son-in-law did for a living, he answered, 'Anything.'"

While Grace waited for the wedding, hoping against hope that Caroline would change her mind, in February and March of 1978 she took part in "Birds, Beasts and Flowers," a program devised by John Carroll to help celebrate International Wildlife Year, which premiered in Pittsburgh, then toured Minneapolis, Philadelphia, Washington, and Princeton and Harvard Universities. In Pittsburgh, Grace, the self-taught intellectual who had never attended college, was overjoyed to receive a doctorate of humane letters from Duquesne University, the first and only honorary university degree she ever received.

By now the wedding date had been set, and Grace knew that Caroline was determined to go through with marrying Junot. Journalist Paul Callan spent a couple of weeks at the Hôtel de Paris covering the wedding and recalled, "I discovered that there was mounting fury that Caroline was marrying Junot. Grace was livid, as was Rainier. And one by one, all these reigning houses, Norway, Sweden, Denmark, Holland, Belgium, and finally Great Britain declined the wedding invitation. And as letter after letter of refusal came in,

Grace got more and more despondent. Prince Charles was originally coming to the wedding but then canceled at the last moment, and that, as well as all the other royals saying no, was her greatest disappointment."

In the end, although the guest list at Caroline's wedding was more star-studded than that at Grace and Rainier's, only Frank Sinatra, Cary Grant, David Niven, and Gregory Peck, plus an assortment of ex-kings and sundry members of international society attended. And perhaps the choice of song that Frank Sinatra opted to sing at the prewedding lunch, which David Niven hosted—"My Way," with its grim lyrics as sung by a dying man, expressing the sentiment that the end is near and he is facing his final curtain—set the tone for the wedding and the marriage that would follow.

At 10 P.M. on June 27, 1978, at a pre-wedding ball at the palace, eight hundred guests dressed in mandatory white tie applauded as Caroline made her entrance on Rainier's arm to the tune of Neil Diamond's "Sweet Caroline." Rainier and Caroline danced the first dance together, as did Albert and Grace. Then Philippe danced with Caroline, while his parents danced with each other. Finally, Grace danced with Philippe. Stephanie was nowhere to be seen.

"Grace said, 'Stephanie, go and put on your nice dress,'" Christian de Massy recalled. "Stephanie stuck her thumb in her mouth and said, 'I wear jeans nowadays.' So Grace said, 'Well, Steffi, it is either jeans and you staying upstairs and watching TV or wearing a dress and going to Caroline's wedding.' Stephanie kept her jeans on and did not go to the wedding."

The ill-fated union between Caroline and Junot was destined to limp on for little more than two years. "Poor Caroline's marriage is not going too well. She's been badly hurt and, God be blessed, she came to Mum and Dad and told us of her unhappiness," Rainier wrote to Rupert Allan in 1980.

"In the end, Junot was in love with Caroline," Christian de Massy said, "but he had done everything to lose her. So he was very down. They were still married, so he went to the palace to try and see her. But she wasn't there, so he asked to see Grace instead. She made him wait for five hours before she saw him. When she did, she told him that Caroline was somewhere in England. When he asked for her telephone number, Grace said she didn't have it."

In the incestuous world of Paris and Monte Carlo, it was impossible to keep the marriage's demise a secret. In an attempt to hide the truth from the press and public, Gwen Robyns, now the Grimaldis' unofficial scribe, was enlisted by Grace and Rainier's press officer Nadia Lacoste to interview Caroline and Junot, then produce a puff piece about their supposed marital bliss.

When Gwen arrived at the Junots' Paris flat, she received a shock. "It was quite clear that Caroline had red eyes and it looked as though she'd been crying," she said, adding, "One day, Caroline just really had enough. She went home weeping, and Princess Grace said, 'Right...' And the prince said, 'Right, you're not going back.' And Caroline stayed home and it was Princess Grace who went over to the flat and she confronted Junot, which I think is very marvelous, and she packed all of Princess Caroline's possessions and then left."

On October 9, Caroline and Junot were granted a divorce. The marriage between the princess and the playboy was over.

21

Full Circle

In February 1980, at the request of William F. Buckley, Grace flew to Rome to make a television program about the Sistine Chapel with David Niven, in which she read a verse from the Bible. But although she looked as radiant as ever, none of the networks bid on the program.

On February 25, according to Judith Balaban Quine, Grace took the Concorde from London to New York, wearing a babushka and very little makeup. Sitting next to her on the plane was twenty-nine-year-old Irish-American businessman Jeffory FitzGerald. At first, he failed to recognize her. Then, after she introduced herself, they chatted for the entire flight. Afterward, the normally circumspect Judith went as far as to write that Jeffory "probably fell in love with Grace on that flight." From that meeting on, Grace met with Jeffory whenever she visited New York.

During her stay in America, Grace met the Catholic priest Father Peter Jacobs, better known as Father Jake. He remembered, "A friend told her that there was a priest in New York whose name was Jacobs but whose mother was a Kelly, so she wanted to meet me. There was an immediate friendship there. Whenever the princess visited Manhattan, we would go to dinner. I took her to a place off the Bowery. She told me that when she was in the theater—long before she went to Hollywood—to get a feeling for her role in a particular play, she spent two or three weeks on the Bowery, then the poorest section of New York, so we ate there.

"Another time, I took her to dinner to Brooklyn, which in those days wasn't fashionable. But she didn't have to go to Le Cirque or to "21"—although she liked it there. She went to Brooklyn and she loved it. She said to her friends,

'Guess where I went to dinner? With my priest friend, Father Jacobs, in Brooklyn!' 'You went to Brooklyn?' 'We went to Brooklyn,' she would say proudly."

After Grace invited Father Jake to Monaco, he learned more of her life there. "When Jimmy Carter gave up the presidency, he restored houses for people in the poorer neighborhoods. Grace did the same thing—she went to the houses of poor people with paint and brushes and cleaned and painted, without any publicity. That's what I liked about her," he remembered.

"When I was a guest at the palace, I would say Mass for Grace. I'd give her Holy Communion. In my moments with her, we'd talk spirit, even other things people would laugh at, like her love for old-fashioned prayer, the rosary, the beads.

"She would ask me to join her on the balcony and watch the changing of the guards with her, just the two of us. She loved music, in particular Mozart, and went to the Salzburg Festival each year. She loved biographies and histories. And she loved her friends. Friends, books, and music—that told me who she was. When she was alive, I said Mass for her in the palace chapel. Then a few years later, I said Mass with her body in the same chapel. That was very hard," Father Jake said, his voice shaking with emotion.

In the spring of 1980, she spent two weeks at Holker Hall, the stately home of Lord and Lady Cavendish of Furness, celebrated for its breathtakingly beautiful formal gardens. There, she opened the Cavendishes' rose show. "I was disappointed when I met her. There was little personality there. She seemed to hate it, the public appearances and everything associated with it," the Cavendishes' butler Alan Selka confided to Randy Taraborrelli.

In November, Grace was in London, promoting *My Book of Flowers*, which she had written with Gwen Robyns. Interviewed by venerable British film critic Alexander Walker, Grace was clearly on her guard. When Walker asked her if she might still consider making a movie comeback, her reaction was extremely revealing. "She looks at me very steadily and then said, 'Oh, come now . . . my last movie, *High Society*, was made 26 years ago.' Then rising: 'And now, I'm afraid I must leave you. One is always trying to catch up. I don't lack things to do, I can assure you,' " Walker recalled.

"The conversation freezes into a second's leave-taking formality—then she thaws as she asks, almost anxiously, 'You haven't forgotten anything?'

"Perhaps it is Princess Grace's serenity which is the most resistant of all veils to pierce—better protection than an iron shutter. 'Grace Grimaldi' plays a role which has lasted longer than any part which Hollywood might have created for her, and she plays it in public with elegance and authority," he wrote.

She had always disliked the press, despised being subjected to their questions and their probing, and loathed the formal events at which she met most of them.

"She dreaded public functions. She hated nothing more than having to stand and greet a thousand people," Robert Dornhelm said. "At the beginning, it was a fairy tale. In the beginning, it was fun. But after a while, when you do it on a daily basis, it gets tedious. After a while it became a chore that she looked upon as such."

Three episodes give a flavor of Grace's public appearances, her dealings with the press and the public and all that they entailed.

The first was when the Whitbread pub first opened in Monte Carlo, and journalist Paul Callan, then a young reporter, was flown over to Monaco for the launch. "This was a British pub abroad, an imitation, a phony," he remembered. "I walked in, had a few beers, and suddenly, in came to open it, the Serene Highness, Princess Grace! She entered with sheer horror on her face. I had to go through a sort of detective who was also her lady-in-waiting to speak to her.

"Finally, I was granted an interview with Princess Grace, but I couldn't think of any questions to ask her. The only thing that came to my mind was, 'Jolly nice for you and Prince Rainier to pop down here for a pint of good old British beer.' And she said, 'I doubt it,' and turned away. She sounded like the Queen of England."

The second was on July 11, 1980, when Andy Warhol and Jamie Wyeth attended the opening of a joint show of their work in Monte Carlo, along with their friends Phyllis and Freddy Woolworth. Afterward, Andy recorded in his diary that when he stood in line to be presented to Grace, "She had a little tummy. We were supposed to kiss her hand but I refused to kiss her hand and so we shook hands and she didn't really like me, she just liked Jamie. And then when Grace found out that Phyllis was a big Du Pont, she was really social climbing, so she was really nice. And then we had to go show her the pictures, and I was trying to be funny but it just didn't go over too well.

"She never let her hair down. And I told her that I heard she paints, and she said she just does collages, she had a big show in France that was a sell-out. And I asked her what else was she doing, and finally she told me that she's on the lecture circuit in the United States reading poetry. And finally after forty-five minutes of chit-chat she decided to go. And when she left she thought the security guard that has the revolver and watches the paintings for the Coe Kerr Gallery was Freddy Woolworth. So it was really funny, she told him she loved the show."

The third was on November 26, 1980, when—fulfilling a request made personally to her by David Niven—she was guest of honor at the *Evening Standard* Film Awards at the New London Theatre, Drury Lane, to present him with a special lifetime award. That night, as the *Evening Standard* deputy film critic William Hall, who was on the committee, remembered, "Princess Grace was absolutely stunning. She had a female minder who stood there, saying nothing. Princess Grace stood at the end of a carpeted area by herself. I thought there would have been millions crowding around her, but somehow, people stayed away. I think people were overawed by her, because she did emanate regality. She had this amazing aura of self-importance. She definitely had her nose in the air, as if to say, 'Approach, if you dare.'

"I looked into her beautiful face, took her ice-cold hand, and said, 'It's a pleasure to welcome you to London. Thank you so much for coming here.' Silence. No reply. Absolutely nothing. She just looked at me. I sensed something was wrong. She wasn't totally relaxed. The tension was palpable. So I said, 'What will you be doing while you're here?' And she said, 'Shopping.' Just one word. I said, 'Oh, good. Is there anything special you're looking for?' She said, 'No.' Then silence. I suddenly realized she didn't want to be there, that she had just used the trip—a first-class flight and three nights at the Connaught Hotel, for her and her minder all paid for—as an excuse to go shopping. But why not?

"An inspiration hit me. I had been in Nice a couple of months before, so I said, 'I was in Nice for the Flower Festival.' And suddenly she relaxed a little, a little softness came into her voice, 'Oh, yes, that's very nice,' she said.

"And then a second inspiration came to me, so I asked, 'Have they named a flower after you?' And she said, 'Yes they have.' And now I'm making a little headway. Not friends yet, but we're getting there. I said, 'I presume it was a rose.' And she said, 'Yes, it was.' I said, 'What color is it?' She just said, 'Pink.'

One word again. No dialogue at all. I thought, this is getting a bit stupid. So I said, 'Was it presented to you by some courtiers at the palace, wearing white wigs?' She said, 'Yes, it was.' I said, 'That must have been a wonderful sight. But supposing you hadn't liked it?' She looked absolutely stunned.

"Then my fellow critic Felix Barker chimed in and said, 'Yes, supposing it had fly weed and mildew!' And he and I started laughing hysterically at the thought. Several moments went by. I looked into that beautiful face and the expression hadn't changed. I looked into a tombstone of disapproval. Her Serene Highness was not amused. Finally, someone came and rescued us, and Felix and I backed away. I have to say I was very disappointed. She really was the ice princess."

By 1981, as Virginia Gallico, Grace's lady-in-waiting, confided to Sarah Bradford, Grace was worn out. "She was in airplanes too much—juggling with her life and her health. When she arrived back at the palace there were so many pressures on her—secretaries asking her things—everything had to be fitted in. Sometimes she would have a moment to rest and sat in her chair knitting."

On March 9, 1981, Grace gave a poetry recital at Goldsmith Hall, at which the young Lady Diana Spencer—newly engaged to be married to Prince Charles—made her first public appearance, wearing a figure-hugging black strapless gown and carrying a single red rose in her hand. When Prince Charles's valet, Stephen Barry, saw Lady Diana dressed and ready to leave for the ball, he was shocked. "But Lady Diana," he said carefully, "perhaps you don't yet know this, but royals never wear black." Whereupon Diana, smiling artlessly, said, "But Stephen, I'm not royal yet . . ."

When Diana arrived at Goldsmith Hall, she was mobbed by a crowd of autograph hunters and well-wishers, and a throng of photographers all screaming for her to look in their direction so that they could get the shot they wanted. She was totally overcome, and quickly escaped into the ladies' room. There she met Grace, to whom she confided her panic. Grace, instead of comforting her, was brutally honest: "Don't worry, dear, it will get worse," she said.

She was right, of course, and Diana didn't take offense at her bluntness. "How wonderful and serene she was. But there was troubled water under her,"

Diana later confided to author Andrew Morton. Later, Diana went farther, telling Caroline that she thought she and Grace were "psychically connected."

In retrospect, Diana wasn't altogether wrong. She and Grace really did have a great deal in common. Apart from the fact that renowned British graphologist Deborah Jaffe, who analyzed Grace's and Diana's handwriting and claims that they are uncannily similar, their lives had strong parallels. They had both been young, shy, beautiful brides, much beloved by the media. Both had married their Prince Charming in lavish wedding ceremonies that caught the imagination of the world. Both became fashion icons, and both contributed a great deal to charity, yet as it transpired, neither would live happily ever after.

According to writer Michael Thornton, Grace said of Diana to the Duchess of Argyll, "Poor thing. I have gravest doubts whether she will stay the course. They have nothing in common. I think he's far too old for her and she is very, very young herself." In some ways, Grace could have been talking about herself at Diana's age, and about Rainier as well.

However, despite Grace's differences with Rainier, his infidelities and hers, unlike Charles and Diana they did indeed stay the course, and on April 19, 1981, they celebrated their silver wedding anniversary at the Palm Springs home of Frank Sinatra, who was now married to glittering blonde Barbara Marx, who bore somewhat of a resemblance to Grace.

That evening, Cary Grant, Gregory Peck, Frank, and Barbara all gave a champagne toast to Grace and Rainer. Rainier was at Barbara Sinatra's table, and she later recalled, "Rainier seems a staid, stern sort of fellow, and it isn't easy for him say what he really feels in his heart, but he toasted Grace and told her what she had meant to him and to their three children. It was a very special moment—one I certainly shall never forget. There wasn't a dry eye in the whole room. Grace was crying. I looked at Cary, and the tears were running off his chin."

On April 24, Grace was with Cary Grant and Frank Sinatra again—this time without Rainier—at a Beverly Hilton fund-raiser for the Dubnoff Center. During the evening, she drew Zsa Zsa Gabor away from the crowds. Zsa Zsa recalled, "She told me how unhappy she was, confiding, 'Darling, I never see my friends anymore. I miss Hollywood, I miss all of you. After all, I'm an American.' "

Despite the display in Palm Springs that she and Rainier had put on of being a happy, united couple, they were fundamentally still estranged and, as

Peggy put it that same year, "They like separate things. When they are apart they have their individual lives. They are even financially independent of each other. It's a nice agreement."

Around that time, too, Grace told Judith Balaban Quine that she was considering buying an apartment in Manhattan so that she could spend more time there. "She," not "we."

With a marriage in name only, in the summer of 1981 Rainier's lack of discretion—even on Grace's home ground—was nevertheless startling. He was photographed backstage at the Broadway production of *The Little Foxes* at the Martin Beck Theater, snatching an illicit kiss from leading lady Elizabeth Taylor.

José Quinto, the photographer who took that picture, remembered, "I was Elizabeth's backstage photographer. Grace was waiting in the dressing room, and Rainier and Elizabeth hid away in a dark corner and kissed for three or four minutes. They were all over each other, more than just kissing in a friendly manner."

Upon learning that Quinto had captured his stolen moment with Elizabeth, when Rainier saw him at a nightclub a week later, according to Quinto, "He pointed his finger at me and said, 'I'll come and get you.' But then we became friends and he tolerated me. He's a nice guy."

On May 15 and 16, 1981, Ralph Wolfe Cowan flew to Monte Carlo to paint Grace again, twenty-four years after the first portrait, and recalled, "One of the first things she said to me is, 'I am twenty-four years older and twenty-four pounds heavier.' And I said, 'You are still gorgeous.' And she was, she was still fabulous. But she was upset because there had been an attempt on that pope's life just two weeks before. She took me on a tour of the palace, but I don't think she often did that, because she didn't know where the light switches were. She kept opening French doors to let the light in.

"She took me upstairs to see the portrait I'd painted of her. I hadn't seen the painting in all those years, and when I saw it again, I went, 'Oh, no!' because there was something technical about it that I didn't like. Grace was really very upset when I told her. And she raised her hand and said, 'Now listen, everyone who has come in here has loved it for more than twenty-four years. My children have loved it, I have loved it, and my husband has loved it for twenty-four years.'"

On July 29, 1981—with Albert by her side, as Rainier was purportedly unwell—she attended Prince Charles's wedding to Lady Diana Spencer at St. Paul's Cathedral. During their stay in London, she and Albert were guests of the Queen at Buckingham Palace.

Although all the other wedding guests sent opulent gifts—the Reagans gave a Steuben glass bowl engraved with the images of noblemen, presidents, and crusaders, the Crown Prince of Saudi Arabia gave diamonds and sapphires—the Prince and Princess of Monaco's wedding gift to the future King of England and his bride was merely a silver picture frame.

In August 1981, *Paris Match*'s Pepita Dupont interviewed Grace. Pepita thought she was wonderful but that she was also troubled. "I felt this person was not well in her life," she observed. "She was so sweet, but I noticed she looked sad. She knew that *Paris Match* was coming, but she was not very well dressed. Her hair wasn't combed. I was surprised. No makeup, nothing. I noticed she had just cried. But I don't know why.

"Albert was there too. He was always near his mother. They were very close. She was very kind to me. She introduced me to her little orange dog, Ollie. She also had a parrot called Berlioz in a little cage. She said she was the only one the parrot would let touch it. She was very warm."

In September, she did a ten-day poetry reading tour, visiting Detroit, Nashville, Durham, Baltimore, Pittsburgh, Philadelphia, and Dallas.

During her visit to Durham, North Carolina, Grace made the somewhat unusual request to tour the Institute of Parapsychology there. She was shown around by research fellow Marilyn Schlitz. "She arrived at the institute with a bodyguard. She had no makeup on, had her hair pulled back, and was gorgeous. We spent half a day together," Marilyn remembered. "She said that she had a strong fascination with parapsychology, because her uncle had been a medium. I got the sense that she loved him and that he'd been a really important person in her life."

While Marilyn doesn't remember the name of Grace's uncle, given her sense that Grace loved him, it is more than likely that George Kelly had not only been a playwright but had also been a medium as well.

"She was so open and had a real natural curiosity about parapsychology.

She was really curious, and thrilled by everything she saw at the institute. I took her to the Game Room, in which there were a bunch of ESP devices, one of which was the Four-Button Machine," Marilyn said.

"I did two rounds of experiments with Princess Grace on the machine, in which she sat in front of a little box with four lights on it and a button in front of each of the lights. Then she had to push one of those buttons and anticipate which light was going to light up. In both experiments, she got significantly less correct hits than you would expect, which meant that she was dubbed a 'misser.'

"Her result was so weird to me, because the way in which we generally interpreted the test was that the 'missers' were the unsuccessful people in life, whereas the 'hitters' were the successful ones."

A month later, highly disturbed that ABC was intending to make a biopic of her life starring Cheryl Ladd, Grace contacted Frank Sinatra, asking him to help her block it.

When all attempts failed, the palace issued a statement: "She is very unhappy about the project. What's so irritating is that there's nothing similar between Cheryl Ladd and Princess Grace." The TV movie was nonetheless made and then broadcast after Grace's death.

She spent Christmas in Monaco with Rainier, the children, Cary Grant, and Fleur Cowles. In the New Year, she and Rainier took a rare trip together, traveling to Bangkok and staying at the Oriental. Afterward, a tabloid reported sources having heard them quarreling bitterly.

On March 16, 1982, she was alone again, and in England, where she read poetry as part of the Chichester Festival's twenty-first birthday celebrations.

At the end of the month, she traveled to Philadelphia for "A Tribute to Grace Kelly, Actress" at the Annenberg Center. Naturally—given that the event was for Grace the actress, not Grace the princess—Prince Rainier did not attend.

"Princess Grace had very few requests," Debbie Adis, assistant to Annenberg Center director Steve Goff, recalled to *Philadelphia Magazine.* "She didn't want the Hollywood stars bothered for autographs, and she wouldn't let us film it for cable TV. If we did that, she told us, she wouldn't come. She didn't want to be on camera all night. She wanted to be there to spend time with her family and friends.

"She didn't throw anybody off the list. She added people. Cardinal Krol was a must. Then, she wanted us to have the doctor from East Falls who delivered her. She was really insistent about that. He was a very elderly man, and he was ill. He couldn't come, but he sent her a beautiful floral display. She took that back to her hotel room. Basically, she was here for the family. It became very much a Kelly family affair. Any Kelly had instant access. She was always available to them. I never saw such a loyal family person. When they got together it was like the stars weren't even here," Debbie said.

As Grace took the stage, dressed in soft pink ruffled gown, her hair braided, her face seemed as youthful as it was when she first stormed Hollywood. She was home again, home where it had all started, in America, the country that she loved.

Frank Sinatra—who had changed his schedule to attend—said from the stage, "Gracie, I'm crazy about you." Then, after telling the same gold record story Grace had at the Festival Hall, he looked into her eyes and said, "God willing, Grace, you'll live to be 150 because I'm planning to live that long." She was fifty-two years old. And just six months later she would be dead. "I feel as though the sword of suffering pierced my heart," Frank Sinatra wrote to Prince Rainier after her death.

In the last month of her life, Grace went on a cruise to Norway with Rainier, Albert, Caroline, and Bettina Thompson, her bridesmaid and friend from the Academy.

All through the cruise, Grace had bad headaches. Around that time, according to Doreen Hawkins, she confided to Hjordis Niven that she was suffering from heart trouble.

And on the night before Grace died, Gwen talked to her on the telephone, Grace said, "I'm so fat and I feel so horrible about myself."

She was going through the menopause, which—when she managed to joke about it—she termed "the angry jaws."

She said to Gwen, "I just don't want to show my body to anyone, it's so awful." Gwen promised to find her a good gynecologist in London, then said good-bye to her.

On September 10, 1982, when Robert Dornhelm arrived to visit her at Rocagel, she was complaining of a cold and allergies. "She was depressed and unhappy," he remembered, adding that all weekend she and Stephanie had dreadful arguments over the fact that seventeen-year-old Stephanie was determined to move in with her boyfriend, race car driver Paul Belmondo, the son of actor Jean-Paul Belmondo.

"She was not in good shape. She had a chest cold, headaches, I think it was a head cold, she said. It was actually the worst state I had ever seen her in and I couldn't cheer her up," Robert said.

"Rainier gave that Rover 3500 in 1972. She'd already had one accident in it, and she hated driving it," Bernard Combemal recalled. "Grace told me many times that since the age of twelve, she had suffered from blinding headaches. She explained to me that that was why she did not like to drive. She practically never drove. The Rover practically had no miles in it.

"She wasn't supposed to drive that day. She was supposed to go back to the palace in the prince's Rolls. Rainier had to leave for appointments, but her dress for the evening wasn't ready. So when Rainier had to leave, she said, 'Fine, I'll take Stephanie with me, and when my dress is ready, we'll go.'"

At 9:30 on the morning of September, 13, 1982, Princess Grace stepped out into the sunshine, into the Rover, and took the wheel of the car.

She was anxious and nervous. She loathed driving, in particular, driving around a particular bend in the road, the bend on which the Rover would crash, then hurtle down the precipice beneath, with Grace and Stephanie in it.

Not too long before she died, Grace and Gwen were driving around that same bend, and Grace said, "You know, someday, darling, somebody's going to have a dreadful accident here."

As Grace's close friend Arlene Dahl recalls, "She had always been psychic. I was with Grace in Monaco six weeks before she died. During that same visit, Grace kept looking at her watch. She said, 'Oh, that Stephanie is almost an hour late for her lesson. That child...' Finally, Stephanie came in – I guess she had had a riding lesson – dishevelled. And Grace said, 'You must go right now into the library and you must apologize to Mr So-and-so for being so late.' Stephanie said, 'Mother, I have to go up and take a bath.' Grace said, 'You will go in right now.' She had lost her temper. Afterwards, she looked at me and said, 'Arlene, she's going to be the death of me.' And six weeks later, she was driving with Stephanie and didn't come out of it. The way she said it... She was a Scorpio and Scorpios are psychic. It haunted me for years afterwards. The way she said it. I'll never forget it."

All her life she had been troubled by disturbing premonitions, by flashes of the future. She believed that she was psychic, and she routinely consulted psychics. In the midseventies, she consulted one of America's most celebrated psychics, Frank Andrews. At the end of their session, which took place at Andrews's house on Manhattan's Mulberry Street, Grace told him that she had one more question.

"I've always had a premonition that I'm going to die in a car crash," she said. "Will I?"

Frank Andrews paused. "Do you really want to know?'

"Yes," she said. "Yes, I do."

He took a deep breath. "Look, I can't say if you will die in a car crash. But I will say this: if you don't change your eating habits and your drinking, you can very easily have a stroke or a heart attack. And that could happen in a car."

She had had a premonition that she would die in a car crash. Psychic Frank Andrews had predicted that she could die in a car, and she firmly believed it. She said as much to a group of friends that night, as they were having dinner at Cleo's on the Upper West Side of Manhattan.

She believed she was going to die in a car, and yet, on the morning of September 13, 1982, she took the wheel of the car and turned it toward the treacherous Corniche.

That Grace—not Stephanie—was driving that morning is incontrovertible, despite all the many rumors to the contrary. In the words of Christian de Massy, "Rocagel is in France, and Grace would never have allowed Stephanie, who was underage, to drive in France.

"Grace planned her career, planned her life. She would never have allowed her daughter to be stopped in France driving illegally. She would never have run that risk, because if the press had found out, the headlines would have been, 'Princess Grace Doesn't Give a Shit About French Law. She Allows Her Underage Daughter to Drive in France.'

"She would never have allowed that to happen. Nine-tenths of the 25-minute drive between Rocagel and the palace is in France, and Grace would never have allowed her to drive there illegally."

Despite her deep-rooted fear of driving, despite the predication that she would die in a car, Grace nevertheless took the wheel that day and drove. So did she want to die that day? Did she want to kill herself? And her daughter, Stephanie, too?

Nothing could be farther from the truth. Despite Stephanie's bull-headedness, her rebelliousness, Grace loved her and wanted her—and all her children—to live and be happy.

She also wanted to live herself. For despite her disappointments—middle age, Rainier's infidelities, her problems with Caroline and Stephanie—Grace loved life. She did believe that she would die in a car crash, but not then, not so soon. After all, she had always been lucky.

Indeed Grace Kelly was born lucky. Exquisitely beautiful, a talented actress, a woman with tremendous sexual charisma, elegant, stylish, intelligent, intuitive, with breeding, money, charm, everything she had ever wanted had always been hers. She had lived many lives: Philadelphia heiress, Hollywood screen goddess, Princess of Monaco, daughter, wife, and mother. And through it all, despite her sometime unhappiness, she had been lucky.

And while she had no doubts whatsoever that she was destined to die in a car crash, Grace still clung to the hope that it wouldn't be then, that it wouldn't be now.

Five months before she died, she said, "No one likes the idea of getting older. It's a question of facing the inevitable and not getting upset about it. One doesn't feel older until you start getting aches and pains and have to curtail or adjust your activities. That hasn't happened to me—yet. I'm lucky and am just looking forward to what comes next."

At twelve noon, on September 14, 1982, Prince Rainier gave permission to switch off the Princess of Monaco's life-support machine.

At 10:35 that night, Grace was pronounced dead.

GRACE PATRICIA KELLY

Born November 12, 1929, Philadelphia, Pennsylvania
Died September 14, 1982, Monte Carlo, Monaco

Appendix I

Celebrated American astrologer John Townley, who pioneered the art of synastry, has published five books including *Dynamic Astrology*. This is his reading of Grace's chart:

You are a person totally gifted by birth with an innate sense of feeling—a grand water trine of Sun and Mars with Moon and Pluto, whose watchwords are character, work, emotion, and faith—through which you instinctively intuit what goes on in the hearts of others, the essence of a performer who must play and actually become the part of another. Plus, with Mercury rising, intelligence and clarity are a natural, and you are a person who is in control of your thoughts and always knows what to say.

With quadruple-Scorpio Sun and Ascendant together with Mars and Mercury, control, reticence and withholding are also built-in, which gives you a sense of external propriety second to none, whatever may be going on underneath. Jupiter conjunct the Vertex means destiny awaits where display, ambition, and the latest fashion are determiners of what must be. It's big-time or bust. The positions of the Moon's nodes, especially with Chiron, indicate that partnerships are critical to your most important life moves, even though they wound you in the process.

Oddly enough, the inspiration—the fire positions in the chart—are crusty Saturn and Uranus, which indicate that what truly moves you is tradi-

tional, and yet unusual. Undiscovered history and older persons with an un-
predictable twist are what really connect you to your inner spirit. A wide but
applying square of Moon to Saturn makes you initially dislike and even fear
the demanding and insistent side of that world, especially your parents and
upbringing, but once you get over it, it actually becomes a lifelong motivation
and rich source of inner support and understanding.

Sadly, your Venus—planet of desire, needs, and inner satisfaction—is in
your hidden twelfth house of trouble and sometimes disaster. What people
think you want, or those they think you love, are not in fact at all as they
seem—and your true heart's desire can bring you hidden and uninvited trouble, providing learning from experience but perhaps not the intended reward.
It may be safest to say that you will ultimately get what you want but may not
be entirely pleased by it, and will keep it to yourself. Watch out what you ask
for, even when it's handed you on a silver spoon . . . and whatever comes,
stoop not to complain . . . As an astrological type, you are one of those few
who are from birth both talented and privileged, have endless energy, and although you do not have to struggle as much for what you achieve compared
to others in the same field, still garner amazing and almost universal admiration. The result is often early success, later overtaken by the backwaters of
missed possibilities in the midst of glory—the classic development pattern
for this kind of horoscope.

Appendix II

ANALYSIS OF GRACE'S HANDWRITING

Distinguished graphologist and scientific handwriting analyst Deborah Jaffe has studied Grace's handwriting. This is her report:

You are a sociable character and enjoy the presence of people from all walks of life. Your ability to integrate on various social levels with both traditional and unconventional types guarantees a diverse group of contacts. However, you are at your most relaxed state with someone you feel you can trust, who will embrace your natural qualities, mirroring your ideals or sharing a similar viewpoint of society.

You are a mercurial type and are intrigued by your environment and able to contribute your views in a stimulating manner. Furthermore, due to your active and curious nature you will be involved and preoccupied with several projects at any one time. You are also adept at playing the part of a perfect hostess, being charming, attentive and intent on making a grand impression especially if this could enhance your status. You are also extremely intuitive and often rely on your "gut feelings." This attribute enables you to assess the nature of your contacts, calculate the subtle nuances of a character and help you to decide how to act accordingly.

Another important facet is your "emotive" and passionate nature. This impacts the way in which you deal with people, projects and your immediate circumstances. You are ultimately a subjective character.

With regard to your "persona," it appears that there are two sides of your character which are consciously projected—as you are very aware of your image. With those with whom you feel comfortable, you are entirely natural and expect to be appreciated as an individual. You have a marked sense of the self, and pride in the grandeur of your status.

Your mentality duplicates your social attitude which is vibrant, and somewhat demanding at times. Furthermore, even though you respect the rules and regulations of society, inwardly you are not a conventional conformist and your ideas reflect your originality.

Your imagination is pictorial and you are capable of rather unusual and unorthodox concepts about which you are usually secretive. Additionally, you are able to display some reserve which undeniably enhances a certain air of mystery.

You attempt to incorporate your ideas into reality, but you are not always aware of what is realistically achievable. However, you have an astute and tenacious nature which you utilize in order to achieve your objectives. Furthermore, your determination can be formidable and if you feel that your "missions" are being meddled with, you will have no reservations about retaliating.

You are certainly a "free spirit" and feel that it is imperative for you to have the freedom to choose what you would like to do, as and when it suits you. However, you do not operate well under pressure and often exhaust your "psychic energy."

Your temperament is slightly histrionic, you are inclined to mood swings and sometimes appear to be emotionally unsettled.

Your self-confidence and judgment of other people appear to waver according to your moods. You use your intuition as a tool and are capable of an "instinctive insight." Consequently, you are able to absorb the feelings of people you encounter and perceive their thoughts in a somewhat abstract manner. Sometimes, this way of dealing with life makes you feel emotionally burdened.

Your gracious, gentle and protective side is reserved for a very select group of people. You are certainly a caring and loving character who relishes the affection of others. However, there appears to have been bitter disappointments with some relationships and your attempts to suppress these feelings have created a certain amount of havoc in your life.

Even though you value your independence, you are at your best when you have the opportunity to play the maternal role. Above all, you possess a unique capacity to touch the souls of other people.

About the Book

Researching and writing a biography of Grace Kelly was a daunting proposition. Gant Gaither, Gwen Robyns, Sarah Bradford, James Spada, Steven Englund, Phyllida Hart-Davis, Jeffrey Robinson, Robert Lacey, and Randy Taraborelli have all published biographies of Grace Kelly. Her bridesmaid, Judith Balaban Quine has written about her marriage and the aftermath. Arthur Lewis has written about the Kelly family; Stanley Jackson, Anne Edwards, and John Glatt have published histories of the Grimaldi family, including extensive material on Grace.

Over twenty years had passed since Grace's death and I judged that my chances of finding even a single interviewee who had known her but hadn't yet talked to any of the other biographers were extremely slim. And even if I did succeed in finding one single, solitary untouched source, the chances were high that he or she wouldn't have anything new to add to Grace's story.

Fortunately, my fears proved to be groundless. During three years of research, I interviewed one hundred and twenty-five on-record sources, including ninety-eight people who had not talked to any previous Grace biographers, including a former head of the SBM, the imposing Bernard Combemal, and Grace's good friend the marvelous Father Peter Jacobs, "Father Jake." I disclosed fifteen of her romances—Bill D'Arcy, Richard Boccelli, Joe Mustin, Philip Barry Jr., Sidney Wood, Robert Evans, Robert Slatzer, Fred Zinnemann, Barney Strauss, Sir Anthony Havelock-Allan, Tony Curtis, Marlon Brando, Malcolm Reybold, Walter Carone, and Graham Binns—who had not been interviewed or written about before by any of her other biographers, and succeeded in interviewing nine of them who were alive at the time of researching the book. After the book was published in America, Grace's friend and fellow MGM star Arlene Dahl told me that Grace had had an affair with Cary Grant.

Biographers are often accused of digging dirt, yet every single one of the most sensational revelations in *True Grace* came to me unsought. When I went to interview Aileen Mehle, the legendary, ever-glamorous society columnist, *Suzy*, on the suggestion of distinguished author and art critic John Richardson, I anticipated that she would relate a few charming anecdotes about encountering Grace at various social events throughout the years. Instead, demonstrating characteristic generosity to another writer, Aileen told me about Grace's letter to Carolyn Reybold.

In the same vein, when I contacted Peter Lawford's widow Patricia Seaton-Lawford, I anticipated that she would tell me a few Hollywood anecdotes that Peter had relayed to her from his time with Grace at MGM. Instead, she volunteered that he had told her about Grace's affair with Sinatra during her marriage to Rainier.

The way I learned about Grace and David Niven is described in the text, and again, the information came to me entirely by accident. As did the Graham Binns story, revealed to me over lunch by journalist Paul Callan, who then introduced me to Antonia Simpson, Graham Binns's former landlady and the recipient of his confidences regarding Grace.

I began my research by drawing on a variety of clippings services and libraries, including *Hans Tasiemka Archives* in London; the George D. McDowell *Philadelphia Evening Bulletin* Collection at the Urban Archives; Temple University; the Press Association; the British Film Institute Library; Kensington and Chelsea Library; the *Philadelphia Inquirer* Library; the Margaret Herrick Library at the Academy of Motion Pictures Arts and Sciences, Los Angeles; the John F. Kennedy Library in Boston; and Freeman's News Service in New York.

This book couldn't have been written without the help, support, and kindness of Grace's first biographer and friend, Gwen Robyns. Her insight into Grace was invaluable and the dedication to this book says it all.

I am immensely grateful to *Sinatra: The Life* authors Anthony Summers and

Robbyn Swan for not only affording me hospitality at their home in Ireland and giving me access to their vast library, but also for introducing me to the invaluable Kelly DiNardo in Washington who succeeded in unearthing the most elusive of telephone numbers for me.

Nemesis author Peter Evans was a great source, a wonderful friend, and a mine of wisdom, as well. Other authors who unstintingly gave their help and advice include Grace biographer Robert Lacey, John Connolly, John Glatt, *Niv* author Graham Lord, John Richardson, Peter Kurth, Gordon Thomas, *File on the Tsar* coauthor Tom Mangold, and Geoffrey Wansell.

Jack King and Terry Sheen at Capa, the study award providers, arranged for a talented and industrious series of interns to work with me on the book: Megan McGuire, Cristine Chambers, Kristen DiLemmo, and Nils Hoger-Lerdal were all tremendous assets, as were my personal assistants, Luisa and Edward Moller, Sarada Earnshaw, Alexis Schumacher, Jess Hill, and Miriam Neuman, all of whom provided terrific support for all aspects of the research. Thanks, too, to Olga Byrne in New York.

After over thirty years as a journalist, during which my work was published in a variety of publications from *The Daily Mail, The Mail on Sunday, The Times, The Sunday Times, The Independent, The Daily Telegraph, The Observer, The Guardian, The Evening Standard*, the *Daily Mirror*, the *Sunday Mirror, The Sun, The New York Post, Hello, McCall's, People, US, Cosmopolitan*, and *Ladies' Home Journal*, I was fortunate in being able to turn to a multitude of journalists and editors for contacts, help, advice, as well as assignments that took me to various research locations, sometimes involving interviews with sources who turned out also to have known Grace and were prepared to talk about her. I owe them all a debt, with special thanks to Jim Gillespie, features editor of *The Daily Mail*, whose contribution was invaluable.

Thanks, too, to Roger Alton, editor of *The Observer*; Gerard Greaves, editor of *The Mail on Sunday's Live* magazine; Caroline Graham of *The Mail on Sunday*; Patricia Towle of *The National Enquirer*; Gary Thompson of the *News of the World*; Patrick McCarthy of *Women's Wear Daily*; Pat Gregor of *The Globe*; Beverly Ecker of *Star* magazine; James Brady of *Parade*; Danielle Baron and Tom McGrath of *Philadelphia Magazine*; Murray Dubin of the *Philadelphia Daily News*; Cindy Reeves of *The Palm Beach Post and Daily News*; as well as to journalists and friends in a variety of related fields who led me to sources who had known Grace, including Sandy Williams, Evelyn Monte, Nina Lerner, Dr. Erika Padan Freeman,

Richard Pollman, Sue Hyman, Paul Hagenauer, Philip Finn, Sandy Whitelaw, James Douglas, Susan Crimp, Marion Collins, Tina Flaherty, Brenda Swanson, Michael Cole, Jean-Pierre de Lukovitch, Marlene Koenig, Nikki Haskell, Catherine Saxton, Paul Callan, and Richard Compton Miller.

I am immensely grateful to distinguished astrologer John Townley, at www.astrococktail.com, who pioneered the composite chart technique, is the author of *Planets in Love*, and did Grace's astrological chart, and to the uncannily accurate graphologist Deborah Jaffe, at dj@btinternet.com, for her interpretation of Grace's handwriting.

During my research for the book, following in Grace's footsteps, I traveled to Philadelphia, where I stayed at the Bellevue Stratford, and was delighted to celebrate the birthday of Grace's still beautiful bridesmaid Maree Frisby Rambo with her. Richard Boccelli, who dated Grace when she was in her late teens, had tea with me at Philadelphia's Four Seasons and drove me to Henry Avenue, where I was able to view the exterior of the Kelly home. In Boston, I interviewed another bridesmaid, the charming Bettina Thompson and also did research at the Kennedy Library.

In Ocean City, Bob and Sally Harbaugh were most hospitable and gave me a guided tour of Ocean City and showed me the letter Grace's sister Lizanne wrote to Bob when she was with Grace in Hollywood during the making of *High Noon*, kindly granting me permission to quote the content in full in this book. However, copyright laws have precluded me from doing so.

In Manhattan, I was fortunate to interview Oleg Cassini who gave me one of his last interviews about Grace before his death in 2006. He was kind, courteous, and clearly proud to have been her fiancé, but touchingly persisted in maintaining the fiction that, apart from Ray Milland, he had been the only man in her life prior to her marriage. Distinguished Presidential historian Barry Landau kindly shared his vivid memories of Grace with me, including the startling story of her visit to Frank Andrews, which she had confided in him not long before her death. The erudite Jones Harris detailed Alice Heine's story for me and generously introduced me to John Richardson who was charming, witty, gallant, and tremendously helpful, introducing me to Reinaldo Herrera, Kenneth Jay Lane, Jamie Niven, and Aileen Mehle.

In Fort Lauderdale, I interviewed Matthew Binns, who shared his memories of his father with me. In Palm Beach, I was fortunate to meet with Malcolm Reybold's daughter by his first marriage, Patricia, and his daughter by

Carolyn Reybold, Nyna. Nyna, wanting to set the record straight about her mother's life and current circumstances, invited me to visit and interview Carolyn in her Long Island nursing home, and accompanied me there.

Carolyn appeared sane and eager to share her memories of Grace with me in a taped interview. Afterward, however, Nyna's elder sister Jyl, who is writing her own book about her mother and whose offer that I collaborate with her on it I declined, was furious that Nyna had taken me to see her mother and that Carolyn had talked to me. She told me in no uncertain terms that she did not wish me to use her mother's quotes. However, Carolyn talked to me of her own volition, on tape, and was fully aware that the interview she gave me was for this book, so I see no reason to bow to Jyl's demands.

In Los Angeles, I stayed first in the Beverly Hills Hotel, just as Grace did on the night on which she won the Academy Award and on many occasions afterwards, and then at the Bel-Air, where Grace once trysted with Clark Gable and which later became her hideaway during the height of her fame as Princess Grace of Monaco. I interviewed a large number of crucial sources, including producer Robert Evans, Alfred Hitchcock's daughter Patricia, and a year before his death, Robert Slatzer. In Los Angeles I also had two long lunches with Robert Dornhelm, who categorically denied that he and Grace had been romantically involved but showed me the most beautiful, romantic photographs of her that he had taken himself in which she wasn't wearing any makeup and her hair was long and flowing.

In Las Vegas I interviewed Tony Curtis, who for the first time ever revealed the fact that he and Grace had had a romantic relationship. In Palm Springs, I interviewed Frank Sinatra's valet, George Jacobs, and producer, George Englund.

During four trips to Manhattan, I stayed at the Waldorf-Astoria where Grace and Rainier danced together at the Imperial Ball before their marriage; at the Regency, where she stayed as a young actress and at the St. Regis, where she stayed as Princess of Monaco. There, I talked to a vast range of sources from the incomparable Patricia Neal to Kathryn Crosby.

In Amsterdam, I had lunch with Dewi Sukarno, who shared her memories of Grace during the seventies. During three trips to Paris, I stayed at the Plaza Athenee, where Grace loved to lunch at the Relais Plaza, and at the George V where she attended many functions. In Paris, Pepita Dupont, *Paris Match*'s former Monaco correspondent, was unutterably generous with her time, her contacts, and her memories, adding a great deal of depth and range to my research. In Paris, I also interviewed Walter Carone's widow Catherine, and Louis Frosio, the celebrated violinist at the palace in Monte Carlo, played for me, while reminiscing about Grace.

During three trips to Monte Carlo, where I stayed at L'Hermitage, the hotel whose décor was created by Grace, and then at the supermodern Meridien, I was able to experience and understand Grace's world. Baron Christian de Massy gave me an interview lasting over three hours; Jeanne Kelly Van Remoortel, Grace's friend, invited me to her restaurant Le Texan, showed me letters written to her by Princess Grace, and allowed me to quote a small amount of our conversation. She did not want to give me an extensive interview as she is writing her own book.

In Portofino, at the Splendido, I was able to experience the romantic atmosphere of the hotel in which Grace and Rainier stole a few days during the early part of their marriage. In Schoenried, Switzerland, where Grace and Rainier rented a chalet for twenty years, I explored the area, viewed the exterior of the chalet and researched Grace's life. Marion Pigache interviewed Monica von Siebenthal, proprietor of Hostellerie Alpenrose, where Grace, Rainier and the children often had dinner.

In London, I conducted a great number of interviews over lunch at Mosimanns, including a lengthy interview with Bernard Combemal, former head of the SBM. I traveled to Gloucestershire to interview Jonathan Binns, to Henley-on-Thames where Sir John and Lady Mortimer shared with me their memories of Grace, and on many occasions to Long Hanborough, Oxfordshire, to see Gwen Robyns.

Some of the sources interviewed for the book—all on tape and all on the record—to whom I am extremely grateful are Karen Amiel, Susan Andreasen, Frank Andrews, Ken Annakin, Jeffrey Archer, Bill Ashmead, James Bacon, Jean-Claude Baker, Tish Baldrige, Patricia Barry, the late Stephen Barry, Frank Basile, Jonathan Binns, Matthew Binns, Susan Binswanger, Lesley Blanch, Dick Boccelli, Sue Bongard, Noel Botham, James Brady, Oleg Briansky, Leslie Bricusse, David Brown, Paul Callan, Catherine Carone, the late Barbara Cartland, Sue Casey, the late Oleg Cassini, Patricia Medina Cotten, Bernard Combemal, Peggy Connelly, Ralph Wolfe Cowan, Antony Cozzi, Kathryn Crosby, Tony Cucurullo, Tony Curtis, Arlene Dahl, Paula Jane D'Amato, Bill D'Arcy, Bruce Davison, Baron Christian de Massy,

Robert Dornhelm, Betsy Drake, Ben Dreyfus, Robin Biddle Duke, Dominick Dunne, Pepita Dupont, George Englund, Peter Evans, Robert Evans, Eileen Ford, Jonathan Foreman, Louis Frosio, Zsa Zsa Gabor, Rita Gam, Massimo Gargia, John Glatt, Lindsey Granger, Bettina Gray, Patrick Guinness, Beth Gutcheon, William Hall, Bob Harbaugh, Lee Harrigan, Nicholas Haslam, the late Sir Antony Havelock-Allan, Lady Sara Havelock-Allan, Doreen Hawkins, Reinaldo Herrera, Patricia Hitchcock, Celeste Holm, George Jacobs, Father Peter Jacobs, Maria Cooper Janis, Jill Duchess of Hamilton, Schuyler Johnson, Jay Kanter, Phil Kellog, Richard Killian, Peter Kurth, Barry Landau, Kenneth Jay Lane, Patricia Seaton Lawford, Robert Levy, David Lewin, Gene London, Paul Lovelace, Mac Macintosh, Aileen Mehle, Sir John Mortimer, Lady Penny Mortimer, Joe Mustin, Patricia Neal, David Niven Jr., Fiona Niven, Jamie Niven, Dale Olsen, Edward Ory, Prince Jean Poniatowski, Gary Pudney, Felice Quinto, Maree Frisby Rambo, Carolyn Reybold, Nyna Reybold, Patricia Reybold, John Richardson, Laura Richardson, Gwen Robyns, Marc Rosen, Arlene Roxbury, Herman Rush, Catherine Saxton, Marilyn Schlitz, the late Robert Slatzer, Victor Spinnetti, Allan Starkie, Barney Strauss, Dewi Sukarno, Taki Theodoracopulos, Michael Thornton, Bob Underhill, Jonathan Van Meter, Jeanne Kelly Van Remoortel, Andrew Vicari, Gore Vidal, Richard Waterman, Antonia Williams, Sidney Woods, Louise Woyce, Valerie Yeomans, and Donald Zec.

I am deeply grateful to my mother for all her encouragement, her work on the manuscript, and her love and support.

To Ellis Fisher Trevor of Thomas Dunne Books for his detailed and inspired contributions to *True Grace*.

And to Tom Dunne himself, for having thrown down that gauntlet in the first place . . . and for having edited the book with his customary flair and brilliance.

Thanks also to the incomparable Four Seasons Resort at Emerald Bay, Great Exuma, where I celebrated finishing the book and which Grace herself would have loved. And thanks to the matchless Halukelani in Honolulu.

And to Claridges — Grace's favorite London hotel.

Notes

This section indicates some of the sources consulted, including interviewees, published sources, and documents consulted. However, it is by no means inclusive. Much information about Grace has been repeated ad infinitum in all the various biographies. Therefore, as often as possible, I have cited the original source that first published the information.

Preface

ix   *Grace, the Vatican, and sainthood*   *Peter Kurth*, Observer Magazine, *November 6, 2005.*

Prologue

1   *description of wedding and cameras obscuring Grace's view*   *Princess Grace of Monaco with Gwen Robyns*, My Book of Flowers; *Alexander Walker, "Regal View of Flower Power."*
Grace and Gary Cooper   *Mrs. John B. Kelly, "My Daughter Grace Kelly"; author interviews with Patricia Neal and Robert Slatzer.*
Grace wanting to marry Bing and threatening to sue for breach of promise   *Author interview with Kathryn Crosby.*
Grace and Rainier's deal with MGM   *John Glatt*, Royal House of Monaco; *Steven Englund*, Grace of Monaco.
2   *Carolyn Reybold witnessing Grace in* **The Father**   *James Spada*, Grace.
"But it wasn't Grace's fault"   *Author interview with Carolyn Reybold.*

Chapter 1

5   *"Jack Kelly was a big man"*   *Author interview with Rita Gam.*

8   *George and Walter Kelly*   *Arthur H. Lewis,* Those Philadelphia Kellys; *John McCallum,* "That Family Called Kelly."

     Walter's career   *Gwen Robyns,* Princess Grace.

9   *Manie Sacks and Levy relationship with Kelly family*   *Author interviews with Sacks's nephew Herman Rush, and with Bob Levy.*

     William Weagley information   *Arthur H. Lewis,* Those Philadelphia Kellys.

     "When Princess Grace came to Philadelphia"   *Author interview with Anthony Cozzi.*

10   *"I remember reading that cable"*   *Sarah Bradford,* Princess Grace.

11   *Schloss Helmsdorf details*   *Marion Pigache interview with Angelika Flemisch, owner of the castle, who revealed that when Grace was Princess of Monaco, her mother traveled to Germany to visit her ancestral home.*

     "We gave her such grief"   *Steven Englund,* Grace of Monaco.

     "I had a good stiff German background"   *Gwen Robyns,* Princess Grace.

     "We were never allowed to sit"   *Gwen Robyns interview with Peggy Kelly.*

     "I met the mother"   *Author interview with Robert Dornhelm.*

     "Oh, that Ma Kelly"   *Steven Englund,* Grace of Monaco.

12   *"We were sitting around the tent"*   *Peter Evans interview with Ava Gardner, tape 1, May 12, 1988, Atticus Productions, courtesy of Peter Evans.*

     Stephanie and Caroline with hand-me-down clothes   *Author interview with Gwen Robyns.*

     boxes of soap   *Ibid.*

     Marks and Spencer trips   *Author interview with Maree Frisby Rambo.*

     giving old gifts away   *Christian de Massy and Charles Higham,* Palace.

     "Sometimes people would receive"   *Ibid.*

     "You owe me five pounds"   *Author interview with Gwen Robyns.*

13   *"Far too stingy"*   *Stanley Jackson,* Inside Monte Carlo.

     Grace and leaving food   *Author interview with Gwen Robyns.*

     "Maree, where are you"   *Author interview with Maree Frisby Rambo.*

     "Grace was very honorable"   *Author interview with Robert Dornhelm.*

     "Once Grace said she'd do something"   *Author interview with Jay Kanter.*

     description of Margaret Kelly   *Gwen Robyns, Robert Dornhelm, Maree Frisby Rambo, who all met her.*

14   *"When we first met"*   *Mrs. John B. Kelly,* "My Daughter Grace Kelly."

     Margaret's career   *Gwen Robyns,* Princess Grace; *Arthur Kelly.*

15   *Jack Kelly's style, Elizabeth Arden, Ellen Frazer*   *Arthur H. Lewis,* Those Philadelphia Kellys.

     "My mother"   *Author interview with Bruce Davidson.*

16   *Margaret's behavior in the face of Jack's infidelity*   *Arthur H. Lewis,* Those Philadelphia Kellys; *John Skow,* "The Princess from Hollywood."

Chapter 2

17   *"I was terribly jealous of her"*   *Grace Kelly interview with* McCall's, 1974.

"Grace was very strong-willed"   James Spada, Grace.

"She was a shy child"   *Margaret Kelly interview with Gwen Robyns.*

18   *Jack forging Kell into instrument of revenge*   Arthur H. Lewis, Those Philadelphia Kellys.

Peggy Miss Personality   *Author interviews with Gwen Robyns and Bob Harbaugh who both know her.*

"My greatest joy in life"   Gwen Robyns, Princess Grace.

Siegfried ill   *Gwen Robyns interview with Dottie Langdon.*

Nativity play   Gwen Robyns, Princess Grace.

19   *Grace swimming at Bel-Air Hotel*   *Author interview with hotel doorman Bob Underhill.*

Jack Kelly and surfboard   Arthur H. Lewis, Those Philadelphia Kellys.

Margaret Kelly and ocean   Ibid.

Jack running for mayor   Ibid.; Gwen Robyns, Princess Grace.

Ocean City background   *Author interview with Fred Miller, Ocean City Museum.*

Jack and politics   Arthur H. Lewis, Those Philadelphia Kellys.

20   *Henry Avenue house*   *Author interview with Bob Levy, who lived next door; Sarah Bradford interview with neighbor Alice Godfrey Waters, Author viewed exterior.*

Don't Feed the Animals   Sarah Bradford, Princess Grace; Gwen Robyns, Princess Grace.

"The woman who played Grace's mother"   Pete Martin, "Luckiest Girl in Hollywood."

21   *"It makes your calves look fat"*   Gwen Robyns, Princess Grace.

"She had a dancer's awareness"   Howell Conant, Grace.

Gaston Duval   Gant Gaither, Princess of Monaco.

outings to the movies   *Author interview with Maree Frisby Rambo.*

22   *"With the deb season coming up upon us"*   Phil Santora, "A Prince for the Girl Who Has Everything."

"Men began proposing to my daughter"   Mrs. John B. Kelly, "My Daughter Grace Kelly."

Harper Davis story   Philadelphia Magazine *interview with Jack Kelly Jr.*

23   *"Grace was an unbelievably"*   *Author interview with Bill Ashmead.*

"I used to pick her up"   *Author interview with Bill D'Arcy.*

"If you wanted to sit ... King bee"   Gwen Robyns, Princess Grace.

24   *"Grace really was a lovely girl"*   *Author interview with Dick Boccelli.*

"She was too rich for my blood"   *Author interview with Joe Mustin.*

Skinny D'Amato information   Jonathan Van Meter, The Last Good Time; *author interviews with Paula D'Amato and Jonathan Van Meter.*

26   *Jack Kelly and Atlantic City Race Track and connection with the area*   William Coe, Atlantic City Magazine, *January 1999.*

"She'd turn up at the racetrack"   *Author interview with Bill Ashmead.*

Yearbook details   Gwen Robyns, Princess Grace.

27   *Caroline unhappy at St. Mary's School and Grace taking her to Henley*   Author interview with Paul Callan.

Chapter 3

28   *"I was talking to JFK about his sisters"*   Mike Mallowe, Philadelphia Magazine, June 1983.

       portrait of Joe Kennedy   Nigel Hamilton, JFK Reckless Youth; John H. Davis, The Kennedys.

29   *Rose to the Paris collections*   Nigel Hamilton, JFK Reckless Youth.

       Margaret with Women's Health Center   Gwen Robyns, Princess Grace.

       "Jack said, 'I fell in love with you tonight!'"   Author interview with Gunilla Von Post. Also in Gunilla Von Post, Love, Jack.

       "Joe wanted Jack"   Michael Beschloss, Kennedy and Khrushchev.

30   *"Grace had a relationship with the president"*   Author interview with Tish Baldrige.

       "She was so scared"   Ralph G. Martin, A Hero for Our Time.

31   *"Grace was like a schoolgirl"*   Author interview with Tish Baldrige.

       Grace on Givenchy dress (which contradicts Tish Baldrige's memory of it being by Yves St. Laurent) and Jack being an all-American boy   Paul Gallico interview with Grace Kelly at the palace in Monaco, June 19, 1965, Oral History Archives, John F. Kennedy Library.

       Grace posing with gun   Steven Englund, Grace of Monaco.

32   *Grace going to White House and Jackie not seeing her*   Philadelphia Inquirer, December 2, 1963.

       Jackie at the feria   Gwen Robyns, Princess Grace; author interview with Barry Landau.

       "I was delighted to meet Mrs. Kennedy"   Philadelphia Magazine, April 27, 1966.

       "That night, at the feria"   Author interview with Barry Landau.

33   *Grace and Bennington*   Jeffrey Robinson, Rainier & Grace; Steven Englund, Grace of Monaco.

       Grace's application to the American Academy   Gwen Robyns, Princess Grace; Sarah Bradford, Princess Grace.

34   *Barbizon details*   Author interviews with Carolyn Reybold and Bettina Thompson; Philadelphia News feature on Barbizon, September 16, 1982; Gwen Robyns, Princess Grace; Sarah Bradford, Princess Grace; Sydney Fields, "Only Human."

       "Grace acted like she was in love"   Author interview with Dick Boccelli.

       Grace losing her virginity   Don Richardson told it to James Spada.

       Grace and Herb Miller   James Spada, Grace.

       "Grace had somewhat of an open door"   Author interview with Bettina Thompson.

       "When one of us dressed"   Sydney Fields, "Only Human."

       "We used to dance"   Author interview with Bettina Thompson.

       "I first met Grace . . . independent"   Author interview with Carolyn Reybold.

35   *Grace at Eastfair*   Ibid.

       description of Eastfair and studio   Author interview with Patricia Reybold.

Malcolm Reybold background   Author interview with Susan Andraesen, Nyna Reybold, Patricia Reybold, and Judith Balaban Quine, Bridesmaids.

Malcolm and Carolyn meeting   Author interview with Patricia Reybold; Judith Balaban Quine, Bridesmaids.

"Malcolm and I"   Author interview with Carolyn Reybold.

36   **"She was obviously well-bred"**   Bernard Scott, "Grace Kelly's Unspectacular Days as a Model."

"Grace was lucky"   Author interview with Carolyn Reybold.

"Grace was not a big model"   Author interview with Eileen Ford.

Chapter 4

37   **"I don't think Grace had formulated"**   Author interview with Laura Richardson.

first meeting with Don Richardson   James Spada, Grace.

38   **"The night we first dated in Hollywood"**   Author interview with Robert Slatzer.

"Don told me that he fell in love"   Author interview with Laura Richardson.

Deborah Kerr accent   Author interview with Gene London.

Grace and clothespin   Robert Lacey, Grace.

"Don never thought Grace was a great actress"   Author interview with Laura Richardson.

Grace's letter to Prudy Wise   Heroes, Legends, Superstars of Hollywood and Rock. All letters from Prudy Wise are from this source.

Margaret Kelly and Richardson   James Spada, Grace.

"One was the Olympic butterfly"   Gwen Robyns, Princess Grace.

39   **Grace dating Philip Barry Jr.**   Author interview with Patricia Barry.

40   **"The four of us . . . in love with acting"**   Author interview with Sidney Wood.

"One afternoon, when Grace was working in television"   Author interview with Carolyn Reybold.

41   **"I was terrible"**   Bruce Caliapin, Time, January 31, 1955.

"She was absolutely stunning"   Author interview with Ben Dreyfus.

the Kellys and the Levys   Author interview with Bob Levy.

"She had a date whom we didn't like"   Author interview with Bob Levy.

42   **"You would ring the Levys' doorbell"**   Author interview with Richard Waterman.

"Frank sang 'Because'"   Author interview with Susan Binswanger.

"Manie was old enough . . . in love with him"   Author interview with Richard Waterman.

Herman Rush quotes on his uncle Manie Sacks   Author interview with Herman Rush; Herman Rush, unpublished biography of Sacks, courtesy of Herman Rush.

43   **"She had become a career carnivore"**   Robert Lacey, Grace.

"I went backstage"   Author interview with Dick Boccelli.

"Grace was the third girl"   Arthur H. Lewis, Those Philadelphia Kellys.

"Don brought Grace to a party"   Author interview with Laura Richardson.

44   **Claude Phillipe**   Ward Morehouse III, The Waldorf-Astoria; Robert Lacey, Grace.

"She had lovely manners"   Sheila MacRae and H. Paul Jeffers, Hollywood Mother of the Year.

Aly Khan   Gwen Robyns, *Grace.*

Aly Khan and the art of **Imsak**   *Author interview with Barbara Cartland, 1976*

"She was like a Patton tank"   James Spada, *Grace.*

Don Richardson and the Academy Award and Grace and Don at dinner years later   *Author interview with Laura Richardson. Over the years, Grace wrote Don a series of revealing letters, but Laura Richardson claims to have burned them all.*

45   *"It was like working on the edge of a precipice"*   James Spada, *Grace.*

"She told me she had done dozens of soaps"   Nancy Nelson, Evenings with Cary Grant.

"She was fabulous"   *Author interview with Dominick Dunne.*

46   *"I thought she was very sweet"*   *Author interview with Rita Gam. Rita Gam was gracious while being interviewed in Manhattan, but when I later contacted her and asked if she knew about Carolyn Reybold's fate said she knew nothing about what had become of her.*

"I was the cameraman . . . so skinny"   *Author interview with Tony Curcurullo.*

George Englund anecdotes   *Author interview with George Englund.*

47   **Shah of Iran**   James Spada, *Grace;* Robert Lacey, *Grace;* Sarah Bradford, *Princess Grace;* author interview with Maree Frisby Rambo.

description of shah's jewels   Judith Balaban Quine, Bridesmaids.

"Grace had a guard outside her front door"   *Author interview with Valerie Yeomans.*

48   **Grace defending Shah of Iran**   Melvin Bragg, Richard Burton.

49   *"Grace would know . . . She was an original"*   *Author interview with Robert Evans.*

Grace dancing for Don Richardson in the nude   James Spada, *Grace.*

50   **Grace dancing the flamenco barefoot on the beach after Alexander**   Gwen Robyns, *Grace.*

Grace dancing barefoot flamenco   *Author interview with Andrew Vicari.*

Chapter 5

51   *"I thought she looked pretty and different"*   James Spada, *Grace.*

"I think she's ours"   Boris Caliapin, Time, January 31, 1955.

52   *"Gene told me he was greatly in love"*   Steven Englund, Grace of Monaco.

"You found in Gene"   Ibid.

53   **information and quotes from Lizanne's letters to Bob Harbaugh**   *Author interview with Bob Harbaugh, who provided access to the letters.*

55   **background on Gary Cooper**   Maria Cooper Janis, Gary Cooper Off Camera; Pete Martin, "Philadelphia Story." Grace's affair with Gary Cooper confirmed in James Spada, *Grace.*

"You should also look at her directors"   *Author interview with Maria Cooper, although she denied that her father had had an affair with Grace.*

"My father told me that Grace had an affair"   *Author interview with Jonathan Foreman.*

"I loved Gary so much . . . she became a princess"   *Author interview with Patricia Neal.*

56   *"She was easy to get into bed . . . really very young"*   *Author interview with Robert Slatzer.*

Chapter 6

60   "**Mogambo** *had three things*"   Hedda Hopper Collection, Margaret Herrick Library, Los Angeles.

61   *background on Clark Gable*   Charles Samuel, The King of Hollywood; Warren G. Harris, Clark Gable.

background on Frank Sinatra   Michael Freedland, All the Way; Anthony Summers and Robbyn Swan, Sinatra; Kitty Kelley, His Way; George Jacobs and William Stadiem, Mr. S; Will Freewald, Sinatra!; Newsweek, June 28, 1999.

background on Ava Gardner   Ava Gardner Museum, Smithfield, North Carolina; Ava Gardner, Ava; Nigel Cawthorne, Sex Lives of the Hollywood Idols; Jane Ellen Wayne, Ava's Men; Roland Flamini, Ava.

details of **Mogambo** *location*   Donald Sinden, A Touch of the Memoirs; Lee Server, Ava Gardner.

"*Grace—Donald—get below*"   Donald Sinden, A Touch of the Memoirs.

62   "*There were things being thrown*"   Ibid.

"*Don't be fooled by his looks*"   Ava Gardner, Ava.

63   "*Gable wanted a night with Ava*"   Author interview with David Lewin, during which he speculated that Grace had been murdered, revealing that the late author Graham Greene led him to believe so. "I saw him soon after Grace's death," Lewin said, "and he told me, 'Grace was murdered. I've been to see the police and they don't want to do anything about it.' I asked him how he knew, and he didn't say. He just said, 'Look, I know.' Graham had contacts in British Intelligence." When I checked with the writer's nephew, Graham Greene, he knew nothing about his uncle having contacted the police regarding Grace's death, nor did Graham Greene the author record any such thing in his diaries.

"*I hate bugs*"   Hedda Hopper Collection, Margaret Herrick Library.

64   "*Gable's first choice was Ava . . . that croc's a prop*"   Author interview with David Lewin.

65   *Grace's memories of Frank in Africa*   Grace Kelly's speech, London Festival Hall, November 16, 1970, when she introduced him in Night of Nights; DVD of Grace's speech and Sinatra's performance that evening. Author was present that night.

"*Ava and Frank behaved so badly at the party*"   Author interview with Lee Harragin.

66   *Ava and Grace*   Ava Gardner, Ava.

"*The moment we arrived back in London*"   Author interview with Maree Frisby Rambo.

67   *Grace pursuing Gable*   Warren G. Harris, Clark Gable.

"*When my father and Tony walked into the Café de Paris*"   Author interview with Jonathan Foreman.

"*We had a ten-day romance*"   Author interview with Sir Anthony Havelock-Allan.

"*Grace used Tony*"   Author interview with Lady Sara Havelock-Allan, who also allowed author to read Sir Anthony Havelock-Allan's unpublished memoirs.

"*When it came to say goodbye to Gable . . . than most people*"   Mrs. John B. Kelly, "My Daughter Grace Kelly."

68   *Grace rendezvous with Clark Gable*   Warren G. Harris, Clark Gable.

"*Grace, you seemed to fall in love all the time . . . these beautiful men*"   Author interview with Gwen Robyns.

Chapter 7

70   *"Jean-Pierre said Grace was so fantastic"*   Author interview with Pepita Dupont.

Hitchcock material   Donald Spoto, The Dark Side of Genius.

71   *"North German or Nordic types"*   Gwen Robyns, Princess Grace.

"I could not think of anything to say to him"   Ibid.

"Maybe she has fire and ice"   Ibid.

"That Gryce"   Robert Lacey, Grace.

"You had to run past 'Jack'"   Author interview with Patricia Medina Cotten.

72   *"He absolutely swore to me"*   Gwen Robyns, Princess Grace.

"Mal was in a desperate situation . . . greatest marriage of all"   Author interview with Doreen Hawkins.

"I think Grace probably . . . gave her another one"   Author interview with Patricia Medina Cotten.

73   *"As an unmarried woman"*   Sunday Mirror, October 28, 1979.

"Grace missed people"   Author interview with Doreen Hawkins.

"Even then I was aware that Grace"   Author interview with Zsa Zsa Gabor for her autobiography, One Lifetime Is Not Enough, by Zsa Zsa Gabor and Wendy Leigh.

"Hedy told me Grace that Grace slept around"   Author interview with Arlene Roxbury.

74   *Lana Turner's one-night-stand with cabdriver.*   Author interview with Schulyer Johnson, whose mother Evie told her. In her day, Evie Johnson was Hollywood's leading society hostess, entertaining a multitude of stars including Humphrey Bogart, Judy Garland, Lana Turner, Frank Sinatra, and Marlon Brando.

"When Grace tried to avoid Howard Hughes"   Nancy Nelson, Evenings with Cary Grant.

76   *"All through the making of **Dial M for Murder**"*   Donald Spoto, Grace.

"She wasn't pretentious . . . we'd go to sleep"   Author interview with Rita Gam.

77   *"Grace loved champagne . . . stop smoking"*   Rita Gam, Actress to Actress.

78   *"Whenever we had lunch"*   Author interview with Maree Frisby Rambo.

"Grace thought she had ESP"   Author interview with Rita Gam.

"Grace had the most incredible ESP"   Geoffrey Wansell, Haunted Idol.

"Grace adored Hitchcock"   Author interview with Rita Gam.

79   *"I think it took him back"*   Lawrence J. Quirk, James Stewart Behind the Scenes of a Wonderful Life.

"Jimmy was working with"   Roy Pickard, Jimmy Stewart.

"Gloria was so worried"   Author interview with Schuyler Johnson.

background on James Stewart   Roy Pickard, Jimmy Stewart; Lawrence J. Quirk, James Stewart Behind the Scenes of a Wonderful Life; Donald Dewey, James Stewart.

"She was anything but cold"   Allen Eyles, James Stewart.

80   *"Grace was my father's favorite actress"*   Author interview with Patricia Hitchcock.

"Grace was so well groomed"   Author interview with Sue Casey.

Chapter 8

82   *"He was a very handsome man"*   Author interview with Donald Zec.

background on William Holden   Bob Thomas, Golden Boy; Donald Shepherd and Robert F. Slatzer, Bing Crosby.

"As for Bill Holden"   Phil Santora, "A Prince for the Girl Who Has Everything."

Holden's psychiatrist   Robert Lacey, Grace.

83   *"In the end, Grace said to MGM"*   Author interview with Kathryn Crosby.

84   *Bing trysting with Grace while his first wife was dying*   James Spada, Grace.

James Bacon material   Author interview with James Bacon.

"In the makeup department...Everybody was"   Author interview with Kathryn Crosby.

85   *"When I arrived, Grace was already there"*   Rosemary Clooney, Girl Singer.

"I listened to Bing...I hated that"   Author interview with Kathryn Crosby.

86   *Tony Curtis romance with Grace*   Author interview with Tony Curtis.

88   *"My father was used to...a straying mode"*   Author interview with Lindsey Granger.

"Grace had one phobia, her behind"   Stewart Granger, Sparks Fly Upwards!

"It wasn't pleasant"   Hedda Hopper Collection, Margaret Herrick Library.

Barney Strauss material   Author interview with Barney Strauss.

89   *"She wasn't in the least bit...beautifully on screen"*   Author interview with Betsy Drake.

background on Cary Grant   Charles Higham and Roy Moseley, Cary Grant; Geoffrey Wansell, Cary Grant, Dark Angel; Gary Morecambe and Martin Sterling, Cary Grant; Maureen Donaldson and William Royce, An Affair to Remember.

"Grace had a kind of serenity"   Nancy Nelson, Evenings with Cary Grant.

"Grace loved and admired Cary"   Ibid.

90   *"Mostly we played roulette"*   Author interview with Betsy Drake.

séance in London   Ibid.

"He had a wonderful sense of humor"   Ibid.

92   *Oleg Cassini details*   Author interview with Oleg Cassini; Gene Tierney and Mickey Herskowitz, Self-Portrait.

93   *"the greatest, most exhilarating campaign"*   Author interview with Oleg Cassini.

"Grace was reserved and distant"   Ibid.

"Grace thought of Oleg as a lapdog"   Author interview with Rita Gam.

"O Leg O Chicken"   Author interview with Betsy Drake.

"The couple planned...they want to think"   John Glatt, Royal House of Monaco.

94   *"Gracie had her heart set"*   Rosemary Clooney, Girl Singer.

Grace at Oscars   Lionel Crane interview with Grace Kelly.

95   *"I thought it would be Peggy"*   Sarah Bradford, Princess Grace.

background on Marlon Brando   Peter Manso, Brando; Marlon Brando and Robert Lindsey, Songs My Mother Taught Me; Patricia Bosworth, Marlon Brando; George Englund, The Way It's Never Been Done Before.

Grace on Oscar night   Judith Balaban Quine, Bridesmaids; Gerold Frank, Judy; Gerald Clarke, Get Happy.

"That night, I was the loneliest person on the planet"   Author interview with Robert Dornhelm.

96   *Brando's Oscar night with Grace*   Darwin Porter, Brando Unzipped. *According to Danforth Prince, Darwin Porter's publisher, Porter's information came from his close friend Edie Van Cleve— Grace's onetime agent and also Brando's. According to Prince, Brando regularly confided in Van Cleve regarding his relationships with women. According to Porter, he and Van Cleve were friends until her death. I requested an interview with Porter, but he was unavailable.*

Chapter 9

98   *history of Monaco and background on Rainier*   Stanley Jackson, Inside Monte Carlo; *Christian de Massy and Charles Higham*, Palace; *Sarah Bradford*, Princess Grace; *Jeffrey Robinson*, Rainier & Grace; *John Glatt*, Royal House of Monaco; *Gwen Robyns*, Princess Grace; *Steven Englund*, Grace of Monaco; *James Spada*, Grace; *Robert Lacey*, Grace; *Anne Edwards*, The Grimaldis of Monaco; *author interview with Christian de Massy.*

109   *"Except for the prince of Monaco"*   Peter Evans, Nemesis.

"With the parliamentary and bank crisis"   Christian de Massy and Charles Higham, Palace.

110   *Onassis's plan for Rainier to marry Marilyn*   Gwen Robyns, Princess Grace.

Onassis's plan for Rainier to marry Eva Marie Saint or Deborah Kerr   Arthur H. Lewis, Those Philadelphia Kellys.

Chapter 10

112   *"After the reception"*   Pete Martin, "I Call on Princess Grace."

"She and Jean-Pierre Aumont waited"   Author interview with Pepita Dupont.

113   *"Grace was showing him the interior of the castle...far away"*   Gant Gaither, Princess of Monaco.

Alec Guinness quotes   Alec Guinness, Blessings in Disguise.

114   *material on the Austins*   Jack O'Brien, "Cupids Tell Real Story of Grace."

116   *"When I saw the way things were"*   Phil Santora, "A Prince for the Girl Who Has Everything."

"She didn't have time to be really in love"   John Glatt, Royal House of Monaco.

117   *"She was playing a princess"*   Gwen Robyns, Princess Grace.

"Grace could sit in front of the fireplace"   Author interview with Robert Dornhelm.

"Once I was fortunate enough to have dinner"   Maurice Zolotow, Cosmopolitan, *December 1961.*

"Grace was a very important actress"   Author interview with David Brown.

"Before Grace left MGM"   Author interview with Gore Vidal; Gore Vidal, Palimpsest.

118   *"Hollywood is a cruel place"*   Author interview with Dale Olson.

"She felt she was getting older"   Author interview with Rita Gam.

"I asked her how much she thought her life would change"   Author interview with Celeste Holm.

"I never wanted just to 'take a husband'"   Sunday Mirror, *October 28, 1979.*

"I did not really give much thought" John Ellison, "Princess Grace."

"I know this is going to be a difficult conversation" Author interview with Oleg Cassini.

119 report of engagement Gwen Robyns, Princess Grace.

Grace and Rainier at Imperial Ball at the Waldorf Olga Curtis, "Grace Kelly Shows Ruby and Diamond Engagement Ring."

Rainier being told that engagement ring was too small Gwen Robyns, who was told by confidential source.

dowry Anne Edwards, The Grimaldis of Monaco.

120 *"Of course, I'm going to continue with my work"* Maurice Zolotow, January 1956.

"I think what happened is her being in love" Maurice Zolotow, "Can a Shy Girl . . . ?"

"The lunch went very well" Author interview with Celeste Holm.

121 *"Yes, dear"* Steven Englund, Grace of Monaco.

"Monaco? It was a great movie set" Author interview with Robert Dornhelm.

"The biggest star of the Metro lot" Joan Collins, Past Imperfect.

122 *"Though involved with Oleg Cassini"* James Spada, Grace.

"Frank, of course, was terribly in love with Grace Kelly" Author interview with Celeste Holm.

"Celeste used to tell me that Frank" Author interview with Frank Basile.

"Dad took me to lunch" Nancy Sinatra, Frank Sinatra.

123 1956 Academy Awards Lionel Crane interview, publication unknown.

Chapter 11

124 *Grace's trousseau* Judith Balaban Quine, Bridesmaids.

"There was such confusion, you know" "Whirlwind After Grace Marries Prince of Monaco."

scene on the dock Author interview with Richard Killian.

125 *"A whole army of journalists"* Author interview with Donald Zec.

Lizanne's farewell Gant Gaither, Princess of Monaco.

stateroom Ibid.

126 *puppy sent as gift from Mr. and Mrs. Alfred Greenfield Jr.* Ibid.

Hitchcock gift Donald Spoto, Grace.

Grace's behavior on voyage Judith Balaban Quine, Bridesmaids; Gant Gaither, Princess of Monaco.

127 *"On the boat she was protected . . . and she laughed"* Author interview with Donald Zec.

"On the boat, it was a fairly raucous scene" Author interview with Richard Killian.

"the equivalent of a hen party" Author interview with Donald Zec.

128 *Walter Carone background* Author interview with Catherine Carone and Pepita Dupont.

"Howell and Walter were in competition" Author interview with Catherine Carone.

"so desperate to find players" Gant Gaither, Princess of Monaco.

"He jumped at the opportunity to get close" Ibid.

129 *"he had never seen Grace so animated"* Ibid.

"Walter Carone was one of the most beautiful men"   Author interview with Pepita Dupont.

"During the voyage, Grace didn't even dance with another man"   Author interview with Maree Frisby Rambo.

"Grace couldn't have had a final fling"   Author interview with Richard Killian.

"Did Grace flirt with Walter?"   Author interview with Catherine Carone.

"Most of the press"   Howell Conant, Grace.

130   *"Without warning . . . toward her new homeland"*   Judith Balaban Quine, Bridesmaids.

Onassis's welcome to Monaco   Robert Lacey, Grace; James Spada, Grace; Peter Evans, Ari and Nemesis.

131   *"she was compelled to receive an American movie star"*   Christian de Massy and Charles Higham, Palace.

"In one of her letters to Don"   Author interview with Laura Richardson.

132   *relationship between Princess Antoinette and Grace and the Kellys*   Christian de Massy and Charles Higham, Palace.

background to wedding celebrations   Judith Balaban Quine, Bridesmaids.

133   *"It was never a fairy tale"*   Christian de Massy and Charles Higham, Palace.

"They thought it was a farce"   Author interview with Gwen Robyns.

details of civil law and ceremony   Judith Balaban Quine, Bridesmaids.

134   *"All the Things You Are" Grace's favorite song*   Author interview with Louis Frosio, who regularly played the violin for her at the palace.

Chapter 12

139   *"When Grace arrived at the cathedral"*   Author interview with Gene London.

"It was a media circus"   Author interview with Rita Gam.

details of Grace and Rainier's deal with MGM,   "The Princess from Hollywood."

140   *"Not only was there pressure before the wedding"*   Pete Martin, "I Call on Princess Grace."

"I was told how magnificent the flowers"   Princess Grace of Monaco and Gwen Robyns, My Book of Flowers.

141   *"After the wedding was over"*   Ladies' Home Journal, September 1982.

"Sometime after, when I was older"   Christian de Massy and Charles Higham, Palace.

"Grace kept saying: maybe we should run off"   John Glatt, Royal House of Monaco.

"I was stationed in Germany"   Author interview with Mac Macintosh.

142   *wedding ceremony*   Judith Balaban Quine, Bridesmaids; Gwen Robyns, Princess Grace.

Sinatra and Ava and the wedding   Sarah Bradford, Princess Grace; Ava Gardner, Ava; David Hanna, Ava.

"Too many movie stars"   Kitty Kelley, The Royals.

"European high society thought the wedding was a joke"   Author interview with Taki Theodoracopulos.

143   *"It was the nicest experrience"*   Gant Gaither, Princess of Monaco.

144   *Peggy saying good-bye to Grace*   Judith Balaban Quine, Bridesmaids.

Grace on the honeymoon   *Ibid.; Gant Gaither,* Princess of Monaco.

145   *"Rainier undoubtedly saw himself"*   *Steven Englund,* Grace of Monaco.

"He liked cowboy movies"   *Author interview with Gwen Robyns.*

"would look alarmed"   *Christian de Massy and Charles Higham,* Palace.

"Rainier was one of the most brilliant men"   *Author interview with Bernard Combemal.*

146   *"nothing more disagreeable to a man"*   *Rainier interview with David Schoenbrun,* Collier's, *1955.*

Rainier, tennis, and the Swifts   *Robert Lacey,* Grace.

147   *"He's just frustrated"*   *Judith Balaban Quine,* Bridesmaids.

"The thing that flabbergasted everybody"   *Dorothy Kilgallen,* Washington Times Herald, *April 24, 1956*

"When Grace arrived back in Monaco"   *Author interview with Pepita Dupont.*

description of palace   *Christian de Massy and Charles Higham,* Palace.

"It was not easy at the start"   *Frederick Sands, "Princess Grace Talks to Woman's Mirror."*

"was in a trap"   *Author interview with Gwen Robyns.*

148   *"They started out having problems"*   *Arthur H. Lewis,* Those Philadelphia Kellys.

"The problem for Rainier"   *Author interview with Pepita Dupont.*

"She certainly had difficulty adjusting . . . difficult for her at the beginning"   *Author interview with Bernard Combemal.*

"'Why,' she said, laughing"   *Maurice Zolotow, January 1956.*

Care packages   *Author interview with Gwen Robyns.*

149   *plastic flowers and "Love" sofa*   *Christian de Massy and Charles Higham,* Palace.

Ponhaus sausage and missing America   *Author interview with James Bacon.*

"Definite anti-American feeling"   *Barbara Walters, "How Now, Princess Grace?"*

"Your father used to work for me"   *Robert Kahn, "What Grace Really Thought About Her Children."*

"We spoke nonstop about hay fever"   *Author interview with Taki Theodoracopulos.*

150   *"I am subject to attacks of claustrophobia"*   *Pete Martin, "I Call on Princess Grace."*

under surveillance   *Sarah Bradford,* Princess Grace; *Gwen Robyns,* Princess Grace; *author interview with Maree Frisby Rambo.*

Grace and protocol   *Author interview with Bettina Thompson.*

"Loss of liberty"   *John Ellison, "Princess Grace."*

"I wouldn't have been able to do my job"   *Sarah Bradford,* Princess Grace.

151   *"After my days as an actress"*   *Sunday Mirror, October 28, 1979.*

"I did exactly what they wanted me to"   *Author interview with Gwen Robyns.*

Chapter 13

153   *Ralph Wolfe Cowan portrait*   *Author interview with Ralph Wolfe Cowan.*

154   *"Rainier was enchanted"*   *Hedda Hopper Collection, Margaret Herrick Library.*

155   *"The Prince laughs at me . . . shell fish"*   *Ibid.*

Rainier filming the birth   Christian de Massy and Charles Higham, Palace.

156   *description of nursery*   Maureen King (their former nanny), "My Life with Princess."

"Remember that your grandfather was a bricklayer"   Author interview with Pepita Dupont.

Grace's letter to Maggi Nolan   Courtesy of Maggi Nolan, who used to run Celebrity Service in Paris, which published Celebrity Bulletin.

157   *"Rainier was very specific"*   Todd Allan, Life After Grace, Meridien TV.

Bill Lovelace story   Author interview with his son, Paul Lovelace.

159   *description of Rocagel*   Gwen Robyns, Princess Grace.

"Rocagel is where we close the door"   Fred Hauptfuhrer, "The Problem on Mother Kelly's Doorstep."

Grace's Hollywood stills in the bathroom   Author interview with Christian de Massy; Howell Conant, Grace.

"Grace told me many times that Rainier was jealous"   Author interview with Gwen Robyns.

160   *"All these actors ... her old environment"*   Author interview with Doreen Hawkins.

lunch with Rainier   Joan Plowright, And That's Not All.

"He was especially awkward"   Christian de Massy and Charles Higham, Palace.

"She was frightened of Rainier"   Author interview with Gwen Robyns.

161   *"She said that the Princess was so sad and lonely"*   Jean-Claude Baker, Josephine.

Chapter 14

162   *"Caroline and Albert were very close together in age"*   Terry Wogan, "The Princess and the D.J."

Caroline putting Stephanie's head in the toilet   Author interview with Christian de Massy.

"I have no power over my daughters"   Author interview with Lesley Blanch.

163   *"The biggest change in my life wasn't the Palace"*   William B. Arthur, "Grace Kelly's Life as a Princess."

"He never stopped having mistresses"   Author interview with Gwen Robyns.

"Most Sundays, Rainier would leave the Palace"   John Glatt, Royal House of Monaco.

164   *"I know he has affairs with other women"*   Sydney Guilaroff and Cathy Griffin, Crowning Glory.

Kings Go Forth Gala   Author interview with James Bacon; James Bacon, Hollywood Is a Four-Letter Town; Art Buchwald, "The Sinatra Gala Chore."

165   *"Frank is bigger than that"*   Sam Zimblast to Gore Vidal.

background on Peter Lawford   Author interview with Patricia Seaton Lawford; Patricia Seaton Lawford, The Peter Lawford Story; James Spada, The Man Who Kept the Secret.

"I have a gorgeous picture ... and she for him"   Author interview with Patricia Seaton Lawford.

166   *"When they were alone on the balcony ... Mr. S. used to call her his 'dream girl'"*   Author interview with George Jacobs; George Jacobs and William Stadiem, Mr. S.

167   *Grace attending Frank's farewell concert*   Author interview with Dale Olson, publicist for the event.

"Once, as they approached a long line"   Judy Klemesrud, "Princess Grace Makes a Movie."

168   *description of Malcolm Reybold*   Author interviews with Patricia Reybold, Nyna Reybold, and Susan Andraesen; Judith Balaban Quine, Bridesmaids.

"Woman adored my father"   Author interview with Patricia Reybold.

169   *"Malcolm was a wonderful guy"*   Author interview with Edward Ory.

The Pursuit of Destiny   Gant Gaither, Princess of Monaco.

Rainier and charades at the Reybolds'   Ibid.

Carolyn Reybold at Grace's debut in The Father   James Spada, Grace.

details on Malcolm, Carolyn, and the family   Author interview with Patricia Reybold; Judith Balaban Quine, Bridesmaids.

170   *"She told me it was over"*   Author interview with Carolyn Reybold, in the presence of her daughter Nyna.

171   *background on Malcolm Reybold*   Author interviews with Patricia Reybold, Nyna Reybold, and Susan Andraesen; Judith Balaban Quine, Bridesmaids; Malcolm Reybold obituary, January 15, 1988.

"We went over to dinner"   Author interview with Aileen Mehle.

"Grace would never have done that"   Author interview with Father Peter Jacobs.

"I've always questioned it"   Author interview with Nyna Reybold.

172   *background to Carolyn Reybold*   Judith Balaban Quine, Bridesmaids; Walter Baron; Janet Midwinter; News of the World, June 4, 1989; Daily Mail, September 14, 1993; Carolyn's story on Hard Copy, September 1993.

173   *"Receiving that letter was the beginning of the downfall"*   Author interview with Aileen Mehle.

Grace leaving Carolyn money in her will   Author interview with Eileen Ford, to whom Carolyn's daughter Jyl revealed it.

174   *"Daddy was very tricky"*   Author interview with Carolyn Reybold, in the presence of her daughter Nyna.

Chapter 15

175   *Jack Kelly's death*   Gwen Robyns, Princess Grace.

Margaret Kelly's death   Press of Atlantic City, January 8, 1990.

Grace breaking down in tears   James Spada, Grace.

"Grace made a sinking boat beautiful again"   Documentary, Life After Grace.

Grace's innovations in Monaco   Author interview with Christian de Massy.

176   *"She organized all the big SBM events . . . when she was dressed up at night"*   Author interview with Bernard Combemal.

177   *Grace's innovations in the palace*   Author interview with Christian de Massy.

"She showed from the first"   Sarah Bradford, Princess Grace.

"She was such a great actress"   Author interview with Reinaldo Herrera.

178   *Khashoggi basing his European operations in Monaco*   Phyllida Hart-Davis, Grace.

August 28, 1960, dinner party on the Christina   Author interview with Reinaldo Herrera.

background on Maria Callas   Giovanni Battista Meneghini, My Wife Maria Callas; Robert Sutherland, Maria Callas.

"I think Maria Callas is a very great artist"   *"A Candid Interview with Princess Grace."*

179   **background on Christina**   *Author interview with Peter Evans.*

"Onassis unquestionably"   *Ibid.*

180   **Grace's four-day cruise on the Christina**   Maurice Zolotow, Cosmopolitan, *December 1961.*

"Onassis wanted to use the SBM for his own business"   *Author interview with Bernard Combemal.*

181   *"Onassis was more interested in maintaining"*   *Ibid.*

"Onassis didn't want to expand"   *Author interview with Taki Theodoracopulos.*

background on Rainier's battle with Onassis   Peter Evans, Ari and Nemesis; *Stanley Jackson,* Inside Monte Carlo.

182   **Grace's spaghetti sauce**   *Author interview with Rita Gam.*

Grace and Rainier at the Splendido in Portofino   *Author visited the hotel, where she saw photograph of them.*

Grace's daily routine   A Look at Monaco, CBS TV, *February 17, 1963; David Taylor,* Sunday Times, *1981.*

183   *"When I used to see Grace"*   *Author interview with Ken Annakin.*

"Grace owned a London taxi"   *Author interview with Jeanne Kelly Van Remoortel.*

184   **background on Nureyev**   Diane Solway, Nureyev.

185   *"Princess Grace was more gracious and royal"*   Anthony Burgess, Observer, *September 26, 1982; background from Roger Lewis,* Anthony Burgess.

Chapter 16

186   **background on David Niven**   *Author interviews with Ken Annakin, Paul Callan, Leslie Bricusse, Phil Kellog, Doreen Hawkins, Aileen Mehle, William Hall, Patricia Medina Cotten, David Lewin, Peter Evans, Graham Lord, David Niven Jr., and Jamie Niven; David Niven,* The Moon's a Balloon *and* Bring on the Empty Horses; *Sheridan Morley,* The Other Side of the Moon; *Graham Lord,* Niv; *David Lewin, "The Last Thing You'd Expect David Niven to Say";* Philadelphia Daily News, *July 30, 1983;* Sunday Mirror, *September 26, 1982.*

"Several of Niv's friends"   Graham Lord, Niv.

David Niven answering Rainier's question about the best sex   *Author interview with Sir John Mortimer.*

187   *"I believe David Niven was Grace's lover"*   *Author interview with Peter Evans.*

"David Niven was a light in Grace's life"   *Author interview with Rita Gam.*

"I would say that David must have been a very, very lucky guy"   *Author interview with Ken Annakin.*

Niven spending evenings at Grace's Paris flat   *Author interview with Robert Dornhelm.*

"David was one of Grace's closest friends"   *Author interview with Phil Kellog.*

"My father was very protective of both Grace and Rainier . . . I really, really loved Grace"   *Author interview with Jamie Niven.*

188 "*I always used to see Grace in the MGM canteen*"   Author interview with George Jacobs.

"*Grace was very friendly with Hjordis Niven*"   Author interview with Bernard Combemal.

"*Grace wasn't nice about Hjordis*"   Author interview with Gwen Robyns.

189 "*all to do with men*"   Graham Lord, Niv.

"*Hjordis told Grace about her infatuation*"   Author interview with Patricia Medina Cotten.

"*We were having lunch at David's beautiful house*"   Author interview with Peter Evans.

Jamie Niven disputing Evans's story   Author interview with Jamie Niven.

190 "*David said, 'We are going out to dinner'*"   Graham Lord Niv.

"*When we were in Lausanne in 1977*"   Author interview with Oleg Briansky.

"*David and Grace both shared a nostalgia*"   Sheridan Morley, The Other Side of the Moon.

191 "*I think what gave Grace an enormous sense of comfort . . . they were really, really close*"   Author interview with Jamie Niven.

192 *David Niven Jr. material*   Author interview with David Niven Jr.

Chapter 17

193 *Caroline's birthday*   Arthur B. Williams, April 11, 1961.

Irish visit   Michael Parkinson, "The Kellys Queue Up to Welcome Grace."

195 "*She is merely spending part of her time in America*"   Donald Zec, "The Hot Iceberg."

196 "*my little holiday treat*"   Ibid.

"*At first Rainier thought . . . a black hole in her life*"   Author interview with Rita Gam.

"*Don showed me Grace's letters*"   Author interview with Laura Richardson.

Grace and Marnie   Patrick McGilligan, Alfred Hitchcock; Frank Goldsworthy, "So Grace Films Again" and "Witness for the Bride"; Donald Zec, "The Hot Iceberg"; Jonah Ruddy, "Grace's Film Must Wait." Author viewed Marnie.

197 "*She was shocked*"   Gwen Robyns, Princess Grace.

"*Caroline told me*"   Author interview with Pepita Dupont.

"*Just knowing Grace and Rainier*"   Author interview with Donald Zec.

"*She lived in a terribly small world*"   Author interview with Doreen Hawkins.

"*I sometimes used to have dinner with Grace*"   Author interview with Lesley Blanch.

198 *John Wayne story*   Aissa Wayne, John Wayne, My Father.

Brando and Grace spending two weekends together on the Riviera   Darwin Porter, Brando Unzipped. It is interesting to note that Brando's costar in Bedtime Story, the movie he was making on the Riviera, was David Niven.

"*She asked me if Dominic's was still the restaurant*"   Tony Curtis and Barry Paris, Tony Curtis.

199 "*As we'd heard from others*"   Judith Balaban Quine, Bridesmaids.

"*Mountbatten was always making passes*"   Author conversation with Jeanne Kelly Van Remoortel.

"*Dinner at the Royal Yacht Club*"   Philip Ziegler, From Shore to Shore.

"*In her wildest of dreams*"   Author interview with Christian de Massy.

"Grace was quite keen"   Author interview with Pepita Dupont.

Grace, Christian de Massy, and Princess Anne   Christian de Massey and Charles Higham, Palace.

200   **The Greatest Story Ever Told** *background*   Judith Balaban Quine, Bridesmaids.

"Stephanie was her daddy's baby"   Gwen Robyns, Princess Grace.

"Stephanie is an interesting child"   Dennis Holman, "Princess Grace Talks . . . About Her Children."

201   *"Grace was insane about her two daughters"*   Author interview with Laura Richardson.

Porto Cervo vacation   Maurice Zolotow, Cosmopolitan, December 1961.

Grace and Vietnam   John Ellison, "Princess Grace."

The Poppy Is Also a Flower   Peter Evans, Daily Express, 1966.

" 'Happy' is not the word I would use . . . in twenty years"   Barbara Walters, "How Now, Princess Grace?"

202   *"He was tubby and smiled kindly"*   Melvyn Bragg, Richard Burton.

Grace's miscarriage   Gwen Robyns, Princess Grace.

Bobby Darin background   David Evanier, Roman Candle.

"The night before the ball"   Author interview with Kenneth Jay Lane.

203   *Rock Hudson and Grace*   Author interview with Dale Olson; Rock Hudson and Sara Davidson, Rock Hudson.

"Grace told me how shocked she was"   Author interview with Dominick Dunne.

204   *"We used some of Rainier's cars . . . closer to the mouth"*   Author interview with Ken Annakin.

Kell's separation   Arthur Lewis, Those Philadelphia Kellys.

London-to-Brighton rally   Margaret Jones, November 1968.

205   *Scorpio Ball*   William Hickey, "It will Be a Ball for Scorpio."

"She had a thing about her shape"   Author interview with Doreen Hawkins.

"Forty is a marvelous age for a man"   William B. Arthur, "Princess Grace at 40."

Grace and Josephine Baker   Author interview with Jean-Claude Baker, Josephine.

Chapter 18

207   *"In the seventies, so many yachts"*   Author interview with Dewi Sukarno.

208   *"resolved to build her life"*   Sydney Guilaroff and Cathy Griffin, Crowning Glory.

"In Monte Carlo restaurants"   Author interview with Dewi Sukarno.

"It was common knowledge around the 'in' group"   Yolande Finch, Finchy.

"We all knew Rainier was a huge playboy"   Author interview with Lesley Blanch.

"Monaco is a very small place"   Author interview with Pepita Dupont.

"In the early 1970s"   Massimo Gargia and Alan Starkie, Jet Set; author interview with Massimo Gargia.

Rainier asking David Niven to find him a flat   Author interview with Sir John Mortimer.

"You know, I have come to feel very sad"   Gwen Robyns interview with Grace Kelly.

"Rainier spent much of his spare time"   Steven Englund, Grace of Monaco.

209   *"Grace had suffered silently"*   Judith Balaban Quine, Bridesmaids.

Mountbatten persuading Grace to take part in Night of Nights   *Author interview with Jeffrey Archer; background from Philip Ziegler,* Mountbatten, *and Brian Hooey,* Mountbatten.

Grace's arrival at Heathrow   *Author interview with Jeffrey Archer.*

Grace's first Festival Hall rehearsal   *November 7, 1970.*

210   **Grace introducing Sinatra at London Festival Hall**   *Author was there;* Evening Standard, *November 14, 1970;* Daily Mail, *November 16, 1970.*

211   **"During Princess Grace's speech"**   *Don Lusher, "Working with Frank Sinatra."*

"Before the show, I watched him"   *Author interview with Jeffrey Archer.*

"She told me she wanted to write . . . but it didn't come to anything"   *Author interview with Peter Evans.*

Grace at the Proust Ball   *Melvin Bragg,* Richard Burton.

212   **Elizabeth Taylor's fortieth birthday party**   *Ibid.; C. David Heymann,* Liz; *Kitty Kelley,* Elizabeth Taylor; *Graham Jenkins with Barry Turner,* Richard Burton, My Brother; *Ellis Amburn,* The Most Beautiful Woman in the World; *"Elizabeth Taylor's Birthday Party,"* Daily Mail, *February 28, 1972; "Elizabeth Taylor's Birthday Party,"* News of the World, *February 27, 1972; "Elizabeth Taylor's Birthday Party,"* Sun, *February 26, 1972; "Elizabeth Taylor's Birthday Party,"* Sunday Mirror, *February 27, 1972; "Elizabeth Taylor's Birthday Party,"* Sunday Times, *February 27, 1972; author interview with Victor Spinnetti.*

213   **Graham Binns's pebbles**   *One was shown to author by Matthew Binns.*

background on Graham Binns   *Graham Binns obituary,* The Independent, *May 13, 2003; John Maxwell,* Jamaica Observer, *May 19, 2003.*

"He was a deeply creative man"   *Author interview with Karen Amiel.*

214   **"Graham was such great fun"**   *Elizabeth Taylor to Nevill Coghill, March 4, 1972, Bodelian Library, Oxford.*

note found in Graham Binns's papers   *Author interview with Matthew Binns. Clearly, that note could well have been from someone other than Grace, but given the relationship that followed—and the fact that Binns kept it until his dying day—it is highly likely that it was indeed written by Grace. His sons, however, did not keep the note, so the handwriting could not be verified.*

215   **"Graham had an open marriage . . . anybody else"**   *Author interview with Antonia Williams.*

"My parents had an open marriage"   *Author interview with Jonathan Binns.*

Chapter 19

216   **"All of Paris"**   *Author interview with Dewi Sukarno.*

Franco Rossellini and Driver's Seat   *Bob Colacello,* Holy Terror.

Marje Proops on Grace wearing white   *Daily Mirror, November 15, 1973.*

Grace not wearing the same outfit   *Author interview with Gwen Robyns.*

217   **Gunther Sachs and Salvador Dalí story**   *Daniel Peres, "Golden Sachs."*

"When I had dinner with Grace and Hitchcock"   *Author interview with Robert Dornhelm.*

Stars on Sunday   *Peter Phillips, Sun, April 20, 1974.*

Grace's Texas barbecue   *Gwen Robyns,* Princess Grace.

1974 Red Cross Ball   *John Glatt*, Royal House of Monaco.

218   *"I got a handwritten note from . . . poorly spelled"*   *Author interview with James Brady.*

219   *"She was operated on . . . have a baby"*   *Author interview with Anthony Cozzi.*

220   *Kell's death*   *James Spada*, Grace.

Grace's life in Paris   *Author interview with Pepita Dupont.*

221   *"She never looked well dressed"*   *Ibid.*

"Grace knew that life"   *Ibid.*

Grace on USS Forrestal   *Author interview with Barry Landau.*

222   *"She was utterly charming"*   *Author interview with Michael Thornton.*

Grace's collages   *Judith Balaban Quine*, Bridesmaids; *Christian de Massy and Charles Higham*, Palace; *James Spada*, Grace; *Gwen Robyns*, Princess Grace; *Robert Lacey*, Grace.

Rainier made fun of her collages   *Robert Lacey*, Grace.

Caroline and Junot   *Christian de Massy and Charles Higham*, Palace; *Judith Balaban Quine*, Bridesmaids.

223   *"Caroline loved my energy"*   *Christian de Massy and Charles Higham*, Palace.

"He was a very charming man"   *Author interview with Bernard Combemal.*

"Grace read it . . . 'Absolutely'"   *Author interview with Jay Kanter.*

"It was a wonderful movie"   *Judy Klemesrud, "Princess Grace Makes a Movie."*

"She was committed"   *Interview with Dennis Stanfill*, Philadelphia Magazine.

Chapter 20

225   *"When the movie was in the can . . . her own profession"*   *Author interview with Oleg Briansky.*

226   *screening in Paris and Dornhelm's reaction to Grace*   *Author interview with Beth Gutcheon.*

"On the night I arrived"   *Author interview with Robert Dornhelm.*

"We filmed her French narration"   *Author interview with Oleg Briansky.*

"I was always honest . . . restaurant together"   *Author interview with Robert Dornhelm.*

228   *"I asked Grace if she wasn't tired"*   *Author interview with Oleg Briansky.*

dancing with Dornhelm   *Author interview with Beth Gutcheon.*

"Grace and I traveled together"   *Author interview with Robert Dornhelm.*

229   *"She started telling me"*   *Author interview with Rita Gam.*

230   *Grace and Shakespeare*   *Gwen Robyns*, Princess Grace; *Judith Balaban Quine*, Bridesmaids.

Caroline engagement announcement   *Gwen Robyns*, Princess Grace.

231   *"It's in the bag"*   *Christian de Massy and Charles Higham*, Palace.

"It was a joke"   *Author interview with Christian de Massy.*

Grace's 1978 poetry tour of America   *Gwen Robyns*, Princess Grace.

"I discovered that there was mounting fury"   *Author interview with Paul Callan.*

232   *Caroline's wedding*   *Gwen Robyns*, Princess Grace.

Stephanie refusing to wear a dress   *Author interview with Christian de Massy.*

Junot waiting five hours for Grace at the palace   Ibid.

233   *Gwen Robyns trying to hide the Junots' unhappiness*   Author interview with Gwen Robyns.

Chapter 21

234   *William F. Buckley*   William F. Buckley, Nearer, My God.

Jeffory FitzGerald   Judith Balaban Quine, Bridesmaids.

"A friend told her . . . That was very hard"   Author interview with Father Peter Jacobs.

235   *"I was disappointed"*   J. Randy Taraborrelli, Once Upon a Time.

"She looks at me . . . authority"   Alexander Walker, It's Only a Movie, Ingrid.

236   *"She dreaded public functions"*   Author interview with Robert Dornhelm.

"This was a British pub. . . . Queen of England"   Author interview with Paul Callan.

"She had a little . . . she loved the show"   Pat Hackett, The Andy Warhol Diaries.

237   *"Princess Grace . . . ice princess"*   Author interview with William Hall.

238   *"She was in airplanes too much"*   Sarah Bradford, Princess Grace.

Diana and Grace   Gwen Robyns, Princess Grace; Kitty Kelley, The Royals.

"But Lady Diana"   Author interview with Stephen Barry, 1981.

"Don't worry, dear"   Author interview with Gwen Robyns.

"How wonderful and serene"   Andrew Morton, Diana.

239   *"Poor thing"*   Author interview with Michael Thornton.

"Rainier seems a staid"   Nancy Nelson, Evenings with Cary Grant.

Grace at Beverly Hilton fund-raiser   Author was there.

" 'Darling, I never see my friends anymore' "   Zsa Zsa Gabor and Wendy Leigh, One Lifetime
Is Not Enough.

240   *"They like separate things"*   Sun, February 18, 1981.

"I was Elizabeth's . . . He's a nice guy,"   Author interview with José Quinto.

Ralph Wolfe Cowan story   Author interview with Ralph Wolfe Cowan.

Grace at Diana's wedding   Gwen Robyns, Princess Grace.

241   *"I felt this person . . . she was very warm"*   Author interview with Pepita Dupont.

September 1981 poetry tour   Author interview with Gwen Robyns.

Grace at the Institute for Parapsychology   Author interview with Marilyn Schlitz.

242   *Cheryl Ladd movie*   Daily Mirror, October 29, 1981.

Grace's last Christmas   Judith Balaban Quine, Bridesmaids; Gwen Robyns, Princess Grace.

Bangkok trip and arguments between Grace and Rainier   Noel Botham, "Princess Grace."

March poetry reading   Daily Mirror, March 17, 1982.

Philadelphia tribute   Steve Goff, Philadelphia Magazine; Philadelphia Daily News, September 15, 1982; Daily Express, April, 2, 1982.

243   *Norwegian cruise*   Author interview with Bettina Thompson.

Grace and heart trouble   Author interview with Doreen Hawkins.

"I'm so fat"   Author interview with Gwen Robyns.

244   *"She was depressed . . . I couldn't cheer her up"*   Author interview with Robert Dornhelm.

"Rainier gave her that Rover ... we'll go"   Author interview with Bernard Combemal.

"You know, someday, darling"   Author interview with Gwen Robyns.

Grace's session with Frank Andrews   Author interview with Frank Andrews.

245   *Grace confirms Andrews's readings and predictions*   Author interview with Barry Landau, who was with her at Cleo's when she revealed it.

Selected Bibliography

Books

Amburn, Ellis. *The Most Beautiful Woman in the World: The Obsessions, Passions, and Courage of Elizabeth Taylor*. New York: Cliff Street Books, 2.

Bacon, James. *Hollywood Is a Four-Letter Town*. Chicago: Regnery, 1976.

Baker, Jean-Claude. *Josephine: The Hungry Heart*. New York: Random House, 1993.

Balaban Quine, Judith. *Bridesmaids: Grace Kelly, Princess of Monaco, and Six Intimate Friends*. New York: Grove Press, 1989.

Baldrige, Letitia. *A Lady, First: My Life in the Kennedy White House and the American Embassies of Paris and Rome*. New York: Penguin Books, 2002.

Beschloss, Michael R. *The Crisis Years: Kennedy and Khrushchev, 1960–1963*. New York: Harper, 1991.

Bosworth, Patricia. *Marlon Brando*. New York: Viking, 2001.

Bradford, Sarah. *America's Queen: The Life of Jacqueline Kennedy Onassis*. New York: Viking, 2.

————. *Princess Grace*. New York: Stein and Day, 1984.

Bragg, Melvin. *Richard Burton: A Life*. Boston: Little, Brown, 1988.

Brando, Marlon, with Robert Lindsey. *Brando: Songs My Mother Taught Me*. New York: Random House, 1994.

Buckley, William F. *Nearer, My God: An Autobiography of Faith*. New York: Doubleday, 1997.

Capote, Truman. *Answered Prayers: An Unfinished Novel*. New York: Random House, 1987.

Cassini, Oleg. *In My Own Fashion: An Autobiography*. New York: Simon and Schuster, 1987.

————. *A Thousand Days of Magic: Dressing Jacqueline Kennedy for the White House*. New York: Rizzoli, 1995.

Cawthorne, Nigel. *Sex Lives of the Hollywood Idols*. London: Prion, 1997.

Clarke, Gerald. *Get Happy: The Life of Judy Garland*. New York: Random House, 2.

Clooney, Rosemary. *Girl Singer: An Autobiography*. New York: Doubleday, 1999.

Colacello, Bob. *Holy Terror: Andy Warhol Close Up*. New York: Harper, 1980.

Collier, Peter, and David Horowitz. *The Kennedys: An American Drama*. New York: Summit Books, 1984.

Collins, Joan. *Past Imperfect: An Autobiography*. New York: Simon and Schuster, 1984.

Conant, Howell. *Grace*. New York: Random House, 1992.

Crick, Michael. *Jeffrey Archer: Stranger Than Fiction*. London: Hamish Hamilton, 1995.

Curtis, Tony, and Barry Paris. *Tony Curtis: The Autobiography*. New York: William Morrow, 1993.

Davis, John H. *The Kennedys: Dynasty and Disaster, 1848–1983*. New York: McGraw-Hill, 1984.

de Massy, Baron Christian, and Charles Higham. *Palace: My Life in the Royal Family of Monaco*. New York: Atheneum, 1986.

Dewey, Donald. *James Stewart: A Biography*. Atlanta: Turner Publishing, 1996.

Donaldson, Maureen, and William Royce. *An Affair to Remember: My Life with Cary Grant*. New York: Putnam, 1989.

Edwards, Anne. *The Grimaldis of Monaco*. New York: Morrow, 1992.

Englund, George. *The Way It's Never Been Done Before: My Friendship with Marlon Brando*. New York: Harper, 2004.

Englund, Steven. *Grace of Monaco: An Interpretive Biography*. Garden City, NY: Doubleday, 1984.

Evanier, David. *Roman Candle: The Life of Bobby Darin*. Emmaus, PA: Rodale, 2004.

Evans, Peter. *Ari: The Life and Times of Aristotle Socrates Onassis*. New York: Summit Books, 1986.

———. *Nemesis: The True Story of Aristotle Onassis, Jackie O, and the Love Triangle That Brought Down the Kennedys*. New York: Harper, 2004.

Eyles, Allen. *James Stewart*. New York: Stein and Day, 1984.

Finch, Yolande. *Finchy*. New York: Wyndham Books, 1981.

Fisher, Eddie. *Eddie Fisher, My Life, My Loves*. New York: Harper, 1982.

Flamini, Roland. *Ava: A Biography*. New York: Coward, McCann, 1983.

Frank, Gerold. *Judy*. New York: Harper, 1975.

Freedland, Michael. *All The Way: A Biography of Frank Sinatra*. New York: St. Martin's Press, 1997.

Friedwald, Will. *Sinatra! The Song Is You*. New York: Scribner, 1995.

Gabor, Zsa Zsa, and Wendy Leigh. *One Lifetime Is Not Enough*. New York: Delacorte, 1991.

Gaither, Gant. *Princess of Monaco: The Story of Grace Kelly*. New York: Holt, 1957.

Gam, Rita. *Actress to Actress: Memories, Profiles, Conversations*. New York: Nick Lyons Books, 1986.

Gardner, Ava. *Ava: My Story*. New York: Bantam Books, 1990.

Gargia, Massimo, and Allan Starkie. *Jet Set: Memoir of an International Playboy*. New York: Barricade Books, 1999.

Glatt, John. *The Royal House of Monaco: Dynasty of Glamour, Tragedy, and Scandal*. New York: St. Martin's Press, 1998.

Granger, Stewart. *Sparks Fly Upward*. New York: Putnam, 1981.

Guilaroff, Sydney, and Cathy Griffin. *Crowning Glory: Reflections of Hollywood's Favorite Confidant*. Santa Monica, CA: General Publishing Group, 1996.

Guinness, Alec. *Blessings in Disguise*. New York: Knopf, 1986.

Hackett, Pat, ed. *The Andy Warhol Diaries*. New York: Warner Books, 1989.

Hamilton, Nigel. *JFK, Reckless Youth*. New York: Random House, 1992.

Hanna, David. *Ava, A Portrait of a Star*. New York: Putnam, 1960.

Harris, Warren G. *Clark Gable: A Biography*. New York: Harmony Books, 2002.

Hart-Davis, Phyllida. *Grace: The Story of a Princess*. New York: St. Martin's Press, 1982.

Hay, Peter, *When the Lion Roars*. Atlanta: Turner Publishing, 1991.

Heroes, Legends, Superstars of Hollywood and Rock. Beverly Hills, CA: Superior Auction Galleries, March 19, 1994.

Heymann, C. David. *A Woman Named Jackie: An Intimate Biography of Jacqueline Bouvier Kennedy Onassis*. Secaucus, NJ: Carol Communications, 1989.

———. *Liz: An Intimate Biography of Elizabeth Taylor*. New York: Carol Publishing Group, 1995.

Higham, Charles, and Roy Moseley. *Cary Grant: The Lonely Heart*. San Diego, CA: Harcourt, 1989.

Hooey, Brian. *Mountbatten, the Private Story*. London: Sidgwick and Jackson, 1994.

Hudson, Rock, and Sara Davidson. *Rock Hudson: His Story*. New York: Morrow, 1986.

Jackson, Stanley. *Inside Monte Carlo*. New York: Stein and Day, 1975.

Jacobs, George, and William Stadiem. *Mr. S: My Life with Frank Sinatra*. New York: Harper, 2003.

Janis, Maria Cooper. *Gary Cooper Off Camera: A Daughter Remembers*. New York: Harry N. Abrams, 1999.

Jenkins, Graham, with Barry Turner. *Richard Burton, My Brother*. New York: Harper, 1988.

Kelley, Kitty. *Elizabeth Taylor, the Last Star*. New York: Simon and Schuster, 1981.

———. *His Way: The Unauthorized Biography of Frank Sinatra*. New York: Bantam, 1986.

———. *Jackie Oh!* Secaucus, NJ: Lyle Stuart, 1978.

———. *The Royals*. New York: Warner Books, 1997.

Lacey, Robert. *Grace*. New York: Putnam, 1994.

Lawford, Patricia Seaton. *The Peter Lawford Story: Life with the Kennedys, Monroe, and the Rat Pack*. New York: Carroll & Graf, 1988.

Lewis, Arthur H. *Those Philadelphia Kellys*. New York: Morrow, 1977.

Lewis, Roger. *Anthony Burgess*. New York: St. Martin's Press, 2004.

Lord, Graham. *Niv: The Authorized Biography of David Niven*. New York: St. Martin's Press, 2004.

MacRae, Sheila, and H. Paul Jeffers. *Hollywood Mother of the Year: Sheila MacRae's Own Story*. New York: Carol Publishing Group, 1992.

Manso, Peter. *Brando: The Autobiography*. New York: Hyperion, 1994.

Martin, Ralph G. *A Hero for Our Time: An Intimate Story of the Kennedy Years*. New York, Macmillan, 1983.

McGilligan, Patrick. *Alfred Hitchcock: A Life in Darkness and Light*. New York: Harper, 2003.

Meneghini, Giovanni Battista. *My Wife Maria Callas*. New York: Farrar, Straus and Giroux, 1982.

Morecambe, Gary, and Martin Sterling. *Cary Grant: In Name Only*. London: Robson Books, 2001.

Morehouse, Ward III. *The Waldorf-Astoria: America's Gilded Dream*. New York: M. Evans, 1991.

Morley, Sheridan. *The Other Side of the Moon: The Life of David Niven*. New York: Harper, 1985.

Morton, Andrew. *Diana: Her True Story—In Her Own Words*. New York: Simon and Schuster, 1998.

Nelson, Nancy. *Evenings with Cary Grant: Recollections in His Own Words and by Those Who Knew Him Best*. New York: Citadel, 2002.

Niven, David. *Bring on the Empty Horses*. New York: Putnam, 1975.

———. *The Moon's a Balloon*. New York: Putnam, 1971.

Pickard, Roy. *Jimmy Stewart: A Life in Film*. New York: St. Martin's Press, 1993.

Plowright, Joan. *And That's Not All: The Memoirs of Joan Plowright*. London: Weidenfeld & Nicolson, 2001.

Porter, Darwin. *Brando Unzipped*. New York: Blood Moon Productions, 2006.

Princess Grace of Monaco, with Gwen Robyns. *My Book of Flowers*. Garden City, NY: Doubleday, 1980.

Quirk, Lawrence J. *James Stewart Behind the Scenes of a Wonderful Life*. New York: Applause Books, 1997.

Reybold, Malcolm. *The Inspector's Opinion: The Chappaquiddick Incident*. New York: Saturday Review Press, 1975.

Robinson, Jeffrey. *Rainier & Grace*. New York: Simon and Schuster, 1989.

Robyns, Gwen. *Princess Grace*. New York: David McKay, 1976.

Rose, Frank. *The Agency: William Morris and the Hidden History of Show Business*. New York: Harper, 1995.

Samuel, Charles. *The King of Hollywood: The Story of Clark Gable*. London: W. H. Allen, 1962.

Server, Lee. *Ava Gardner: Love Is Nothing*. New York: St. Martin's Press, 2006.

Shepherd, Donald, and Robert F. Slatzer. *Bing Crosby: The Hollow Man*. New York: St. Martin's Press, 1981.

Sinatra, Nancy. *Frank Sinatra: My Father*. Garden City, NY: Doubleday, 1985.

Sinden, Donald. *A Touch of the Memoirs*. London: Hodder & Stoughton, 1982.

Solway, Diane. *Nureyev: His Life*. New York: Morrow, 1998.

Spada, James. *Peter Lawford: The Man Who Kept the Secrets*. New York: Bantam, 1991.

————. *Grace: The Secret Lives of a Princess*. Garden City, NY: Doubleday, 1987.

Spoto, Donald. *The Dark Side of Genius: The Life of Alfred Hitchcock*. Boston: Little, Brown, 1983.

Summers, Anthony, and Robbyn Swan. *Sinatra: The Life*. New York: Knopf, 2005.

Sutherland, Robert. *Maria Callas: Diaries of a Friendship*. London: Constable, 1999.

Taraborrelli, J. Randy. *Once Upon a Time: Behind the Fairy Tale of Princess Grace and Prince Rainier*. New York: Warner Books, 2003.

Thomas, Bob. *Golden Boy: The Untold Story of William Holden*. New York: St. Martin's Press, 1983.

Tierney, Gene, and Mickey Herskowitz. *Self-Portrait*. New York: Wyden Books, 1979.

Van Meter, Jonathan. *The Last Good Time: Skinny D'Amato, The Notorious 500 Club, and The Rise and Fall of Atlantic City*. New York: Crown, 2003.

Vidal, Gore. *Palimpsest: A Memoir*. New York: Random House, 1995.

Von Post, Gunilla, with Carl Johnes. *Love, Jack*. New York: Crown, 1997.

Walker, Alexander. *It's Only a Movie, Ingrid: Encounters on and off Screen*. London: Headline, 1988.

Wansell, Geoffrey. *Cary Grant, Dark Angel*. New York: Arcade, 1996.

————. *Haunted Idol: The Story of the Real Cary Grant*. New York: Morrow, 1984.

Wayne, Aissa, with Steve Delsohn. *John Wayne, My Father*. Dallas: Taylor Publishing, 1998.

Wayne, Jane Ellen. *Ava's Men: The Private Life of Ava Gardner*. New York: St. Martin's Press, 1990.

Zec, Donald. *Put the Knife in Gently! Memoirs of a Life with Legends*. London: Robson Books, 2003.

Ziegler, Philip, ed. *From Shore to Shore: The Final Years. The Tour Diaries of Earl Mountbatten of Burma,*
    1953–1979. London: Collins, 1989.
———. *Mountbatten.* New York: Knopf, 1985.

Newspaper and Magazine Articles

Allen, Rupert. "Grace Kelly." *Look*, June 15, 1954.

"Amazing Grace." *Ladies' Home Journal*, September 1982.

"The Amazing Grace." *Sunday Mirror*, October 28, 1979.

"Amazing Grace and Her Girls. Deadly Drugs and Dangerous Men." *Star*, March 12, 1996.

"Amazing Grace Gives a Real Oscar-Winning Performance." *Star*, August 1, 1995.

"And Now Here Comes The Bride." *Life*, April 9, 1956.

"Another Girl Guide." *Life*, January 25 1963.

"Anthony Burgess on the Loss of Princess Grace." *Observer*, September 26, 1982.

Arnold, Eve. "With the Grimaldis." January 30, 1963.

Arthur, William B. "Grace Kelly's Life as a Princess." May 2, 1957.

———. "Monaco Gets a New Prince." *Look*, May 27, 1958.

———. "The Princess and the Palace." *Look*, August 18, 1954.

———. "Princess Grace After Five Years." April 11, 1961.

———. "Princess Grace at 40." *Daily Sketch*, December 5, 1969.

———. "Will Princess Grace Lose Her Throne?" *Look*, July 31, 1962.

"At the Barbizon, A Royal Memory." *Philadelphia Daily News*, September 16, 1982.

"Ava and the Princess . . . The Old Rivals Meet Again." *Sunday Dispatch*, February 7, 1960.

Barker, Dennis. "Her Grace." *Guardian*, January 15, 1976.

Battelle, Phyllis. "Grace Kelly, Monaco Prince to Marry, Live on Riviera." *Los Angeles Examiner*,
    January 6, 1956.

Bell, Christopher. "Three Years of Grace." April 25, 1954.

"The Birth of Prince Rainier's Son and Heir: Monaco Rejoices." *Illustrated London News*, March
    22, 1958.

"Bombshell New Book Rips Lid Off. Clark Gable's Red-Hot Affair With Grace Kelly." *Globe*,
    May 14, 2002.

Botham, Noel. "Princess Grace: 'Our Marriage Is Over.'" *National Enquirer*, July 6, 1982.

Bowers, Ronald. "Grace Kelly." *F.I.R.*, November 1978.

Buchwalk, Art. "Grace Talks About That Wedding." *Express*, March 28, 1956.

Buchwald, Art. "How Grace Really Met Rainier." *Los Angeles Times*, January 13, 1956.

———. "Kismet and Kelly—I Have the Real Story." *Daily Express*, January 10, 1956.

———. "The Question Is: Does Miss Kelly Care?" *Evening Standard*, September 21, 1955.

———. "The Sinatra Gala Chore." *New York Herald Tribune*, June 19, 1958.

Burrows, George. "Co. Mayo Home for Princess." *Sunday Telegraph*, November 20, 1977.

"A Candid Interview with Princess Grace." *Playboy*, January 1966.

Capettini, Roger, and John Blosser. "Princess Grace's Mom Dies—Believing Her Daughter Was Alive." *National Enquirer,* January 25, 1990.

Carlton, Peter. "Living With the Memories." November 15, 1989.

"Caroline and Junot's Split." *Daily Mirror,* December 2, 1980.

"Caroline and Junot's Marriage." *Sunday Mirror,* October 12, 1980.

"Caroline Overwhelmed." *People,* May 28, 1978.

"Caroline's Annulment." *Daily Mail,* July 23, 1979.

Cassa, Anthony. "Grace Kelly: The Lady Had Class." *Hollywood Studio Magazine,* n.d.

"Charges Against Frank Sinatra." *Daily Express,* July 22, 1972.

Childe, Leslie. "Vatican Cool Over Priest's Call to Beatify Grace." *Daily Telegraph,* September 17, 1983.

"Coca-Cola Warehouses are Eyesores." *Standard,* September 17, 1982.

Conant, Howell. "Princess Grace Prepares for Her Baby." *Collier's,* January 4, 1957.

Cook, Jim. "Rainier's Ma: The Quiet Years." *New York Post,* February 12, 1956.

Crane, Lionel. "A Picture, No Doubt, She'd Rather Forget." *Sunday Mirror,* July 21, 1963.

Crewe, Quentin. "The Actress." *Evening Standard,* June 17, 1953.

Curtis, Olga. "Beauty Kissed Prince, Grace Kelly Is Irked." *Herald Express,* January 7, 1956.

———. "Grace Kelly Shows Ruby and Diamond Engagement Ring." *Herald Express,* January 6, 1956.

———. "Kept Their Romance Secret Until Time to Be Revealed." *Los Angeles Herald and Express,* January 10, 1956.

———. "Prince Won Over Many Suitors." *Herald Express,* January 9, 1956.

Curzon, Shirley. "A Tribute to a Gracious Lady." *Majesty,* November 1982.

Daily Express, November 6, 1959.

"David Niven Refutes Stroke Rumors." *Sunday Mirror,* September 26, 1982.

David, Lester. "Even a Prince Needs Privacy." *This Week Magazine,* January 13, 1957.

Davis, Victor. "My Darling David Wanted Me to Commit Suicide with Him." March 6, 1994.

"Definitive Accident Findings." *Daily Mirror,* September 17, 1982.

"Did Prince Know That Kisser?" *Los Angeles Examiner,* January 9, 1956.

Downs, Hugh. *20/20.* ABC News. September 23, 1982.

Dryan, Riva. "Grace Cheated on Rainier With Old Flame Cary Grant." *Celebrity Plus,* January 1989.

"Ecuadorian Upset Over Kiss Given Prince." *Los Angeles Times,* January 9, 1956.

Edwards, John. "Shattered Rainier Ventures Out, and the Painful Past Is Recalled at His Every Turn." *Daily Mail,* September 17, 1982.

"Elizabeth Taylor's Birthday Party." *Daily Mail,* February 28, 1972.

"Elizabeth Taylor's Birthday Party." *News of the World,* February 27, 1972.

"Elizabeth Taylor's Birthday Party." *Sun,* February 26, 1972.

"Elizabeth Taylor's Birthday Party." *Sunday Mirror,* February 27, 1972.

"Elizabeth Taylor's Birthday Party." *Sunday Times,* February 27, 1972.

Ellison, John. "Princess Grace." *Daily Express,* February 16, 1968.

————. "Princess Grace Is a Star Again—to Boost Monte." *Daily Express*, October 22, 1965.

"Eternal Grace." *Examiner*, May 22, 2001.

Evans, Peter. "The Private Lives of the Secret Agents." May 18, 1965.

————. "Six Years Since She Made a Film—And the Old Image Won't Be Good for Business." *Daily Express*, March 27, 1962.

————, and Yul Brynner. "Grace Kelly Returns—for a Dollar a Week." *Daily Express*, February 24, 1966.

"Fans Say Goodbye to Atlantic City Race Course." www.fresnobee.com.

Fielding, Henry. "A Night Without the Royal Tiara." February 6, 1968.

————. "Still in the Kingdom of Kelly." *Herald*, March 15, 1958.

Fields, Sydney. "Only Human." *Daily Mirror*, December 9, 1953.

Finn, Philip. "Wife Sees Mugger Gun Down Grace's Brother." *Daily Express*, December 29, 1982.

Fliegers, Serge. "Palace Emergency." *News of the World*, August 29, 1965.

————. "Terror at Sea—And the Prince Saves Us." *News of the World*, September 5, 1965.

————. "When the Royal Children Saw This Scene . . ." *News of the World*, September 12, 1965.

Frederic Laurent on Albert of Monaco. *Independent*, July 13, 2005.

"French Police Baffled by Accident." *Standard*, September 16, 1982.

Gee, Jack. *Daily Mail*, March 18, 1968.

"George Smith Gives Grace Lessons." *Myerscough Voice—Alumni*, March 9, 1981.

"The Gifts and the Headaches." *Life*, May 30, 1956.

"The Girl in White Gloves." *Time*, January 31, 1955.

Glynn, Prudence. "Princess Grace of Monaco: Perfect Typecasting." *Times*, May 9, 1972.

Goldsworthy, Frank. "Bored, So Grace Films Again." *Daily Express*, March 20, 1962.

————. "Witness for the Bride." *Daily Express*, March 24, 1962.

"Goodness Grace What a Time to Choose." *News of the World*, March 25, 1962.

Gourlay, Logan. "Why Was Grace Lured Back to Hollywood?" *Daily Express*, March 20, 1962.

"Grace." *Daily Mirror*, February 12, 1957.

"Grace: A Dear Friend, Sinatra Stunned by Grace's Death." *Philadelphia Daily News*, September 15, 1982.

"Grace and Hollywood." *Sunday Mirror*, October 28, 1979.

"Grace and Jackie Kennedy." *Daily Express*, December 13, 1963.

"Grace and Rainier Begin Month Visit." *New York Journal American*, November 24, 1958.

"Grace Awaits Third Child, Friend Says." *Los Angeles Times*, April 22, 1959.

"Grace, Hollywood, and Hedda Hopper." *Sunday Mirror*, October 28, 1979.

"Grace Is Here, Doesn't Care Where She's Wed." *Mirror News*, January 10, 1956.

"Grace Kelly Allowed to Leave Bed Briefly." *Herald Express*, January 24, 1957.

"Grace Kelly and Her Dad." www.ushistory.org.

"Grace Kelly and Monaco Prince Will Be Married." *Los Angeles Times*, January 6, 1956.

"Grace Kelly as a Regular Guy." *Standard*, September 16, 1962.

"Grace Kelly Hints Prince Romance." *Los Angeles Times*, January 5, 1956.

"Grace Kelly Keeps a Date with Prince." *Evening Standard*, January 5, 1956.

"Grace Kelly Picks 8 Attendants and 4 Flower Girls for Wedding." *Los Angeles Times*, February 22, 1956.

"Grace Kelly Selects Another Bridesmaid." *Herald Express*, February 21, 1956.

"Grace LeVine and Bobby Marx Engaged." *Daily Mail*, December 17, 1980.

"Grace Loved at 2nd Sight." *Mirror News*, January 9, 1956.

"Grace on Board of Directors." *Daily Mail*, November 10, 1976.

"Grace on Princess Caroline's Image." *Daily Mail*, July 23, 1979.

"Grace on Style and Exercise." *Look*, December 1969.

"Grace, Prince to Have Not One—but 2 Weddings." *Los Angeles Examiner*, February 7, 1956.

"Grace Upset Over Stephanie and Miguel Bose Romance Rumors." *People*, March 1, 1981.

"Grace Visits London." *News of the World*, 1957.

"Grace Waits for Her Baby." *Picture Post*, November 26, 1956.

"Grace Walks 8 Hours After Surgery." *Los Angeles Times*, April 4, 1959.

"Grace Weds in Spring." *Mirror News*, January 6, 1956.

"Grace's Niece Is Penny Wise." *New York Post*, October 25, 1963.

"Grace's Sister on Romance." *Sun*, February 17, 1981.

Gris, Henry. "Princess Grace: It Is Highly Unlikely That I'll Ever Make Another Picture." *National Enquirer*, September 10, 1972.

Guinness, Alec. "Who Slipped the Tomahawk in Grace Kelly's Bed?" *Evening Standard*, February 3, 1956.

Hamilton, Jack. "Princess Grace: A New Role." February 12, 1963.

Hartt, Julian. "Grace Kelly Here; Quite Indifferent On Wedding Site." *Los Angeles Examiner*. January 11, 1956.

———. "Prince Describes Ideal Woman." *Los Angeles Examiner*, January 6, 1956.

Hauptfuhrer, Fred. "In Her Own Words." *People*, April 5, 1982.

———. "Life's No Fairy Tale." *Sunday Mirror*, April 18, 1982.

———. "The Problem on Mother Kelly's Doorstep." *People*, May 29, 1975.

Herbert, Ivor. "Grace." *Evening News*, December 8, 1966.

Hickey, William. "Irish Give Grace Her Last Wish." *Daily Express*, September 29, 1982.

———. "It Will Be a Ball for Scorpio on Princess Grace's Birthday." *Daily Express*, October 23, 1969.

———. "The Truth They Can't Tell Grace Kelly's Mother." *Daily Express*, September 7, 1983.

Hoffman, Werner. "Behind the Glitter: New Bio of the Star Who Married a Prince." *New York Tribune*, May 24, 1984.

"Hollywood Amuses." *Daily Mirror*, August 11, 1980.

Holman, Dennis. "Princess Grace: 'How I'm Raising My Three Children.'" *National Enquirer*, June 23, 1974.

———. "Princess Grace Talks to New Reveille About Her Children." *Reveille*, April 19, 1974.

Hughes, Emmet John. "A Romance That's Got Everything." *Life*, January 16, 1956.

"I'm Still Terrified When I Meet People." *Woman's Mirror*, May 22, 1959.

"Inside Story of Grace Kelly's Incredible Rise to Stardom." *Star*, October 12, 1982.

"It's Snake Eyes for College in Monte Carlo: Grace Kin." *Sunday News*, March 29, 1970.

"James Stewart Will Miss Princess Grace." *Daily Mirror*, September 15, 1982.

Johnson, Erskine. "The Luck of the Irish? It's Unneeded." *American Daily*, November 10, 1954.

Jones, Bridget. "She's Changed Meaning of Sex Appeal." *Reveille*, May 3, 1955.

———. "She's Making Girls Wear Glasses." *Reveille*, May 10, 1955.

"Jyl Affected by Princess Grace's Passing." *Daily Mail*, September 14, 1993.

Kahn, Robert. "What Grace Really Thought About Her Children." *Sunday People*, September 19, 1982.

Kashner, Sam. "The Loneliest Guy in the World." *GQ*, November 1999.

Kelly, Grace, and Debora Murdoch. "My Style." *Daily Mail*, October 7, 1969.

Kelly, John B. "Grace's First Date at 13; Walked to Game." *New York Journal American*, January 16, 1956.

———. "My Grace In Love." *Sunday Pictorial*, January 15, 1956.

Kelly, Mrs. John B. "Began Getting Proposals at 15; Death Took Her Real Love." *New York Journal American*, January 17, 1956.

——— "Crush on Clark Gable Like That of a Schoolgirl." *New York Journal American*, January 20, 1956.

———. "Decided Early to Be an Actress; Helped Pay Tuition by Modeling." *New York Journal American*, January 18, 1956.

———. "Fiction Outdone by Real Romance." *New York Journal American*, January 23, 1956.

———. "My Daughter Grace Kelly." *Los Angeles Examiner*, January 15–20, 1956.

———. "My Daughter Grace Kelly." *New York Journal American*, January 15, 1956.

———. "Overcomes 'You're Very Good, But Too Tall,' to Get First B-way Role." *New York Journal American*, January 9, 1956.

———. "Sister Wed—Where Is Prince Charming?" *New York Journal American*, 1956.

———. "Studio Dreamed Up Those 'Heavy Dates.'" *New York Journal American*, January 21, 1956.

"The Kelly's Cool Film Beauty." *Newsweek*, May 17, 1954.

Kenny, Mary. "Memories of Princess." *Sunday Telegraph*, September 19, 1982.

Key, Ivor. "Rainier Is Set to Wed Niven Wife." *Daily Express*, January 1, 1994.

Kilgallen, Dorothy. *Washington Times Herald*, April 24, 1956.

Killian, Richard. "Grace! Your Serene Highness." *Daily Express*, January 6, 1956.

King, Maurine. "My Life with Princess." *News of the World*, August 22, 1965.

"The Kiss at the Waldorf." *Daily Express*, January 19, 1956.

Klemesrud, Judy. "Princess Grace Makes a Movie—But It's No Comeback." *New York Times*, December 18, 1977.

Knight, John. "Farewell to a Princess." *Sunday Mirror*, September 19, 1982.

"Krol Extols Kelly as Wife and Mother." *Philadelphia Daily News*, September 18, 1982.

Lamb, Bobby. "On Tour with Frank Sinatra." June 9, 1962.

"The Last Fling of Princess Grace." *Daily Mirror*, October 2, 1982.

Leach, Robin. "Anguished Princess Grace Tries to Nip in Bud Her Son's Hot Romance With Beautiful Actress." *National Star*, December 18, 1979.

Lecler, Rene. "Grace Kelly." *Illustrated*, November 20, 1954.

"The Legacy of Princess Grace." *Life*, March, 1983.

Lewin, David. "The Last Thing You'd Expect David Niven to Say." *Daily Mail*, October 23, 1978.

"A Life of Grace." *People Weekly*, September 27, 1982.

Littlejohn, Norah. "Princess Grace Tells Her Secrets." *Reveille*, November 29, 1956.

Lockhart, Lloyd. "Grace Kelly Says: 'I Can't Believe I've Been So Lucky.'" *Star Weekly*, March 17, 1956.

Lusher, Don. "Working with Frank Sinatra." 1971.

MacLaurin, Barbara. "Princess Grace of Monaco." *Women's Wear Daily*, April 26, 1974.

Maksian, George. "The Princess Is Peeved." *TV Scene*, October 28, 1981.

Marja, Fern, and Marcy Elias. "Does Anybody Here Know Kelly?" *New York Post*, April 3, 1955.

Martin, Pete. "I Call on Princess Grace." *Saturday Evening Post*, January 23, January 30, February 6, 1960.

————. "Key Witness." *Sunday Graphic*, March 20, 1955.

————. "The Luckiest Girl in Hollywood." *Saturday Evening Post*, October 30, 1954.

————. "Philadelphia Story." *Sunday Graphic*, March 9, 1955.

"Masked Ball to Benefit Flood Victims." *Daily Mail*, September 11, 1967.

McCallum, John. "That Family Called Kelly." *World Telegram and Sun Saturday Magazine*, August 18, 1957.

McPherson, Mervyn. "Bringing Up My Baby." *Star*, March 1, 1957.

————. "The Private Life of Princess Grace." *Star*, November 26, 1956.

"Meet Me Tonight in Atlantic City." *Scotsman*, July 12, 2003.

Miller, Fred. "Rescuing History." www.ocnjmuseum.org/ocmpages/exh_grace.html.

"Monacans Want Big Wedding at Palace." *Los Angeles Examiner*, January 10, 1956.

Mosley, Leonard. "How I Would Fuse Such Talents." *Daily Express*, March 30, 1962.

————. "She's a Girl Who Cringes at a Kiss." *Daily Express*, March 27, 1962.

————. "This Is the Script I Would Write for Her . . ." *Daily Express*, March 28, 1962.

"Most Beautiful Women in International Society." *New York Journal American*, August 18, 1958.

Muller, Robert. "I Wanted to Be an FBI Agent." *Daily Mail*, February 3, 1959.

Munch, Jennifer. "Grace Kelly: A Philadelphian at Heart," n.d.

Murray, James. "British TV Bans Princess Grace's Last Show." February 7, 1983.

Musel, Robert. "A Little Princess Acts Up." United Press International, October 7, 1959.

————. "Love Still Binds Grace, Rainier." *New York Journal American*, October 5, 1959.

"Mystery Woman Kisses Prince, Irks Grace Kelly." *Los Angeles Times*, January 8, 1958.

Nemy, Enid. "Kelly Women Together at a Philadelphia Party." *New York Times*, April 8, 1973.

Nevill Coghill Obituary. *Times*, November 10, 1980.

"The New Prince Albert." *Sunday Times*, July 10, 2005.

Nickels, Thom. "Memories of Grace Kelly." Philly1.com, April 21, 2004.

"Now Grace Expects Her Fourth Baby." June 30, 1967.

O'Brien, Jack. "Cupids Tell Real Story of Grace." *Los Angeles Examiner*, January 10, 1956.

O'Connor, Ulick. "Princess Grace Drops a Secret." *Sunday Mirror*, August 24, 1969.

O'Donnell, Edgar. "Sink or Swim." *Press of Atlantic City*, August 7, 2003.

"On Set with Sinatra." *Newsweek*, June 28, 1999.

"101-Gun Salute Sets Off Wild Rejoicing Throughout Monaco." *Los Angeles Times*, March 14, 1958.

Parkinson, Michael. "The Kellys Queue Up to Welcome Grace." *Daily Express*, June 14, 1961.

Parsons, Louella O. "Grace Sails April 4th for Monaco Wedding." *Los Angeles Examiner*, February 15, 1956.

Peres, Daniel. "Golden Sachs." *W*, May, 1999.

Poole, Shona Crawford. "Define Time: Princess Grace's Rare Elegance." July 6, 1967.

"Prince and New Bride." www.ibiza-spotlight.com.

"Prince Rainier and Princess Grace's Silver Anniversary." *Daily Mail*, n.d.

"Prince Rainier Rules With Strong Hand," n.d.

"Prince Rainier Still in Charge." *Daily Express*, January 8, 1981.

"Princess at the Opera." *Guardian*, January 15, 1976.

"Princess Beatrix to Wed Claus Von Amsberg." *Newsweek*, March 14, 1966.

"Princess Caroline on Marriage." *Sun*, April 16, 1982.

"Princess Diana at Grace's Funeral, Grace Quotes." *Sunday Mirror*, September 19, 1982.

"Princess Grace Against Hollywood Story." *Daily Mirror*, October 29, 1981.

"Princess Grace as Someone's Wife." *Sunday Mirror*, October 28, 1979.

"Princess Grace. Broken." *Daily Express*, January 9, 1963.

"Princess Grace: Cause of Death." *Standard*, September 15, 1982.

"Princess Grace: Cause of Death, Efficient Police Force." *Observer*, September 19, 1982.

"Princess Grace Comes Home With Her Dream." *National Star*, April 27, 1974.

"Princess Grace Comes to the Rescue." *Daily Sketch*, August 9, 1965.

"Princess Grace Consults With Swiss Doctors." *Los Angeles Times*, April 1, 1959.

"Princess Grace Dances with David Niven at Rose Ball." *Daily Mail*, April 21, 1976.

"Princess Grace Gives Thanks." *Daily Mirror*, April 10, 1958.

"Princess Grace Hosts Red Cross Gala Ball." *News of the World*, n.d.

"Princess Grace: It's True." *Sunday Express*, August 25, 1957.

"Princess Grace Loses Her Baby." *Daily Mirror*, July 7, 1967.

"Princess Grace: A New Role." *Look*, February 12, 1963.

"Princess Grace Presents Award at New Standard British Film Awards." *Daily Express*, November 26, 1980.

"Princess Grace Puzzling to Residents of Monaco." *Los Angeles Times*, July 12, 1956.

"Princess Grace Visits President Kennedy's Grave." www.pophistorynow.com.

"Princess Grace with Richard Burton's Relatives." *Daily Express*, March 8, 1972.

"Princess Grace's 50th Birthday." *Daily Express*, November 18, 1979.

"Princess Grace's Final Thoughts." *Daily Mirror*, September 16, 1982.

"Princess Grace's Marriage on the Rocks." *National Star*, June 7, 1975.

"Princess in Chichester Festival Theater." *Daily Mirror*, March 17, 1982.

"Princess Margaret on Stormy Seas." *News of the World*, September 5, 1965.

"Princess of Monaco Christened." *Los Angeles Times*, March 4, 1957.

"Princess on a Conquest of Paris." *Life*, October 26, 1959.

"A Princess Stars Again But Just For The Night." March 17, 1982.

"The Prisoner Princess by Grace's Pal." September 19, 1982.

"Rainier and Grace Have a 54-Footer." *Life*, July 9, 1965.

"Rainiers Expect Child; Monaco Bursts with Joy," n.d.

"The Real Grace Kelly?" n.d.

Richards, Denise. "The Girl Princess Grace Will Play." *Evening Standard*, March 22, 1962.

Richardson, John. "Monte Carlo—The Last Romantic Haven." *Vogue*, November 1981.

Rittenberg, Madeline. "Life in Tiny Monaco Entirely Different From Glamor of Being a Movie Star." *New York Journal American*, January 11, 1956.

Robbins, William. "Philadelphians Honoring One of Their Own, Princess Grace." *New York Times*, March 29, 1982.

Robyns, Gwen. "The Princess Makes Do." *Sunday Graphic*, July 10, 1957.

———. "A Touch of Grace." *Daily Star*, September 16 and 17, 1982.

"Royal Visitors in Eire." *Sphere*, June 24, 1961.

Ruddy, Jonah. "Grace's Film Must Wait. Yacht to Please." *Evening News*, October 26, 1962.

Ryttenberg, Madeline. "Filmland Prepared Grace for Her Role." *New York Journal American*, January 9, 1956.

———. "French Beauty Gave Up Stage Career to Sail on Rainier's Yacht." *New York Journal American*, January 10, 1956.

Sands, Frederick. "Princess Grace Says: 'Gossips Reported Me Dying or Divorcing—Here's the Real Truth About My Life.'" *National Enquirer*, April 5, 1977.

———. "Princess Grace Talks to Woman's Mirror." *Woman's Mirror*, May 22, 1959.

Santora, Phil. "A Prince for the Girl Who Has Everything." *Daily News*, January 9 and 10, 1956.

Satchell, Tim. "Princess Grace Puts on The Big Sell . . ." *Daily Mail*, November 26, 1980.

Schallert, Edwin. "Critic Sees Monaco's Gain as Filmland Loss." *Los Angeles Times*, January 22, 1956.

Scott, Bernard D. A. "Grace Kelly's Unspectacular Days as a Model." *National Enquirer*, November 12, 1974.

Sharpley, Anne. "They Are Absolutely In Love, Says Father Tucker," n.d.

Sims, Victor. "Girl Like Grace Kelly?" *Sunday Chronicle*, October 16, 1955.

"Sinatra Was a Racetrack Stockholder." *Press of Atlantic City*, August 12, 1993.

Skow, John. "The Princess From Hollywood." *Time*, September 27, 1982.

Smith, Godfrey. "A New Life for Princess Grace." *Sunday Times*, June 8, 1958.

———. "Squire in a Palace." *Sunday Times*, June 1, 1958.

Smith, Sydney. "Rainier Talks About His Troubles." February 25, 1957.

Spada, James. "Nation of Film Fans Happy to Say Grace." *Boston Herald*, May 31, 1987.

"Speaking Out in Princely Fashion." *New York Sunday News*, October 10, 1971.

"Stephanie Kicked Out of St. Dominiques." *Sunday Mirror*, October 4, 1981.

Stephen, Schaeffer. "Unseen Grace." *US*, November 21, 1983.

Stephens, Peter. "Grace Is Going to Have a Baby." *Daily Mirror*, August 3, 1956.

"Storm in a Port as Actor Niven Hits Out," n.d.

Suzy. "Mystery Solved." *Daily News*, February 25, 1983.

Tanfield, Paul. "I Said to Princess Grace." *Daily Mail*, August 8, 1960.

"This Baby Boy IS My Son, Admits Albert." *Daily Mail*, July 7, 2005.

"This First Meeting Was a Magazine Stunt!" *The People*, January 8, 1956.

Time magazine. January 31, 1955.

Tory, Peter. "When Bing Caught Kelly's Eye." *Daily Mirror*, February 4, 1983.

"Two Children Enough Says Rainier." *New York Journal American*, November 26, 1958.

"Two Princesses." *Daily Mirror*, January 26, 1957.

"The Typical American Matron (As Seen in Grace Kelly)." June 2, 1959.

Vine, Brian. "Sinatra's Tribute to Grace." April 21, 1981.

Vinocur, John. "For Princess Grace, a Forlorn Farewell." *New York Times*, September 19, 1982.

———. "High Society." *New York Times*, May 18, 1978.

Walker, Alexander. "Regal View of Flower Power." *Sunday Telegraph Magazine*, November 9, 1980.

Walters, Barbara. "How Now, Princess Grace?" *Ladies' Home Journal*, November 1966.

Ward, Vicky. "My Dad Was a Flamboyant Personality, but He Never Flaunted His Infidelities." *Daily Mail*, March 10, 1998.

Warwick, Christopher. "A Principality's Farewell." *Majesty*, November 1982.

Weinman, Martha. "Hollywood's Queen Becomes a Princess." *Collier's*, March 1956.

Wharton, Kate. "Bizarre Cult of St. Grace." *Sunday Mail*, September 18, 1983.

"What a Swell Party That was." *Daily Mirror*, April 21, 1981.

"What Is Grace Up To?" April 23, 1956.

"When Grace Had a Jewish Lover." *New York News*, March 20, 1994.

"Where Is Royal Wedding to Be?" *Herald Express*, January 10, 1956.

"Whirlwind After Grace Marries Prince of Monaco." *Ladies' Home Journal*, September 1982.

Whitaker, James. "I Carried Stephanie From the Car and Put Her Down Nearby. She Just Sat There and Cried." *Daily Mirror*, September 16, 1982.

White, Sam. *Evening Standard*, October 16, 1969.

———. "Grace and the Monaco Match-Maker." *Evening Standard*, September 17, 1982.

———. "Princess Grace's Indiscretion: Will De Gaulle React?" *Evening Standard*, March 8, 1968.

"Why Princess Grace Goes Into Porn Shops." *Globe*, July 1, 1980.

Winters, Nancy. "Princess and the Purse." *Fame*, November 1989.

Wiseman, Thomas. "I Kept a Date with Grace Kelly." *Evening Standard*, February 27, 1956.

———. "Is Mr. Hitchcock Staking Too Much on Princess Grace?" *Sunday Express*, March 25, 1962.

"Witnesses to Princess Grace's Accident." *Daily Mirror*, September 16, 1982.

Wogan, Terry. "The Princess and the D.J." February 25, 1981.

"Writer, Actor David Niven Charmed His Audiences." *Philadelphia Daily News*, July 30, 1983.

Yves, Debrain. "The Kelly Touch." January 21, 1957.

Zec, Donald. "Grace, The Queen of Hollywood." *Sunday Mirror*, March 13, 1955.

———. "The Hot Iceberg." *Daily Mirror*, March 23, 1962.

————. "Look Who's Holding Hands!" *Daily Mirror*, June 16, 1958.

————. "Two Faces of Grace." *Daily Mirror*, March 26, 1952.

————. "Untarnished Goddess." *Sunday Mirror*, September 19, 1982.

Zolotow, Maurice. "Can a Shy Girl Who Became a Movie Star Carve Out a New Career—As a Princess?" *American Weekly*, April 22, 1956.

————. *Washington Post and Times Herald*, April 22, 1956.

Index